LABOUR STRUGGLES

IN SOUTHERN AFRICA 1919–1949

New Perspectives on the Industrial and Commercial Workers' Union (ICU)

Edited by David Johnson, Noor Nieftagodien, Lucien van der Walt

HSRC
PRESS

WITS
UNIVERSITY

Published by HSRC Press
Private Bag X9182, Cape Town, 8000, South Africa
www.hsrcpress.ac.za

First published 2023

ISBN (soft cover) 978-0-7969-2641-8
ISBN (PDF)

© 2023 Human Sciences Research Council

This book has undergone a double-blind independent peer-review process overseen by the HSRC Press Editorial Board.

The views expressed in this publication are those of the authors. They do not necessarily reflect the views or policies of the Human Sciences Research Council (the Council) or indicate that the Council endorses the views of the authors. In quoting from this publication, readers are advised to attribute the source of the information to the individual author concerned and not to the Council.

The publishers have no responsibility for the continued existence or accuracy of URLs for external or third-party Internet websites referred to in this book and do not guarantee that any content on such websites is, or will remain, accurate or appropriate.

Copy edited by Jacqui Baumgardt
Typeset by Shane Platt
Cover concept by Clair Durow; finalised by Shane Platt
Printed by Capitil Press, Cape Town, South Africa

Distributed in Africa by Blue Weaver
Tel: +27 (021) 701 4477; Fax Local: (021) 701 7302; Fax International: 0927865242139
www.blueweaver.co.za

Distributed in Europe and the United Kingdom by Eurospan Distribution Services (EDS)
Tel: +44 (0) 17 6760 4972; Fax: +44 (0) 17 6760 1640
www.eurospanbookstore.com

Distributed in the US, its possessions, Canada, and Asia by Lynne Rienner Publishers, Inc.
Tel: +1 303-444-6684; Fax: +1 303-444-0824; Email: cservice@rienner.com
www.rienner.com

Suggested citation: David Johnson, Noor Nieftagodien and Lucien van der Walt (eds) (2023) *Labour Struggles in Southern Africa, 1919–1949. New Perspectives on the Industrial and Commercial Workers' Union (ICU).* Cape Town: HSRC Press

Table of Contents

Acknowledgements

Our first debt of thanks is to Mthunzi Nxawe at HSRC Press, who has been an excellent commissioning editor – professional, patient, receptive, and always prompt in responding to our many emails. Siphokazi Mdidimba, the editorial project manager, has done a magnificent job in seeing our collective labours through to publication. This volume had its origins in a series of panels on the ICU at the June 2019 Southern African Historical Society conference at Rhodes University, Makhanda, South Africa, and the one-day symposium on the ICU that followed. Organised by the History Workshop at the University of the Witwatersrand and the Neil Aggett Labour Studies Unit at Rhodes, these events took place a century after the founding of the ICU. We are immensely grateful to those who contributed papers to the panels, to the generous audiences whose engaged questions invigorated our fascination with the ICU, and to the participants in the colloquium, especially Dinga Sikwebu of the Tshisimani Centre for Activist Education based in Cape Town. The panellists of 2019, together with the additional contributors recruited en-route, have displayed great patience during our long journey to publication: without them, this volume would not exist. The HRSC Press's anonymous reviewers provided incisive critical feedback, which was invaluable in helping us to fine-tune the final draft. We are grateful to the National Library of South Africa (Cape Town) for providing a high-resolution copy of the image used for the cover (John C. Scott's cartoon 'When He Awakes', published in the Workers' Herald of 28 July 1926 and of 10 August 1929); to Harrie Carr for restoring the image; and to Clair Durow for her striking cover design. For permission to reproduce the map of ICU branches in Southern Africa, we are grateful to Historical Publications of Southern Africa. Henry Dee's efforts in seeking out (and finding) the many missing references in Phil Bonner's unpublished paper were essential to preparing this especially rich chapter. We extend our thanks to Phil's widow, Sally Gaulle, for permission to publish it. We are also indebted to Laurence Stewart for invaluable editorial work and to the History Workshop for funding his work.

DJ, NN, LvdW

List of Abbreviations

AMCU	Associated Mineworkers and Construction Union
AMEC	African Methodist Episcopal Church
ANC	African National Congress (known as the SANNC between 1912 and 1923)
APO	African Political Organisation (known as the African People's Organisation from 1919)
British TUC	British Trades Union Congress
Comintern	Communist International (also known as Third International)
CPSA	Communist Party of South Africa
CPGB	Communist Party of Great Britain
COSATU	Congress of South African Trade Unions
FOSATU	Federation of South African Trade Unions
ILP	Independent Labour Party
Independent ICU	Independent Industrial and Commercial Workers' Union of Africa
ICU	First called the Industrial and Commercial Union; then known as the Industrial and Commercial Workers' Union between 1919 and 1925; and later named the Industrial and Commercial Workers' Union of Africa between 1925 and 1929
ICU yase Natal	Industrial and Commercial Workers' Union yase Natal
ICWU	Industrial and Commercial Workers' (Amalgamated) Union
ICF	Industrial and Commercial Workers' Federation of the Cape Province
IWA	Industrial Workers of Africa
IWW	Industrial Workers of the World
JCEA	Joint Council of Europeans and Africans
JCEN	Joint Council for Europeans and Natives
KTC	Kroonstad Town Council
NAB	Native Advisory Board

NCWA	Native and Coloured Workers Association
NNC	Natal Native Congress
NRC	Native Recruiting Corporation
NP	National Party
ORCVA	Orange River Colony Vigilance Association
Pact	National Party-South African Labour Party coalition government
PEICWU	Port Elizabeth Industrial and Commercial Workers' Union
PEAICCNWU	Port Elizabeth Amalgamated Industrial and Commercial Coloured and Native Workmen's Union
PECC	Port Elizabeth City Council
PEMCNEA	Port Elizabeth Municipal Coloured and Native Employees Association
SACP	South African Communist Party
SACTU	South African Congress of Trade Unions
SAIRR	South African Institute of Race Relations
SAR&H	South African Railways and Harbours
SALP	South African Labour Party
SAP	South African Party
SANNC	South African Native National Congress (known as the ANC from 1923)
SATUC	South African Trades Union Congress
SRNA	Southern Rhodesian Native Association
SWAPO	South West African People's Organisation
TAC	Transvaal African Congress (previously Transvaal Native Congress)
TNMCA	Transvaal Native Mine Clerks' Association
UNIA	Universal Negro Improvement Association
WNLA	Witwatersrand Native Labour Association
YCL	Young Communist League

Map of ICU Branches in Southern Africa, 1919–1930

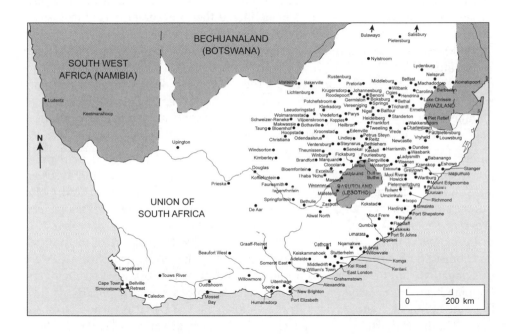

Introduction

David Johnson, Noor Nieftagodien and Lucien van der Walt

The Industrial and Commercial Workers' Union of Africa (ICU) was the largest black trade union and political organisation in Southern Africa in the 1920s. With between 100 000 and 150 000 members in South Africa alone at its peak in 1927, it dwarfed the African National Congress (ANC) and the Communist Party of South Africa (CPSA).[1]

In the century since the ICU so dominated Southern Africa's political landscape, successive generations of historians have filtered their interpretations of its history through perspectives marked by their respective contexts. Under segregation (up to 1948), the earliest informal histories by ICU members like Clements Kadalie and sympathisers like C.L.R. James and Leonard Barnes proclaimed the ICU as the harbinger of freedom for black Southern Africans. Such optimistic accounts were soon displaced by more critical popular histories of the ICU by disillusioned members like A.W.G. Champion and H.D. Tyamzashe, moderate supporters like W.G. Ballinger and Winifred Holtby and hostile CPSA critics like Albert Nzula.

Under formal apartheid (1948–1994), academic histories succeeded their popular precursors, with scholarly interventions by *inter alia* Sheridan Johns, Eddie Webster, Jack and Ray Simons, Phil Bonner, Paul La Hausse, William Beinart and Colin Bundy, and two major monographs – Peter Wickins's *The Industrial and Commercial Workers' Union of Africa* (1978) and Helen Bradford's *A Taste of Freedom: The ICU in Rural South Africa, 1924–1930* (1987). Produced by the pioneers of the radical-revisionist South African historiography initiated in the 1970s, these histories were in sympathy with the aspirations of the ICU and its black working-class members. Popular histories by a new generation of trade unions and labour activists, like the Federation of South African Trade Unions (FOSATU), also turned afresh to the ICU's dramatic story. Seeking lessons in the mistakes and failures of the ICU, however, academic and popular histories alike subordinated the ICU's contribution to the freedom struggle to those of the higher profile anti-apartheid organisations that dominated subsequent decades. Bradford's conclusion to her seminal work encapsulates how the ICU was relegated in the pantheon of liberation organisations:

> Sixty years later [since the collapse of the ICU], the South African countryside is still a cesspit of poverty and misery, and neither the racist state nor capitalism have been overthrown. There is no quick and infallible route to liberation; there is no easy way forward for the millions scrabbling for survival on farms and in rural ghettoes. There is but the certainty that the ANC and the Communist Party have long since surpassed the organisational and theoretical capabilities of the ICU.[2]

With the prestige of the ANC and the SACP at its zenith in the mid-1980s, the two organisations are thus cast as the heroes of South Africa's freedom struggle, with the ICU a charismatic but flawed supporting character in the early scenes of an unfolding drama. Similar critical interpretations also emerged from FOSATU and its allies, which emphasised industry-based unionism and strong workplace organisation, and deprecated the 'One-Big-Union' approach of the ICU.

Re-reading Bradford's words three decades after the end of apartheid, certain continuities stand out: rural Southern Africa remains 'a cesspit of poverty and misery', and capitalism is still dominant. Arguably more striking, however, are the contrasts. The racist state *has* been overthrown, superseded by the post-apartheid state. But a jarring note is struck in a second contrast, namely in Bradford's generous acclamation of the 'organisational and theoretical capabilities' of the ANC and SACP. Once the paragons of national liberation struggle, the ruling alliance is now the object of the most searching criticism, as it has mutated into a state (or state-aligned) centre of power mired in bureaucratic ineptitude, ideological confusion and endemic corruption. Moreover, post-apartheid South Africa has been increasingly blighted by mass unemployment, widespread poverty, high levels of gender-based violence and infrastructural deterioration – all of which the ANC has failed to ameliorate.

The mounting criticisms of the ruling political alliance have focused especially upon the obstacles to economic emancipation, with the role of trade unions in serving Southern Africa's working class fiercely debated. The Congress of South African Trade Unions' (COSATU) compromising alliance with the ANC has come under especially intense scrutiny, as has the declining influence of trade unions and of workers' control within the large unions. The questions this collection accordingly confronts are: How does the changed context of post-apartheid South Africa – the continuities as well as the ruptures – affect our historical understanding of the ICU, one of Southern Africa's most significant liberation movements outside the hegemonic ANC-SACP-COSATU alliance? And how does the ICU's achievement of building a radical and inclusive mass movement independent of established political parties and the state speak to our post-apartheid present?[3]

The contributors to this volume answer these questions in a wide variety of ways. Drawn from different disciplines (social and labour history, political studies and literary studies) and from different generations, and far from unanimous in their assessments of the ICU's history and its contemporary significance, the chapters in this collection provide a provocative range of new interpretations of the ICU.

Post-apartheid perspectives (1): From South Africa to Southern Africa

The post-apartheid period has been characterised by a fundamental reconfiguring of South Africa's relationship with its Southern African neighbours. In the South African liberation movement's discourse of the 1980s, the frontline states were loyal comrades united in the fight against apartheid. Nelson Mandela's momentous speech at Cape Town's Grand Parade on 11 February 1990 acknowledged South Africa's debt to its neighbours: 'we thank the world community for their great contribution to the anti-apartheid struggle. Without your support, our struggle would not have reached this advanced stage. The sacrifice of the frontline states will be remembered by South Africans forever'.[4]

That Mandela overestimated South African memories soon became apparent: four years later, the Minister of Home Affairs warned that the 'aliens who are pouring into South Africa' were competing for scarce resources, stealing the fruits of 'our' democracy.[5] Mandela's appreciation of the sacrifices made by the frontline states was echoed by Thabo Mbeki, whose ideological project of the African Renaissance embraced not only the peoples and cultures of the frontline states, but all Africans. In 1998, for example, Mbeki paid tribute to 'the pyramids and sphinxes of Egypt, the stone buildings of Axum and the ruins of Carthage and Zimbabwe, the rock paintings of the San, the Benin bronzes and the African masks, the carvings of Makonde and the stone sculptures of the Shona'.[6] Mbeki's inclusive Pan Africanist rhetoric, however, always co-existed with the prioritisation of South African economic interests in the region, a tightening of immigration controls and neo-liberal economic policies, which devastated the working classes of the subcontinent. Comparative research published in the same year as Mbeki's African Renaissance speech indicated that South Africa has amongst the highest levels of anti-immigrant sentiment in the world. Driven by intense competition for jobs, escalating township and rural poverty, mass unemployment and state-sponsored South African nationalism, 'regional xenophobia' directed against migrants from neighbouring states continued to increase apace.[7]

Since the turn of the millennium, hostility towards non-nationals has escalated into violence at frequent intervals: in May 2008, widespread attacks on non-nationals left 62 dead and nearly 100 000 displaced; in November 2009, 2 500 Zimbabwean farm workers in the Western Cape were forcibly evicted from their homes; in May–June 2013, four Somali shopkeepers were murdered, with many more injured and killed in subsequent attacks; and in April and October 2015, attacks on Somali, Pakistani and Bangladeshi shopkeepers in Durban, Johannesburg and Makhanda (Grahamstown) met with negligible policing or state sanctioning.[8] In the same year, Lindiwe Zulu, the Minister of Small Business Development, observed, 'Foreign business owners in South Africa's townships cannot expect to co-exist peacefully with local business owners unless they share their trade secrets'.[9] Unsurprisingly, attacks have continued, with non-nationals killed, injured and displaced in Tshwane in June 2016; in Durban in March 2019; and in Johannesburg in September 2019. In June 2021, the anti-immigrant organisation, Operation Dudula, led a march through Soweto, drawing significant support, and in April 2022, striking farm workers in the Sundays River Valley in the Eastern Cape demanded the expulsion of all foreign workers recruited as cheap labour by commercial farmers. And the state continues to collude in such violence: in January 2020, Aaron Motsoaledi, the Home Affairs Minister, reiterated the sentiments of his predecessors, alleging, 'Most people are not documented because they came here to commit a crime. They came as criminals, not as migrants'.[10]

What this snapshot suggests is that anti-immigrant sentiment, particularly against African non-nationals, has become embedded in South African politics, reversing the international solidarity that characterised the anti-apartheid struggle. How have these developments influenced the post-apartheid historian? For the historian of the ICU specifically, one consequence has been a heightened awareness of and sensitivity to the contributions of non-South African nationals to the ICU in the 1920s. This regional dimension of the ICU was barely examined under apartheid, when labour historians aligned to the independent black union movement focused primarily on South Africa. Contending with the political conflicts within the South African trade union movement and the imperatives of the *national* liberation struggle, transnational connections and processes were secondary, with the result that the crucial transnational dimension of the ICU was neglected.[11] From its beginnings, the ICU sought to organise across Southern Africa, with branches formed in six countries in the early 1920s, and it continued to flourish in Northern Rhodesia (now Zambia) from the 1930s and in Southern Rhodesia (now Zimbabwe) up until the mid-1950s.[12]

As a response to the changed political context, as well as a corrective to the earlier national histories of the ICU, our first section accordingly foregrounds the ICU's Southern African networks, with three chapters on the connections with the neighbouring states. The section opens in South West Africa, with Lucien van der Walt's chapter, 'The ICU, the Mines and the State in South West Africa, 1920–1926: Garveyism, Revolutionary Syndicalism and Global Labour History'. Van der Walt describes how sections of the ICU were set up in South West Africa in 1920; in Southern Rhodesia and Swaziland in 1927; in Basutoland in 1928; and in Northern Rhodesia in 1931. Following the establishment of a branch in Lüderitz in December 1920 by the South African worker, Jimmy La Guma, the ICU played a key role in organising workers on the docks, in the diamond fields, and in the fishing industry. From its base in Lüderitz, the ICU grew on the back of a wave of strikes and protests, taking root amongst South African, Afro-Caribbean and Liberian immigrants, but growing to include Nama as well as black migrant workers, with a branch in Keetmanshoop in the midst of karakul farms, and sections in workers' compounds in the mining town of Elizabeth Bay and the Walvis Bay harbour.[13] Van der Walt's account of the South West African ICU pays close attention to its politics, activities and transnational connections, notably those with the Industrial Workers of the World (IWW), the Universal Negro Improvement Association (UNIA) and the ICU sections in South Africa.

In Chapter 2, Anusa Daimon's 'The Rabble-rouser: Robert Sambo's ICU Stint in Rhodesia', the discussion of the ICU's networks moves to Southern Rhodesia. Damon relates how the ICU spread north of the Limpopo in 1927, when Clements Kadalie deployed a fellow Nyasa representative, Robert Sambo, to establish a branch in Southern Rhodesia. Operating from Bulawayo, Sambo, with the assistance of another Nyasa, John Mphamba, agitated effectively from February to June 1927.

Organising urban workers, Sambo appealed to working-class solidarity, attacked the government, and demanded basic rights, sowing the seeds of a radical labour movement in Southern Rhodesia, which spread to the countryside in a second wave of ICU activity in 1928. Sambo's activities constituted the most radical challenge to colonial capitalism and the white-ruled state to date, provoking the authorities to deport him. Sambo's deportation, however, did not end the ICU's impact, as Rhodesian trade unionists such as Masotsha Ndlovu rebuilt the ICU, laying the basis for Benjamin Burombo, Reuben Siwela, Josiah Maluleke and Jasper Savanhu to form their own unions. Furthermore, those recruited into trade union politics through the ICU sustained their radical commitments, most notably ICU veteran, Charles Mzingeli, who was the leader of the Reformed ICU that dominated Salisbury politics after 1945. Damon reconstructs the history of Sambo's remarkable five-month stint in Southern Rhodesia, demonstrating how one 'undesirable foreigner' spread the ICU's liberatory message within a hostile and paranoid colonial state; how the ICU was able to re-emerge and expand in even the most repressive of contexts; and how the ICU exerted a long-term impact on the resistance cultures of Southern Rhodesia.

The third chapter by Henry Dee, 'Organising the Unorganised: ICU Internationalism and the Transnational Unionisation of Migrant Workers', extends the discussions of the ICU's Southern African networks to ICU workers from Central Africa, and assesses the remarkable stance the ICU leadership adopted in relation to the question of 'foreign' labour in South Africa. Noting that the ICU started out as a trade union led by immigrant workers, Dee argues that the ICU operated on a transnational basis because South Africa's labour force was transnational – in the 1920s, around half the 200 000 workers on the gold mines were Mozambican, and Johannesburg's domestic service industry was dominated by Central Africans. Dee foregrounds the many hardships faced by immigrant workers in the 1920s: representatives of South African labour – both white and black – pursued anti-immigrant agendas based on the dogma that migrant workers forced down wages; the government shifted from a laissez-faire to a state-controlled immigration regime; calls for the restriction of immigration and deportation of black immigrants intensified after Johannesburg's anti-immigrant riots of 1927; and the 10-year old South African state was actively promoting an exclusivist ideology of South Africanism. In such a hostile context, the ICU defended workers' rights to free movement, and demanded a minimum wage, arguing that pay was undercut by bosses not immigrants. Dee argues further that as the ICU's constituency was made up of migrants working in different industries, its 'One-Big-Union' strategy – as opposed to organising separate unions for individual industries – was entirely appropriate.

Post-apartheid perspectives (2): From national history to local and regional histories

The muted response to the ICU's centenary in 2019 contrasts with the brouhaha that accompanied the centenary of the ANC's founding in 2012.[14] Aside from proving yet again that history is written by the victors, recent ANC historiography reveals a second way in which post-apartheid perspectives on twentieth-century resistance history are quite different from their apartheid-era precursors.[15] Whereas histories written in the final decades of apartheid sought to recover the heterogenous local histories of forgotten black peasants and workers, biographies of nationalist leaders have dominated the South African history-publishing landscape in the post-apartheid period.[16] The transition was occasioned by the ANC's tactical decision in the late 1980s to replace the emphasis on collective struggle with the elevation of iconic leaders. As one historian-biographer explained, 'the ANC has shifted its policy of a collective image to the tactical utilisation (with Tambo's keen participation) of Mandela as an icon of the struggle against apartheid'.[17] The ANC's strategic switch from attributing agency to the collective masses to elevating the individual leader in the 1980s has continued to be zealously executed, with best-selling biographies of the leading nationalists dominating the History sections of publishers' lists – Anthony Sampson's *Mandela: The Authorised Biography* (1999), Elinor Sisulu's *Walter and Albertina Sisulu: In Our Lifetime* (2002), Luli Callinicos's *Oliver Tambo: Beyond the Ngele Mountains* (2004) and Mark Gevisser's *Thabo Mbeki: The Dream Deferred* (2007), to name but the most obvious examples.[18] In all cases, the individual leader's life-story, the ANC and South Africa's collective history are (roughly) synchronous, as the nationalist biography functions metonymically for the teleological history of the nation's journey from racist state to liberal democracy. Even when criticising the ANC or its leaders, such works preclude raising doubts about the inviolable historic destiny of their chosen subject(s) or contemplating the claims of alternative traditions of resistance.

It would be easy for new histories of the ICU to embrace the post-apartheid celebration of individual struggle leaders, to provide biographically centred chapters on the ICU's equivalents of Mandela/Sisulu/Tambo – pre-eminently Clements Kadalie and A.W.G. Champion. Within the pages of this volume, there are indeed discussions of Kadalie and Champion, as well as of numerous other key members, supporters and critics of the ICU – James La Guma, Robert Sambo, Keable 'Mote, Eva Kubedi, Selby Msimang, Winifred Holtby, William Ballinger, Ethelreda Lewis, Mabel Palmer and H.D. Tyamzashe.

However, the primary emphasis, especially in this second section, is less on the individual ICU leaders, but instead on the many workers who made up the membership of the ICU – the women and men, the urban labourers in many different industries, and the farm workers, labour tenants and peasants in branches across South Africa. In this respect, the collection re-affirms the commitment of the social historians who prioritised recovering the forgotten voices of black peasants and workers. In the specific context of ICU history-writing, this commitment was evident in the re-examination of government reports on the ICU's activities, and even more so, in the extensive use of oral history as a route to recovering the memories of rank-and-file ICU members. The hundreds of interviews conducted by the University of Witwatersrand Sharecropping and Labour Tenancy Project (SLTP) between 1979 and 1987 produced unique insights into the distinctive experiences of ICU members in the different regions of the country.[19] Examples abound. In Kroonstad in the Orange Free State, Lucas Nqandela recalled Kadalie at first 'insulting the whites and promising us liberation from oppression', but he then complained how at a later stage, as the ICU foundered, Kadalie 'just vanished like water vanishing under the ground'.[20] In Mooi River in Natal, Charles Kumalo remembered, 'The ICU fought for freedom. Those of Congress also fought for freedom but didn't talk about money. The ICU was concerned with wages [and helping evicted tenants] back onto the farms'.[21] And in Middelburg in the Transvaal, Rose Mthimunye reminisced about how the ICU gave black workers the confidence 'to be free to move on pavements, walking side-by-side with the whites and rubbing shoulders with them'.[22] In order to account for these – and the many more – different experiences of ICU members in South Africa, the seven chapters in Section B focus on ICU branches in specific towns and regions, foregrounding the variations in membership, organisational cultures, and successes and failures.

Section B opens with the first of three chapters on the ICU in the Orange Free State. Peter Limb and Chitja Twala's chapter, 'The ICU in Free State Dorps and Dorpies', argues that the histories of workers' movements in small rural towns ('dorpies') shed important light on the national events and developments of the 1920s. Foregrounding the neglected histories of early twentieth-century black politics and labour in the Orange Free State, Limb and Twala assess the political, industrial, intellectual and cultural histories of the ICU in rural towns such as Harrismith, Bethlehem, Bethulie, Parys and Winburg, noting especially their connections to the larger towns and cities. Other issues fundamental to the history of the ICU in the Orange Free State that are explored include: the tensions between the ICU's national bodies and its local branches; the different roles played by teachers, women, farm workers, urban workers and traders in ICU politics; the alternately symbiotic and contradictory relationships between political and trade union activism; and the ICU's complicated relationships with the different regional ANC bodies. Focusing on the two decades (1920s and 1930s) when ICU branches flourished in the 'dorpies' and hinterlands of the Orange Free State, Limb and Twala provide an alternative history of early twentieth-century liberation movements in the Orange Free State.

In the second of the chapters on the ICU in the Orange Free State, 'The ICU and Local Politics: Kroonstad, from the Late 1920s to the 1930s', Tshepo Moloi notes that notwithstanding the early presence of a branch of the South African Native National Congress (SANNC, renamed the ANC in 1923) in the town, Kroonstad's African locations were politically quiescent before the arrival of the ICU. After Keable 'Mote established an ICU branch in Kroonstad in 1926, however, the town's political culture was transformed. Together with Henderson Binda, Eva Kubedi and other local leaders, 'Mote mobilised the location's inhabitants, delivering fiery speeches at a number of large public gatherings and initiating political campaigns that challenged the authority of the Native Advisory Board (NAB) and Joint Council for Europeans and Natives (JCEN), most notably the campaign to boycott the paying of rates and taxes. Emphasising the crucial role played by the Women's Section of the

Kroonstad ICU branch, Moloi delineates the distinctively radical trajectory of the ICU in Kroonstad which inspired Kadalie's boast that 'the ICU have never failed in Kroonstad'. Moloi's chapter concludes with an analysis of the demise of the ICU in Kroonstad, elaborating the personal and political disagreements between 'Mote and Kadalie that ultimately undid the ICU's political achievements in Kroonstad in the late 1920s.[23]

In Chapter 6, 'Trouble Brewing: The ICU, the 1925 Bloemfontein Riots and the Women Question', Nicole Ulrich demonstrates that the ICU's proletarian focus enabled a different gender politics which recognised women as workers and equal members. Examining how the Bloemfontein branch of the ICU related to black proletarian women, the chapter first outlines the significant if uneven inclusion of domestic workers in a pioneering campaign for a general minimum wage. In a reassessment of the Bloemfontein protests of 1925, Ulrich traces their trajectory from an initial altercation between women beer brewers which the ICU leaders successfully escalated into a successful stayaway (a township-based general strike), as they defended women's rights to brew traditional African beer. Ulrich proceeds to register the limitations of the ICU's efforts on behalf of African women beer brewers: the ICU leaders were unable to appreciate the full significance of the women beer brewers' vernacular forms of protest, which operated beyond the bounds of formal trade union organisation. As a result, the ICU failed to create lasting solidarities with proletarian women operating outside the formal waged economy. Notwithstanding these qualifications, the ICU's approach to women workers – inconsistent as it was, and not always realised in practice – was radical for its time, and contrasted sharply with the conservative gender norms of other liberation movements such as the ANC.

The focus in Chapter 7 shifts to the Western Transvaal, as Laurence Stewart highlights the varied character and politics of the ICU in this region. In 'The ICU in the Western Transvaal, 1926–1934: Re-imagining Ideological, Spatial and Political Realities', Stewart analyses the unique political contribution and the ideological character of the ICU in this region. The ICU was most active in this region from 1926–1934, well after the time when the ICU has been assumed to have disintegrated elsewhere in the country. First entering towns on the periphery of the Western Transvaal and Cape Province in 1926, the ICU grew rapidly after the mine workers' strike in Lichtenburg, where Kadalie and 'Mote delivered speeches to the workers, and the ICU helped to organise the 5, 000 miners who went on strike. After the strike, the ICU expanded its appeal to recruit farmworkers and location residents, developing their strongest following in the Bloemhof-Schweizer-Reneke-Wolmaransstad triangle. Based upon close analyses of the oral testimonies of ICU workers, Stewart argues that in addition to achieving important material victories, the ICU's activism 'punctured' the dominant economic and political norms, in the process creating a 'new subjectivity'. Stewart identifies two elements to this process: ICU leaders generated a distinctive vocabulary of freedom, subversion and ridicule, delivering public speeches which roused their audiences' imaginations, encouraging their demands for economic and social change. Secondly, the ICU's public meetings created a space which constituted a public sphere operating beyond the control of the state and white employers. In both these ways, dominant norms were breached, generating a new discursive and spatial consciousness in ICU members.

In Chapter 8, 'The ICU in Port Elizabeth: The Making of a Union-cum-Protest Movement, 1920–1931', Noor Nieftagodien demonstrates that the ICU was the pre-eminent organisation of the black working class in Port Elizabeth in the 1920s, eclipsing both the CPSA and the ANC. In 1920, the union had 4 000 members, a high proportion of the town's black workforce, most of whom were employed in the state-run harbours and railways. By the end of the decade, however, it had declined to a few hundred. This chapter examines the history of the ICU in Port Elizabeth. Reflecting experiences elsewhere in Southern Africa, the ICU in Port Elizabeth was a product of the intensification of working-class contestation after the First World War. One of its successes – mirroring the achievements of the ICU in Lüderitz and Cape Town – was the joint organisation of African and coloured workers, thus establishing the basis of a non-racial trade unionism in the town which endures till today. While its core membership in Port Elizabeth was drawn from industrial areas, it mostly operated in the town's black locations, mobilising on a variety of issues that transcended the traditional concerns of industrial unions. As such, it is defined as a union-cum-protest movement. The ICU's multifaceted characteristics were reflected in the organisation's eclectic ideological influences. The unique socioeconomic character of Port Elizabeth created forms of working-class politics that were peculiar to the town and which confounded the national leadership, which in turn generated conflicts amplifying the organisational frailties of the ICU. Rather than offering a 'rise and fall' narrative, Nieftagodien argues that an historical account of the movement in Port Elizabeth offers a useful lens through which to engage with the early efforts of the black working class to produce distinctive ideologies, politics and organisational forms.

The final chapter focuses on the complex but hitherto neglected history of the ICU on the Witwatersrand in the second half of the 1920s, making available a previously unpublished paper by Phil Bonner (1945–2017), one of the pioneers of South Africa's labour and social history – '"Home Truths" and the Political Discourse of the ICU'.[24] Bonner provides an economical sweep of existing scholarship on the ICU, arguing that the crucial role of its discourse – the language of the ICU – has received relatively little attention. Bonner addressed this gap by demonstrating how central mass meetings, extravagant rhetoric and the ICU press were pivotal to ICU activities and in attracting state surveillance and repression. Mining the rich seam of information that documents ICU meetings and ICU speeches in the form of police reports, Bonner locates his study in the Witwatersrand of the late 1920s, arguing that ICU leaders in Johannesburg, Benoni, Germiston and Roodepoort successfully articulated outrage at the innumerable indignities to which the black populace was subjected, and sought to insult and offend those responsible for their plight. Public oratory was used by ICU speakers to rouse passions, to voice outrage, to stir indignation, to inspire confidence, to register a flat collective refusal, to kindle hope and to imagine a better future. Language itself, excessive or otherwise, was one of the chief political weapons in the arsenal of the ICU; the spoken word, Bonner concludes, was the ICU's most potent resource.

Post-apartheid perspectives (3): Factions and legacies

The final section explores the factions within the ICU, as well as its influences, legacies and historiography. The best of the ICU historians writing during the apartheid era were keenly aware of the ICU's contending factions. Bradford, for example, lists several: 'traditionalists with their radical beliefs about land; ... *abaphakathi* familiar with separatist Christianity and Garveyism; ... white intellectuals propagating socialism; [and] landlords adhering to economic liberalism'.[25] The ICU's short-lived achievement was to effect a working unity between these disparate factions. How they did so – and why the ICU's broad front ultimately collapsed – is a question with a direct purchase upon a post-apartheid political culture dominated by factional antipathies, sulphurous rhetoric and shifting alliances, not only within the ruling party, but also in trade unions and civic organisations.

Section C opens with a chapter discussing the relationship between the ICU and the ANC by focusing on the career of Selby Msimang, founding member of the SANNC in 1912, and president of the ICU in 1920. Sibongiseni Mkhize's chapter, 'Leadership Contestations and Worker Mobilisation in the Early Years of the Twentieth Century: Selby Msimang and the ICU, 1919–1921', examines Msimang's involvement in the ICU during his years of activism in Bloemfontein in 1919–21. Msimang's mobilisation of municipal workers in Bloemfontein under his own Industrial and Commercial Workers' Union (ICWU) raised his stature and elevated worker struggles to the national level, attracting the attention of Clements Kadalie, who had led the ICU from its beginnings in 1919. Their brief association fostered the merger of the ICU, the ICWU, the Industrial Workers of Africa, and other emerging unions under the banner of the ICU in Bloemfontein in 1920, with Msimang its president from 1920 to 1921. Despite this early ascendancy, Msimang failed to sustain this position, as his critical attitude towards strikes and boycotts brought him into conflict with his fellow trade unionists. He was also confounded by the challenge of negotiating with charismatic figures like Kadalie, who were impatient with the cautious and pragmatic approach favoured by ANC leaders like Msimang. Though often overlooked, the history of Msimang's work for the ICU therefore both highlights the divisions that beset the ICU from the start and demonstrates the limitations of reading its history exclusively through the deeds of towering figures like Kadalie and Champion.

In Chapter 11, 'The Communist Party of South Africa and the ICU, 1923–1931', Tom Lodge notes how the relationship between the CPSA and the ICU evolved in two distinct phases. First, between 1923 and 1926, the CPSA was encouraged to ally with the ICU, both by the Comintern and by South African CPSA leaders, who recognised the need to influence black African workers. CPSA leaders accordingly began to proclaim the importance of African rights in their programmatic statements. Increasing number of CPSA members joined the ICU at this stage, with several black and coloured communists becoming key ICU organisers at both the national level and in rural branches. At the end of 1926, joint membership of the ICU and CPSA was prohibited, effectively precipitating the expulsion of the communists from the ICU, a dramatic event conventionally interpreted as the immediate prelude to a rightward turn of the ICU and its descent into organisational chaos. Lodge demonstrates *contra* that there was a significant second phase of ICU/communist relations during which the CPSA sustained its support in branches where individual Party members had been the animating personalities. Indeed, in different local settings, the CPSA mobilised mass support, enabling it to act to as an effective agent of black political mobilisation. Local communists emerged at the helm of (often rather successful) rebellions against taxes and other new kinds of restrictions affecting urban residents, including efforts to subject women to pass regulations. In these mobilisations, communists would appeal to their neighbours and followers as householders, protectors of the family, Christians and members of a subjected race – deploying the same language they had used as ICU organisers. Lodge thus demonstrates that the history of interactions between the CPSA and ICU after 1926 were in fact substantially more complex than has hitherto been acknowledged, and further, that the focus on splits at the national level has contributed to an under-estimation of the ICU's resilience in local branches.

Elizabeth van Heyningen in Chapter 12, 'Illusion and Disillusion: White Women and the ICU', traces the histories of several influential white women who promoted and assisted the organisation. Continuing the historical analyses of women in the ICU by Moloi (in Chapter 5) and Ulrich (in Chapter 6), Van Heyningen focuses upon Winifred Holtby, Mabel Palmer and Ethelreda Lewis, distinguishing at the outset their respective political orientations, with Holtby and Palmer identified as socialists and internationalists (not 'liberals'), and Lewis as a romantic conservative. The chapter considers their voluminous writings, ranging from published works such as Holtby's novel *Mandoa, Mandoa* (1933), Lewis's novel *Wild Deer* (1932) and Palmer's academic and journalistic essays, to their many unpublished letters and diary entries. In tracing each woman's relationship with the ICU – and their relationships with each other – Van Heyningen analyses how they brought (or did not bring) a feminist sensibility to bear upon their political advocacy and activism on behalf of the ICU; how they influenced both general policies and specific strategic decisions adopted by the ICU (often behind-the-scenes and hence hitherto under-appreciated); and how their views on black politics and trade unionism evolved in the course of their dealings with the ICU. By focusing upon the histories of these three women and the ICU, Van Heyningen sheds light upon broader debates about the relationships between feminism and racism, and between imperialism and modernity.

In the final chapter, 'The Romance and the Tragedy of the ICU', David Johnson argues that the historical accounts of the ICU to date have been framed by the alternating genres of the anti-colonial romance and the didactic tragedy. In an analysis of the historiography of the ICU, Johnson first discusses the early ICU histories framed as anti-colonial romances by Clements Kadalie (1923–1928), Ernest Gitsham and James F. Trembath (1926), G.M. Godden (1928) and Leonard Barnes (1930). The discussion proceeds to consider the histories framed as liberal tragedy by A.W.G. Champion (1928), Winifred Holtby (1927–1934) and W.G. Ballinger (1929–1934); pauses briefly to examine the history of the ICU framed as farce by H. D. Tyamzashe (1941); and then continues to the histories framed as communist tragedy by Albert Nzula (1935), Edward Roux (1948), and Jack and Ray Simons (1969). The survey of the historiography of the ICU concludes with a brief consideration of the two major monographs on the ICU by Peter Wickins (1978) and Helen Bradford (1987), contending that both reproduce the deep structure of the anti-colonial romance. Demonstrating the limitations of reading the history of the ICU in terms of the genres of romance or tragedy, the balance of the chapter proposes an alternative generic frame for narrating the history of the ICU derived from C.L.R. James's suggestive insights into anti-colonial historiography.

Conclusion

In May 2013, Blade Nzimande, General Secretary of the SACP and ANC government minister, addressed over a thousand workers at a rally hosted by the ANC- and COSATU-affiliated National Union of Mine Workers. On the defensive after the killing of 34 miners by the South African Police at Marikana on 16 August 2012 and threatened by the rapid rise of the new Associated Mineworkers and Construction Union (AMCU), Nzimande excavated a century-old insult to impugn the rival union. AMCU, he told his audience, was guilty of 'Kadalism', an offence he defined as the attempt to 'divide the workers and liberation movement'[26]

Nzimande thus joined a long roll-call of public figures to have vituperated the ICU, beginning in the 1920s with racist politicians, white mine, factory and farm owners, and conservative ANC leaders. Unpacking fully Nzimande's insult in 2013 would require several paragraphs; instead, let us end with a mischievous question. In post-apartheid South Africa, how are we to interpret an attack upon a long-defunct liberation organisation (like the ICU) by a leading representative of the ruling alliance that is itself in deep crisis? There is little doubt that such attacks made in the 1980s – when the ANC, SACP and COSATU enjoyed unparalleled moral authority – might have been devastating. But do such insults, charges and accusations carry the same weight after the Marikana massacre, which took place under the regime of Jacob Zuma, the SACP and COSATU's favoured candidate during the power struggle with Thabo Mbeki? With this open question, we invite our readers to turn the page and re-assess the ICU.

SECTION A

The ICU in Southern Africa

1 The ICU, the Mines and the State in South West Africa, 1920–1926: Garveyism, Revolutionary Syndicalism and Global Labour History

Lucien van der Walt

Introduction

The Industrial and Commercial Workers' Union of Africa (ICU), formed in Cape Town, South Africa, in 1919, was not just the largest black and coloured ('mixed race', 'brown') protest movement in 1920s South Africa, it was also a transnational movement in aim and fact.[1] Resolving at its July 1920 congress at Bloemfontein, South Africa, on 'one great union of skilled and unskilled workers of Africa',[2] it spread into South West Africa in 1920, Swaziland around 1926, Southern Rhodesia in 1927, Basutoland in 1928 and Northern Rhodesia in 1931. As Henry Dee notes in this volume, it also had enthusiasts in Nyasaland and Mozambique,[3] although apparently no organised presence.

The ICU articulated a range of ideas, visions and grievances. It blended a class-based socialist language, directly derived from revolutionary syndicalists like the Industrial Workers of the World (IWW, 'Wobblies') later buttressed by some Marxism, with Pan-African nationalism (notably Garveyism) – and Christian, liberal, Marxist and social-democratic influences.

The ICU in South Africa and Southern Rhodesia developed into mass movements.[4] The other sections in the subcontinent were more modest: for example, there were two delegates from Basutoland at the ICU's July 1920 conference in Bloemfontein, and two again at its December 1927 conference in Durban, but branches were only founded in 1928, and proved short-lived.[5] The South West African ICU was another of the smaller sections. It operated in a large but sparsely populated territory, claimed by the German empire in 1884 but conquered by its southern neighbour, South Africa, during the First World War. Following military occupation in 1915, South Africa – a British Dominion and the most powerful, developed state in the region – ruled the colony under a League of Nations mandate.

The South West African ICU was centred on relatively cosmopolitan Lüderitz,[6] a small port town linked to local diamond fields and the fishing industry. However, from 1922, it also had a presence to the east in Keetmanshoop, around 330 kilometres inland by rail, a small administrative centre and railway hub in the midst of sheep farms; by 1926, to the south in Elizabeth Bay, a diamond mining town 25 kilometres from Lüderitz; and that same year in Walvis Bay, 750 kilometres to the north, a South African exclave that dated to the 1790s.[7]

It was tiny in comparison to the two big ICUs, but the historical significance of an organisation is not simply an outcome of its size. The South West African ICU was the first labour union based amongst black Africans and coloureds in that colony. It was also one of the first unions with a large membership of workers of colour in Southern Africa outside of South Africa.[8] It was preceded only by the 1911 *Associação das Artes Gráficas de Lourenço Marques* in Mozambique.

Thirdly, the South West African ICU appears in a different light when located within regional processes of class formation and struggle, rather than viewed in isolation. It was, after all, part of a larger ICU movement that aspired (in the words of an ICU organiser in Southern Rhodesia) to burn 'like veld fire' across and beyond the subcontinent.[9] As the global labour history approach notes, the 'methodological nationalism' of traditional labour (and political) history – where the nation-state's territory is taken as the self-evident unit of analysis – ignores transnational processes.[10] An examination of cross-border connections, and the development of multi-country comparisons, can shed new light on labour movements in Southern Africa, including the ICU.[11] The full story of the ICU requires not just fuller attention to the nuances of its complex politics, but a reframing of its history around a regional rather than a national framework, and a fuller account of the history of its smaller sections. [12]

This chapter, besides providing a partial reconstruction of the history and politics of the South West African ICU, is particularly interested in explaining why the union emerged when and where it did, and the factors that enabled and shaped, as well as limited its activities, spread and concerns. It was the first ICU outside of South Africa by far, emerging within two years of the mother body, which was founded in Cape Town in January 1919. It proved far more durable than the small ICU sections established in Basutoland, Northern Rhodesia and Swaziland, lasting over five years. Yet, it shared with them an inability to develop a mass base, or a countrywide character, unlike the South African ICU and the ICU *yase* Rhodesia.

Besides contributing to the larger study of the ICU movement, this chapter also contributes to the history of labour and protest in Namibia, and to a fuller understanding of the complexities of well over 150 years of connections, overlaps and entanglements between South Africa and South West Africa. The analysis draws heavily on the global labour history approach, in rejecting nationalist narratives, in paying close attention to cross-border connections and processes, and in using comparisons to identify some key issues.

This chapter argues that the ICU was an important pioneer of labour unionism and socialist ideas in South West Africa, intersected with the local Garvey movement in important ways, and can only be adequately understood by taking its connections with South Africa seriously. The South West African ICU championed the interests of a diverse range of people of colour, including South African coloured and local black African migrants, local workers, Afro-Caribbeans and West Africans, and not just proletarian, but also small business, interests. It intersected with the Garveyite movement in important ways but was a distinct formation. Its rise and fall cannot be understood outside of the context of a rapidly growing, highly concentrated but small, multi-racial and multi-national working class in southern South West Africa, centred on primary industries, in a repressive, racist colonial context.

Historiography and the South West African ICU

There is a significant, if largely dated, body of literature on the largest ICUs, those of South Africa and Southern Rhodesia. While the South West African ICU makes occasional appearances in studies of the South African body, it has received little attention. This is partly because of the paucity of work on the history of labour and the larger left in South West Africa: labour studies centre on an exposé of grim colonial (more recently, post-colonial) labour markets and working conditions, or studies of the new union movement established from the late 1970s, and linked to the (illegal) nationalist South West African People's Organisation (SWAPO), which was founded in 1960.

Yet unions emerged sixty years earlier, around 1914: later than Mozambique or South Africa, but contemporaneously with the rise of unions in the Rhodesias, and slightly ahead of Angola. A trade union was established in the port of Lüderitz by 1914,[13] by the small and then largely German-speaking white working class that emerged in the German period.[14] White workers were concentrated in harbours, mines and railways, with 702 whites and 8, 740 black Africans employed in mining and prospecting in 1924.[15] By 1920, there was a small union federation, stretching all the way to the Tsumeb copper mines in the far north near Angola, with its own weekly, the *Volksblatt*.[16]

Black African workers went on strike as early as 1893, and first unionised in 1920 with the ICU. At this time, socialist literature was also readily available, from Germany (including the social-democratic *Freiheit* and communist *Rote Fahne*) and South Africa, whose revolutionary syndicalist International Socialist League was also active in the colony.[17] Around 1928, the *Arbeiterverbandes für Südwestafrika* applied to join the International Federation of Trade Unions (as did the South African ICU);[18] it also sought to affiliate to the multi-racial South African Trade Union Congress.[19] Numerous other unions emerged from the 1930s onwards, and there was a strike wave in the 1950s. A South West African Labour and Farmers' Party was formed in 1931, with W.H. Fischer of the *Arbeiterverband* winning the seat for Kolmanskop, a mining town near Lüderitz.

There is, nonetheless, very little in the way of a labour or social history of the working class in Namibia. Such gaps are partly the result of the very limited literature on many elements of Namibian history and society. This does not, however, quite explain why some periods and themes rather than others have been largely ignored. Several other factors need to be noted.

One is the long-established tendency by writers across the intellectual and political spectrum to analyse the country primarily in terms of inter-group relations between races and ethnicities e.g., 'the whites', 'the Herero', 'the Nama', and 'the people'. Divisions within these neatly bounded groups are then typically reduced to differing views on what the group should and could do. In more left-wing and nationalist accounts, the inter-group relations approach remains, but framed by an emphasis on the evils of German and South African colonial rule, and a teleological story of 'popular resistance' developing into that of an emergent Namibian nation.

There is not much scope, within these essentially pluralist approaches, for attention to structured internal conflicts and cross-cutting divisions on class lines. The reduction of 'resistance' to a vaguely defined anti-colonialism makes it difficult to consider issues like class struggles between African aristocrats and commoners, or workers' opposition to capitalism as such. Working-class struggles matter here only as purported examples of national struggle; there is no real place here for things like white trade unions, readers of *Freiheit*, anarchists in 1920s Windhoek, [20] or local Black Consciousness and Trotskyism. [21]

The conflation of labour activism and nationalist politics, a recent survey notes, has profoundly 'inhibited our ability to conduct meaningful studies of labour relations, labour policy and the history of workers'. [22] It has led, *inter alia*, to misunderstanding the timeline and complexities of the labour movement. Thus, the SACP's South West Africa expert Ruth First would claim, in 1963, that unions first emerged with two short-lived efforts in Lüderitz in 1949–1952, after which there were supposedly 'no unions'. [23] Even in the early 1980s, the main labour organisations in the country were long-established white or formerly white unions, not SWAPO-linked bodies. [24]

Further, perceptions of Namibian history have been deeply structured by the crudest variant of the preceding approach: the assiduously promoted patriotic history that presents the rise of SWAPO and the start of its armed struggle in the north in 1966 as the inevitable and obvious culmination of a century of resistance.

But this effort at naturalising nationalism and SWAPO cannot explain why mass nationalism was absent for most of the colonial period, or why SWAPO's influence was always so limited in the southern half of Namibia. In South West Africa, as elsewhere, nationalism is demonstrably only one of many responses to colonial and national oppression, and indeed, just one current within national liberation struggles – consider, for example, the role of anarchism in Korea or Ukraine, or Marxism-Leninism in Angola or Vietnam. It also rests, obviously, on a methodological nationalism that assumes the borders of South West Africa constitute the container of the Namibian story, with activities understood as exile, international solidarity, or as South African colonialism.

The SWAPO nationalist narrative is a significant obstacle to labour history in its effacement of class divisions, its presentation of workers and unions as simply adjuncts to nationalism, and its heavy focus on older rural uprisings, presented as antecedents of its own largely rural armed struggle, concentrated near the Angolan border.

Against this backdrop, it is not surprising that the South West African ICU is substantively discussed in only three works: Gregory Pirio's 1982 paper on Garveyism in the making of Namibian nationalism, the notes in the published Marcus Garvey papers, and Tony Emmett's pioneering 1987 PhD on 'The Rise of African Nationalism in South West Africa/Namibia, 1915–1966'.

Pirio, working on the Marcus Garvey Papers Project, focused on demonstrating the influence of Garveyism on 1920s South Africa and South West Africa, especially on the ICU.[25] Despite fundamentally incorrect claims that the ICU was the 'labour wing of the Garvey movement', and Garveyism the 'ideological underpinning' of 1920s mass black politics in both Namibia and South Africa,[26] Pirio provided the first analysis of the ICU in Lüderitz, and its connections to South African-based ICU activists including J.C. Gumbs, Clements Kadalie and S. Bennet Ncwana, editor of *The Black Man* from 1920, which was (briefly) an official ICU organ.[27]

The Africa volumes of the published Marcus Garvey Papers, which appeared in 1995 and 2006, include notes on the Lüderitz ICU.[28] Like Pirio, the editors were primarily interested in the ICU (and other formations) only insofar as they intersected with Garveyism and seemed to affirm its influence. For example, the discussion of the Watch Tower movement skipped over almost all its religious doctrines in order to hone in on a few Garveyite traces.[29]

Emmett's work on Namibian resistance history, on the other hand, had a far wider scope, and provided a more balanced view of the ICU.[30] It had two main limits. First, the work on the ICU was narrowly concerned with the early years of the Lüderitz ICU. Secondly, it was framed by Emmett's interest in finding 'the origins of Namibian nationalism' within earlier struggles against 'colonial authority', which were retroactively dubbed an 'early and "underdeveloped" expression of nationalism',[31] as if these were self-evidently 'nationalist' or invariably led to 'modern' nationalism.

A new approach to the South West African ICU

Thus, key approaches to the study of Namibian history struggle to deal with the South West African ICU, which had a multi-national membership, preceded the SWAPO unions by 50 years, was southern and urban, was highly political but independent of parties, emphasised class rather than a Namibian nationalism, and which was so firmly embedded in the regional ICU that its branches sent delegates to ICU congresses in South Africa rather than hold their own national congresses (see below).

By moving away from methodological nationalism and nationalist histories, it becomes possible to construct a richer and more balanced account of the ICU movement, including in South West Africa. This requires rejecting general accounts of colonial oppression in favour of class analysis, dispensing with nationalist teleologies, in order to understand the rise, durability and limitations of the union.

The brute fact of oppression simply cannot explain why the ICU emerged when and where it did, what it did and why, or why it was not able to move beyond a fairly narrow zone of southern and coastal Namibia. This requires, at the least, attention to transnational processes and movements, and avoiding selective, often anachronistic and sometimes false nationalist mythologies.

It is useful to consider the ICU in a different way. In what follows, I suggest that the following factors must be considered in explaining its rise and characteristic features: the consolidation of a stratified, urban working class in the colony; the importance of transnational processes of class struggle as well as cross-border connections through immigrants and the circulation of dissident ideas, news and papers; and the peculiar characteristics of the urban enclaves in which the ICU operated. These self-same factors, which enabled the ICU in important ways, also limited it profoundly, accounting in substantial part – but not entirely – for its failure to develop a mass base and colony-wide presence.

Working-class formation: A basis for the ICU

The lush north of South West Africa, towards the Angolan border, was home to large Bantu-language-speaking black African farming societies: the Ovambo alone accounted for over half the colonial population of 200 000 in the 1910s. It was largely barred to whites outside of a few mining concessions. In the east, there was a small Tswana-speaking population, with connections to neighbouring Bechuanaland.

The arid central and southern region of South West Africa, or *Polizei-Zone* (later, the 'Police Zone'), was far more sparsely populated, largely by San (so-called 'Bushman') hunter-gatherers, pastoralists both Bantu-speaking (like Herero) and Khoi (so-called 'Hottentot', like Damara); the latter blurred into Afrikaans-speaking Baster,[32] coloured, Oorlam and Nama pastoralists who trekked from South Africa from the 1700s. Windhoek, the German colonial capital, was actually founded by Oorlam in 1840.

A mixture of diplomacy and war opened the Police Zone to white settlement, especially a brutal German imperial war against Herero and Nama rebels in 1904–1908 that killed off more than half these populations. This war was followed by devastating land and livestock expropriations. By the end of German rule, half of the total land area was opened to whites on a freehold basis. The Namib desert made up much of the zone, and the dry, hot climate and limited vegetation of the remainder helped ensure that sheep farming on vast ranches was predominant.

Many white farmers, even in the early South African period, were under-capitalised and relatively poor: given low wages and a shortage of labour, it was common for workers – predominantly Nama – to also receive grazing rights for their own herds.[33] Although several reserve areas were declared in the Police Zone, notably the Berseba Hottentot Territory (later 'Namaland') north of Keetmanshoop, these were overcrowded and highly stratified. With farm labour unattractive and reserve life precarious, many sought urban jobs in the southern towns, especially Keetmanshoop and Lüderitz.[34]

Given absolute labour shortages, as well as specific gaps in key jobs, other labour supplies were tapped. German workers, especially artisans, were brought in on a large scale before the South African occupation. By 1914, there were 14, 000 whites in the colony, of which 12, 000 were Germans, with most of the rest Afrikaners.[35] Afrikaners started to arrive in the ill-fated *dorsland* treks of the 1870s – pastoralist migrations that reached into Angola – while others came as transport riders in the 1900s. Given that the number of whites involved in agriculture was tiny – there were just 500 white farms in the Police Zone in 1907, rising to 1 300 in 1913 –[36] it is obvious that most whites were urban, and a great many were reliant on wage labour.

While around half the German population was (mostly forcibly) repatriated after the occupation, provision was made for the rest to access South African citizenship and white South African immigration was meanwhile encouraged, partly to shift 'poor whites' to the new territory, and partly to fill empty posts on the mines and elsewhere. By 1926, the white population had almost doubled to 24 000, of which half were Afrikaans-speaking, and 10% English-speaking, including Jews.[37]

Secondly, under German rule there was also substantial use of black African and coloured workers from outside the colony in a range of jobs. Coloured and black workers were actively recruited in Cape Town from 1904, including men from the Eastern Cape, Xhosa-speaking areas.[38] The Cape Coloured population was substantial enough to sustain cultural associations and a local version of the Cape Town Carnival.[39] This sort of recruitment continued to some extent under South African rule;[40] coloureds from South Africa were a mainstay of Lüderitz crayfish operations into (at least) the 1950s.[41]

South West Africa was, at the time, one of the most attractive labour markets in Southern Africa,[42] and these non-Namibian workers were able to secure rights and wages substantially better than locals employed on the farms, or the migrant labour recruited in the north. Increasing use was made in the south of black men recruited north of the Police Zone. Most were from Ovamboland, followed by adjacent Kavongo, but a few came from Angola; Walvis Bay also used migrants, but drew heavily from South Africa itself. These men were 'migrant labourers' in the Southern African sense: men whose families maintained rural homesteads, while they worked elsewhere on fixed contracts, especially in mines and rail as, in South Africa and the Rhodesias, such men were increasingly housed in closed compounds and under contracts that amounted to indenture.[43]

It is essential, when understanding this growing working class, to note, first, that South West Africa was, and remains extremely sparsely populated. With the local or indigenous population estimated at 200 000 in the 1910s, the total population was 214 000 on the eve of the First World War. This was less than the population of Johannesburg at the time,[44] although South West Africa was two-thirds the size of South Africa. Only a third of the total was in the Police Zone, either near the coast or in the scrublands of the east.

These South Africans were prominent in ports like Lüderitz and Swakopmund, along with Afro-Caribbeans, Cameroonians and Liberians (the latter were so-called 'Kroo-boys', or 'Kru'). Many were employed by German shipping companies, which relied heavily on West Africans, but many Liberians moved into jobs in finance, government, mining, railways and restaurants.[45] Liberians and black and coloured South Africans were the largest groups of 'foreign' workers, after Germans and South African whites.[46]

Not only were the rural areas of the zone sparsely populated overall, but its towns were also tiny by South African or Rhodesian standards. In 1916, Lüderitz had just 1 600 white residents, predominantly Germans.[47] Lüderitz, founded in 1883 as a trading post, was the colony's only harbour besides Swakopmund before 1920. It was also a railway hub, with a line running east through the surrounding Namib desert completed in 1908 when it reached Keetmanshoop, the key town in the sheep farming region in interior.

But Lüderitz really took off when diamond fields were opened in the desert to the south from 1908. This led to the declaration of a large *Sperrgebiet* for the exclusive use of diamond companies and the establishment of a line of mining towns in the desert, running from Kolmanskop through Elizabeth Bay, Pomona and Bogenfels, linked up by a private railway line. These were company towns, not municipalities with power over large rural hinterlands like Lüderitz and Keetmanshoop. Kolmanskop, the largest and richest, had a population of just 1 100 in the late 1920s, including 800 black migrant workers.[48]

The diamond boom was not the start of capitalist mining in South West Africa, as this started at Tsumeb in 1900, but it made the colony profitable for the first time.[49] It made Lüderitz an extremely important town, and it seemed possible that it would displace Windhoek as the capital.[50] It became a crucial adjunct to the diamond industry, the site of a local Chamber of Mines, the first stock exchange, of engineering and ship repair works, and a key place for importing machinery, food and fresh water. It became the 'the major industrial enclave in Namibia' at the time,[51] although it should also be seen as a key node in the complex of diamond mining towns and the colonial transport infrastructure in the Police Zone, and as closely connected to Keetmanshoop in the interior. There was also a growing fishing industry (including processing and canning).

These small urban centres that accommodated the working class were crucial to the formation of a stratified working class in South West Africa. This was concentrated in large private capitalist operations, like mines, or state operations, like railways, harbours and municipalities. Migrant labourers, as well as the local people of the Police Zone, were enmeshed in a labour relations system rooted in restrictions on land ownership and livestock and centred on coercion and a system of registration books (under the Germans) and passes (under South Africa).[52] By contrast, most of the Caribbean, West African and South African white workers were more-or-less free labour in the classic sense, but were further divided by race, skill and nationality.

Like Lüderitz and Keetmanshoop, the mining towns were typically segregated into three: a white area, an out-of-sight 'location' for black and coloured people – usually a grim slum – and compounds for migrant workers. The residential parts of the white area, in turn, were divided between the homes of the elite, more modest family housing, and hostels for single working men.

The South African take-over had some effects but did not fundamentally affect the social structure. German investments were fairly rapidly displaced by South African private capital, notably the diamond mines where Consolidated Diamond Mines, an Anglo American Corporation operation, established a monopoly from 1919. The South African state took control of state lands, engaged in a renewed round of land seizures, and its state corporations expanded across the colony. Thus, SA Railways and Harbours (SAR&H) took over the Lüderitz docks as well as the railways through its South West African division, and further integrated the railways into the South African grid with a new line running from Upington to Keetmanshoop. The South African state retained some demarcations and regulations like the Police Zone and *Sperrgebiet* in the colony, but made some reforms, such as replacing the registration book system with an internal passport ('pass law') system, and increasingly ruled South West Africa as a fifth province.

The rise of the South West African ICU

Clearly, objective conditions now enabled the emergence of something like the ICU. However, the rise of the ICU, as an actual working-class movement, required something more, and here it is essential to take account of both local dynamics and transnational processes.

Exactly how, or when, the Lüderitz ICU was established remain murky but its emergence was closely linked to the great wave of strikes that rocked Southern Africa from 1917–1925, including in South West Africa.[53] As elsewhere, post-war inflation was an important cause of this transnational working-class rebellion, although of course this intersected with local dynamics.[54] The diamond industry was closed down during the early part of the First World War, leading to substantial wage losses. Workers like the Kru were also aggrieved by losses incurred due to being conscripted into the German war effort, and by declining wages and employment under South African rule.[55] From 1917, South Africa detailed German abuses and racism as part of its war-time propaganda and in order to buttress its post-war claims on the territory.[56] There were hopes that its rule would lead to real improvements, and the dashing of this hope contributed directly to strike action on the mines of the south.[57]

In July 1919, white workers won a strike on the diamond fields in the face of martial law,[58] doubtless inspiring other workers to similar actions. In 1920, rumours of a general strike swept Lüderitz. On 3 May, 'Ovambos (about 250 of them) and 5 Cape Boys [i.e., coloureds] struck work at Charlottental, and marched to Lüderitzbucht with all their kit and chattels', followed by strikes at Bogenfels, Ponoma and

Stachslager, again including compound and daily workers, among the latter coloureds, 'Hottentots' and Liberians.[59]

At this point, the importance of cross-border connections through immigrants and the circulation of a dissident press becomes important. While the Ovambo went back to work (and their compounds) at Ponoma, 30 daily-paid workers – coloureds, Kru and Khoi (most probably, Nama from the east) – refused to return without concrete wage gains. They were then expelled to Lüderitz on a special train.

The Lüderitz magistrate believed that South African coloureds 'had fomented the trouble all along the line' and identified one 'Laguma' as an instigator at Ponoma; he recommended he be deported, an opinion shared by the local police. 'Laguma' was Jimmy La Guma, a young coloured worker from Cape Town with some familiarity with socialist literature, who had worked in South West Africa since 1910, on a farm, the railways and then the diamond fields.

La Guma's own account of the Ponoma events matches that of the Lüderitz magistrate, although it gives the year of the strike as 1918.[60] It provides important details that fill out the story and underline the importance of radical immigrants: apparently, he helped initiate a workers' committee including (South African) Xhosa, local Khoi and Ovambo; he was secretary while another coloured, William Adriaanse, was chair. The committee issued a letter of demand to management and, receiving no response, workers downed tools. La Guma, in taking such actions, drew on his 'mainly theoretical knowledge of the class struggle and the trade union movement'.[61]

Adriaanse and La Guma were among those shipped off to Lüderitz, where they would help found the ICU a few months later. La Guma was not deported from the colony, but he was 'black-balled' on the mines. He survived by working on ships at the harbour and threw himself into protests by coloureds against efforts to put them under the pass laws and was arrested as a ring-leader.[62] Among others arrested was a certain Pieterse, described by La Guma as a 'one-armed school teacher', also a coloured, who authorities suspected of being an ICU agent from Cape Town.[63]

Much of the initiative to form an ICU section came from these immigrants. According to La Guma, white workers did show some sympathy with black and coloured strikers, who marched to the trains under a tattered red flag cobbled together from a stick and a borrowed neckerchief. As 'the trains steamed slowly away' from Ponoma, the 'German artisans working in the machine-shops looked up … lowered their tools and raised their clenched fists in salute'.[64] But these workers, the best paid and best treated, and predominant in the skilled jobs, seem to have shown little interest in organising across the colour line.

But why, then, did Adriaanse and La Guma not form a completely new union of their own? Here the transnational circulation of dissident ideas, news and publications was crucial. La Guma was deeply impressed by reports of the joint December 1919 strike on the Cape Town docks by the ICU and the syndicalist Industrial Workers of Africa (IWA), against the SAR&H as well as the private shipping and stevedoring firms.[65]

These were the very same types of employers who predominated in Lüderitz. It also worth noting at this point that many ICU struggles in South Africa in the early years, including at Bloemfontein, Cape Town, East London and Port Elizabeth, involved workers in municipalities or on the state-run harbours and railways. Interest in the ICU's anti-capitalist rhetoric has tended to obscure the extent to which it was, at least before the mid-1920s, a union substantially based in the state sector. The ICU would surely have seemed a good fit for Lüderitz, and for La Guma himself, with his railways background and current employment at the port.

Copies of the ICU's *Black Man* also circulated in Lüderitz at the time, with John de Clue, Afro-Caribbean and owner of one of four black businesses in the Lüderitz 'location',[66] listed as its local agent; evidently, he corresponded with Ncwana.[67] The paper carried enthusiastic reports on ICU progress, including details of the July 1920 congress which saw the IWA and other unions merge under the ICU banner. Its programme, insisting on coloured/ black unity, abolishing pass laws, and organising all workers regardless of sector, sex or sector,[68] would have spoken directly to the experiences and concerns of men like Adriaanse, La Guma and Pieterse.

The ICU's 'one great union' model probably also seemed ideally suited to Lüderitz, which was not based on a large concentration of workers facing a single employer like the diamond towns. Rather, the workforce was split between employees of shipping and stevedoring firms, the SAR&H, the municipality, the fishing companies, and small firms, such as engineering workshops and restaurants.

Emmett asserts the ICU was founded in December 1920.[69] The leadership included Adriaanse, De Clue and La Guma; Pieterse and one Hannibal, also an Afro-Caribbean storekeeper, were also founder members; a Nama, Jacob Jantjes, would serve on the committee.[70] The secretary post was a paid one, held by La Guma and after his return to South Africa in 1921, by Adriaanse.[71] Adriaanse remained active for some time, as did a Mr Wood.[72] Unlike the ICU in the Rhodesias, Kadalie's Nyasa compatriots provided neither agitators nor a communications network for the union in South West Africa. The immigrants that counted in spreading the union to the northern colony were coloured South Africans.

The formation of a South West African body was reported at the January 1921 conference of the ICU in Cape Town, and De Clue of Lüderitz attended the October 1921 ICU congress in Port Elizabeth.[73] In 1922, the ICU was established in Keetmanshoop, which, like Lüderitz, had a (relatively large) population of several thousand: these were the two biggest towns in the south. Keetmanshoop started as a Nama settlement and Rhenish mission station in the 1860s. In the 1900s, it was a growing town, benefitting from its role as a military centre, and its growing importance as an administrative centre, covering 34 farms in 1913.[74] Keetmanshoop had a larger white population than Lüderitz and a black population of 1 720 in 1929.[75] But like Lüderitz, its importance from the 1910s rested increasingly on its role as a transport hub. It connected the railway from Lüderitz to a north–south line running that reached Windhoek, 460 kilometres to the north, in 1912, under the Germans; under South Africa, it was connected to Upington, South Africa, 470 kilometres to the south by the SAR&H.

The town was thus crucial to the railways – the main transport infrastructure in the southern interior – and to the growing number of sheep farms; it was also the site of shops and services and an important administrative centre. It was by rail and through Keetmanshoop that Ovambo and other migrant labourers from the north reached the mines of the south. In addition to the town 'location', home to coloureds, Herero, Nama and Ovambo,[76] there was a railway compound 'set apart for natives and coloureds, in which there were some hundreds of natives', some apparently with families.[77] It seems clear that the union spread along the railway line.

The South West African ICU was never designated a separate national section, unlike the ICU *yase* Rhodesia; rather, its branches sent delegates to ICU congresses in South Africa, as was the case with the ICU in Basutoland. The two early South West African branches had seats at the January 1923 congress in Cape Town, both represented by Jimmy La Guma, who was resident in South Africa from 1921. There do not seem to have been delegates at the January 1924 conference in East London, but De Clue was present at the April 1925 congress in Johannesburg.

In October 1922, the ICU's President-General, J.C. Gumbs, visited both Lüderitz and Keetmanshoop. He presumably met the Keetmanshoop branch when he visited the town in 1922.[78] Gumbs did not report on the branch at the 1923 ICU conference where La Guma, acting as its representative, also provided no details. The conference recorded, only, that it was donating £5 to the ICU's printing press fund (Lüderitz gave £10).[79] The Keetmanshoop local government, unlike that of Lüderitz which engaged in surveillance of the ICU, also paid little attention to the local ICU. Thus, there are few details available regarding the Keetmanshoop branch.

Urban peculiarities, private and state investments, and the ICU

It was in the small, southern urban areas that black and coloured unionisation started with the ICU. It was based on the larger, more concentrated workforces around large private operations, such as Anglo's Consolidated Diamond Mines, and big state operations, such as SAR&H. The ICU emerged in the two biggest municipalities in the south, Keetmanshoop and Lüderitz, both of which played a crucial role as transport hubs.

In these early years, the union was not structured around workplaces but in the locations. It also seems to have been centred in the urban strata lying between the mass of unfree migrant labourers and farm labourers at the bottom, and the white workers above. The available evidence suggests that the founder members in Lüderitz were fairly typical of that branch as a whole: mainly black and coloured workers and marginal petty bourgeois traders, resident in the town's location; it was there, too, that the union held its meetings.

Government officials recognised this situation and were demonstrably concerned that the ICU would break out into the farms and compounds.[80] Like German officials before them,[81] they also feared South African coloured workers would incite locals. At Lüderitz, systematic efforts were made to block the union's access to compounds, and especially to the Ovambo workers, and to keep ICU emissaries off the diamond fields. [82] Police found that Pieterse was trying to recruit Ovambo:[83] he was given a warning and placed under surveillance. After Gumbs' tour, which apparently included a visit to the railway compound at Keetmanshoop,[84] there was a *de facto* ban on ICU leaders from South Africa touring the colony.[85]

Thus, the Lüderitz ICU was largely denied access to two of the major concentrations of workers – the compounds and the diamond towns – while operating in a town where the workforce was divided between numerous employers, some quite small. The densely populated, relatively small, segregated Lüderitz 'location', with its slum conditions, was the best concentration of workers available.

Compound managers were crucial to thwarting the union, but over time, the ICU made inroads into the compounds. In 1926, two black South Africans, named as Timothy and Naphtali in the records, held ICU meetings and collected funds in a compound at the South African exclave of Walvis Bay.[86] Walvis Bay was, from 1922, administered as part of South West Africa, but continued to draw on South African labour. The two men were deported, although Naphtali seems to have managed to return to the town later that year. [87]

There was a more sustained ICU branch in the southern diamond town of Elizabeth Bay, which was based on deep diggings. It was led by Standright Mackenzie, Garnet Tshabalala and Kegapilee Moogoris, and active in 1926 and 1927.[88] These were black men, apparently South Africans,[89] who lived in the mine compound. In January 1927, the branch held a protest meeting where 'the local chairman and several Executive Committee members made strong speeches' against a rash of repressive and racist bills before the South African parliament.[90] This meeting, which resumed in the evening when the speakers again 'waxed hot', was part of a larger ICU campaign.

Again, we see that the ICU emerged where workers were concentrated – and again where workers lived, not the workplace itself. Perhaps these men were among the delegates from South West Africa that reportedly attended the December 1927 ICU congress at Kimberley, South Africa,[91] easily reached by rail via Keetmanshoop and Upington.

The politics of the South West African ICU

These same conditions that enabled the rise and spread of the South West African ICU also shaped its activities and concerns. It is profoundly mistaken to suggest, as Pirio did, that the ICU was essentially, the 'labour wing of the Garvey movement', or that Garveyism presented as the 'ideological underpinning' of 1920s mass black politics in either South Africa or its colony.[92]

Certainly, Garveyism and the UNIA were among the myriad influences on the ICU, including in South West Africa, and there was also some overlap in membership, the key example being De Clue, adherent of both. But the politics of the ICU were far more complicated, evolving and diverse than conflations like Pirio's admit.

There was little similarity between the programme of ICU in South West Africa and that of the Universal Negro Improvement Association (UNIA). As elsewhere there was, for instance, a substantial influence from revolutionary syndicalism, including the IWA and the Industrial Workers of the World, and of class politics more generally.

The rules and regulations members adopted by the ICU in Lüderitz make no mention of any goals beyond improving the 'social, moral and intellectual interests' of members, including 'equitable rates of wages, and reasonable hours of labour, to regulate the relations between employer and employee'.[93] Whites could join, but not serve as leaders, unlike the UNIA, while the ICU also stressed class politics: the union would cooperate 'with the worker [sic.] of other unions for the advancement of the whole working class'.[94] This helps explain why the ICU did not engage in the UNIA's characteristic activities in South West Africa, such as selling rosettes, raising money for projects like halls and business schemes, benefit schemes, recruiting chiefs, requesting the colony be handed to Garvey, or spreading millenarian promises of liberation by black America.

While the Lüderitz ICU does not seem to have organised any workplace structures, nor negotiated with any employers, nor undertaken any industrial actions, this outpost of the 'one great union' focused on the sphere of social reproduction. It highlighted the lack of education and hospital facilities for blacks and coloureds, segregation on the trains, taxation and licensing fees, including for black businesses, pass laws and abusive police. De Clue gave a long, fiery report on these matters at the October 1921 ICU conference in Port Elizabeth,[95] which led directly to the decision to send Gumbs to the colony. Likewise, the ICU in Elizabeth Bay joined an ICU campaign against proposed new laws – but does not seem to have been able to engage in battles around wages and workplace conditions.

An alternative view of the ICU is presented by Emmett, who tended to dismiss the Lüderitz ICU as basically a vehicle for more elite interests, mainly concerned with 'privileged urban groups' and petty traders.[96] But while the union had little to do with the workplace, it raised issues affecting black and coloured residents in general, most of them working class. While centred on a stratum that was treated better than the migrants and the farm labourers, it hardly represented an elite. Even the best-off small traders like De Clue were on the margins.

It is true that ICU in both South Africa[97] and South West Africa often sent delegations to the authorities, seeking redress of grievances. This was less a sign of innate reformism than a result of its strategy. Since the ICU in South West Africa did not build workplace power, or show any ability to organise strikes from its bases in 'locations' or compounds, it had very little leverage, and was often fobbed off with excuses and vague promises. Not much was gained, beyond a circular to municipalities in the early 1920s stating that Cape Coloureds were to be exempted from passes, curfews and various segregationist by-laws, and treated, as far as possible, 'on an equal footing with Europeans', including being allowed to live outside the locations.[98]

The challenges of small town and farmlands

At the same time, the very factors that allowed the ICU to emerge in South West Africa – small towns with large workforces and segregated, concentrated residential areas, compounds that gathered hundreds of workers, large investments by private capital and the state – also created substantial obstacles to its operations.

Small municipalities and company-run diamond towns lent themselves to surveillance, harassment and controls over movement. This was evident in the ongoing monitoring of the ICU in Lüderitz, the ongoing and clearly effective measures taken to isolate the early ICU from the compounds and the farms, direct pressure placed on Pieterse, the deportations at Walvis Bay, and the capacity to block visits from South Africa. For example, following his address at the October 1921 ICU congress, which was reported in the press and attracted the ire of officials, De Clue was targeted 'by the local authorities in the Protectorate',[99] and subjected to threats like the revocation of his business licence.[100]

Furthermore, the Police Zone was not just sparsely populated, but most of the population was rural. Few farms had large workforces, and the different farms were isolated by the large size of the farms, the great distances between settlements, and the rudimentary transport infrastructure. Moreover, the rural sector of the working class was immersed in labour-repressive and paternalistic relations. There were occasional strikes, including in 1918, but unionisation never took place.

This alone cannot explain why unions (or the ICU) did not emerge in the rural areas. In South Africa and in Southern Rhodesia, the ICU developed into a mass movement, and in both, it grew explosively once it entered the countryside.

In South Africa from 1925, the ICU connected up with the tens of thousands of black tenant farmers on white farms, then being forced into wage labour by the final roll-out of the 1913 Land Act.[101] The ICU *yase* Rhodesia, initially based in the black townships of Bulawayo and Salisbury, the two main towns, grew rapidly when it managed to penetrate the reserves from the end of the 1920s. Here, the peasants and chiefs were feeling the blows of the 1930 Land Apportionment Act, which drastically reduced black access to land. [102]

But the conditions facing the South West African ICU were different. In South Africa and Southern Rhodesia, the large-scale development of white commercial farming in the 1920s centred on breaking peasant (including tenant) farming and was associated with rapid urbanisation. There was no major restructuring in South West African colonial agrarian relations in the Police Zone until the 1950s, despite a massive boom in the karakul industry from the 1930s.[103] There was rural unrest in the early 1920s: mostly localised and small scale, it faded in the face of 'the preponderant power of the state'; the armed rebellion of the Bondelswarts, over 200 km south of Keetmanshoop, was triggered by an 'absurdly high tax' and crushed with overwhelming force, with 100 killed.[104]

Conclusion: *The importance of politics*

This paper has tried to show how the ICU was shaped by, and operated in, the very specific conditions of 1920s South African-ruled Namibia. That said, it must be emphasised that while objective conditions enabled, shaped and constrained the union, they provide only a partial explanation of its evolution and features.

Due account must also be taken of the political choices made by the union and its militants. The UNIA – despite all its weaknesses and utopian character, and despite its manifest inability to do anything to change the conditions of farm labourers and reserve residents – was able to develop a short-lived presence in the rural areas around Keetmanshoop. The authorities were convinced, in hindsight correctly so, that the ICU could penetrate the compounds, yet there was not much achieved in this regard before 1926.

In part, the limitations reflected the weaknesses of the ICU everywhere. Its ideas were a *sui generis* and unstable mixture:[105] ICU discourse shifted between, and sometimes mixed, ideas of international class solidarity, black racial unity across classes, social revolution, constitutional reform and self-help business schemes. It drew, variously and to different degrees at different times, on Garveyism, Christianity, Marxism, liberalism, and revolutionary syndicalism; these influences jostled and overlapped, in an unstable and changing mix of ideas and politics.

This enabled a remarkable degree of flexibility in how the ICU could position itself and adapt to changing circumstances. Yet this also mitigated – as later unions in South Africa emphasised – against the adoption of any clear strategy, concrete, democratic and patient workplace organising, strikes and the careful building of a bottom-up, self-managed working-class counter-power, backed by education and a proletarian counter-culture.[106] Rather, the ICU relied on rallies, speeches, sweeping promises and raising great hopes, and increasingly, on personality politics. In the end, it could not be sustained. There is much to be admired in the ICU, as a pioneer of trade unionism, of black and coloured workers' unity, of political awakening, anti-colonialism and anti-racism, and of immense bravery and sacrifice – and, perhaps of especial interest today, of a working-class globalisation-from-below. But it is important, too, to honour its legacy by learning from its limitations.

2 The Rabble-Rouser: Robert Sambo's ICU Stint in Rhodesia

Anusa Daimon

Introduction

In February 1927, the South African-inspired ICU spread its tentacles beyond the Limpopo River, when its leader Clements Kadalie deployed fellow Nyasa Robert Sambo, to establish a sister section in Southern Rhodesia. Clandestinely operating in and around Bulawayo and Salisbury, Sambo, with the assistance of another Nyasa, John Mphamba, challenged the colonial establishment for five months; by June 1927, his nascent movement had been effective enough to get him deported from Rhodesia. The movement struck a new note of radicalism in Rhodesian black African politics, offering the most vocal challenge yet to colonial policies, appealing to working-class solidarity, attacking the government, and demanding basic rights.[1] Sambo's transformative politics and *blitzkrieg* success alarmed the authorities in Rhodesia and other neighbouring colonies, always on the lookout for ICU agents.

He was thrust into the deep-end, with a state that was not as tolerant of African unionism and agitation as that which his leader, Kadalie, experienced in neighbouring South Africa. Although the Rhodesian administration unceremoniously expelled him, all was in vain because Sambo had sown the seeds for the emergence of a radical new labour movement organised around urban, mine and farm workers. According to Ranger, the ICU represented a process of political expansion and democratisation and thus attracted peasants, builders, clerks, domestic servants, factory workers, municipal workers and miners.[2] Sambo's short stint left an indelible legacy, inspired Rhodesian Africans like Masotsha Ndlovu and Job Matabasi Dumbutshena (who revived the Rhodesian ICU in 1928), Charles Mzingeli (an ICU stalwart who revived it in 1946), Benjamin Burombo and others to form their labour unions between the 1930s and 1950s. Sambo laid the base for urban social movements – a crucial antecedent for modern mass nationalism.

While the legacies of the ICU have been well addressed in a nuanced Zimbabwean historiography, not much is known about Sambo himself, who was so crucial to these developments.[3] Unlike other ICU activists in Rhodesia like Mzingeli, the literature is generally silent on his biography, including his brief but dramatic encounters with the Rhodesian state. Sambo appears as a footnote in the Zimbabwean ICU, which talks rudimentarily about his deployment to and banishment from Rhodesia. His life before, and the details of how he executed the colossal task of promoting radical worker consciousness within a rigid and intolerant colonial state is not well detailed. What he did after his deportation is also hazy, despite the international ramifications of this move by the Rhodesian state and how Kadalie used Sambo's deportation for the general benefit of the ICU. The story of what Sambo did after his deportation is also missing: he did not immediately return to Nyasaland as assumed in the orthodox narrative, but first detoured to South Africa through Mozambique, before returning to his ancestral homeland. He continued to be connected to the broader anti-colonial politics in Nyasaland but surprisingly not with labour unionism, choosing to join the millenarian Christian movement instead.

Using archival and secondary literature, this chapter reconstructs a biographical narrative of Sambo, showcasing how he, dubbed an 'undesirable native alien' by the authorities, accomplished the mission of establishing a rabble-rousing movement against a hostile state, as well as the aftermath of this struggle. It argues that Sambo's relatively brief ICU stint was critical in the overall emergence and evolution of the ICU and trade unionism in Rhodesia, and in developing Kadalie's strategy of spreading the ICU across Southern Africa. Other than radicalising Rhodesian Africans, it offered Kadalie as well as later Rhodesian trade unionists valuable lessons in confronting and coping with Rhodesian repression of radical African political consciousness.

Reading Sambo: Historiographical silences and the quest for sources

The historiography of the ICU in Zimbabwe has few details on the Sambo era. Very little is dedicated to him other than his deployment by Kadalie in February 1927 to establish the ICU in Rhodesia, and his deportation in June 1927. Not much is known about his life, education and family before his five months stint in Rhodesia, or of his life after deportation. In contrast, the Rhodesia ICU narrative is more extensive on the period from 1928. Dealing with the organisation's revival by Sambo's successor, Ndlovu, the literature is exceptionally detailed on its growth, weaknesses and impact.

There is some limited material on Sambo in the secondary literature. The absence of Sambo in the historiography is rooted in the dearth of sources on him. Sambo is one of those ICU luminaries with a very small, highly fragmented paper trail for researchers. One has to literarily scavenge from a few available sources. A primary reason is the nature and attitude of the Rhodesian state towards what it deemed subversive elements. From the onset, the state was unfriendly and went to great lengths to thwart their influence on the general African population. This included censoring the ICU in public newspapers such as the *Rhodesian Herald* and the *Bulawayo Chronicle*. However, the ICU also found an audience in the local and international media, particularly the US-based *Negro World*, the UK-based *New Leader* and ICU's *Workers' Herald*, casting some light on Sambo in the process, especially after his deportation from Rhodesia.

The Rhodesian and South African states, in their quest to track the activities of the ICU, did generate intelligence and policing reports on the ICU where Sambo is mentioned, as well as correspondence concerning Sambo deportation between different departments as well as the two states. But Sambo, as Kadalie's lieutenant, was operating under the colossal shadow of his leader, the main figure attracting concern by colonial regimes. Most colonial investigations were dedicated to Kadalie, at the expense of his emissaries like Sambo, who appeared in cameos as part of a supporting cast.

Unfortunately, even this archival residue is incomplete because critical listed files on the ICU activities in Rhodesia cannot be located in the National Archives of Zimbabwe in Harare and elsewhere.[4] Sambo also never wrote an autobiography: not even a picture can be found. His successors, Ndhlovu and Mzingeli, were both interviewed by later researchers, and their lives are richly represented in the literature: Sambo's was not.[5] Kadalie himself says very little about Sambo in his autobiography, *My Life and the ICU: The Autobiography of a Black Trade Unionist in South Africa*.

All these sources, few as they are, are critical in reconstructing a crucial part of Zimbabwe's ICU and trade unionism history. They illuminate to some extent a biographical account of Sambo and his short rabble-rousing stint and legacy in Rhodesia. They also reflect on the nature of the Rhodesian state in relation to other regional regimes, as they responded to the trail-blazing ICU challenge across Southern Africa.

The rabble-rousing 'undesirable native alien'

Sambo was born in the 1890s in Rumphi in Karonga district, Northern Malawi. He belonged to the Henga, a sub-ethnic group of the Tumbuka ethnic group. He was an alumnus of the famed Overtoun Institution of Livingstonia Mission in Bandawe, like his friend Kadalie and other Malawian luminaries like Mphamba, later associated with the ICU. He joined thousands of able-bodied men migrating from Nyasaland to neighbouring countries in Central and Southern Africa in search of wage employment: the consequence of limited money-income opportunities, harsh taxes and low wage rates for Africans in colonial Malawi. In the matrix of the regional colonial economy dominated by South Africa, Nyasaland became a labour reservoir including for manual migrant workers under the infamous *chibharo* system, as well as for more skilled black white-collar workers like clerks.[6] This saw both ordinary Malawians and educated men, including luminaries like Dunuza Chisiza Kadalie, Elliot Kamwana, Mphamba and even later Malawian president, Hastings Kamuzu Banda, moving south across the labour frontier, in the process influencing and reshaping the region's political economy.

Sambo seems to have left Nyasaland earlier than Kadalie, and initially worked in South Africa before returning to Nyasaland in 1912, two months after the formation of the South African Native National Congress.[7] This development inspired him, on his return, to join Levi Mumba and Simon Muhango in founding the North Nyasa Native Association in 1912, one of the earliest 'interwar secular political pressure groups lobbying for the improvement of African welfare in Nyasaland.'[8] This was followed by the West Nyasa Native Association formed in 1914, the Mombera Native

Association in 1920, the Southern Province Native Association in 1923, the Central Province Native Association in 1927 and the Chiradzulu District Association in 1929, all playing an influential role in the early stage of Nyasaland nationalism.

These associations tried to advance the social, economic and political interests of the indigenous population, including through self-help. The *Livingstonia News* published by the Livingstonia Mission at Khondowe, Rumphi, reported that Sambo started a movement in Karonga 'encouraging my people in agriculture':

> It is now high time for the Africans to rise up and work out their own salvation… For nothing can come without struggling for it and the mission being the chief captain who recruits and drills us for this salvation I am encouraged to write you for this, and I hope you will be interested in it, as it is part and parcel of your noble duties among us.[9]

These associations were precursors of the Nyasaland African Congress in 1944, which led Malawi towards independence.

Sambo would subsequently return to the southern labour markets where Kadalie was already causing colonial disharmony with his fledgling ICU, which was founded in 1919. Described by the Cape Town MP and Advocate Will Stuart as an 'unparalleled colossal phenomenon – an African Xavier', Kadalie had an unhappy stay in Rhodesia from 1915 and 1918 where he faced racism and witnessed exploitation before finding his way to South Africa.[10] The experience was decisive in radicalising him.[11] He worked at the Shamva mines as a clerk, first in the compound office and later in the general manager's office.[12] In 1916, he moved on to Salisbury (now Harare) but could not find any work, then south to the notorious Mvuma mine, then to Bulawayo, where he worked as clerk on the Rhodesian Railways.[13]

Kadalie's move to South Africa in February 1918 would totally transform his life and the course of African labour activism in the region.[14] He vowed to address the 'evils of the mining recruiting system and the systematic torture of the African people in Rhodesia that kindled the spirit of revolt in me'.[15] He had unfinished business in Rhodesia, the liberation of Rhodesian blacks always high among his priorities.[16] Further, the ICU was committed, from 1920, to organising northwards up to the Zambezi.[17] In a letter Kadalie sent to a relative in early 1926, he reported:

> Yes, I have been in communication with many people in Southern Rhodesia, and most of these gentlemen expressed the desire that branches of the ICU ought to be opened in Southern Rhodesia. As soon as we get into touch with an influential person, we shall authorize him to proceed with work there.[18]

Although there were earlier contacts in Southern Rhodesia, the formal decision to establish a sister section in Rhodesia was made at the 1927 ICU annual conference, in response to a telegram from African workers requesting that Kadalie extend his union and its activities to Central Africa.[19] A central voice for African economic and political protest in the early 1920s in South Africa, the ICU was a model and inspiration for workers north of the Limpopo.[20] As Scarnecchia also notes:

> Bulawayo, situated on the rail line between Salisbury and South Africa, always seemed to import South African political influences and currents before they reached Salisbury's African townships. But Salisbury also belonged to the greater network of Southern Africa's urban areas, and word would have spread about tough-talking African politicians in South Africa, Nyasaland, and Northern Rhodesia. Politically minded township residents would have heard of Kadalie and perhaps have heard him speak as they travelled along the main railway lines and roads from the north to the south.[21]

Consequently, the request from Rhodesia was quickly approved. As Van der Walt notes, the conference agreed to establish a Southern Rhodesian ICU, which was supposed to transfer 20% of its income to the parent body.[22]

Kadalie delegated Sambo for the mission since he could not come to launch the Rhodesian ICU in person: he had been deemed *persona non grata* by the Rhodesian administration a year before. Driven by the fear of the ICU spreading, the Rhodesian state was generating intelligence reports on Kadalie as a potential political leader that could inspire Rhodesian natives.[23] He was blacklisted as a prohibited immigrant under Section 2(1) Ordinance 7 of 1914.[24] Sambo, his friend, had already been in Rhodesia and was not yet blacklisted.

Sambo spent six months in early 1926 in Nyasaland where he made contact with leading men and tried to shake 'those sleeping people' into a political alliance with their fellows in the south.[25] It is not clear when exactly Sambo left Nyasaland for Rhodesia, but Ewing places him in Gwelo (now Gwero) in late 1926, which was on the railway between Salisbury and Bulawayo, where he was working. He was also the Assistant General Secretary of the Gwelo Native Welfare Association, 'a front organisation for ICU and Garveyite propaganda before its establishment'.[26] In an anonymous letter to the *Workers' Herald*, Sambo pledged to work for the ICU until 'the matches Kadalie had lit into a blaze run like veld fire from South Africa to Nyasaland and thence to East Africa'.[27]

At some point he moved to Bulawayo, where he worked with Mphamba, a fellow Nyasa, and infuriated the state with five months of ICU activity.[28] He announced the arrival of the ICU by a series of meetings, militant speeches, a poster campaign and a general denunciation of government labour policy: an unexpected, intoxicating message to the African workers.[29] The new radical ideas about working-class solidarity across race and ethnicity were unprecedented in Rhodesian politics. The movement struck a new note of radicalism in Rhodesian African politics, appealing to working-class solidarity, attacking the government, demanding basic rights and targeting the weak defence of African rights by missionary groups.[30] Sambo declared: 'The time is now come... when all natives should be united with one body in the name of Africa... So, I ask you this day to join the movement and we fight for our Africa... Take away the word'.[31]

Rhodesia's deplorable labour situation, which Kadalie had witnessed, was conducive to a positive reception of the ICU message. Rhodesian Africans worked under appalling conditions on farms, mines and urban jobs, receiving very low wages and suffering extreme racial discrimination. Sambo combined an interest in the organisation of urban workers with attention to the conditions of agricultural labourers on white Rhodesian farms.[32] He carried out a survey of working conditions and compiled facts and figures about the customarily poor conditions and low wages.[33] Sambo noted that:

> In most of the farms, my people work from 12 to 14 hours a day. Their quarters are not fit for human beings, and their food is cheap or rotten meal and salt; to get meat is to wait until one beast is dead. If they cry to their masters for being overworked, their masters hit them. When they go to the nearest police station to report and get their assistance, the police officers instead of calling the master to come and answer the charge against him he only talks to him through the phone. Having received the reply that 'The bloody niggers were loafers and that they did not wish to work', the police officer then answers that alright, 'I will fix them up', he then slaps them on their faces and commands them to go back to work or else they will get arrested if you leave your work again... [34]

Sambo felt he was the voice of the oppressed and thus argued that:

> I, being the eyewitness of these things and having seen the affliction of my people joined the aforesaid organisation who in turn appointed me to be an agent and an organiser of my fellow workers throughout the Colony of Southern Rhodesia, in order to create for them a channel through which they could lay all their grievances against masters.[35]

The ICU public meetings were held on Saturdays and Sundays, and hordes of people from townships attended to hear speakers denounce Native Affairs Department officials as oppressors, and condemn the way black people were being treated by employers and white people generally.[36] Although such attendance did not usually translate into paying membership, Sambo's message attracted much wider support than the existing, moderate black welfare associations. The ICU appealed to a broad spectrum and by March 1927, the union had 155 paid-up members and its ideas were spreading rapidly.[37]

Through fiery propaganda, Sambo's transformative ICU message became an object of concern to the state and white community. Bulawayo's Superintendent of Natives summarised some of the 'objectionable utterances and contemptuous propaganda' at ICU meetings:

This is a native land and I am prepared to die for it

Today India is clamouring for independence. How long will Africa sleep

White people are frightened of the ICU

We must be bold; we are the aborigines and the country is a black man's country

We are oppressed because we are black

The churches are assisting the Government to keep us under foot

There has been no rain in the country since the white man came into it

I am not content to be under the white man

White men are afraid we will come together and fight them.

We are the reformers who can assist you. The ICU stands for all workers. I include the Police who have to patrol the lanes in their bare feet for a few pounds

How much longer must our oppression continue. Oppression makes people rise.[38]

The Superintendent of Natives pointed out that, 'the constant allusions to oppression of the black races by the white can only produce bitterness, leading to hostility'.[39] He concluded that 'it appears that many of their utterances border on sedition, and if unchecked and uncontradicted, can easily result in bringing the government and its officials into disrepute, and in creating a state of antagonism against all authority, if not open rebellion amongst the native population'.[40] West argues that the authorities felt that 'the ICU had created a "Hyde-Park"-type atmosphere in which contempt and hatred of white men, and government of white men, were sedulously taught.'[41]

Nipping it in the bud: Rhodesian state response to Sambo's ICU

The developments in Rhodesia were part of a larger process. As noted by Van der Walt, the ICU became 'an international body, a transnational movement whose tentacles spread into South West Africa in 1920, Rhodesia in 1927, and Northern Rhodesia in 1931'.[42] There were also short-lived ICU branches in Basutoland in 1928. The expansion of the ICU was almost inevitable, as it was intertwined within an exploitative regional colonial economic system based on a cheap, regional, mobile black labour force. Accordingly, it grew and expanded along a migrant trail into the 'urban centres, mining and farming districts, and rural areas of Southern Africa, attracting not just labourers but also sharecroppers, peasants, and even more radical sections of the African petty bourgeoisie'.[43] As Van der Walt explains, the spread of the ICU into the Rhodesias was directly linked to the flow of labour between Nyasaland, Rhodesia and South Africa.[44] Crucially, the network of educated Nyasas mainly from the Overtoun Livingstone mission from which Kadalie, Sambo and others influential Malawian had hailed, was central in trans-nationalising the ICU from the 1920s onwards.[45]

The emergence and subsequent spread of the ICU created alarm among the colonial authorities as the ICU became a transnational labour movement. Thus, colonial states systematically began to monitor constantly ICU activities in the region, fearing that 'one-big-union' would emerge.[46] Kadalie testifies, for example, that 'the neighbouring governments were always on the lookout for the ICU agents and we were consequently debarred from entering Basutoland and South West Africa, where we had two branches, and Transkei',[47] the latter an African reserve in South Africa.

Gripped with the fear of a militant and more radical labour organisation, the Rhodesian regime sought, from the onset, to nip Sambo's ICU in the bud. The state was very cognisant of the impact of the ICU in South Africa and went to great lengths to thwart its emergence and influence on the Rhodesian African population. As early as 9 May 1926, the Bulawayo Superintendent of the Criminal Investigation Department (CID) in Rhodesian police (BSAP) reported to the Chief of Staff, Defence Forces in Salisbury:

> I have to inform you that Clements Kadalie, a notorious extremist and native of Nyasaland, has been a resident in the Union [of South Africa] since 1921 … he has been appointed National Secretary of the ICU a powerful organisation … Kadalie is, I have been authoritatively informed, associated with communism and one SP Bunting, who is in direct communication with Moscow… [and] is also associated with the Universal Negro Improvement Association and African Communities League, has relatives employed in the government service of Northern Rhodesia.[48]

It was this same report that recommended (successfully) that Kadalie be barred from entering Rhodesia by being listed a 'prohibited immigrant'. The Chief of Staff jotted at the bottom of the report that, 'this may be of importance to us in view of the spread of this movement in the Union of South Africa'.[49]

The Rhodesian state was also perturbed by the tolerance that South Africa had towards subversive elements, such as the Communist Party of South Africa, and could not fathom such an approach. For Rhodesia, South Africa was not doing enough to curb the rise of militant African-initiated labour and political formations in the aftermath of the First World War.[50] It allowed the ICU almost free rein to establish branches, recruit followers and hold annual congresses, and tolerated the circulation of papers like the ICU's *Workers' Herald* (published in Johannesburg) and Garvey's *Negro World* (published in Philadelphia).

Rhodesia was much tougher on seditious elements. For instance, it closely monitored such early movements like the Rhodesian Bantu Voters' Association and the Southern Rhodesian Native Association and arrested and deported Nyasa leaders of the Watch Tower movement and the 1927 Shamva miners' strike. Repression continued in the decades that followed, with the monitoring, disruption and outright banning of many millenarian, labour and political organisations, and the censorship of the press: for example, the *African Daily News* was banned in 1964.[51]

As soon as Sambo set the ICU in motion in Bulawayo, the authorities began monitoring and discussing his movements and activities. Detectives were deployed to his meetings to follow the proceedings. They religiously recorded and reported his speeches and actions, and often harassed ICU members. According to West, the colonial regime viewed the ICU as a more serious threat than any of the other political formations, and consequently it faced unprecedented levels of surveillance, harassment, and outright persecution, the likes of which would not be seen again until the rise of mass African nationalism in the late 1950s.[52] Few ICU meetings, in the Sambo period and after, were free of police surveillance, with the police also intercepting the correspondences of ICU activists and some private citizens.[53] Scarnecchia comments that it is truly remarkable that the ICU even managed to establish branches and expand into the early 1930s.[54]

Sambo's deportation was not abrupt. The authorities debated its legality, thus taking considerable time to come to a decision. For instance, in May 1927, the Commissioner of Police felt that it was premature to deport Sambo, suggesting he be kept under observation instead.[55] However, the Chief Superintendent CID thought it advisable that Sambo be dealt with under Section 1 of the High Commissioner's Proclamation, 30 June 1891, or Proclamation no. 1 of 1920.[56] The Rhodesian Premier was unsure, querying:

> do one or other of these proclamations give us the necessary power if it is required to use it; and is there no danger, apart from the possibility of his subversive propaganda being secretly conducted and thus making headway amongst indigenous and other natives, that we may prejudice our powers of deportation under the undesirable immigration laws, by delaying action.[57]

Pressure also came from white employers, who were bluntly in favour of Sambo's expulsion. The Acting Secretary of the Eastern Fort Victoria Farmers Association, J. Rademeyer, wrote to the Ministry of Native Affairs on 20 February 1928 after the deportation, notifying him that the Association had 'unanimously resolved to approve your action (Sambo deportation), and it is hoped that the government will continue to put its foot down very severely on any further ICU, or other mischievous propagandists'.[58]

Denunciations of the ICU were not restricted to white economic and political elites, as rival local African organisations joined in. In particular, the Southern Rhodesia Native Association, 'playing to nascent nativism with an especially anti-Nyasaland bent, hailed by colonial officials as "purely Rhodesian", denounced the ICU activists as alien provocateurs or agitators from the Union … endeavouring to import into our colony the Union atmosphere'.[59] According to West, the Association leaders were not just opportunistic but genuinely alarmed by the ICU's popular appeals, self-proclaimed and brash proletarian style, and emphasis on the working class.[60]

Deportation ramifications

The Rhodesian authorities arrested Sambo in the autumn of 1927 and deported him from the colony on 24 June 1927. Sambo's deportation was a 'crude political surgery' which, however, did not fully achieve the desired results.[61] Instead, it put an unwanted spotlight on Rhodesia, as the fallout went far beyond the Rhodesian borders. Ranger argued that the protest that followed Sambo's deportation must have shown the Rhodesian administration that it was dealing with a new sort of movement.[62]

First to condemn the act was the foreign labour media. The British-based *New Leader* took the matter head-on, arguing that the act was 'an intolerable infringement of the right of association...we are having the matter raised in the House of Commons'.[63] It reiterated its sentiments on 30 September 1927 stating that 'Robert Sambo, the agent of the ICU in Southern Rhodesia, has been deported to Portuguese territory... This flagrant invasion of the rights of our coloured comrades ought to be vigorously challenged in the House of Commons'.[64] Second, South African black leaders also joined the outcry. Eddie Khaile of the African National Congress (the renamed South African Native National Congress) contested on behalf of its Free Speech Defence Committee: 'our rights, the rights of all peoples, of free speech and association are being grossly violated'.[65] Khaile, a member of the Communist Party, had formerly been expelled from the ICU in 1926 but clearly remained in solidarity.

Labour Members of the House of Commons in the UK did raise concerns over the matter in November and December 1927. MP Walter Baker quizzed the Secretary of State for Dominion Affairs whether he was aware that 'the natives of Southern Rhodesia have been prevented from organising themselves in a trade union, and that punitive measures have been taken against a native, Mr. Robert Sambo, who endeavoured to form a branch of ICU, which was in breach of Article 41 of the Southern Rhodesia constitution'.[66] Baker was furious as the matter was 'of most serious moment to the natives, and it is unsatisfactory that an organisation which is allowed freely to operate within the Union should be barred across the border'.[67]

The Secretary, Mr Amery, claimed not to have enough information to respond adequately, but promised to look into it. He, however, asserted that Southern Rhodesia was a country possessing responsible self-government, and that it was only in matters affecting the position of the natives that the special reservations enjoyed by the High Commissioner in regard to Rhodesian governance could be exercised.[68] Mr Baker then raised the issue to the British Prime Minister, Stanley Baldwin, in December 1927 asking him:

> Whether he will ascertain the nature of the activities which, in the opinion of the Southern Rhodesian Government, were likely to cause unrest among the native community and which led to the deportation of Robert Sambo; whether he will cause inquiries to be made as to the grounds upon which it was decided to deport to Portuguese territory a

native with a British domicile; and whether he will obtain information as to the endeavours which are being made in Southern Rhodesia to prevent the organisation of natives in trade unions?[69]

The Prime Minister was evasive: 'the question relates to matters entirely within the discretion of the Southern Rhodesia Government, and for this reason I cannot undertake to make further inquiries on the subject.'[70] In addition 'protests were also made at the 1928 meeting of the Southern Rhodesian Missionary Conference where John White described the deportation as deeply embittering to African feelings'.[71]

Third on the scene was the ICU and Kadalie. Kadalie was in Europe when Sambo's expulsion occurred. He was incensed but adeptly used the issue – and the incarceration of another ICU activist, Isa MacDonald Lawrence in Nyasaland, who got three years hard labour for importing the *Workers Herald* and the banned *Negro World* – for a campaign.[72] He managed to arouse the British Labour Party, through the person of Mr Wallhead, to protest in the House of Commons Sambo's deportation and Lawrence's heavy sentence. Wallhead charged the Rhodesian government with slavery.[73] Mr Wallhead fumed:

> I should like to know why the Rhodesian authorities prevent the formation of branches of ICU, and why they take the line which they do take against allowing the natives to organise themselves in protective bodies in order to improve their conditions and standard of life… I wish to know is there is any chance of revision of sentence, which seems a particularly harsh one for the offence of taking into the district a few newspapers…[74]

Meanwhile the *Workers Herald* reported on 17 July 1927 that while Sambo had been deported, Kadalie 'is working hard for his liberation, and the right of the organisation to unrestricted expansion in Southern Rhodesia'.[75]

Kadalie sent a defiant letter to the Rhodesian Prime Minister, Howard Moffat, protesting Sambo's deportation. He insisted on:

> regarding the Rhodesia territories as… a legitimate sphere wherein to extend my Union activities… as a result of Sambo's activities, your Government saw fit to order him to leave its territory, which he did, notwithstanding the fact that he was a resident of many years' standing… This action appears to us to be singularly arbitrary and unfair, as, in accordance with the foremost traditions of British justice, every citizen is entitled to know the nature of any charges preferred against him and to a trial before conviction and punishment.[76]

Kadalie took the opportunity to reiterate the various injustices against Africans in Rhodesia, noting that:

wages paid to native workers in your territory compare most unfavourably with those paid in the Union, where, in all conscience, they are bad enough… your average wage seems to be about 2 pounds per month, often without food and accommodation… these are starvation wages and they presuppose living conditions which make an agitation for improvement not merely necessary, but imperative, to all lovers of justice.[77]

Then Sambo himself came out publicly in a protest letter to the colonial government in Nyasaland that, interestingly, drew heavily from Kadalie's letter. Written on 10 January 1928 from Durban, South Africa, it was directed to the Governor of Zomba in Nyasaland. It stressed the grave injustice of a deportation for a noble cause: 'I wanted to organise my fellow workers for the labour union'.[78] He reminded the Rhodesian government of the sacrifices that migrant labourers were making to that state, asserting:

we Nyasaland natives have helped to build Rhodesia industrially, commercially as well as in agriculture since her emancipation; and whose number is (36 000 as per report of 1923) swamping all other natives from all her sister colonies, as well as aboriginals throughout all industries and commercials of Rhodesia; could not hold our peace while we see her drifting away in wages from good to worse.[79]

Sambo's life after Rhodesian expulsion

The ICU literature tends to ignore Sambo after 1927; what he did after his deportation is hazy and brief. Although it is often supposed that he was expelled straight to Nyasaland, he in fact entered Portuguese Mozambique where, upon reaching Beira, he 'altered course at Beira for the Union where I could have the freedom of protesting against the Rhodesian Government'.[80] He entered South Africa through Komatipoort in the Northern Transvaal, five kilometres from the Mozambican border.[81] The South African Secretary for Native Affairs lamented on 4 January 1928 that 'through the carelessness of a Native Constable at Komatipoort, Sambo obtained a travelling pass [on 30 August 1927]and proceeded to Natal and is now domiciled at the ICU headquarters at No. 25 Leopold Street, in Durban'.[82]

Sambo stayed in Durban from September 1927 until March 1928. It is not quite clear why Sambo went to domicile with Allison W. Champion, the powerful Zulu leader of the ICU branch in Durban, rather than his friend Kadalie.[83] This is even more puzzling when we note there were significant tensions between Kadalie and Champion at the time, leading to Champion taking a large part of the ICU membership away into a new ICU *yase* Natal in late 1928 – the first big split in the ICU. He may simply have not known, or cared, about the fight, of course.

Meanwhile, Sambo was deemed to have illegally entered the Union and thus ran afoul of the law. He was deported from South Africa on 7 March 1928 under the 1913 Prohibited Immigrants Act.[84] Considering his convictions and passion, and the suffering he underwent for the ICU cause, it is intriguing to find that after his return to Nyasaland, Sambo moved away from labour unionism. Although there was little scope for union activity in the colony, it is odd that he did not seem to connect up with other ICU sympathisers in the territory, of which there were a number.

Instead, Sambo found inspiration in the rising African separatist church movement. He joined hands with four other middle-grade Livingstonia mission graduates, three of them school teachers, to establish the African National Church in 1928 at Deep Bay and Florence Bay in Karonga district. One was Simon Kamkhati Mkandawire, a mission printer; the others were Paddy Nyasulu, a mission storekeeper and subsequently a government clerk, and Levi Mumba, later a leader of the Nyasaland African Congress.

The church spread to other parts of Nyasaland, Mkandawire opening branches in Mzimba district, and Nyasulu doing so around Karonga and into the Unyakyusa-Rumgwe region of southern Tanganyika.[85] For his part, Sambo opened and organised branches in the Ntcheu and Lilongwe districts, and by 1940, the church had accrued over 3 000 members in the country, almost all of them within the Livingstonia sphere.[86]

Going the independent church route could have been either a calling for Sambo or an alternative outlet to vent his frustrations over his deportation and the injustices of the colonial system. According to Ewing, the African National Church offered Sambo a new and more protective platform through which to work for the development of the continent.[87] It baptised its adherents according to the orthodox Christian rite, but was liberal on issues such as communal drinking and polygamy.[88] The church drew its membership initially from 'the intelligentsia of the Livingstonia Mission who had been excommunicated for polygamy'.[89] With his wide experience in politics, Sambo became central to carefully working out and drawing up the church's constitution and testament of principles.[90]

Conclusion

Though Sambo remains a footnote in the historiography of the ICU and labour activism in Zimbabwe, his brief ICU stint between February and June 1927 was critical in the development of radical African politics in the country. The episode was pivotal in the overall emergence and evolution of the ICU and indeed black trade unionism more generally in Rhodesia. His transformative politics and the strategy of public meetings, fiery speeches and propaganda laid the template for future radical labour and nationalist organisations. Lessons were also learnt by both Kadalie and Sambo's successors on how to cope with the rigid and intolerant Rhodesian colonial state. His deportation moreover gave Kadalie the platform to expose the harshness of the Rhodesian state as well as the plight of Rhodesian Africans on the European stage.

In spite of Sambo's deportation, Kadalie promised the Rhodesian administration that 'we shall find means, as we have done in the past, to get our message to our fellow workers, and we shall find men and women in your colony to raise and uphold the banner of freedom…All form of oppression and the deportation of our agents shall not deter us'.[91] Just like Kadalie, the deported Sambo defiantly threatened that '…unless natives and native workers are set on a better footing there will often be unrest and as the result we shall look to England and the League of Nations for help than in our local authorities'.[92] These were not empty threats, as new ICU leaders, especially Ndlovu and Dumbutshena, relaunched the ICU in Rhodesia after 1928, and Mzingeli built it in Salisbury; this time, it spread into the capital as well as into small towns and into the countryside. Sambo's work also helped inspire Benjamin Burombo, Reuben Siwela, Josiah Maluleke and Jasper Savanhu to form their labour unions between the 1930s and 1950s. Moreover, the people who entered politics through the ICU stayed in radical politics for decades afterwards; Mzingeli as leader of the Reformed ICU dominated Salisbury politics after 1945.

Ironically, Sambo became more influential in absentia, as his five-month, rabble-rousing stint episode left an indelible mark that 'served as a training ground for political activity and provided the beginnings of a base for later mass urban party movements; one of the most important forerunners of modern mass nationalism'.[93] He managed this with all odds against him, working under the colossal shadow of Kadalie and operating in treacherous waters and under an intolerant regime that set out to kill the ICU at its birth. Nonetheless, the fuller details of Sambo's story require further study. While his fragmented paper trail ends with the African National Church in Nyasaland, his childhood, family, his encounters in South Africa and why he chose to domicile with Champion in Durban and not Kadalie after his ejection from Rhodesia, and his death, still need to be probed.

3 Organising the Unorganised: ICU Internationalism and the Transnational Unionisation of Migrant Workers

Henry Dee

Introduction

The mobile and transnational nature of the Southern African labour market has compelled trade unionists in the region to address the entangled politics of race, migration, empire, nation and class.[1] Critically situating the ICU within these debates, this chapter compares the trade union's transnational organisation of black workers, regardless of nationality, into a single general trade union, with the strategies of other contemporary labour organisations (white and black alike). While other labour leaders attempted to raise wages by restricting migration and calling sectional, industry-specific strikes, the ICU hoped to increase workers' pay by calling general strikes and replacing the transnational recruitment networks used by Southern Africa's docks, farms and mines with a scheme of minimum wages, ICU-run labour bureaus and the broader principle of employing 'free labour in a free market'. Although the ICU fell well short of these heady ambitions, its understanding of the inter-relationship between migration, wages and work mattered at both an economic and a political level. Challenging narrow, exclusionary ideas of race, nation and class, the ICU contested the dominant contemporary theories of white trade unionists, socialists and communists, as well as moderate black leaders within the African National Congress (ANC).

First, this chapter lays out the transnational character of Southern Africa's interwar working class, and the internationalist agenda that the ICU pursued in response. Second, in light of these factors, the chapter explores how the trade union hoped to challenge transnational recruitment networks, demonstrating how and why the trade union expanded to Johannesburg, and beyond. Third, the chapter addresses why the ICU's expansion faltered and failed when challenged by capitalist interests and the emergence of increasingly exclusionary forms of African nationalism. Significantly – with relevance to debates about worker mobilisation today – recognition of the ICU's expansive transnational strategy helps clarify debates about whether or not the organisation was an effective trade union, superseded at the end of the 1920s by industrial unions focused on specific sectors in specific towns.[2] In a context where highly mobile black migrant workers constituted a significant proportion of Southern Africa's working class, it made economic sense for the ICU to operate as a transnational, mass-member general trade union, unionising local and immigrant workers. Furthermore, when cognisant of this context, the political imperatives behind the trade union's pronounced socialist internationalism also become explicit.

The transnational nature of Southern Africa's working class

During the interwar period, urban centres across Southern Africa relied heavily on migrant workers, often drawn from across colonial state borders. From the 1860s, the mines of Kimberley and Johannesburg drew in hundreds of thousands of African and Asian workers – from across Southern Africa and East Asia – alongside tens of thousands of white miners from Europe, Australasia, and America.[3] Robert Kadalie was among the thousands of Malawians subsequently recruited by the Witwatersrand Native Labour Association (WNLA) between 1904 and 1913, with his younger brother, Clements Kadalie, following in his footsteps in 1918.[4] By the 1920s, hundreds of thousands of Mozambican and Basotho men dominated the gold mines' workforce, while Basotho women and Malawian men had a disproportionate presence in Johannesburg's domestic service sector (the city's second largest employer).[5] Black workers in South Africa's new interwar industries were, similarly, described as a cosmopolitan mix of 'Blantyres, Nyasaland boys, Zulus and Sesutos'.[6] In particular, Central African workers from Nyasaland, Southern Rhodesia and Northern Rhodesia constituted a considerable proportion of workers on South Africa's new platinum and copper mines at Rustenburg and Messina, the diamond diggings around Lichtenburg and new cement factories run by the Pretoria Portland Cement Company.[7] By the 1920s, South Africa's docks, equally, relied on a conspicuously transnational workforce. West African 'Kru' and West Indian winchmen were employed alongside local coloured and African workers on Cape Town's shorefront, while Durban's docks and railways employed a mixture of Zulu and Basotho alongside some Malawian migrant workers.[8] Similarly in Southern Rhodesia, ICU leader Robert Sambo emphasised how Malawian men were 'swamping all other natives from all her sister colonies, as well as aboriginals throughout all industries and commercials'.[9] White farmers across the vast rural stretches of Southern Africa, likewise, were heavily dependent on exploited immigrant labour. Below Salisbury, 'practically all the farm labour' in Southern Rhodesia was 'from Nyasaland'.[10] Natal's sugar plantations were dominated by Mozambicans, while significant numbers of Mozambican, Malawian and Zimbabwean workers were employed on large-scale industrial farms in the Transvaal, such as the Zebediela Citrus Estate in Potgietersrust, the Esrael Lazarus estates in Bethal and the Medalie brothers' farms near Kinross.[11]

Accordingly, a large proportion of the leadership and membership of the ICU were made up of highly mobile migrant workers, often born outside Southern Africa. In Cape Town, the ICU unionised a considerable number of West Indians and West African Kru, including James Gulam Gumbs, the ICU's long-standing president, and Emmanuel Johnson, the ICU's junior vice-president, who originated from St Vincent in the Caribbean and West Africa respectively; the trade union's first secretary and first assistant secretary, Clements Kadalie and Peter Nyambo, were both from Nyasaland; and James Thaele, a member of the ICU executive, was born in Basutoland.[12] In South West Africa, the ICU was led by a West Indian, John de Clue.[13] In Natal, the ICU was initially led by an Eastern Cape Xhosa migrant,

Alexander Maduna, while the membership included many Basotho and Indians, alongside Zulu migrant workers.[14] In the Free State, the ICU was led by Keable 'Mote, Jason Jingoes and Robert Sello (all of whom were born in Basutoland).[15] And in the Transvaal, Abdul Mohamed, the Lydenburg ICU branch secretary, originated from Zanzibar.[16]

Through extensive letter-writing networks and individual migrants who moved across state borders, the ICU became 'well known' in Southern Rhodesia and Portuguese East Africa, where workers were soon 'desiring to identify themselves with us'.[17] 'Regarding [the] Rhodesian territory as an integral part of [the] Subcontinent', two Malawians, Robert Sambo and John Mphamba, alongside two South Africans, Martha Ngano and Josephina Zulu, established new ICU branches in Bulawayo and Salisbury between 1926 and 1929 (as Anusa Daimon sets out in his chapter).[18] Mozambican radical Dick Khosa, in turn, claimed that the ICU was in contact with 100 000 Mozambicans on the Rand, while Kadalie hoped that two other Malawians, John Lawrence and Isa Macdonald Lawrence, could organise black dockworkers at the port of Beira, and in Nyasaland itself.[19] ICU branches were also founded in Basutoland and Swaziland during the late 1920s, while Joseph Kazembe opened an ICU branch as far north as Livingstone, Northern Rhodesia, in 1932.[20] Although these ventures were often short-lived, they indicate the ICU's willingness to organise all workers – coloured, African and Indian alike, regardless of nationality – and the transnational scale of the trade union's ambitions.

Over the course of the 1920s, however, the ICU's internationalism was seriously challenged by solidifying colonial state borders. Since the late 1890s, when restrictions were first imposed against Indian immigrants in Natal, South Africa had been a global pioneer of immigration controls.[21] At the behest of white labour, further restrictions were introduced on the Rand gold mines, blocking the employment of Chinese and Central African immigrant workers in 1907 and 1913 respectively.[22] The 1913 ban was based on the criminally high mortality rates of 'tropical' workers, but was, notably, pushed through by politicians from the South African Labour Party (SALP), in particular Frederic Creswell, who were 'strongly opposed to the importation of more and more primitive natives from beyond the borders of South Africa, which not only increased the black population but also removed from our own natives opportunities to improve their circumstances'.[23] White workers' fears of replacement endured over subsequent decades. During the economic downturn from 1921 to 1923, Jan Christian Smuts' South African Party (SAP) vigorously deported Mozambican women from Johannesburg and unsuccessfully pushed for the restricted employment of Mozambican men on the gold mines.[24]

Despite these efforts, a key factor during the 1924 general election was the widespread belief that 'the Smuts Government were ready to permit, if not to assist, unscrupulous industrialists to eliminate as far as possible the white men from the industries of this country, replacing them with blacks imported from East or Central Africa'.[25] After winning the election, J.B.M. Hertzog's National Party (NP) and Creswell's SALP pushed for further restrictions on Asian and African immigration. In June 1927, the NP-SALP 'Pact' government produced the first formal policy on the position of Central African immigrants in South Africa, initially resolving 'to continue the laissez-faire policy of not removing extra-Union natives unless they had criminal convictions'.[26] After riots targeting Central African immigrants in Johannesburg and the Lichtenburg diamond diggings, however, the Native Affairs Department issued a new decree in June 1928 establishing a scheme of self-funded repatriations and labour bureaus, directing 'foreign labour' to farms.[27] The 1928 Mozambican Convention, in turn, not only reduced the quotas of Mozambican workers employed on the gold mines, but also banned the employment of Mozambicans outside the mines. As a result, the government started repatriating workers employed on Natal's sugar estates in early 1928.[28]

As recognised by ANC leader Z.K. Matthews, 'when white leaders spoke of the "nation" of South Africa, they meant only the white nation'.[29] Nevertheless, many moderate black South African nationalists actively supported these exclusionary policies. After breaking with Kadalie's ICU, the ANC Minister of Mines and Industries, Henry Selby Msimang, for example, published regular articles in *Umteteli wa Bantu* condemning the 'unrestricted immigration of foreigners'. Envisaging a 'closed' national labour market, blocking the 'unregulated influx of labour in[to] industrial or other centres' and halting the erosion of wages, Msimang asserted that 'Union Natives' should 'endeavour to clear redundant labour by imposing restrictions against non-Union Natives'.[30] Bennet Ncwana (another former ICU leader who had become a prominent ANC moderate by the mid-1920s), similarly, condemned 'the disastrous policy of supplementing Union Labour by about 80 000 natives from Portuguese territory', asserting that it was a 'condition of happiness for the state to find within its own limits all the labour it requires for its industries'.[31] Integral to these anti-immigrant sentiments was a patriarchal anxiety to control women and counter sexual 'deviancies' introduced by men who crossed colonial borders. Msimang condemned Malawian immigrants, in particular, for 'exploiting the weakness of our womenfolk without shame or pity'.[32]

In this increasingly hostile environment, the ICU was denounced as a 'foreign' influence throughout Southern Africa. The South African government's 1925 Native Churches Commission explicitly critiqued 'the fact that several of its leaders are foreign-born natives', while white South African politicians insisted that Kadalie was 'a foreigner without right to a permanent domicile in the country'.[33] Challenging the legitimacy of ICU leaders, such as, 'Mote, from the wilds of Basutoland, or Kadalie, from Nyasaland', black South African moderates similarly questioned how, 'in the name of all that is sensible, could civilised people, and Christians at that, allow such pagans and barbarians as 'Mote and Kadalie to lead them?'[34] The moderate black newspaper, the *African Voice*, denounced the ICU leadership as a bunch of 'foreign agitators', while *Umteteli wa Bantu* was adamant:

> There is no demand for foreign leaders… Many South African Natives are endowed with all the essential qualities of leadership, and it would

be an unfortunate business if they permitted their functions to be usurped by men from Central Africa, the West Indies and America whose only claim to South African Natives' sympathy and support is their colour.[35]

Leaders of the Transvaal African Congress (TAC), likewise, opposed Kadalie's advance to the Rand and demanded that those workers 'who had joined the "ICU" followed him back to Nyasaland'.[36] Similarly in Southern Rhodesia, the ICU was accused of having a foreign leadership and importing foreign ideas, with the moderate Southern Rhodesian Native Association (SRNA) denouncing ICU leaders as alien provocateurs who misled locals.[37] Building on these sentiments, colonial states made draconian use of their borders to combat the ICU. Clements Kadalie was banned from entering South West Africa, Southern Rhodesia and Portuguese East Africa, as well as the South African province of Natal; Abdul Mohamed was deported from South Africa; Robert Sambo and John Mphamba were deported from Southern Rhodesia; and Isa Macdonald Lawrence was deported and imprisoned for three years' hard labour after importing copies of the *Workers' Herald* and attempting to establish a branch of the ICU in Nyasaland.[38]

These 'foreign' labels, nevertheless, were often instrumentalised by the ICU leadership. Kadalie and his comrades revelled in the popular perception that they were external 'agitators' – in particular 'American Negroes' – who were 'free of all tribal affiliations'.[39] Alexander Maduna relished the fact that 'being a foreigner in Natal and the Free State, I destroyed the seemingly impregnable walls of the above places, and emancipated the Zulus and the Basutos from slavery'.[40] When Kadalie was threatened with deportation, he made clear that his 'birthplace is a few miles away from the Chamber of Mines building as in comparison with a distance of thousands of miles between South Africa and the home of these foreign adventurers who are sucking the blood of the people of this continent'.[41] Robert Sambo in Southern Rhodesia, similarly, explicitly denounced the passing of 'Laws and Bye Laws all to the Slavery of a Native, both Aboriginals and Foreign', and enthusiastically envisaged the ICU spreading 'like veld fire from South Africa to Nyasaland and thence to East Africa'.[42] Theo Lujiza (the ICU's leading East London official), meanwhile, claimed that Kadalie's outsider status 'didn't matter except [for] the enlightened class [who] used it as an excuse'.[43] The ICU newspaper, the *Workers' Herald*, in turn, mocked those who perpetuated the colonial divisions imposed by whites:

> Stop destroying the nation with white people's deceiving words. White people say Kadalie is not welcome (he is a Nyasa), only Thaele is welcome (he is a Msotho). All the morons are deceived with those words by white people. Go visit the compounds, and elsewhere, they are packed with Sothos, the Nyasas, the Xhosa and the Pondos.[44]

From its formation in 1912, many of the 'enlightened class' in the ANC actively fought against 'tribalism' in South Africa and fostered connections with African nationalists in Southern Rhodesia (although key figures such as John Dube already disapproved of Congress' early transnational solidarities).[45] The ICU, in contrast, was far more explicit in its expansive, transnational scope and its deliberate engagement with local and immigrant workers. ICU newspapers reported how 'workers in Nyasaland, South West Africa [and] Portuguese East Africa are waiting for the arrival of your industrial emissaries', while ICU poetry declared:

> You young man of Kadalie
>
> You have come to unite
>
> Flocks that spurn each other,
>
> Shangaans, coloureds,
>
> Son of the black man
>
> In the land of our ancestors.[46]

While occasionally working with some African nationalists, the ICU eclipsed the ANC during its heyday in the 1920s and denounced exclusionary forms of nationalism in favour of internationalist conceptions of race and class. Rather than through the leadership of moderate nationalists in the ANC or SRNA, salvation would be achieved through working class power.[47] In 1927, Kadalie declared that the ICU was 'utterly opposed to nationalism. Our goal is international socialism'.[48]

The struggle against transnational capitalist recruitment

The ICU as a new all in general union argued that it was essential to organise all workers regardless of skill, across colonial borders, if wages and working conditions were to be improved. In stark opposition to other trade unions, the ICU championed the 'free movement' of black workers across Southern Africa and campaigned for minimum wages to ensure that bosses did not undercut workers' pay. Quoting nineteenth-century abolitionist literature, the ICU transformed liberal imperialist ideas of work into a radical agenda – promising that it would 'strive by every constitutional means to fight aggressive capitalism or white labour [and], while doing so we shall educate the African workers "to supply free labour in a free market"'.[49] At a local level, the ICU opposed pass laws and segregationist controls on black urbanisation, lambasting white trade unionists for 'believing in the efficacy of artificial restrictions'.[50] As Alfred Ngaleka questioned in the Workers' Herald: 'why should we restrict members of the working class in their movement or labour? Why not start from the other side by introducing a compulsory minimum wage for unskilled as well as skilled labour thereby ending the bogey of Native competition once [and] for all?'[51] Similarly at a transnational level, the ICU called for 'free labour within the Union of South Africa and elsewhere in the continent'.[52]

The ICU's ideal of 'free labour' across southern Africa, however, was fundamentally challenged by the power of large-scale, cross-border capitalist recruitment networks – most notably Chamber of Mines' WNLA, which recruited workers from beyond South Africa's borders, and Native Recruiting Corporation (NRC), which recruited migrant workers within the Union of South Africa. While the trade union had 'very little quarrel' with the system as a 'means of keeping a regular supply', the ICU asserted that, in practice, mine recruitment was 'nothing but highway robbery'.[53] As the *Workers' Herald* made clear, under the system of mine recruitment, 'the African workers are debarred from forming themselves into an industrial union, quite apart from the interferences and jurisdiction of the Chamber of Mines. The system is there to supply scab labour in the event that the African workers have withdrawn their labour'.[54] Beyond the gold mines, other key economic sectors, such as the sugar plantations, farms and docks, were also heavily reliant on recruited labour. As such, when low-wage workers were employed to work at the Cape Town docks (threatening to undercut the local minimum wage established by the ICU), the trade union responded with the assertion:

> we shall welcome and encourage free labour in a free market at a proper rate of pay, but when we know that natives are being recruited for the purpose of creating more industrial kings and mine magnates, then, sir, you can rest assured that the tongue of the agitators shall not be idle.[55]

Perhaps with this in mind, Kadalie became close friends with the radical Mozambican journalist and businessman, Brown Dulela, who campaigned successfully to safeguard the property of Mozambican miners in Johannesburg before being banned from South Africa in 1927.[56]

From the mid-1920s, the ICU poured considerable resources into organising the huge concentration of migrant workers in Johannesburg. The interests of mine workers were at the forefront of the ICU's submission to the 1925 Economic and Wages Commission, and by 1926, the ICU's head office had relocated to the Rand on the basis that Johannesburg was 'the chief industrial centre of Africa', with 'well over half a million non-European workers engaged in its great industries and commerce'.[57] The ICU enjoyed a degree of success turning the mines' workforce against their employers. On the Crown Mines, in particular, the trade union quickly enrolled 'a good number of members, including some African clerks'.[58] Escorting Kadalie to the Crown Mines' compound, Mildred Ngcayiya – a former school teacher on the trade union's local executive – introduced the ICU leader to Allison Wessels George Champion, the president of the Transvaal Native Mine Clerks' Association (TNMCA). Champion subsequently attended a number of ICU meetings and resigned his position within the TNMCA to formally join the ICU in mid-1925.[59] In central Johannesburg, Champion was soon telling audiences: 'Had the natives been organised at the time of the [1920] strike on the mines, they would have succeeded in getting more money. They failed because they were not organised'.[60] In March 1925, the ICU led 600 workers from the Nourse Mine to demand an increase in the minimum wage per shift from one shilling two pence to two shillings per day. The miners' demands were rejected by the Chamber of Mines, but the call for a 2s minimum wage endured long after and became central to the

ICU's transnational strategy – 'not to be regarded as an end in itself, but as a stepping stone to the ultimate achievement of the full economic rights of the native workers'.[61]

In criticising the mines and docks' recruitment networks, the ICU soon singled out African chiefs as important collaborators with capitalists. As acerbically recounted by the ICU's leading Rand radical, Thomas Mbeki, chiefs addressed NRC meetings after being bribed with cash and liquor, imploring their followers to go 'to the mines', where they would 'get pudding, jam, cake and other nice things'.[62] Ultimately, however, the trade union aspired to work through chiefs. Kadalie emphasised:

> [It is] of vital importance that we should get into touch with the territories, for is not there that the Chamber of Mines has a reservoir of cheap and docile labour? The sooner we educate the chiefs and their people that our trade union movement in urban areas does not suggest disloyalty to constituted government or any disloyalty to the chiefs themselves but is calculated on a 'bread-and-butter' struggle for ourselves, our women and children – a holy and noble struggle – we shall then be nearing our goal to economic emancipation.[63]

By 1925, Kadalie felt assured that '[o]nce we succeed to capture the Transkei and convince the chiefs with our aims and objects we can rest assured that we are drawing nearer to the time when this Organisation shall be dreaded by the Mine Owners of the Rand.'[64] James Thaele, likewise, asserted that 'chiefs must be made conversant with the [ICU's] policy' with 'a view to tie up and bring to a standstill, even if for a fortnight, the "recruiting system" in the Native territories so as to paralyse within 24 hours the Mining Industry.'[65] In certain settings, the ICU did attain chiefly support. Mbeki 'converted' a number of chiefs in the Transvaal between 1925 and 1926.[66] In Natal, Chief Stephen Mini of Pietermaritzburg was well known for his 'strong ICU tendencies', while Chief Dirk Siyoka was alleged to be 'under the employ of the ICU'.[67] Numerous Swazi chiefs supported the ICU.[68] At the same time, Keable 'Mote organised seven ICU branches in Basutoland with the support of Chief Jonathan Malapo Moshesh, while another Basotho chief, Motsoene, visited the ICU Workers' Hall in mid-1928.[69]

Through the cooperation of chiefs, the trade union's leaders also hoped to supplant mine recruitment through a network of ICU-run labour bureaus.[70] Significantly, Kadalie argued that these bureaus needed to encompass Mozambican workers if they were to be viable, with police reports recording his belief:

> that it would be no good [simply] condemning the recruiting system as conducted at the present time, because the Chamber of Mines would then recruit natives from the Portuguese Territories; they would, therefore, have to organise the Portuguese natives in a similar way to that which was suggested by him with regard to themselves, otherwise the action suggested by him regarding native labour offices would break down.[71]

Frustrated realities: The fate of the ICU's internationalism

Throughout the second half of the 1920s, the ICU sustained contact with thousands of migrant workers in and around the Rand. A leading Malawian socialite, Stanley Highboy, helped Kadalie organise dances at the ICU Workers' Hall, while at the end of 1926, a prolonged ICU campaign ensured that domestic servants could not be dismissed without notice – something that directly benefited numerous Malawians, in particular.[72] In January 1927, Theodore Ramonti addressed hundreds of Mozambican colliery workers at Witbank, calling for an end to the pass laws and a 5s per day minimum wage.[73] In August 1927, Josephina Zulu, a 'notorious prophetess' from Natal, addressed a Johannesburg ICU meeting about the organisation of workers in Southern Rhodesia.[74] In November 1927, 2 000 Mpondo miners flocked to ICU meetings led by Thomas Letshoedi in Randfontein.[75] And in July 1928, Kadalie and Gumbs led a mass meeting of Central African workers at the ICU Workers' Hall.[76]

As Phil Bonner demonstrates (see Chapter 9 of this volume), however, already by August 1925, it was apparent that ICU organisers had effectively been locked out of Johannesburg's mines. Through the compound system, effective private policing, a strict policy of non-recognition, and a network of informers (that included key ICU leaders such as Keable 'Mote), individual ICU members soon found themselves dismissed from work. ICU shop steward Thibedi William Thibedi noted that mine workers were 'always threatened with expulsion or dismissal if they are observed to associate with the Workers' Union – the ICU'.[77] Simultaneously, the South African government's 'civilised labour policy' attacked the ICU's established membership base among railway and dockworkers, as white and coloured workers displaced their African counterparts.[78] By October 1926, ICU railway workers were looking to organise a transport section with its own officials, asserting that they desperately needed 'leaders of action who know how to organise the workers'.[79] Despite early efforts at organising women workers, Tyamzashe concluded by December 1926 that the ICU on the Rand had also 'failed to draw into our ranks the female workers who in other countries are to be found in the vanguard of the organised proletariat'.[80] Theo Lujiza similarly recalled that there were 'very few members from Nyasaland and Mozambique though there were very many from both territories on the mines'.[81] The ICU's particular failure to organise Mozambican workers may lie in the prejudices harboured by some ICU officials.[82] Leaders, such as Kadalie and James Thaele, consistently attacked 'old tribal differences' between South African and Mozambican workers.[83] But the trade union's moderate vice-president, Alexander Mac Jabavu, received enthusiastic applause at the ICU's 1926 annual conference for declaring:

> At present the Chamber of Mines prefers the Portuguese Native, not because he is more efficient but because he works for half the wage of the Union Natives, and he can stand more humbug and kicks... the first claim for labour lies with the Union Natives, and the Portuguese Natives should be told to look for work in their own country.[84]

In response to the ICU's setbacks in Johannesburg, the ICU redoubled its existing organisational efforts in the northern Transvaal, Transkei, Pondoland and Southern Rhodesia, and sent feelers into Nyasaland and Portuguese East Africa. Kadalie told members:

> We must organise the mine natives and it must be done in their homes and through their chiefs... The ICU movement has spread all over the country and now we have thousands of followers, but not enough; we want hundreds of thousands – enough to make a big noise [...the mine management] must not sleep.[85]

In the Transkei, ICU leaders systematically targeted NRC meetings, heckling and interrupting speakers, and causing mine officials to worry that the NRC would soon be unable to 'induce British South African Natives to engage for mine work'.[86] Addressing a crowd in King Williams Town, Kadalie asserted: 'It is necessary for us to unite and be like the Native Recruiting Corporation' – who always spoke 'with one view' and was engaged in 'robbing and sucking the blood of the black man'.[87] Over the course of 1926 and 1927, innumerable additional branches were established across the Transvaal (particularly in the east of the province) under the initiative of Thomas Mbeki, with at least 23 000 joining the ICU.[88] As many as 70 000 joined the trade union in Natal.[89] As a result, when NRC officials toured South Africa in 1927, from 'East London to Kokstad workers clamoured for an increase in the minimum wages paid'.[90] Meetings 'singled out the glaring disparity between the highest wages of skilled African workers and the minimum wage of "an unskilled and incompetent European who is put to supervise them"', and in districts 'in which the ICU propaganda has spread they are now asking for a specific minimum rate of 4/- to 5/- per die four to five shillings per day].'[91]

Nevertheless, the bourgeoning ICU in Natal soon faced considerable resistance from established capitalist interests linked to the sugar plantation economy and the local SAP. Men such as William Campbell (the manager of Natal Estates Ltd), George Higgs (an Empangeni sugar planter) and Charles George Smith (the chair of the Illovo Sugar Estates and the Natal leader of the SAP) were extremely hostile to the ICU and closely connected to two Natal SAP MPs who were some of the most outspoken critics of the ICU in parliament, John Sydney Marwick and George Heaton Nicholls (himself a Zululand sugar planter). Both Marwick and Nicholls acted as lobbyists for Natal sugar interests (ensuring that Zululand planters retained the right to recruit 'illegal' Mozambican immigrants, even after the 1928 Mozambican Convention).[92] In parliament, they objected to the ICU, at least in part, because they wanted to ensure 'an increased and more constant supply' of labour to key industries, championing chiefs as key mediators in the 'kraalhead system'.[93] As such, they both actively supported the 1927 Native Administration Act because it strengthened the power of labour recruiting chiefs – explicitly pitching them against the ICU.[94] As a means of propping up the 'kraalhead system', the Natal SAP also channelled considerable resources and funding towards a number of moderate black leaders in Natal who staunchly opposed the ICU – most notably men such as Bennet Ncwana, and John Langalibalele Dube, and a new, conservative Zulu organisation, Inkhata ka Zulu.

Black moderates, in turn, clearly had their own reasons for working with the SAP. Writing from his home in Ohlange, Dube told Marwick that the ICU was initiating the 'breaking down of parental control and restraint, tribal responsibility and our whole traditions – the whole structure upon which our Bantu nation rests'.[95] *Ilanga lase Natal*, Dube's paper, incessantly attacked the ICU for affiliating 'with the Socialism, Communism and Bolshevism as is carried on at present in some European countries', complaining that the 'masses' were being 'gulled into joining such foreign organisations the antecedents of which they know nothing'.[96] In August 1927, *Ilanga* reiterated in a letter from Chief Solomon Dinizulu that Zulus 'do not even know' Kadalie, and 'do not know how far he has already gone in putting things right in his own land'.[97] The same month, Dube 'spoke in condemnation of the aims and objects of the ICU' at a well-catered 'anti-ICU festival' on the Campbell sugar estates, insisting 'that the time had not come for the Zulu workers to organise a trade union, more particularly in the sugar fields, because they were still raw'.[98] Bennet Ncwana attacked the ICU at numerous meetings in Natal between 1926 and 1927, provided Marwick with material for his anti-ICU speeches, and repeatedly called for Kadalie's deportation.[99] In October 1927, an embattled Champion asked Ncwana directly 'whether you and Mr Dube are trying to surround the ICU'.[100] The *Workers' Herald* lambasted Ncwana, insisting that it was 'not only the Union of South Africa that must unite in a brotherhood spirit, but the whole of the African continent'.[101] But there is evidence that Dube and Ncwana's arguments did gain influence among some ICU officials as they encircled the trade union. Arguing that 'Ncwana was attempting to publish a paper dealing with the affairs of the ICU and that this Bennet Ncwana was actually being financed by the Chamber of Mines', Kadalie alleged that 'there were officials of the ICU interested in the publication of [Ncwana's] paper', and that there were some 'men within the ranks of the ICU who had introduced tribal differences and had stated that because he, Kadalie, came from Nyasaland he should not be given the opportunity to lead South African Natives'.[102]

Tensions between Malawian and other workers were also coming to a head more widely in a series of events that drove some ANC leaders into direct conflict with the ICU. Malawian workers, on the one hand, and Basotho and Xhosa, on the other, first started fighting on the Lichtenburg diamond diggings at the end of August 1927, resulting in the displacement of around 350 Malawian men and their families from the area.[103] In September 1927, Henry Selby Msimang addressed a meeting of the Basotho-dominated TAC in Western Native Township, where he promoted a new ANC-led 'African Labour Congress' and asserted that 'all foreigners coming to South Africa quickly made the black man their slaves'.[104] Champion rebuffed Msimang's new rival labour union as a 'mushroom organisation, which would just collect money and then die out'.[105] Subsequently, at the end of December, a further 400 Malawians had their huts burnt amid a four-day rolling brawl with Xhosa and Basotho workers at Lichtenburg; while on 25 December 1927, a riot between Malawian domestic servants and Basotho in Johannesburg's Western Native Township resulted in 'heavy casualties', followed by further violence the next day in Newclare, where six Malawians were killed. In response, the TAC called a meeting where Eddie Khaile, the ANC general secretary, 'presided over (and induced) a handful of ignorant Native workers' to 'pass a hand-over-fist resolution asking for the repatriation (or deportation) of all Blantyre Natives', alleging that Malawians drank heavily, started fights, undercut wages and stole wives.[106]

Richard Selope Thema, Sol Plaatje and Richard Msimang (Selby's brother) contended that the TAC had only 'fortified themselves behind the barbed wire of racialism and provincialism' because it had 'lost the sway which it once held over the people'.[107] In response to the resolution, the ICU declared that it would have 'nothing to do with' the Congress, condemning the emergence of 'tribal jealousy' within the TAC.[108] The *Workers' Herald* asserted: 'Not many weeks ago, the Congress passed a resolution asking for the repatriation of all Blantyre Natives. Can anything more diabolical be imagined? Fancy the silly and mischievous idea of stirring up African against African'.[109] With ambiguous undertones, Josiah Gumede, the ANC president, retorted that the Congress would 'not alter its plan to please Kadalie and will pursue its course of uniting the SA natives to help themselves'.[110] More explicitly, Msimang fully endorsed the TAC resolution, contending that if 'the restrictions against Indians are a means of self-preservation for the European trade, more should be done to lend ear to the petition of Union Natives for their measure of self-preservation'.[111] Into 1929, Simon Peter Matseke, the TAC's Marabastad leader, continued to tell meetings: 'We will ask the government to deport Clements Kadalie. We don't want him here. He does nothing for us, [and] is only causing trouble'.[112]

Many ICU leaders saw the calls to repatriate all Central Africans as the latest move in an ongoing campaign to deport Kadalie. Addressing 'a combined meeting of the ICU and their Rhodesian comrades' alongside Kadalie at the Workers Hall, police reported that the ICU president, James Gumbs, declared:

> he knew what was really behind the minds of those who advocated the repatriation of the Rhodesian [sic] natives. They wanted him (Clements Kadalie) to leave the Union of South Africa. He said their comrades in Rhodesia had requested the assistance of the ICU in this matter, but until they became members of the ICU he could not assist them; he urged all Rhodesian natives present to join the ICU and most of them did so.[113]

The TAC's deportation campaign led to numerous meetings over the course of 1928 and 1929, but most Central Africans do not appear to have turned to the ICU in this moment of crisis. The ICU's Scottish adviser, William Ballinger, noted in 1929 that Central Africans 'never joined the ICU'.[114] Lujiza concurred that the 'opposition used to ask why this was the case as Kadalie was from Nyasaland – surely he was not sincere if he could not organise his own people'.[115] Instead, many appear to have rallied around the more moderate Johannesburg-based Nyasaland, Rhodesia and East African Native Congress led by a Malawian Pentecostal church minister, John George Phillips.[116]

There were numerous factors behind the ICU's disintegration, but anti-immigrant politics certainly played a key (and hitherto under-appreciated) role in the growing dissension within the trade union. It is well established that the Durban ICU, outraged by Champion's suspension for financial misconduct, formally broke away from the 'mother body' in May 1928, and that subsequently at the end of June 1928, a 'Clean Administration Group' led by Doyle Modiakgotla, Alexander Maduna and Keable 'Mote called for Kadalie's resignation. Kadalie and Champion both believed, however, that Ncwana and Msimang were the moving forces in this 'sinister campaign among higher officials of the ICU'.[117] From Kadalie's perspective, '[u]nder-lying the cry for "Clean Administration" and the ICU *yase* Natal is that I should be sent out of the country'.[118] He later wrote:

> For a time, the president [Gumbs] and I were able to keep together the various elements that were antagonistic to each other, but as time wore on, I was in turn marked out for attack, owing to my being born outside the Union of South Africa. When Champion broke away the fact of my birth was used by him to rally the Zulu workers around his leadership.[119]

Champion himself staunchly rejected Kadalie's accusations of 'tribalism'[120] but a number of his lieutenants certainly did mix their appeals for provincial autonomy with anti-immigrant slurs. At heated ICU meetings, Zulu leaders told Kadalie that they refused to 'be treated like boys by a Nyasalander like you', while Jim London, the chair of the Durban ICU, told a meeting in late April 1928: 'We are angry, terribly angry, but let us show Kadalie we Zulus are gentlemen, and will not be interfered with by a man from Nyasa'.[121]

Similar assertions were repeated as the ICU disintegrated further over the course of 1928 and 1929. Pressured into resigning his position as ICU general secretary in January 1929, Kadalie initially intended 'to interest myself in the affairs of the natives in this country from Rhodesia and East Africa – many of them are my own countrymen', who were 'now being deported – illegally in my opinion'.[122] Ultimately, however, he decided to launch a rival Independent ICU in March 1929. Independent ICU leaders continued to invoke Kadalie as a 'prophet sent by God from Nyasaland to come to organise the native[s] of South Africa'.[123] Many who remained within the original ICU of Africa, however, were soon repeating anti-immigrant attack lines. In East London, John Mzaza asserted that Kadalie was a 'drunkard', 'not fit to be a leader of the ICU', who 'should [be] told to go back to Nyasaland to where he belongs'. Gardiner Jamela, likewise, claimed that Kadalie aimed to 'deceive the Amaxosa, because he cannot deceive his own people in Nyasaland'.[124] In Parys, Samuel

Mbulawa, told a rowdy and antagonistic audience that the trade union's bankruptcy was Kadalie's fault, and reminded the crowd that Malawians 'would have nothing to do with him saying that you have failed to assist others, how can you assist us[?]'[125]

Amidst these clear divisions, the economic depression put a final nail in the ICU's coffin. At an individual level, ICU leaders were threatened by the 1930 Riotous Assemblies Act, which NP politicians hoped would specifically target 'agitators coming from Swaziland, Nyasaland, and some from Zululand', and ensure that there were 'few agitators of the Kadalie and [Bransby Ndobe] type to stir up the natives'.[126] Soon after the act was passed, Kadalie was banned from the Rand and Champion was deported from Durban. On a macro level, in turn, black South Africans increasingly called 'for restricting work in the mines to Union Natives'.[127] After consulting moderate leaders and chiefs, the 1930 Native Economic Commission noted that, in particular, '[f]eeling among Union Natives against these Nyasaland natives [was] indeed very bitter'. He continued:

> Just as white people in the Union have determined that their standard of living and civilisation should not be jeopardized by permitting unrestricted immigration into the Union of Europeans of low character and civilization, so the Natives of the Union claim that they should be protected from immigration[.][128]

Exploiting this sentiment, the government attempted to create jobs for black South Africans through the mass deportation of 'foreign' workers from mines and urban areas.[129] These schemes were costly and ineffective, but nevertheless contributed to a climate of fear and hostility that fatally undermined solidarity. Amidst a final round of schisms which crippled the Independent ICU in mid-1932, rival officials resolved that they 'did not wish to be led by a foreigner anymore'.[130]

Conclusion

Despite clear setbacks, the ICU was undoubtedly at the forefront of migrant worker organisation in the 1920s, cognisant that capitalism in Southern Africa operated on a regional basis. Because capitalist 'oppressors' were 'organised both nationally and internationally', Kadalie insisted that unless 'the workers exert their strength internationally, they are doomed to defeat'.[131] In contrast to other trade unions, the ICU directly championed the need to organise Mozambican and Central African workers, attempted to outflank capitalist employers by working beyond the borders of South Africa, and critiqued emerging forms of exclusionary nationalism that hindered these organisational efforts. Inescapably, however, the ICU failed to overcome existing and emergent forms of exclusionary nationalism. Already by the 1920s, it was clear that the politics of black trade unionists, nationalist leaders and clergy alike were shaped by the logic of colonial borders – across South Africa at the end of the 1920s, the various ICU schisms were 'more or less aligned tribally'.[132]

These differences are key to understanding the ICU's failings and its ultimate collapse. But it is also significant that the first major black trade union organised in opposition to these divisions on an internationalist platform (far outstripping contemporary nationalist organisations in terms of mass membership), and that these broader solidarities had a clear economic rationale. While migrant workers on the mine compounds were not organised effectively until the rise of the National Union of Mineworkers in the 1980s, the ICU set important precedents that would be built on over subsequent decades.

SECTION B

Local and Regional Histories of the ICU

4 The ICU in Free State Dorps and Dorpies[1]

Peter Limb and Chitja Twala

Introduction

In writing ICU history, many scholars give prominence to events in major urban centres, for good reason. Yet, ICU growth in small Free State towns was an important part of this history. This chapter uncovers the history of neglected persons in a variety of rural towns, how farm and urban workers fitted into ICU politics, and relationships between ICU national, regional and local structures and personalities. We focus on small-town political life as expressed in meetings and other forms of ICU agitation. Perceptions by historians that significant events largely took place in large cities have influenced the marginalisation of rural and Free State history. When we de-centre this assumption to factor rural–urban interaction into the equation, a variant story emerges that enhances the importance of ICU history across the Free State.

Territory, language, power

Scholars researching the ICU have mapped its prodigious, if brief, rural growth including in the Orange Free State (OFS); a few, notably Bradford, have presented evidence of its presence there, while accepting it was difficult to organise farms. However, there is less attention to actual organising in rural dorps, and ICU history has not been written on a provincial scale. Yet, Bradford's sensitive treatment of the memories of sharecroppers and ideologies of organisers, together with Wickins' account of branch history and recent works by Moloi on Kroonstad, Mkhize on Selby Msimang in Bloemfontein and Neame's magisterial synthesis of ICU factions, including synergy or conflict with the African National Congress (ANC) and Communist Party (CPSA), lay a foundation for better understanding of its politics.[2]

ICU discourse, to Bradford, reveals much about class origins; to Wickins, speeches to rural audiences were 'composed largely of general complaints, … vague talk of the recovery of freedom', while some emphasised wages. Bonner views ICU discourse as 'millenarian syndicalism' often delivered in a top-down manner with little audience participation, apparent in our cases too, though we find instances of the crowd speaking back. Refracting discourse through the lens of police reports, an often-hostile press or interviews with sharecroppers, we must allow poetic licence, particularly in small towns, little more than service centres for agricultural hinterlands, 'a neglected area of study', if of late given more attention.[3]

The ICU was less a *trade* than a *political,* general union. We explore how its political unionism played out in the language and actions of activists who blended class, race and political tropes across the rigidly regulated terrain of OFS dorps (towns).

Leaders organised a web of branches but faced big problems maintaining them. They had to secure bases using novice officials lacking resources and get across programmes resonating with local cultures, a process helped by national union policies of better wages and land schemes, but also by attention to grassroots demands, articulating policies in diverse, sometimes idiosyncratic ways, mixing unionism, reformism, revolution and black nationalism, delivered largely orally, using an array of metaphors, advice and dire warnings.

Rural connections with political movements from below were explored by Bradford, Bundy, Beinart and others yet there is little treatment of small OFS towns or how they interacted, save Murray, who shows how Barolong politics straddled Thaba 'Nchu and Bloemfontein. Keegan charted the development of capitalism on the southern highveld but in the period before the ICU. The white-centred chronicles that litter OFS settler historiography remind us that local history too should be 'history from below'. Overcoming this neglect requires close attention to municipal and black politics on which there is work on larger towns, but we broaden this to cover a wide range of rural dorps where the ICU was active.[4]

The municipal could even lead the national – as in the drive for women's passes and the Land Act by white town councils or pass law protests by women. Crucial battles over policy play out at municipal level, with conflict between peoples and elites when the state is emerging, as on the southern highveld. As in other places with emerging labouring classes, so OFS towns, too, had crowds who flocked to rallies, and nascent middle strata from among whose ranks would emerge ICU activists who, as Tilly observed more generally, 'followed available scripts, adapted those scripts' and 'like troupes of street musicians, drew their claim-making performances' from often-limited repertoires. There were scripts available to ICU activists from labour movement, ANC, Garveyite and CPSA political cultures, and their performances recorded in the press and by police are major sources of local ICU history. In focusing on activists, we assert the '"small town" theme' as an 'important feature of urban history'.[5]

OFS ANC branches gave some attention to farm labour but the strictures Govan Mbeki would take up about rural neglect applied here too. ICU provincial secretary T.W. Keable 'Mote raised the need to address the countryside as early as 1923. Neame refers to ICU-led 'peasant revolt'. Yet a mood of revolt never became an uprising and rigid agrarian relations constricted autonomy, seen in how symbiotic paternalism in the life of sharecropper Kas Maine discouraged direct ICU involvement on farms.[6]

In the archives, political peasants are glimpsed in interviews with sharecroppers that provide insights into working lives and ICU politics. Ndie Makume recalled ICU meetings on farms near Lindley, how sharecroppers donated cattle to the union, but that it was better to keep quiet. Tolo Manoto heard Clements Kadalie speak in Phiritona on Sundays when labourers could escape the farms, yet 'never knew clearly what type of movement it was' and did not join. To John Mosina, who worked near Frankfort, the ICU 'meant freeing people from slavery'. He 'and most blacks joined'; they elected local delegates 'from some of the educated people'. Philip Masike remembered how Kadalie in 1928 promised land but 'went away with our money'. To Jameson Molete in Winburg district, the ICU organised effectively but 'never lasted long'. Labane Rakabaele, working on farms in Marquard then Kroonstad, did not understand ICU policies but attended their gatherings on football grounds and later joined, recalling how it recruited labourers who travelled from farms to meetings, which as Keegan notes, helped rural peoples use 'the political arena to forward their own agenda'. Historians synthesised such voices to gauge the mood towards the ICU but gave less attention to what actually happened in dorps.[7]

Political economy and political unionism

The ICU faced major problems: widely scattered towns thwarted easy interaction, scant industrialisation restricted the pool of workers who might join, and protest was constrained on regimented farms. In the two reserves, union prospects were bleak: Witsieshoek was a closed society, ruled by a white commandant, with little employment; the patchwork-quilt land holdings of Thaba 'Nchu produced few industrial workers; once-politicised black farmers were in decline due to the Land Act; and there was rising debt. The economy remained overwhelmingly rural yet by the 1920s, notes Bradford, 'it was in the Free State where proletarianisation was furthest advanced in both town and countryside', referring more to land uprooting than incorporation in an urban proletariat. Compensation was below a living wage: in Bethlehem district, only land was offered; in Edenburg, merely a sheep and food.[8]

Urbanisation was underway. By 1904, black people had become majorities in Bloemfontein, Kroonstad and Harrismith. Most remained on the land: in 1921, 421 978 of the black population still lived in rural areas, only 60 235 in towns. Yet black urban numbers grew – between 1911 and 1921, it roughly doubled in Bethulie (529/1 025), Harrismith (3 056/3 547), Kestell (242/486) and Vrede (600/1 605). Bethlehem skyrocketed from 3 000 in 1922 to 29 289 by 1936.[9]

Black mine employment grew to average 10 000 in 1911 but by the time of the ICU had declined: in 1922, there were only 1 600 at Viljoen's Drift, 595 further south. Despite some growth from 163 engineering units in 1904, the iron and steel industry never took off. Limited industrialisation outside of Bloemfontein meant few larger factories, with workers found notably in municipal employ, railways and stores. In the few places where factories opened, the ICU, even with a local branch, was rarely in a position to capitalise, as when the Harrismith wool factory reopened in 1927. Similarly, while the ICU attracted women and had female officials in Bloemfontein and Kroonstad, by the time the flow of women migrants increased in the 1930s, its branches had largely folded.[10]

White unions rarely took strike action: 80 railwaymen stopped work in Frankfort in 1924, clothing and brick workers in Bloemfontein in 1926/27; the latter included black labourers whose conditions ICU officials monitored. Black workers struck more often, but invariably faced repression: as early as 1895–1896, strikers in Koffiefontein were shot; in 1903, 500 at Cornelia mine were arrested and put in cattle trucks; in 1907, 500 miners at Voorspoed marched on Kroonstad only to face police rushed from Bloemfontein. In 1920, a police train sped to confront Jagersfontein strikers.[11]

This was a turbulent, formative period of black politics. In Bloemfontein, ANC leaders exuded moderation though a spate of farm shootings in the 1920s roused some to action. There were big protests by women in 1913 and 1920 against passes, a 1918 strike and 1925 'riots'. In all this, there was at first only an ephemeral ICU presence but national ICU policies on wages aroused local interest and received a boost when it won wage gains in Bloemfontein. Ideological tussles were blunter than on the Rand; the CPSA and unions were weak here, so too the black press. Msimang's short-lived *Morumioa*, the initial ICU organ, folded in 1920. The ICU's *Workers' Herald* and CPSA's *South African Worker* made the rounds in small numbers while Chamber of Mines-owned *Umteteli wa Bantu* with superior resources won wider readership, red-baiting ICU leaders as 'semi-educated blatherers'; 'aggressively stupid'.[12]

The first attempt to form a national black union, the Industrial and Commercial Workers' Union (ICWU), was at Bloemfontein in 1920, attracting delegates not only from the Cape but other OFS towns: E.W. and Wesley Mbete, P. Makhetha (Heilbron), L. Mablame (Kroonstad), C.D. Modiakgotla (Westminster), Agent Rakanoane (Winburg), G. Liphoko (Bethlehem), Rev. Leuta (Harrismith) and delegates from Viljoensdrift, Jacobsdal and Vredefort. George Mocher, born in Bloemfontein, was the first ICWU secretary. But the ICU soon shifted its base to the Rand and not until 1926 would rural OFS delegates again take part.[13]

Relations with other movements were complex. Congress had convened the ICWU conference and the ICU tended to view it as its political arm. Founding ICU members Walter Makgothi and James Mogaecho of Winburg were active in the ANC, Makgothi as provincial secretary, Rakanoane as president, in which capacity he spoke out on labour conditions. Over two-thirds of delegates at the 1927 ICU congress were ANC members. As forced removals increased in Waaihoek, ANC and ICU leaders protested. Some wore two caps. Modiakgotla was secretary both of the OFS ANC and ICU Kroonstad, urging an ICU meeting in Mangaung in 1927 to abandon *hamba kahle* petitioning and 'sit down, throw away their passes and refuse to pay taxes.' Rising repression encouraged closer relations with sympathetic ANC leaders, J.T. Gumede and Z.R. Mahabane, the latter based in Vrede. There also was tension. In Kroonstad, where the ANC was weak, Robert Sello observed that his ICU members treated the union as 'a pseudo-political body'; they could thus be allies or rivals and some criticised ANC prevarication: John Mancoe told the 1928 ICU conference the ANC had done little to combat passes. The 1925 Bloemfontein riots saw divisions. Thomas Mapikela steered the ANC tiller away from the ICU in Mangaung, and the Bethlehem Location Advisory Board expressed hostility.[14]

There were short periods of CPSA-ICU cooperation in Mangaung, where three union leaders joined the party, and where white communist Sam Malkinson lived in the township, and in Kroonstad, where S.P. Bunting visited to court 'Mote, who briefly wrote for the *South African Worker* in 1926 lauding 'victory of socialism' if all oppressed 'unite and proclaim the dictatorship of the proletariat', but then voted to expel communists from the ICU. Mutual suspicion abounded: Roux argued 'the average native intellectual' like 'Mote was 'willing enough to speak on our platform' but viewed his opportunism as a danger. Such flirtations barely filtered down to dorpies. In the northeast, ICU leader Robert Dumah combined communist and Garveyite ideas but there the ICU was very much on its own.[15]

Cramping ICU initiatives was government and employer hostility. Municipalities, politicians and farmers drove forward into national legislation the Land Act. In 1927, Hertzog told the OFS Congress of his ruling NP, which had tabled 11 motions condemning the ICU that farmers should unite against the union. To J.G. Keyter, Member for Ficksburg, 'this is a white man's country'. The white male-only electorate of only 47 279 in 1922 elected 16 members, 17 of them NP.[16]

Despite such antagonisms, ICU branches exploded from a single centre, Bloemfontein, in 1925 to 22 branches by 1926, gaining 16 more in 1928, the summit of its influence when it reached most sizeable towns. Yet that year at least nine branches closed. Initiatives came from Johannesburg, keen to boost funds, Bloemfontein, and, after an early 1929 split led by 'Mote, Kroonstad. Most branches formed too late to catch the earlier wave of union consolidation, resources remained weak, supply lines stretched, and wage gains won in bigger cities rarely filtered down to dorpies, but the experiment would be a bold one.

Case studies: The Northeast

In terms of an urban workforce, northeast towns in what is today Thabo Mofutsanyana District Municipality could offer the ICU little, but it had a large population of farm labourers. Patterns of ICU work, tropes employed by its organisers and inner divisions had much in common with other areas distant from ICU centres of Bloemfontein and Kroonstad. 'Mote, with an interest in agriculture and concern for rural workers, signalled as early as 1923 a desire to organise there, urging Sesotho readers to join, and predicting its envoys would go as far as Harrismith by November, but it was not until late 1926 that progress was made by founding 11 new branches.[17]

Farm worker conditions were 'oppressive and tantamount to chattel slavery' reported journalist Richard Thema in 1927. In Senekal, he heard of 'ruthless warfare against the ICU'; any members were 'dismissed... or evicted'. Despite hostility, it made great strides in 1926–1928. Kadalie wrote admiringly in his memoirs of 'prominent propagandists' 'Mote and Simon Elias, with their 'able and good' secretaries the 'twin brothers [Esau and Jacob] Nhlapo at Bethlehem and Reitz' plus Dumah, who 'did a lot to stir the central province to action'. If much recorded ICU discourse here came from visiting officials, local activists added their own take, blending elements of Garveyism and rural utopian communism, manufacturing distinctive, syncretic ideological reactions to rural-based class and racial conflict.[18]

Into Memel, a village with 358 black people, nearby Verkykerskop, and Kestell further south, stepped maverick union activists Dumah and David Stebe. This was tough terrain for the ICU. In June 1929, when Memel secretary Stebe held a meeting in Verkykerskop, he was summoned for trespassing on a local farmer's land just to get there; the previous week, he had travelled that way to Bethlehem and Paul Roux to assist others similarly arrested. He urged listeners to 'fight with the law for better wages and liberty', then announced the Universal Negro Improvement Association (UNIA) had invited 10 men to America but the sergeant recording the speech felt the 135 or so present were 'not much in favour' of the idea.[19]

Stebe likely took his Garveyism from Dumah who had taught in Herschel where he was Native Teachers' Association secretary, gravitated to the UNIA, then ICU, becoming secretary there later in Vrede. He too was arrested for union work. After the 1929 ICU split that produced the Independent ICU (IICU), Dumah joined the latter but left to become local UNIA secretary. His admixture of ideas is clear in his March 1929 speech to 50 people at tiny Kestell. He wanted to 'find a way to organise the ICU' but saw William Ballinger (white adviser who displaced Kadalie from ICU leadership) as a 'dictator' and so had closed ICU offices at Vrede and Memel, instead forming 'the African movement'. The crowd, reported police, 'all listened attentively and cheered'. In 1929, Jacob Nhlapo addressed a 50-strong meeting there, arguing ICU success in gaining a fixed wage in Bloemfontein meant 'smaller towns must follow too'. The crowd swelled as churchgoers came out and, denouncing the pass laws, he was cheered. Next month Dumah addressed 250 people in Memel, criticising the town clerk for aiming to 'do away with the ICU'. Reframing local Afrikaner history, he thundered, 'Let us be black de Wets' – Christiaan de Wet had led the 1914 Boer rebellion which started in the town. He then made the startlingly false claim that all ICU leaders had now joined the CPSA.[20]

'Mote, who in 1928 had been arrested in Memel and refused bail, returned to the dorpie on 15 December 1929 with Dumah. Addressing a 400-strong meeting, now under UNIA auspices, Dumah spoke first, invoking history: 'white people are celebrating Dingaan's Day... We must also celebrate.' His anti-capitalism mixed with calls for freedom. 'Time has come for free and better wages and to have our own parliament.... I say Africa for the Africans.' 'Mote then asked everyone to pay £1 to 'contribute to buy lands' but cautioned: 'Don't expect to get rich the first year.' That July, Dumah had forcefully told a crowd of 150: 'You must sjambok these constables and police ... [and] farmers, who ill-treat you.'[21]

Farm labourers around Christina hamlet were prominent among the 130 who heard Stebe for three hours in January 1929. 'If the employer breaks the agreement the ICU is here to fight the employer,' he emphasised, the ICU ticket 'is a stick to fight your employer.' Returning in March with Dumah for a five-hour meeting, he promised, 'if your employer strikes you this organisation will put him in jail.' Dumah talked up the Garvey movement, then, in a flurry of radical, contradictory metaphors first invoked anti-colonial battles of Moshoeshoe and added, 'I am speaking in Johannesburg next week as a communist... We are coming in aeroplanes and in storms and we must destroy the capitalists... We want to establish the black republic and if the Communist Party is against us we will kick it to hell too.'[22]

Harrismith and nearby Witsieshoek with their higher populations offered possibilities but despite some occasional strikes and land protests, the ICU at first made little headway. In 1926, the local magistrate condemned denial of free labour contracts producing 'a large, discontented hopeless' populace with 'no activity' in formation of societies and 'no unrest' – seemingly stony ground for the ICU. The push to found branches, first mooted by 'Mote in 1923 and tentatively attempted in 1924 by Paul Twala, came in October 1926 when 'Mote spoke at a flurry of gatherings at Harrismith. Housing, he stated, was 'altogether too shameful for human habitation'. At an enthusiastic open-air meeting, then in the evening at a packed church and next day on the square, he urged higher wages. Staying on to meet farmworkers after a church service, he advocated strikes as 'our great industrial weapon', and 'a large number' enrolled. In a fortnight, he returned to meet women about passes and wages. The next morning, he addressed rail-workers, then spoke to a crowd of 300, 'a goodly proportion' from farms, again hammering low wages. His performance, police observed, was supplemented by calls to sing the African anthem when enthusiasm waned. Next day, he held a recruitment drive. Being a workday, only 80 people arrived but, improvising, he led them singing in a demonstration through the streets.[23]

The ICU put down tentative roots. Josiah Mochoko, earlier active in the Vigilance Committee fighting women's passes, was an active Harrismith secretary, also covering Witsieshoek, calling for more membership cards. But with splits, there was little consolidation and, by January 1929, it was the Garveyite Dumah whom Mochoko hosted at a meeting attracting barely 60 people, Mochoko remarking on insufficient progress made. Dumah took up worker complaints against police for failure to investigate employer assaults, but the branch proved ephemeral. When 'Mote revisited in 1931, he found little left of the ICU, though veterans assisted Hyman Basner's radical election campaigning in the mid-1930s.[24]

Further south, Ficksburg, Fouriesburg and Clocolan, astride the border, presented different problems. 'Mote, born in Leribe, pushed to recruit in Basutoland where Chief Joseph Molapo let them open branches and offered to sell maize to the union. A Ficksburg branch formed in April 1927, and still had a secretary, L.J. Rakhajane, in 1929 when Jacob Nhlapo, previously a powerhouse in Reitz ICU, addressed a gathering of 300–500 people. He conceded things had not gone 'too well with the ICU', blaming the audience for 'not supporting us' and reminding them to 'be obedient to your masters.' He said little concrete about Ficksburg and, naively, assured them a petition would solve any grievances. Predictably, his speech provoked 'very little interest'.[25]

Paul Roux village was part of an ICU tour in late 1928, and in March 1929, Aaron Mhelpu of Bethlehem branch addressed a 30-strong meeting there. A year later, a correspondent reported the ICU had left an imprint in this 'town of the Boers' giving a glimmer of hope black people could be treated fairly, but Boers had responded with evictions. ICU 'lions' promoted community land purchases but with the pain of evictions and as money given to the ICU disappeared, people became depressed. Branch leaders, Elizabeth Maine and Rosina Thakedi, stood their ground, and in 1933, Peter Malepe, previously Parys ICU chair, was in charge of a surviving, if small, organisation.[26]

The regional centre of Bethlehem had earlier hosted the Eastern Native Vigilance Association that took up farmworker conditions but when the ICU formed a branch there in 1926, led by Obed Dhlamini, the Advisory Board adopted a 'capitalist offensive against [ICU] activities'. In a district where, as 'Mote noted, workers were 'not paid, but only given ALMS DISGUISED AS WAGES', the ICU grew. Esau Nhlapo replaced Dlamini, dismissed for graft, in 1927. He encouraged Stimela Jingoes, a clerk, to continue organising. Nearby towns, recalled Jingoes, who viewed the ICU more as a trade union, were 'a wide open field'. He worked hard with Nhlapo and Dumah but his syndicalism did not mesh with their more political style. By 1929, Dumah was Bethlehem district secretary, but moved away from the ICU. In 1931, 'Mote returned, recalling how when in 1926 he first arrived in this 'big city', women and girls too had joined. Now talk was all on 'Native trade' and they had to be patient with the ICU.[27]

Further north in Vrede, the ICU was more active. District secretary Dumah had intensified work there after action taken against him for ICU involvement while teaching at the Wesleyan school. In December 1928, addressing 175 town and farm workers, he focused on better wages and wanted to organise workers by sector. In the following February, after the split, Joe Kokozela from Johannesburg addressed an ICU meeting of 150 people. He assured farmworkers the union was pushing for written contracts but despaired that the local committee had disintegrated. Dumah was present, but Kokozela was frank: 'I want you to get rid of Dumah.' In April, Dumah and Stebe responded by resigning and joining the UNIA. Dumah, who saw himself as another Langalibalele, a 'black Julius Caesar', on 15 June 1930 organised a rally against the Riotous Assemblies Act, with 1 200 attending including numerous farmworkers; many joining the UNIA. Dumah also identified as a 'strong supporter' of the CPSA. In 1931, he exposed farmworker evictions in *Negro Worker*, noting the ICU had died back in 1929, as had the UNIA 'a few days after its inception in Memel', but 'Garveyism teaches self-consciousness… Long live the black African republic! Workers of the World Unite!' Dumah, like 'Mote in his radical phase, spliced a syndicalist African liberationism with rural communism in his own repertoires of protest.[28]

Across the northeast, small branches struggled, buffeted by splits, employer and state repression, and corruption. Those on the ground urged branches be taken seriously. In 1929, 'Mote complained, 'almost [all] my branches have not received any issues of the *New Africa*' (IICU organ). Do not despise small branches,' he warned, begging Kadalie to address small branches 'very anxious to see you', and reporting wide demands for membership cards. Head office was impressed to learn 'small branches are playing their part' but pointed out their logistics were difficult, as they 'never get an acknowledgement'.[29]

The South

Little populated or industrialised, the south was still part of ICU attempts to build a provincial structure. Sizeable clusters of black miners in Jagersfontein and Koffiefontein had diminished by the 1920s. Distant from major ICU offices, small southern towns served pastoralists and were difficult to visit regularly, therein lying a tension between local and central structures evident at ICU meetings. From 1926 to 1929, new branches sprang up but just as soon disappeared.

These ephemeral structures lasted less than two years. Wickins' calculations based on branch payments suggest only three were financially viable by 1927: Jagersfontein, Springfontein and Zastron, although Bethulie, Fauresmith and Koffiefontein also feature on a list of conference delegates.[30] Intrepid ICU organiser and encyclopaedist John Mancoe detailed officials in his 1934 *Directory*, including James Mogaecho, southern secretary; Absalom Goduka, regional organiser; C.J. Mabuza, Springfontein chairperson; Jacob Mitchell, Jagersfontein organiser; Michael Moleko, Senekal-Jagersfontein secretary; and in Wepener, A.J. Lepotane, 'first lady Branch Secretary-Chairwoman', with Philbert Makosholo secretary and Kemul Motalingoene chair. Lepotane was still active in 1936, attending the All African Convention, and addressing a rump ICU conference.[31]

Bethulie, a small, isolated town scarcely mentioned in ICU histories, witnessed women's anti-pass protests in 1923 and later that decade poor wages and housing, and harsh application of laws inclined some residents to back the ICU. The town council sought to expel those lacking a permanent job and maximise fees via ruthless bureaucracy: in 1927 'old and weak … unfit for work' Jappie Mbusha could not pay fees but bluntly was told by Superintendent J.H. Cloete to 'pay or clear out.' Isaac Mothibili, who had undergone a serious medical operation and had no income, had to pay all arrears. Abraham Finger with severe arthritis could not work, but his application for exemption was rejected. David Smith, despite 20 years plumbing experience was refused residency as he did not work for white people.[32]

At a mass meeting in February 1929 at which residents complained of police bursting into their homes at any time and of location superintendent Cloete slapping youth, Isaac Letali, Bethulie ICU leader and Advisory Board secretary criticised the superintendent and resigned from the board in protest. In response, Cloete vowed 'to deal with agitators of [his] type.'[33]

In late 1928, Absalom Goduka, an ICU regional organiser, who had been arrested for organising in Springfontein, held meetings in Bethulie. The first attracted 130 people, the second 250. Assuring listeners the ICU had not abandoned them, he used metaphors of farm labour, lamenting they were born with an ox-hide strip around their necks. When workers complained, white farmers said they 'would loosen it tomorrow' but then said 'wait until next year.' Goduka offered little more than a promise of central intervention – 'If you have trouble, wire us at Johannesburg or

Bloemfontein, we will come to you' – praised Cloete for allowing the meeting, and gave scant attention to building a strong branch. In trying to sting listeners to action, he abused them: 'Your heads are small. You are lying; we are doing the work.' Police noted 'no questions were asked and the speaker was treated as if he was rather a joke'. Distant and out of touch with local complaints, he would have gained few kudos for praising Cloete.[34]

Into this situation, a few months later and after the IICU split, came Elias. To a meeting of 200–300, he enunciated ICU principles of justice and unity. Asked the reason for the split, he replied in class terms: Ballinger 'associates with the Chamber of Mines and is now living in Parktown, leading a parasitical life.' Detailing their low wages, he urged people to 'organise yourselves, work out your cost of living … then go to your superintendent', advice that also would have fallen on sceptical ears.[35]

In April 1930, Goduka returned to find the old branch, opened only the previous year, 'dead', including a women's section that 'had such a good female secretary'. He berated a crowd of 200: the ICU had 'no faults, it is you people… Here the blacks don't know how to organise'. None of this endeared him to the audience. He questioned the integrity of Letali, now local IICU secretary, who retorted that whenever Goduka came he told 'a different story' and did not consult. Makie, a teacher, asked Goduka to explain differences between ICU bodies, but he refused. The following week Goduka lectured a small crowd 'no longer supporters of the ICU'. Mrs van Vuuren told him, 'I'm leaving the ICU, for the money my child has to pay is very much if… caught' by police for brewing. Goduka dismissed her comment as irrelevant but more attention to local issues may have bolstered the dying branch.[36]

Philippolis also hosted Elias. In April 1929, he spoke to a crowd of 300, calling on residents to demand higher wages from the town council or leave their service. He detailed local prices – a bag of coal cost twice that in Bloemfontein – and criticised how residents were 'fenced in, like ostriches', but added he now had 'nothing to do' with Kadalie. Yet the following month he addressed a meeting in Kroonstad of Kadalie's Independent ICU. Residents, like those in Bethulie, must have been confused by the split.[37]

Rouxville and Zastron linked to wider networks also incorporating Herschel, Burgersdorp and Aliwal North traversed by activists scouting new branch possibilities. Albert Nzula cut his teeth in the ICU, working with James Leeuw in Rouxville Location, before becoming CPSA national secretary. But organisers were vulnerable in such remote places. In 1927, 'Mote was arrested after the Rouxville Council refused him permission to organise despite Advisory Board support. The ICU also faced religious conservatism. After Elias addressed 'a very large' meeting in Zastron calling for higher wages and termed the Dutch Reformed Church (DRC) 'the Church of Satan', a local DRC teacher, Stephen Tshepe, left the meeting in disgust. He was not only a police informer but also *Umteteli* correspondent and urged the ICU 'to choose people we will be able to follow.' Nevertheless, Elias enrolled 129 members that day.[38]

Another problem facing organisers was denial of temporary residence permits. This was the case in Springfontein, where C.J. Mabuza was ICU chairperson. It had seen determined anti-pass protests in 1923 and as a railway junction staffed by workers offered recruitment prospects to the ICU. But in 1928, 'Mote, Mancoe, Elias, and Goduka were all arrested there for organising, 'Mote using the presence of a large court gathering to rail against the town council's 'unreasonable and autocratic attitude'.[39]

Covering such vast territory with so few resources was not helped by internal divisions. 'Mote, touring the south with James Mogaecho, southern secretary in 1927, complained to head office that it had authorised Goduka to organise in the province, a 'gross violation' of the ICU constitution for, as provincial secretary, he had not been informed, and monies collected had not been satisfactorily accounted for.[40] The small workforce brought in little cash to ICU coffers, another barrier to growth. Inability to implement grassroots control that could have given local people a stake in the movement aggravated these problems.

Centre and North

The north and centre, covered in other chapters, are treated briefly with the emphasis on surrounding dorps. Bloemfontein, where the union first gained a base, won a key wage increase, had (like Kroonstad) female officials, and nourished a vibrant union culture, was, by 1927, in decline. Surrounding towns were patchily covered. In 1929, Secretary Walter Makgothi still reached out to Bultfontein. To the east, Thaba 'Nchu only ever had an ephemeral ICU presence. In contrast, in Ladybrand, when 'Mote visited in 1926, he claimed (with hyperbole) 'the whole population rose to the occasion' and in 1929, Jacob Nhlapo attracted 2 000, stating that once the ICU 'gets things right at Bloemfontein' by organising along trade lines, 'all the smaller towns must fall in.' But viable branches did not emerge from these relatively sizeable gatherings. At subsequent meetings, Nhlapo's 'very moderate' speeches attracted only 50 and 100. A similar small crowd heard Mancoe address the pass laws. That local leaders, Andries Matlhare and Fredericks Brandis, do not feature in reports suggests the ICU here over-relied on outside speakers.[41]

In 1927, 'Mote moved to Kroonstad as provincial secretary and, despite town council hostility, made it his base – it became third most financial of all branches – for expansion to other towns. In speeches in Frankfort in 1927, he blended Biblical and communist metaphors, and expressed solidarity with the Chinese revolution but took care to detail local conditions. The Parys branch, deduced Moloi, was second in provincial strength, unusual in being more farm-based. In a speech in May 1927, 'Mote urged a wage of 8s. a day in shops or on farms. Parys and Heilbron branches in the early 1930s lobbied over withheld farm wages and support of aged workers but as the depression bit, they faded away.[42]

From 1929, Benjamin Mazingi from Johannesburg became IICU Kroonstad district secretary. Addressing a small audience in Petrus Steyn that year, he promised to fight for higher wages and buy them land. In 1930, he addressed a 100-strong meeting in Villiers, condemning Masters and Servants' laws and women's passes. He urged subscriptions to help the ICU purchase a farm near Frankfort so 8 000 Africans 'need no longer work for a Baas' – a project treated by listeners with scepticism. At Edenville meetings of 350 and 150 people in 1929, 'Mote and Alex Maduna hammered the need for wage increases and written contracts. But divisions widened. Maduna spoke on behalf of the 'ICU of the Free State' and 'Mote refused to let Kokozela, from 'Ballinger's ICU' speak. Two weeks later a poorly attended meeting of only 40 heard Henderson Binda and Sello praise Ballinger's 'new way of safe keeping their money'. Police fretted that 'Mote, in the dying embers of his radicalism, pushed the League of African Rights in villages and Bunting had slept overnight at his home and met farm workers.[43]

In May 1930, Thema compiled a report on worker conditions in Reitz, Frankfort, and Lindley districts: forced to work continuously for 12 months, conditions on farms and in towns were 'tantamount to slavery'. He met clerics 'once antagonistic to the ICU' now 'willing to assist'.[44] But only a shell of the ICU remained. As in the south and northeast, the need for a strong ICU was never more evident.

'Mote and Sello attempted a national ICU unity conference in 1931 at Kroonstad but none of the old leaders appeared, save Selby Msimang, sent by conservative ANC president Seme; the 57 delegates came overwhelmingly from the OFS. 'Mote's revolutionary fire had gone; he now praised Seme and preached 'goodwill towards an established and orderly Christian government.' A revival conference hosted by Heilbron secretary, I.B. Moroe, also failed. Some skeleton bodies persisted: Mrs E. Benjamin, a hospital worker, was Bloemfontein secretary (1937–1939) but, in rural towns, most branches folded.[45]

Conclusion

In the short term, the ICU in OFS dorps failed. Emblematically, in 1929 at remote Hoopstad, activists Elias Mahumapelo and J. Segale wanted action but, leaderless, requested 'an official reside in their midst to help them', to no avail.[46] Resources were now dwindling. Yet while many branches withered, some lasted longer, and in the absence of black unions, kept alive organisational ideas and techniques of improving working conditions. Support from rural ex-ICU members to radical electoral candidates E.T. Mofutsanyana and Basner in the mid-1930s and revival of a spirit of revolt in the late 1940s in Witsieshoek speak to the sparking of a political consciousness that would smoulder on in isolated outbreaks of defiance and border penetration by exiles in coming decades as people in rural towns cherished memories of this once inspiring organisation.

In the Free State, harsh material conditions and social tensions made rural people more amendable to the ICU message. But the calling of meetings and founding of branches and the challenge to authority this represented owed more to the considered campaigns, drive, and language of activists using imaginative as well as standard repertoires of protest. ICU political discourse followed the impulse, detected by Bonner, audaciously to reverse the gaze of the state's panopticon, but for successful leaders, it also involved a fusing of rhetorical flourish with close attention to local complaints. This made the ICU in these oft-neglected dorps and farms, if the Achilles heel of the body, more relevant to the grassroots.[47]

5 The ICU and Local Politics: Kroonstad, from the Late 1920s to the 1930s

Tshepo Moloi

Introduction

In 1931, Thabo Keable 'Mote formed the Federated Free State Industrial and Commercial Workers' Union of Africa as an alternative to the official branch of the Industrial and Commercial Workers' Union (ICU) of Africa in Kroonstad, which was already struggling to survive. According to Davenport and Saunders, '[I]t led no more than a twilight existence until its final disappearance in 1933'.[1] The situation was worsened by the refusal of many branch members to pay membership fees when they realised that the ICU could not deliver on its promises. This crisis in the branch stood in sharp contrast to the organisation's heyday when it infused radical and militant politics in the black locations of Kroonstad. A primary contributor to the demise of the branch was the tension and infighting between the ICU leaders, particularly 'Mote and Clements Kadalie.

Prior to the founding of the branch of the ICU in 1926 Kroonstad's black locations remained quiescent politically. This was largely due to the passive character of the branch of the South African Native National Congress (renamed the African National Congress (ANC) in 1923), and the pacifying role of the Native Advisory Board (NAB) and the Joint Council for Europeans and Natives (JCEN). However, towards the end of the 1920s, the ICU in Kroonstad, led by 'Mote, Henderson Binda and Eva Kubedi, amongst others, changed this situation. It mobilised the locations' residents to boycott increased rates and to oppose the NAB and JCEN, which they accused of not advancing the interests of the residents. The militant and radical activism infused by the ICU in the area led Kadalie to boast that 'the ICU have [sic] never failed in Kroonstad'.[2]

Although the ICU played an important role in shaping Kroonstad's history of political resistance, it has received little scholarly attention.[3] Writing about the formation of the ICU in rural areas, Bradford alludes to the role played by the ICU Women's Section in Kroonstad.[4] Similarly, Dee, when discussing the inconsistencies in Kadalie's biographies, also notes the active role played by women in the branch of the ICU in Kroonstad.[5] Wickins' doctoral thesis refers to the establishment of the ICU and its local leaders, ranging from the district to branch leaders, and briefly discusses the tension that developed between Kadalie and 'Mote.[6] Johns elaborates on this key point and writes about 'Mote's attempts to '... keep together several branches of the ICU in one organisation' after Kadalie's resignation from the ICU in 1929. Specifically related to Kroonstad, Johns recounts the conference 'Mote convened in Kroonstad to form a new trade union movement'.[7] Ntantala's autobiography recalls the names of the leaders of the ICU in Kroonstad indicating their lasting influence in the area.[8] Finally, Keegan, in his book *Facing the Storm,* records that black labour tenants in the rural Orange Free State (OFS) joined the ICU and some of them like Lucas Nqandela attended meetings of the ICU in Kroonstad's old locations.[9]

This chapter builds on the existing scholarship by locating the emergence of the ICU in the context of the changing conditions in the black locations of Kroonstad and residents' growing dissatisfaction with the inability of existing organisations to deal effectively with their problems. As was the case elsewhere in the country, the ICU was seen as a more militant alternative to the moderate ANC and certainly more prepared to engage in protest action. I also demonstrate that the failure of the ICU's national leaders to assist the members of the ICU at local level caused the latter to lose faith in the union and its leaders, which contributed to the demise of the Kroonstad ICU branch. A central factor in this equation was the tension between 'Mote and the national leadership of the ICU, which accelerated the fragmentation of the organisation.

This chapter draws extensively on newspaper reports, particularly *Umteteli wa Bantu,* the minutes of the Kroonstad Town Council and ICU material such as a report written by William Ballinger about the branches of the ICU of Africa. Most importantly, I have also relied on oral history interviews with some of the residents of Kroonstad's old locations. Although the informants interviewed were not members of the ICU, their insights shed light on the conditions in the old locations. I demonstrate that the role of the radicalised elite and women, led by the ICU's women's section, marked an important break with old elite politics and helped to introduce radical politics in Kroonstad.

Kroonstad

Kroonstad, situated in the northern Free State province (formerly the OFS), was founded in the 1850s and proclaimed a municipality, with its own local government in 1875.[10] Black people who migrated to Kroonstad during this period first lived in the area today known as 'town', the current central business district. They called their settlement 'A Location', which was in close proximity to the white residential areas. At the beginning of the twentieth century, whites began to complain about the growing inter-relationships between white men and black women caused by the afore-mentioned close living arrangements. However, the absence of segregation regulation meant they could not yet successfully demand the removal of black people. This was to change decisively in the early part of the twentieth century because of the spread of scarlet fever in 1915 and the influenza epidemic in 1918, which killed about 229 whites and blacks in the town.[11]

This presented whites and the authorities with a pretext to campaign for the removal of black residents. Despite evidence to the contrary, they blamed black people for the spread of disease and thus threatening their own lives. From this point, the demand for decisive residential segregation enjoyed overwhelming support from Kroonstad's white population. In 1920, the residents of A Location used the compensation they received from the Kroonstad Town Council (KTC) for their properties in town to purchase plots and built their own houses in the new settlement, about 1.6 kilometres from town, which they also named A Location. They became standholders. Subsequent locations were established after the promulgation of the Natives (Urban Areas) Act of 1923, which became the key piece of legislation that empowered urban local authorities to set aside sites for black occupation (but not ownership) in separate areas described as 'locations'.[12] Although the adoption of the Act was optional, the KTC enthusiastically welcomed it and moved swiftly to establish locations for its black inhabitants.

In this effort, it was assisted by the *Bantoe-administrasieraad* (Bantu Administration Council) that, despite its name, was an informal committee made up of some of the male inhabitants of A Location. Setiloane wrote that the new A Location consisted between 200 and 300 houses and comprised a mixed population, made up of Sesotho, Setswana, isiXhosa and few isiZulu-speaking people, and a number of Afrikaans-speaking people.[13] In the next four to five years, after the establishment of A Location, the black population grew in Kroonstad due to inward migration. At the time, blacks came from as far afield as Bechuanaland in search of employment opportunities and a place to stay.[14] This forced the white authorities to establish another location, which they named B Location but was popularly known amongst the locals as Marabastad after Jan Maraba, who built the first house there. The last residential area for blacks to be established was D Location, also known as Matikaring (the diggers), west of Marabastad. Setiloane noted that this location mainly accommodated people 'from the neighbouring farm districts' and people from the mines, hence 'the diggers'.[15] In 1925, the white authorities in Kroonstad, in line with the government's segregation laws, established a settlement for coloured people east of the black locations. This area came to be known as Cairo (or C Location). Setiloane estimated that 'some 300 coloureds lived there after its establishment'.[16]

The establishment of the new locations coincided with a new wave of migration by blacks from the surrounding regions, as well as Basutoland. A combination of factors caused this. Firstly, the Land Act of 1913 squeezed many people off their land to seek employment and places to settle in urban areas. Secondly, in 1923, the Smuts government relaxed the regulations, which had restricted black women from migrating to the urban areas. Thirdly, the drought that had started in 1927 and peaked from 1932 to 1934 forced many black people who lived and worked on the farms dotted across the OFS to leave the farms.[17] For Wickins, this latter group included the independent black farmers who 'would not submit to lowering of their status and accept employment on white farms as labour tenants'.[18] Some of these people settled in Kroonstad.

The Pact government, which came to power in 1924, was especially concerned about the disruptions these changes caused in the rural areas. In her important study of the transformations underway in rural areas at the time, Bradford argued that the authorities 'tended to be extremely sensitive to the interests of the white petty bourgeoisie and to farmers' fears of a labour shortage'.[19] This was especially noticeable among smaller urban local authorities in largely rural provinces. Kroonstad was a case in point. From the mid-1920s, the town council introduced stringent by-laws to control the influx of black people into Kroonstad and to maintain law and order in the locations. It issued passes and permits to the inhabitants. Police raids were stepped up and became common features in the locations as the authorities aimed to 'decrease the amount of "inessential" Africans …' in the area.[20]

Furthermore, in line with the Natives (Urban Areas) Act, the KTC established a separate native revenue account with funds collected from fines, fees, rents and beer-hall takings. The creation of this account was ostensibly to fund further housing development and to improve conditions in the locations, without the white authorities having to carry the financial responsibility. Considering the pervasive poverty among black residents, the funds collected in this way was always inadequate to meet even the basic needs of residents. In fact, Kroonstad's old locations remained in a slum-like state. There was little or no visible improvement through most of the period under discussion. In A Location, for example, 'half of the houses were built with bricks and half with mud'.[21] Although the majority of the inhabitants had built themselves three- or four-roomed flat-roofed mud houses, 'none of the houses had running water or an inside toilet'.[22] They used communal taps placed strategically at the end of streets. For Ntantala, who lived there in the 1930s, 'poverty was all around'.[23]

Life in the old locations was a mixed bag. This was largely due to the kind of employment and earnings the residents of the old locations could find. Professionals such as teachers and blacks employed at the South African Railways were relatively well-off. Although they earned meagre salaries, they earned enough to build modern houses that were larger than the average abodes in the location, with a 'dining room, a living room, kitchen and a bathroom'.[24] John Setiloane, who was born in 1920, averred that from the £4.10 monthly salary his father earned as a South African Railways labourer, he was able to build a big house. He recalled 'after they had been moved [from town], my father built his house at B Location. It was a five-roomed house. In addition, he also built two extra rooms outside'.[25] Some of the residents of Kroonstad's old locations were not so fortunate to earn as much as Setiloane senior did. They took home a pittance. Isaac Schepera, using the returns submitted by employers to the Wage Board between 1926 and 1929, records that in Kroonstad some adult males employed during this period earned as little as 10 shillings per day.[26]

Survival in Kroonstad was made more difficult by the fact that the town lacked industries. Thus, the majority of Africans were employed as unskilled labourers in the municipality and in the service sectors such as retail shops and hotels. Employment for black women was even more limited, with most of them employed as domestic labourers or as washerwomen. Parkies Setiloane recalled that his mother was a washer-woman and earned £1 in 1937.[27] It can be safely estimated that before 1937, black women might have earned even less.

Unemployed black women had few survival options available to them, with the sale of home-brewed beer being the most common. The government deemed such business illegal and attempted to stamp it out. For example, the Native (Urban Areas) Act No. 13 of 1928 prohibited the supply and delivery of any liquor to blacks. The municipality established a beer hall to monopolise and control the brewing and sale of beer. As in other areas, the white authorities in Kroonstad also enforced a total ban on the purchase and consumption of liquor by blacks in the old locations. To enforce adherence to the new regulations, the municipal police mounted regular raids on households suspected of trading in home-brewed beer, which made it even more difficult for the unemployed black women in the old locations to survive.[28]

They were not the only women to suffer under the municipality's new stringent rules. Black women who owned houses rented out rooms as a means to generate income and, as such, maintained a degree of autonomy and resisted the efforts of the authorities to push them into low-paid menial jobs. Rent from lodgers was an important and steady source of income. Not surprisingly, the authorities found this entrepreneurial practice by black women intolerable. The KTC issued lodgers' permits only to those blacks who it had given permission to be in the urban area. Tenants were also required to pay a fee for their lodger's permit, which caused a strain on their finances, making it more difficult to pay rents to standholders.

All sectors of the black population of Kroonstad felt the tightening of oppressive laws from the mid-1920s. Soon after ascending to power, the Pact government intensified the assault on the economic base, the political rights and the ideological role of the black middle classes. One of the main effects of the civilised labour policy was that it further limited work opportunities for blacks as the government sought to prioritise white employment in all categories from skilled to unskilled jobs.[29] Faced with increasing unemployment, more black people in the town turned to trading. The Kroonstad authorities deemed such trading as illegal and its hand was strengthened with the promulgation of the Urban Areas Amendment Act of 1930, which empowered it to refuse granting trading rights to blacks.[30] Although this did not apply to all trading, the effect was to push large numbers of traders to operate illegally. In response, the municipal police organised more raids in the location to arrest traders who faced imprisonment or heavy fines.[31]

Finally, the stringent measures imposed by the local municipality also affected those blacks who held certain status within the community. From the early 1920s, the state made it ever more difficult for petty bourgeois blacks to maintain the earlier privileges of the 'izimteti' (exemption). For example, people like 'Mote who were part of the elite, found themselves continually harassed by the police who were enforcing various new regulations.[32] Undoubtedly, the stringent attitude displayed by the local municipality made life unbearable for the majority of blacks living in the old locations. It also unintentionally created a fertile environment for discontent. This made it easy for the ICU to recruit members and mobilise the community against the local white authorities. The chapter now turns to the role and activities of the ICU in Kroonstad. However, before this, a brief discussion about the roles of the moderate structures which existed in the old locations prior to (and after) the formation of the

ICU is necessary.

'Ineffective responses by the moderates'

It is unclear when precisely the ANC was launched in Kroonstad but there is evidence of branch activity in 1915 in the old A Location. In that year, the ANC held its fourth annual meeting in the town.[33] The local branch was led by members of the elite such as Robert Sello and Reverend Pitso who followed the mother body's politics of petitions and refrained from confronting the white authorities in Kroonstad.

In 1920, when some of the black residents of the old A Location attempted to resist removals from their settlement, the branch of the ANC failed to intervene in support of their campaign. In fact, there is no evidence to suggest that it was ever active, even in addressing the day-to-day hardships experienced by the inhabitants of the black location. In this sense, the local branch practised the same approach as the leadership of the OFS. Limb noted that 'despite the economic difficulties and legal provocations, OFS congresses' leaders generally emphasised moderate tactics'.[34] As a result, in the 1920s, the branch of the ANC in the Kroonstad's old locations had become moribund.[35]

After the removals, the residents of the old locations briefly shifted their hopes to the Administration Council, mentioned earlier, comprising a handful of black male inhabitants of Kroonstad, to advance their communal interests. However, there is no evidence to suggest that this body played any significant role to actively represent the interests of the broader community. After 1923, an Advisory Board and a chapter of the Joint Councils for Europeans and Natives were established to mediate relations between the black population and whites. The Advisory Board was created under the Urban Areas Act and only had an advisory role. In fact, the white local authorities were not even obliged to take its views into account when formulating policies for the locations.[36] Like other areas, Kroonstad's NAB was powerless. There may have been some hope that this body would represent the interests of the black population and channel their grievances to the authorities. This changed when the residents, aggrieved by the constant municipal police raids, particularly on Sundays, searching for homes of beer brewers and those who defaulted paying their lodgers' permits, voiced their dissatisfaction against the KTC. When the NAB failed to convince the KTC against the heavy-handed way it dealt with blacks, the residents of the old locations slowly lost faith in the NAB.[37]

The Joint Councils aimed to bring whites and Africans together in bi-racial committees for consultation and discussion.[38] In Kroonstad, this body was established in September 1928 and its black members were largely drawn from the 'respectable' section of the community, including teachers and church ministers.[39] 'Mote and Binda, key figures in local politics, were also members of this body, which they viewed as a lobby group, particularly on the issue of trading rights for blacks in the old locations.[40] However, the local JCEN did not question the government's discriminatory policies, which limited its impact even among the elites. Soon after its founding, criticisms began to be mounted against its ineffectiveness in challenging the authorities. 'Mote, in his capacity as the provincial secretary of the ICU in the OFS, led the attacks on the JCEN and he was eventually forced to resign. Until the late 1920s, the elites dominated politics in Kroonstad and participated in various organisations and structures to advance their own interests and to mediate relations between the black population and the white authorities. Their politics were largely characterised by deference to authority and they deliberately avoided any form of militant opposition. The emergence of the ICU marked a departure from this approach and introduced, for a short period, a militancy to black resistance politics in Kroonstad.

The ICU and the radicalisation of local politics

Peter Hlaole Molotsi, former resident of Kroonstad's old locations and later a leading figure in the Pan Africanist Congress, recalled that his father, a former teacher, was a member of the old ICU of Kadalie in Kroonstad in the 1920s. He further added that from his father's stories, he learnt that Africans resisted white domination and foreign rule.[41] From Molotsi's anecdote, we can deduce the effect the ICU had in influencing blacks to mount resistance in Kroonstad. The ICU was only established in Kroonstad in 1926, some years after it had spread across the country from its origins in Cape Town. There are a number of reasons behind the delay. Firstly, until 1923, the ICU remained mainly a largely Cape-based organisation.[42] Secondly, because of the removals (and blacks gradually migrating into Kroonstad), the community of the old locations remained disparate and unorganised until the mid-1920s. Finally, the reliance on the ANC and, later, the NAB and JCEN seems to have restrained the residents of the old locations from participating in confrontational politics. This was evident in their subdued response to the campaign initiated in 1920 by the Industrial and Commercial Coloured and Native Workers' Union of Africa (ICWU), which was an attempt to fill the political vacuum left by the South African Native National Congress (SANNC), by mobilising the residents to demand better wages.[43] In that year, a member of the ICWU from Bloemfontein was sent to Kroonstad. There he addressed a community meeting attended by about forty blacks. He instigated them to demand 10 shillings and six pennies per day for skilled labourers and seven shillings and 5 pennies per day for unskilled labourers, and four shillings and 6 pennies per day for male and female servants living in town.[44] However, this organisation changed name in 1921 after it joined forces with Kadalie's ICU and it became the Industrial and Commercial Workers' Union.[45]

The non-existence of the branch of the ICU in Kroonstad should not be construed to mean that nothing was happening in the OFS. After the 1923 ICU conference, which decided 'upon a nationwide publicity campaign to induce Africans to organise themselves into one-big-union, the ICU "invaded" the OFS in its expansion campaign'.[46] In 1925, the ICU established a branch in Bloemfontein, the first in the OFS. A year before this, however, 'Mote, a Mosotho from Basotholand, had been recruited to join the ICU.[47] The latter had been a member of the passive SANNC branch in Kroonstad.[48] 'Mote was later to play an important role in mobilising for the ICU in Kroonstad. In 1925, the ICU changed its character and began to operate as a union-cum-protest organisation, taking up both rural and urban socioeconomic and political issues.[49] Commenting on this new approach, Johns argued:

> In April 1925, the ICU was on the verge of becoming an organised movement of mass protest. It tried to maintain its trade union character. But in a situation where any question regarding non-white labour was inevitably a political one, the pronouncement and actions of the ICU and its leaders took on an increasingly political colour.[50]

The following year, 'Mote, who lived in Kroonstad, replaced Alex Maduna as the provincial secretary of the ICU in the OFS. The change in provincial leadership seems to have accelerated the process of establishing a branch of the ICU in Kroonstad. Four months into his new position, a branch of the ICU had been established in the old locations 'and it was transferring money to the headquarters of the union.'[51] Among its early recruits were teachers, such as Joseph 'Joe' Kokozela, who was born at Beaconsfield, in Kimberley, where he began his teaching career. After a stint in Johannesburg, where he joined the ICU possibly in 1924 when Kadalie met him there for the first time,[52] Kokozela moved to Kroonstad to take up a position as the headmaster at Bantu United School.[53] He emerged as a key figure in local black politics and, in 1929, rose to prominence in the struggles of the old location. He also reflected the growing support among middle-class blacks for the ICU from the mid-1920s.[54] This was a direct response to the government's attack on the black middle class, which blurred the grievances of the black middle class and those of the unskilled and lowly paid blacks.

The turning point for the ICU in Kroonstad came in 1927. In that year, the delegates attending the ICU's conference discussed very little in the way of 'traditional' trade union concerns. Instead, they were mainly concerned with political issues, particularly the government's segregation bills. After that conference, the members of the ICU developed an assertive attitude towards whites.[55] In line with this, members of the ICU in Kroonstad began to directly oppose the white local authorities. 'Mote, for example, is said to have been very vocal against the government's discriminatory laws and the stringent laws employed by the white local authorities in Kroonstad to control black people. His fiery speeches gained him popularity amongst the black people in and around Kroonstad. In 1927, at an ICU meeting held in Parys, he was introduced by Simon Elias, who addressed about 600 people, as 'My Jesus' and when 'Mote ascended the platform to speak the crowd broke spontaneously into song 'God Save Africa'.[56]

Buoyed by such support, the leaders of the ICU in Kroonstad ventured out to mobilise black people living and working on the farms within the Kroonstad district. Lucas Nqandela was one of those who joined the ICU. Writing about Nqandela's life experiences, Keegan remarked: 'Nqandela, a land tenant on farms in the OFS, recalled that Kadalie's ICU began to organise farm workers in about 1927. He took out a membership in the union, paid his fees and received a membership badge'.[57]However, because of the blatant and random attacks and killings of blacks by whites on the farms, Nqandela and some of his fellow members of the ICU attended the union's meetings in Kroonstad's old locations.[58] 'On Sundays Lucas and his fellow members', Keegan added, 'rode into Kroonstad to attend meetings at an open-air bus stop in the black township to hear Kadalie and his lieutenants insulting the whites and promising us liberation from their oppression'.[59] Because of active mobilisation, the membership of the branch of the ICU in Kroonstad increased rapidly. In his annual report, Henderson Binda, the branch secretary, recorded that from 1927 to 1928, 10 813 members joined the ICU in Kroonstad.[60]

The presence of the ICU and its assertive politics, particularly evident in the militant speeches of its leaders, changed the mood among local black people. They became more emboldened to challenge their subordination by whites. John Setiloane remembered that his father, who worked for the South African Railways, was not intimidated by whites:

> I can recall whenever I took food for my father at his work not even once did I see a master and servant relationship. He spoke as he pleased with the whites and they did the same with him. You'll hear him say *Jy sien ek hierdie ding gemaak* (You see I have made this thing). And a white employee would respond and say *Ja ek sien Willy* (Yes, I see Willy). His name was William. I always felt proud when I heard hm talking like that.[61]

The ICU Women's Section and the boycott

Black women were also encouraged to become politically active by the ICU. At the height of its activities in the town, a women's section was formed. Dee avers that women were encouraged to join the ICU from its foundation in 1919.[62] Although the executive leadership of the ICU at all levels remained male-dominated, the ICU had some of the most active and militant women members. These included Mabel Klaasen (Bloemfontein), Mary Jane Lenono (Durban), Soshankana (Adelaide) and Annie Mashinini (Port Elizabeth).[63] In Kroonstad's old locations the ICU was boosted by the membership of Eva Kubedi, the secretary of the ICU Women's Section, a 'dauntless platform speaker'.[64] Emily Machoba was another active member of the Women's Section, 'famous for her organising ability'.[65] In 1928, the women members of the ICU mounted the first-ever recorded protest in Kroonstad.

Amidst the constant raids by the KTC police, detentions and fines for trading illegally, dubious administration of lodgers' permits, and other stringent measures used by the white local authorities to 'keep black people in line', the Council arbitrarily decided to hike rates by six pennies a month in the old locations.[66] Paltry as this may seem, the majority of women, who were standholders, were unemployed; they relied heavily on the rentals from their lodgers. For them the increment was monumental and unwarranted. When the ICU, on behalf of the standholders, challenged the matter in court, the standholders boycotted paying the increment. The ICU Women's Section was at the forefront of this. For Bradford, the women's leading role in this standoff was largely influenced by their '*struggle* against proletarianisation'.[67] Although the boycott did not result in a victory, 'Mote praised the women and remarked that they were 'real fighters'.[68]

The boycott took place during the period when the ICU national leadership regularly used the legal route to mount opposition to various laws and local regulations.[69] This tactic was pursued despite the union's mounting financial difficulties due, *inter alia*, to embezzlement and financial mismanagement by some of the leaders.[70] It was during Allison Wessels George (A.W.G.) Champion's tenure as acting general secretary (Kadalie was overseas), that the ICU approached the courts to intervene on behalf of the standholders in Kroonstad. The KTC countered the ICU by escalating the case to the Supreme Court, where it emerged victorious.[71] Faced by arrears and the possibility of being ejected from their houses, the standholders and members of the ICU, expected the ICU to intervene and assist them to meet the Council's demand for the arrears owed to it.[72] However, the union failed to come to their rescue and the KTC moved swiftly to evict standholders who were in arrears. 'Mote and Kadalie, who had returned from his visit overseas, distanced themselves from the boycott, which left the local standholders in limbo. The ICU promised that the National Council Sub-Committee would investigate the matter but nothing came of this. The ICU's callous response came as a huge disappointment to its members and supporters.

The disturbing trend that had developed amongst the national leadership of the ICU to abandon its local branches or members when in trouble was not new or peculiar to Kroonstad. Jack and Ray Simons note that when the coal miners in Natal, many of whom were union members, went on strike in June 1927, the union's officials denied responsibility and even declared that the strike was illegal. Similarly, the union's national leadership failed to help the dockworkers at the Point in Durban, 'the union's main centre', after they had come out on strike twice within a short period. Finally, again, the leadership was found wanting when men employed at Karzene, the railway depot in Johannesburg, called a strike for higher wages. Instead of assisting and guiding the workers, Henry Tyamzashe, the Complaints and Research Officer, advised them 'to resume work pending a discussion of their grievances'. When the workers refused, they were dismissed.[73]

The KTC used the opportunity to strike a blow against the leadership of the ICU and singled out 'Mote as the prime instigator of the boycott, even though it is not clear if he was in Kroonstad during the boycott. 'Mote had been transferred in 1928 to Bloemfontein and was replaced as the district secretary by Conan Doyle Modiakgotla who hailed from Griqualand West.[74] This notwithstanding, 'Mote's popularity made it easy for the Council to point the blame in his direction.

The ICU crisis and the collapse of the Kroonstad branch

When the residents of Kroonstad's old locations embarked on the boycott, the national ICU was already in the middle of a serious crisis. Misunderstandings and tensions had developed between the leaders, each accusing the other of embezzlement and/or mismanagement of the union's funds. Consequently, the ICU conference held in Bloemfontein in April 1928 decided to expel Champion.[75] After the expulsion of Champion, the branch of the ICU in Durban seceded from the ICU and formed a new union, the ICU *yase* Natal (ICU of Natal) and elected Champion as its general secretary. Disgruntled with Kadalie's 'despotic' leadership and seeming non-existence of the union's financial statements, some of the leaders, both national and provincial, led by Modiakgotla, formed a 'Clean Administration Group', of which 'Mote was a member.[76] This group agitated for the expulsion of Kadalie.[77]

The tension between Kadalie and 'Mote can be traced to when Kadalie returned from Europe. Before he left, Kadalie had been an uncompromising and fiery public speaker, who displayed an 'image of "bad boys" who refuted white leadership'.[78] 'On his return from Europe', wrote the Simons, 'he declared that he would transform the ICU into a "true trade union", cooperate with the white union, and repudiate any African who was anti-white'.[79] In his attempts to instil his new approach within the ICU, Kadalie found 'Mote too radical and anti-white. 'Mote, as he had been doing since joining the ICU, lambasted the whites-only KTC and agitated the residents against whites in the Joint Council. This contrasted with Kadalie's newly found moderate approach. Kadalie, whom the government had threatened to deport to Nyasaland, distanced himself and the ICU from 'Mote and his actions in Kroonstad. Soon rumours that 'Mote was embezzling the union's funds began making rounds. According to Johns, 'complaints were made that 'Mote ... whose speeches particularly disturbed white South Africans, was spending union funds illegally'.[80] To monitor him (and possibly to discipline him), the union decided to transfer him to the Transvaal. 'Mote threatened to secede from the ICU but was persuaded to reconsider this step. However, Kadalie and others used this episode as grounds to suspend 'Mote,[81] which irrevocably severed relations between the two.

Meanwhile, the working relationship between Kadalie and William Ballinger was also deteriorating, because of allegations of corruption and poor leadership levelled against Kadalie, whom Ballinger described as 'one of the worst scoundrels I have met'.[82] On 28 February 1929, the ICU's Sub-Committee accepted Kadalie's resignation. With the backing from ICU supporters in the Reef, two months later Kadalie established his new union, the Independent ICU. In turn, the ICU, now firmly under the leadership of Ballinger, countered by changing its name to ICU of Africa and, in June 1929, it held its conference in Kroonstad.[83] The crisis within the ICU of Africa confused its membership. As a result, in Kroonstad, the ICU of Africa lost a significant number of members. Binda, the local branch secretary, reported that, in 1929, only 503 members joined the ICU of Africa.[84] The explanation Nqandela offered Keegan for terminating his membership is telling. It is worth quoting Keegan in detail:

But what spurred his disillusionment further was when he saw the whites attend the meetings in Kroonstad wearing the white lapel badge of membership; for he began to wonder whether the union's message was not perhaps a ploy by the *Boers* to impoverish the blacks still further by inducing them to pay money into the organisation's coffers. He wondered how could whites be involved in an organisation that referred to them as 'white pigs'? So, when he was ordered to pay membership fee for his invalid father and mother, he refused. 'This is nonsense', he declared.[85]

It is also possible that the membership of the ICU in the old locations was affected by the Proclamation 252 of 1928, issued under the Native Administration Act. This Act prohibited any meetings, except for religious or domestic purposes, of more than ten Africans in any reserve throughout Natal, the Transvaal and OFS, without the permission of a chief and magistrate.[86] Fearing drastic repercussions for defying the government, members of the ICU likely opted to stay away from meetings organised by the union in the old locations, and subsequently lost interest in the ICU of Africa. This Act, and probably the heavy-handed manner in which the KTC responded to the boycott, also contributed to the inaction of the branch of the ICU's Women's Section in Kroonstad. There is no evidence to suggest that it continued with its activities after the boycott had been crushed.

In spite of the declining membership and dwindling funds, the branch of the ICU of Africa in Kroonstad continued with its activities. In September 1929, it attended the Wage Board meeting sitting in Kroonstad. Ballinger, Kokozela, the secretary, and Binda, the district secretary, represented the union in demanding a minimum wage of £8 per month or five shillings/4d (pennies) per day. Their argument was based on the fact that residents spent approximately £7 per month on basic needs.[87] There is no evidence to suggest that the ICU of Africa won any of its demands, and this seemed to be its last effort in establishing a presence in the town.

After Ballinger had taken over the leadership of the ICU of Africa, 'Mote seems to have operated alone, trying to win over the former branches of the ICU. Johns notes that after Kadalie's resignation from the ICU and the formation of the ICU of Africa, in the OFS 'Mote laboured to keep together several branches of the ICU in one organisation.[88] *Umteteli wa Bantu,* describing 'Mote as 'a dead letter at (sic) Kroonstad', reported on his presence at a meeting in Kroonstad addressed by Sidney Percival Bunting, a member of the Communist Party of South African (CPSA) and founder of the League of African Rights. However, these efforts also seemed to have failed,[89] reflecting the diminished influence of 'Mote in the old locations.

The poor attendance at this meeting was likely caused by residents being unsure about which ICU 'Mote was representing. A number of bodies had been created, all claiming to be branches that had seceded from the 'mother body'. Despite these challenges, 'Mote soldiered on, seemingly confident that his former popularity would create a following for his new political ventures. In an attempt to mobilise black people in the old locations, he supported the anti-pass campaign organised by the CPSA and led the ICU branches in the OFS in a joint campaign with the CPSA in commemorating this campaign on Dingaan's Day on 16 December 1929.[90] A similar campaign was organised by the CPSA in Potchefstroom, in the Western Transvaal.[91] The government did not take kindly to such a campaign, claiming it would heighten animosity between black and white people.

By this point, the branch of the ICU of Africa in Kroonstad had been paralysed. There are no reports of its activities. 'Mote, in his capacity as a community leader, continued his vociferous opposition against the Joint Council of Europeans and Africans (JCEA). Because of this, his membership in the local chapter of the JCEA was terminated in 1931.[92] In his correspondence to John David Rheinallt-Jones, the founder of the Johannesburg Joint Council and later the chief organiser of other joint councils, Father Martin Knight, an executive member of the JCEA in Kroonstad, emphasised the body's exasperation with 'Mote when he informed him about the speech 'Mote made in a meeting organised by the JCEA. He wrote: 'Rather a disturbed meeting of the Joint Council last night. 'Mote was introduced as a visitor and let off his usual hot-air. I doubt if he will be given another opportunity.'[93]

In his final attempt to revive his political standing and that of the ICU, in April 1931, 'Mote convened a conference in Kroonstad of ICU branches in the OFS and Western Transvaal. At the meeting, 57 delegates formed the Federated Free State ICU of Africa, and elected Selby Msimang president and 'Mote secretary.[94] However, there is no evidence to suggest that this new body existed beyond its name. Before 1935, after a period of about three years of active organisational work in Kroonstad's old locations (and the surrounding farms), the branch of the ICU in Kroonstad ceased to exist.

Conclusion

Kroonstad's old locations, a settlement for black people in the northern Free State, remained politically sedentary until the establishment of the branch of the ICU in the mid-1920s. The inactiveness of the SANNC and the pacifying role played by the moderate bodies such as the NAB and JCEN had contributed to this state of affairs. The emergence of the branch of the ICU in Kroonstad, formed in 1926, a year after the 'mother body' had decided to change its *modus operandi,* from being a traditional trade union to a trade union-cum-political movement, attracted large numbers of supporters to oppose the enforcement of arbitrary by-laws by local white authorities. This infused radical politics in the old locations. Unlike in other areas, these were led by the radicalised elite and women, who led a boycott against rent and taxes in the old locations. However, the tension which had developed between the ICU's national leadership and local leadership throughout the country affected the branch of the ICU in Kroonstad and ultimately caused its demise prematurely. In spite of the efforts to resuscitate it, by 1935, the ICU branch in Kroonstad had ceased to exist. Nonetheless, it left a legacy of political protest that many activists continued to reference for decades.

6 Trouble Brewing: The ICU, the 1925 Bloemfontein Riots and the Women Question

Nicole Ulrich

That the time has come to admit women in the Workers' Union as full members, and that they should be allowed to enjoy all privileges and receive the same rights as male members, and there should be female representatives in our Conference. Further, that women workers receive equal pay, men and women, for the same work, done, and that all members of the Conference should do all they can to get women to join the Workers' Union of the different towns.[1]

Report on First Black Labour Conference, Bloemfontein, 1920.

The women got up [and] went to the constables and Malinghoe, one of the women, struck the European constable with an empty paraffin tin [and] also threw sand after them. The women made a great noise…I was very much frightened by the attitude of the women who obviously wanted to fight the police.[2]

Eyewitness account of the altercation between beer brewers and the police, Bloemfontein, 1925.

Introduction

Much has been written about the ICU's kaleidoscope of ideologies and various styles of organisation at the local, national and transnational levels and across rural and urban terrains. Bloemfontein was an important site of black women's struggles, and this chapter investigates how the Bloemfontein branch of the ICU related to local black proletarian women.

The ICU adopted a distinct proletarian political style, which not only countered the moderation of black political elites, but also allowed for a different kind of gender politics that recognised women as workers and as equal partners in the struggle for freedom. The ICU's Bloemfontein branch appealed to women domestic workers in its minimum wage campaign and was also drawn into the 1925 riots, started by beer brewers. However, the branch did not organise black proletarian women in any meaningful way.

Women and workers

In her work on the political characterisation of black women's protest and the early liberation movement, Nomboniso Gasa considers how we ought to write about black women as political, historical agents. She calls for an open approach that transcends a narrow heroic narrative, and that takes women on their own terms to grasp the 'rich, textured, layered and complex discourses and experiences of women making sense of their own lives and finding new agency and ways of being'.[3]

Women, not just black proletarian women, participated in or related to the ICU in multiple ways (for example, see the chapter by Elizabeth van Heyningen). The ICU's national and provincial leadership centred on 'big' men such as Clements Kadalie, Selby Msimang and A.W.G. Champion, but as David Johnson and Henry Dee note:

> Up to a third of the ICU's members were women, and individual women members played prominent roles – Mildred Ngcayiya was on the executive of the Johannesburg branch of the ICU, and Bertha Mkhize, Rhoda Champion, Mary Lenono and C.T. Ntombela were well to the fore in Durban ICU campaigns. Collectively, women ICU members were vital in establishing the ICU co-operative in Natal in 1926–27; in waging the 1929 campaign against municipal beer halls in Durban; and in sustaining the strike in East London in 1930.[4]

The most notable ICU protest by black proletarian women – and amongst the most violent protests in the history of the ICU – was the 1929 beer hall boycott in Natal.[5] In this instance beer brewers recruited by the ICU *yase* Natal, played a key role in the Women's Auxiliary that championed and enforced the boycott of municipal beer halls and demanded the legalisation of brewing African traditional beer. According to Helen Bradford, numerous demonstrations erupted in the towns surrounding Durban in which '[t]ypically women marched through streets, chanted war songs, raided beer halls, [and] assaulted male drinkers' who broke the boycott.[6]

The black women of Bloemfontein played a leading role in the 1913 anti-pass protests. In 1920, the first black labour conference that launched the ICWU, also held in Bloemfontein, broke with the gender conservatism of men-only organisations such as the ANC by recognising women – in industry, but especially in domestic work – as a key constituency and accepted women as fully fledged members.

The ICU's Bloemfontein branch, the first to be established outside of the broader Cape that centred on organising dockworkers and municipal workers, found that a relatively large proportion of the city's proletarians were women. (The gender composition of the black population of Bloemfontein proved relatively even and stable and in 1904 women constituted as much as 44% of the black population).[7] By the 1920s, half of Bloemfontein's black women worked in the domestic sector, while the other half worked on their own account[8] as laundry women (who earned money by washing and ironing clothes at the municipal washhouse for a fee), beer brewers (who brewed and sold traditional African beer as well as other alcohol concoctions) and sex workers.

Some labour scholars may quarrel with defining women who work on their own account as genuine proletarians. For decades, scholars within labour studies have questioned the dominant focus on waged, male, industrial workers and have drawn attention to other important forms of work and labour relations under capitalism, especially in colonial contexts.[9] Even so, historians have yet to develop robust conceptual categories for non-waged, unpaid, own-account, service/reproductive, and coerced work.[10] Conceptual categories such as 'informal' and 'precarious' workers apply to the present condition of global capitalism and cannot easily be projected onto the past. This is especially true of the 1910s and 1920s when a barrage of racist legislation and regulations such as the 1913 Land Act, pass laws, and poll tax passed by the newly constituted South African state accelerated the proletarianisation of African people, reorganising work and labour relations in the process. Scholars of present-day capitalism recognise that precarious workers tend to be women. However, feminist scholars worry that the significance of domestic, or reproductive, work – which is to reproduce labour power (or create 'the capacity to work') under capitalism – has been lost.[11]

Laundry women, beer brewers and sex workers were not engaged in waged work, but their subsistence was no longer tied to land. There were some women from elite households who dabbled in the illicit beer and alcohol trade, but most women who worked on their own account were economically marginal with tenuous rights to stay in the city. Together with waged domestic workers, their reproductive work was integral to capitalism, and they constituted a significant proportion of the permanent urban proletariat of Bloemfontein as well as one of the largest concentrations of black urban proletarian women in South Africa during the 1920s.

Living in Bloemfontein

It is necessary to get a sense of the local context in which the ICU branch organised. The small black population of Bloemfontein, which became the capital of Orange Free State (OFS) in 1854, increased markedly in the 1870s, with the discovery of diamonds in the Orange River Valley and Kimberly, and again in the 1890s, with the completion of the Cape to Johannesburg railway line. Bloemfontein's total population almost doubled from 3 000 in 1890 to 5 800 in 1899 and the black population's composition changed when those designated as Indian were prohibited from living and trading in the Republic.[12]

The total population increased significantly during the Anglo-Boer South African War, largely due to the destruction of rural livelihoods by the British military's scorched-earth policy that forced people into towns in search of work. Bloemfontein was occupied by the British in 1900 and incorporated into the British empire as a garrison town. By 1904 the total Bloemfontein population was 33 883 with approximately 18 382 being black residents – although, much of this growth included war refugees and was not permanent. By 1913, the total population was approximately 26 500.[13]

After the First World War, urbanisation continued, largely due to the complex processes of dispossession set in motion a decade before by the 1913 Land Act, and included tenant families who were pushed off white-owned farms. By 1919, the town's population consisted of approximately 15 700 white and 16 500 black residents. They were joined by an exodus of thousands of Basotho women in the 1920s. These were not the 'runaway' wives who migrated to Bloemfontein in the 1890s, but the abandoned and destitute wives of migrants in search of work.[14] Local authorities regarded Basotho women as 'riff-raff' and did not want them in Bloemfontein, especially since they were associated with the illegal trade in alcohol and sex work.[15]

Not all those who lived in Bloemfontein were poor or proletarian and a relatively large group of *Amarespectables* – educated and skilled black men and women – settled in late 1890s. *Amarespectables* were drawn from different parts of the country and ethnicities (Griqua, Korona, Baralong, Basotho, Mfengu, Zulu and Oorlams), but shared an adherence to Christianity. This elite included the notable group of independent or self-employed men, skilled traders such as cart drivers, shoemakers, masons, carpenters, wagon makers and café owners.[16] For widows, or those wives and daughters who had to contribute to the family income, renting out rooms to lodgers, selling produce from livestock and dressmaking were options.

Amarespectables, especially skilled men working in the building trade and women renting rooms to lodgers, benefited from the significant population increase during the Anglo-Boer South African War.[17] However, after the First World War, they too were placed under increasing economic pressure due to rising inflation and the erosion of their ability to work independently. The costs of 'work on own behalf' licences were increased, and eventually restricted to black men who were either disabled or old and who had lived in Bloemfontein for a long period.[18] Young, able-bodied men were expected by authorities and employers to find proper employment.

From 1861, black residents were compelled to stay with their employers or designated locations.[19] The locations included K****fontein for Mfengu and Baralong and a separate location for coloureds, although this separation does not appear to have been maintained. Waaihoek was established in 1891 but was not able to accommodate all and the 'Brickfield Camp' was erected on the west side of Bloemfontein. After the Anglo-Boer South African War, local authorities became concerned that overcrowding undermined racial segregation – with Africans, coloureds and a sprinkling of poor whites living in Waaihoek. As a result, Waaihoek was expanded southwards with the construction of 'Bethany'. A separate coloured area, 'Cape Stands', was erected in 1906, partly due to a campaign by the pro-segregation 'Cape Boys', and the 'Number 3 Location' was created for railway workers in 1907.[20] However, authorities' concerns over segregation lingered – coloured residents continued to live in Waaihoek and there were fears the location would spill into neighbouring white residential areas. In 1918 the town council decided to move residents of Waaihoek – Africans to Batho Location and coloureds to Heidendal.[21] But not enough funds were allocated to these schemes and, throughout the 1920s, residents complained of an 'acute shortage of housing' and the high cost of building materials.[22]

Black political opposition

Bloemfontein's *Amarespectable* played an influential role in shaping modern black opposition politics locally and in South Africa more generally through the creation of organisations such as the Orange River Colony Vigilance Association (ORCVA). Established in 1904 by African men, the ORCVA represented 'civilised and tolerably educated Natives who have entirely disregarded the customs and practices of such natives as are still living in a tribal fashion'.[23] Members identified as loyal British subjects and aimed to 'further the interests of His Majesty's Native Subjects in this colony, materially, politically, and religiously'.[24] The ORCVA articulated a very particular vision of modern black, genteel, opposition politics that was echoed by the South African Native National Congress (SANNC) established in 1912, also in Bloemfontein.

Some coloured residents followed Dr Abdurrahman's African Political Organisation (APO) that supported African and coloured cooperation.[25] For example, in 1908, the ORCVA and the APO petitioned local authorities regarding the deplorable state of Waaihoek. However, the most formidable political challenge in Bloemfontein came from *Amarespectable* African women.

Educated and propertied African men could be exempted from carrying passes, but such exemptions were not available for women. Night passes date back to the 1860s, and from 1872, black residents (all women and proletarian men) had to carry cards signed by employers, and from 1880, black residents were required to pay six pennies for a certificate issued by the town council.[26] Pass raids became more frequent and in 1898, the 'wives of householders in the location' sent a petition to President Steyn to object to passes, but to no avail.[27]

Male delegates at the National Convention in 1909 objected to passes for African women and were especially annoyed that the bodily integrity of their wives, sisters and mothers was violated by police in pass raids and arrests.[28] The issue came to ahead in Bloemfontein with a notable intensification of pass raids and arrests and, on 28 May 1913, women held a mass meeting in Waaihoek and declared that 'no matter what happened' they would refuse to carry passes.[29] Their passive resistance campaign spread to other parts of the Orange Free State in which women went to prison rather than carry passes.

Bloemfontein's town council was forced to make concessions and eased arrests, but the pass laws were not officially changed. Even so, the anti-pass protests were remarkable. Unlike the ANC that relied on deputations, the courts, and appeals to royal authorities, African women pre-figured openly confrontational forms of protest and, while led by elite women, the fight against passes was inclusive of all African women and viewed as part of a collective tradition of struggle.

The struggle for a minimum wage, 1919–1925

By the 1920s, Bloemfontein had become the commercial and administrative hub for the surrounding farmlands. However, black residents were placed under increasing pressure. The cost of living increased by 60% between 1914 and 1919, creating economic hardship even for *Amarespectable*. In addition, black residents faced tighter segregation measures and restrictions on their mobility, which were extended and consolidated under the 1923 Urban Areas Act.[30]

After the anti-pass campaign of 1913, the town council did not enforce passes for African women. This attracted much criticism from Bloemfontein's white madams who objected to the shortage of domestic workers and who wanted to see black women working on their own account forced into domestic work. As one letter to *The Friend* complained, not without some irony, '…this is a white man's town, and we [the white women of Bloemfontein] have every right to demand that every able-bodied native woman should work…'.[31] However, the town council did not want a repeat of the 1913 anti-pass campaign and avoided measures that would 'interfere with the liberty' of black women, including a proposal to set up a Labour Servants Agency to place black women into domestic work.[32]

While the anti-pass protest continued to haunt local authorities, the ANC branch was no longer active[33] and the political energy of black residents appeared, at first, to be effectively channelled into the Advisory Board set up by the town council. One Advisory Board served Bloemfontein's locations and consisted of three African men appointed by local authorities and 12 blockmen. The town's locations were divided into 12 blocks, and it is notable that blockmen were elected by each of the 12 sections.[34] The Advisory Board was a male affair – women were not able to serve as blockmen, and only black men over the age of 21 and who had lived in the location for more than six months were eligible to vote for blockmen.[35]

It is difficult to grasp the political character of the Advisory Board. The Joint Councils had no influence in Bloemfontein and a significant part of the Advisory Board consisted of elected representatives. There were conservative members on the Advisory Board, but they were not always able to control decisions and, to remain legitimate, the Advisory Board had to keep in touch with residents' concerns. The Advisory Board supported deputations to the town council from widows, standholders, traders and laundry women, and brought practical issues such as roads, water and electricity supply and grazing rights to the attention of the municipality.[36] Radical leaders could – and were – elected to the Advisory Board. However, the Advisory Board did not have much power to make significant changes.

In February 1919, Selby Msimang stepped into the political breach and organised a campaign for a minimum wage of 4s 6d a day.[37] Msimang, who moved to Bloemfontein in 1915, was the son of a religious minister; had previously worked as a court interpreter and clerk in the Volksrust office of Dr P. Ka Seme, an African lawyer; and edited a newspaper, *Morumioa Inxusa*. He identified the economic difficulty experienced by workers as a pressing concern and did not organise under the auspices of the ANC, even though he was a member. The minimum wage campaign consisted of public meetings – some that attracted up to 1 000 people – at which Msimang spoke. Msimang appears to have had an ambiguous relationship with the Advisory Board. On the one hand, he was a vocal critic and in 1917, publicly exposed Advisory Board members who were secretly receiving money from the municipality. [38] Yet, he invited a couple of Advisory Board members – J. Ntlintise and J.H. Kenny – to speak at public rallies for a minimum wage.[39]

Msimang's campaign captured the imagination of black proletarians in Bloemfontein – even domestic servants asked for wage increases.[40] Employers were quick to respond. On 17 February 1919, the *Friend* reported on 'an important meeting of large employers of native labour', with representatives from the 'South African Railways; Provincial Public Works Department; the Corporation of Bloemfontein, the *Friend* Newspapers Ltd.; Messrs C.A. Fichardt Ltd.; Mr C.W. Champion; the South African Breweries, the Master Builders Association and others' that appointed a sub-committee to come up with a united response and to determine a minimum wage for unskilled workers.[41] The sub-committee recommended that 2s 3d per day should be paid to those workers who had worked for less than six months at an establishment; 2s 6d per day to those workers employed for more than six months but less than a year; and 2s 9d per day to those workers who had worked for more than a year. For semi- skilled workers, the committee proposed that employers make special terms.

Much like places such as East London, Bloemfontein's private and government employers were willing, even if reluctantly, to negotiate better wages for black workers.[42] However, this attempt at bargaining draws attention to the intrinsic limitation of trade union approaches that focus narrowly on wages, especially with regard to organising women. It is unlikely that the minimum wages proposed applied to home-based domestic workers. In addition, a focus on minimum wages automatically excluded those who worked on their own account and did not relate to their specific concerns regarding rights and legality, tightening municipal regulations, and tariffs (such as laundry fees) that increased their operating costs.

The proposal of the sub-committee was rejected by Msimang.[43] At this point, authorities became concerned that the movement for higher wages would spread to other parts of the country.[44] On Friday, 1 March 1919, Msimang was arrested and charged with inciting public violence under the Public Welfare Act.[45]After hearing about Msimang's arrest, approximately 400–500 black residents gathered outside the police station in which Msimang was held and demanded his release.[46] The *Cape Times* reported that those who gathered were '…very excited and riotous and many carried sticks'.[47] The demonstration moved into the location, apparently ransacking the house of a '…councillor…' (of the Advisory Board) along the way, and gathered at a café. Here the demonstration was confronted by policemen, who dangerously fired '…over the heads of the crowd…', and arrested demonstrators.[48]

The Friday disturbance in the location alarmed the white residents of Bloemfontein. The *Friend* reported that 'criminals' and 'undesirables' were to blame for the riot and raised the possibility of black workers calling a general strike on the 3 March.[49] The Mayor wanted to prevent any further protests and addressed a public meeting on

Monday.[50] He insisted that Msimang was arrested for inflammatory speech and not for his participation in the minimum wage campaign. Despite the Mayor's claims, further meetings in the locations were prohibited.[51]

The ANC passed a resolution condemning the arrest of Msimang and the intimidation of black workers.[52] The Industrial Socialist League set up a defence fund to raise bail for Msimang (which was set at an astounding 500 pounds) and money for legal representation.[53] Out of all of those who rallied to the defence of Msimang, it was Kadalie's letter of encouragement that resulted in further action.[54] Msimang was greatly impressed by Kadalie, secretary of the ICU (which was at this stage a union for dockworkers in Cape Town). At the end of 1919, the minimum wage campaign was consolidated when Msimang formed the Native and Coloured Workers' Association (NCWA).[55] The general union adopted the ICU's constitution and Msimang expressed a desire that the NCWA amalgamate with the ICU.[56]

Msimang and Kadalie arranged the first black labour conference, which aimed to unite all black labour organisations, from 12 to 13 July in Bloemfontein at which the ICWU was launched.[57] Msimang would prove a relatively moderate politician over time, but the conference signalled a significant development in modern black opposition politics in South Africa. This distinctly proletarian focus was part of a global shift after the 1917 Russian Revolution that allowed for alternative political traditions with broadly socialist aims that centred on championing the cause of the workers and the poor.

The ICWU was inclusive from the start and organised 'coloured' and 'Native' workers south of the Zambezi, including those engaged in agricultural work.[58] Most notable were the resolutions on women: the conference resolved to fight for equal wages for men and women and include women workers as full members (as noted above). Helen Bradford partly attributes this progressive stance on women to the intervention of the formidable Charlotte Maxeke, a key women's rights activist and intellectual and president of the Bantu Women's League.[59] Importantly, Maxeke's call for the full integration of women was readily accepted by the labour conference. This is notable since the SANNC, to which Maxeke's Bantu Women's League was affiliated, had not done the same. In addition, the newly formed ICWU aimed: 'To see that all females in industries and domestic services are protected by the organisation, by encouraging them to enrol in all branches of the Union to help them maintain a living wage'.[60] This means that the first black labour conference was officially committed to organising women, especially domestic workers, and included them in a campaign for a living wage. In so doing, the ICWU's proletarian approach offered the possibility of an alternative gender politics.

In 1920, the ICU set out to organise women factory workers in Cape Town and the recognition of women as workers and equal participants in the struggle for freedom was confirmed in the 1925 and 1927 constitutions and echoed in ICU rhetoric and material.[61] However, this idea was not developed into a coherent or consistent position on the women's question, and existed, often awkwardly, alongside – and was sometimes eclipsed by – traditional notions of gender hierarchies within the labour movement. For instance, in his letter discussing the Bloemfontein branch in the September 1923 issue of the *Workers' Herald*, John Mancoe noted that 'the black worker today realised that it was time for *him and for her*, for their future progeny, to demand a living wage' (my emphasis).[62] In the same issue, the poem 'Workers of Africa' promoted the idea that the African worker was masculine and the sole breadwinner and encouraged workers to: 'think of the rags your wives and children wear/ Put aside your soul-wrecking apathy; if you call yourself a man'.[63] The conference's attempt at unity failed and the black workers' movement fractured. Soon after the July 1920 conference, the Cape Town ICU decided to remain separate from the ICWU and by the end of the year, the ICWU in Port Elizabeth broke with the ICWU and joined forces with Kadalie.[64] Msimang continued to organise the ICWU but confined his activities to the Cape.[65] His absence impacted negatively on the ICWU in Bloemfontein, which collapsed in 1921.[66]

In 1923, Kadalie returned and established an ICU branch in Bloemfontein. The branch started with a membership of about 1 000 and John Mancoe was appointed branch secretary.[67] In the *Workers' Herald*, Kadalie reported on Bloemfontein, in which he reaffirmed the branch's focus on minimum wages, including for domestic workers:

> I came into contact with working men and women. As in other towns young African girls are engaged in domestic services, and these are paid at the rate of not more than 20/- per month…that the minimum rate paid to the African male worker by the leading firms, such as *The Friend* Newspaper Ltd., The Municipality, G.A Fichardt Ltd. and Champion Ltd., was 15/- per week raising to 26/6. The Railway Administration laying down their minimum scale of pay to be 12/6 per week, rising after 21 months service to 22/- per week.[68]

The branch accelerated its minimum wage campaign at the end of 1924. The *Workers' Herald* reported on a public meeting in Waaihoek, held on 26 December. However, this time Keable 'Mote and John Mancoe did not include domestic workers in their proposal that:

> Bloemfontein's Native workers respectfully request the town council to approach the employers of labour and urge that every Native working man should earn a sufficient wage to enable him to maintain his family in civilised comfort, Christian decency and citizenship and that we are very much in favour of a minimum wage.[69]

Perhaps 'Mote and Mancoe resorted to the idea of workers being male breadwinners because they wanted to encourage other groups with conservative notions of gender hierarchies to join the ICU's delegation to the town council, including Congress, the Advisory Board and the League of Native Churches.

On the 9 February 1925 Kadalie led a delegation to 'acquaint' and 'interest' the town council in a minimum wage. A report in the *Workers' Herald* both warned and praised the town council:

> There are 20 000 Natives in our Bloemfontein Location, ninety-five per cent of which are workers. The ICU is determined to capture these workers under its banner…a strike of these workers may paralyse all trade for many a day…The question of the minimum wage is engaging the serious attention of local Natives and they have placed their implicit confidence to the City Fathers to secure for them full and reasonable wages. We must say we cannot help to mention the name of our Location Superintendent Mr. J.R. Cooper who introduced the delegation. We shall always support this magnanimous gentleman.[70]

Public meetings continued to take place in Waaihoek and at the end of February the *Workers' Herald* reported on an open-air meeting that 'lasted for two hours' and was attended by 'some 1 500 to 2 000 Native men and women'. Here Kadalie lunched his guiding message for the year, which captures the uneven integration of women in the ICU's vision: 'You must be free men and free women in the land of your fathers. Let that be your vision for the year. Get together everywhere and breath the word: I want to be a free *man* (my emphasis)'.[71] The meeting also raised two important issues – the demand for a Minimum Wage Bill (in response to the Wage Bill proposed by government) and the abolition of the pass system (in response to night passes for women in the Transvaal).

The Bloemfontein branch sent five male delegates (J. Gaba, J.B. Mancoe, S.M. Elias, J. G. Mpinda and A.B. Dilape) and three female delegates (Mrs Emma Lande, Mrs Maria Elias and Mrs J. Mancoe) to the Fifth Annual Conference of the ICU (Third African Labour Congress) that met in Johannesburg from 13–19 April. The Bloemfontein branch's minimum wage campaign was celebrated. However, this campaign mainly consisted of public meetings and lobbying local authorities, with polite hints of a possible strike, to convince employers to award black workers a minimum wage. Little was done in the way of establishing durable trade union structures or organising workers at specific workplaces or in a key sector, including domestic workers. And, in spite of the 1920 resolutions and the promise of gender equality, the ICU's appeal to domestic workers and proletarian women proved inconsistent and uneven. The conference ended on 19 April, but as delegates 'were buttoning their coats up tightly and making ready for departure… unexpected trouble' was already brewing in Bloemfontein.[72]

Riots and the limits of formal organisation

The riots started on the afternoon of 19 April 1925, when Police Constable Pieter Muller and black Police Constable, P.C. Stanford, went out on patrol to search for beer parties. When they passed a vacant plot on the western side of the Bethany location and Monument Road, they saw a group of 700–800 men and women standing around, with a separate group of women sitting near the trees. Later a witness to an inquest by Magistrate Streak, conducted a few weeks later, confirmed that these women were having an open-air beer party.[73] Finding no commotion, the constables turned back before they reached the beer party. According to Mahmookho Namai, who was one of the women who organised the party, the beer brewers were divided on what to do about the police. Ma Sannel addressed the women and appealed to them to be sensible and 'when the police come here', she said, 'we must throw the beer out and let them arrest us'.[74] However, most beer brewers were angry and followed a woman named 'Malingwa' (also 'Malinghoe') who went after the police.

Malingwa struck Muller with an empty paraffin tin and grabbed Stanford by his coat. Stanford claimed that she was not drunk, 'but very infuriated'.[75] 'The crowd following the woman then picked sand up and threw it in the constables' faces and started to throw stones. Muller also claimed to have been hit with a sjambok on his back.[76] Stanford testified that the crowd was 'excited' and he heard someone shout: 'We have long been threatened by police, today we will get them'.[77] Another witness claimed that the women 'appeared ready to fight'.[78] This was confirmed by Namani, who testified that 'the police were in danger of th[eir] lives; in fact, God helped them'.[79] The constables made it to the corner of Falck and Watkey Streets, where they managed to flag a taxi. They went to the Waaihoek Police Station to report the matter.

This altercation may have been spontaneous but was not unexpected and was part of ongoing skirmishes between beer brewers and police. The town council was eager to end the illicit beer trade in the locations. Rather than implement the same beerhall system as in Durban, the Advisory Board suggested that it may be better to restrict the sale of 'momela' (sprouted corn), by giving each family permission to grow their own 'momela' and to brew no more than four gallons of traditional African beer a day for their own consumption.[80] This proposal was discussed over a number of years, but only officially enforced after the 1923 Native Urban Areas Act was passed.

The Bloemfontein model meant that all women were subject to police searches for illicit beer, which residents felt encroached on their rights to brew a traditional food staple. Women of Bloemfontein had already strongly demonstrated their objection to police searches and arrests.[81] Many women complained that when police did find beer, they would tip it out and then exaggerate amounts to magistrates. After the 1923 Natives Urban Areas Act raids and arrests were intensified. In 1920, records indicated that 25 women were arrested for their involvement in the illegal beer trade.[82] In 1924, 215 residents were arrested for drunken behaviour, 250 for participating beer gatherings, 80 for being in possession of large quantities of beer, and 42 for the possession of liquor other than beer.

Beer brewers were tired of police harassment. One witness, Thuys Zeekoe, claimed that when he visited a friend on the 12 April, he passed a group of Basotho women at the *spruit* near the community hall. They were having a meeting. He heard a woman say, 'We are not to brew [African] beer, but we are going to brew it…if they do attempt to arrest us we will hit them.'[83] This hostility was not new and beer brewers had a history of attacking the police during raids. It was for this reason that white policemen were required to accompany black constables on their patrols.[84] In addition, this willingness to confront the police, even violently, points to a vernacular form of protest crafted by proletarian women who occupied a space of illegality that would be echoed in the 1929 beerhall protests in Natal.

The response by the police was heavy-handed. A squad of men, under Lieutenant Mathews, including three mounted police who were armed with revolvers, and 20 police on foot, returned to the vacant square.[85] They were joined by white civilians, some armed, who congregated on the lower end of Monument Street.

There events leading up the shooting of an innocent by-stander, Simon Dibi, are contested. The police who later gave testimony to the inquest emphasised the unruly behaviour of residents. Mathews claimed that when his squad arrived at the vacant square, that there was already a crowd of approximately 3 000–4 000 unruly residents who booed the police.[86] The squad had trouble dispersing the crowd and were surrounded and stoned from all directions. The police had to retreat and called for reinforcements.

Jacob Sesing, a blockman for the Bethany location who would play a key mediating role between the crowd and the Superintendent, gave a very different account.[87] Sesing did not see a crowd of thousands of residents, but a group of beer brewers on the open square with many black men and women onlookers who were standing outside their houses. Without any justification, the police charged at a group of onlookers and chased them down the street, firing their guns at them. Only after the police had attacked residents and shots were fired, did a group of youngsters, none of them older than 16, throw stones at the police.

Simon Dibi was shot dead near the *spruit* and the open square off Monument Road, on the west side where the beer brewers were congregated.[88] It is not clear who shot Dibi – the shot could have come from the armed mounted police or one of the white civilians who had entered the fray. The crowd was reportedly 'seething with rage and indignation' and demanded that the policeman who killed Dibi be handed over to them.[89] Mathews called for reinforcements and sent an urgent message to Colonel Beer, the Deputy Commissioner of the Police for the OFS.[90]

Beer's testimony confirms that of Sesing. When he arrived he saw a crowd 'varying from 200 to 800 approximately' who were in an excited state. Behind them, at a distance, 'some thousands' of residents stood quietly.[91] However, there was a fear that the protest was escalating quickly. By the time J.R Cooper arrived, 'sticks were brandished' and 'women with aprons full of stone came up'.[92] Beer claimed that more people congregated in front of the police and that 'many women there were armed with stones and excit[ed] the men by words and gestures to become more turbulent.'[93]

Cooper tried to engage with the crowd. He called for a doctor to examine Dibi and assured the crowd that a proper enquiry would be held concerning Dibi's death and also conveyed the crowd's demand that the police must retreat.[94] Lt. Mathews declined, stating at one point, 'I cannot move back one inch,' but Beer agreed to leave the location ground and moved the police onto the street junction between Monument and Falck streets.[95] Cooper then attempted to call a meeting with 'responsible natives'. He managed to locate a few blockmen but claimed that the 'rowdier element gave us no chance', he was 'unsuccessful in arranging a meeting'.[96]

The crowd had made its position clear – people would disperse and return home once the police and white civilians withdrew from the location.[97] Beer refused to withdraw the police and tensions mounted. Finally, a hailstorm temporarily defused the standoff with most of the residents running for shelter and the police withdrawing from the location.[98]

With the locations free from white intrusion the protest was transformed into a disciplined political struggle.[99] James Mpinda – Advisory Board chair and ICU member – played a central role in the mobilisation of residents. Meetings were held throughout the night and a stayaway was called for the next day.[100] During the night symbols of police authority were targeted – the houses of black constables were ransacked and burnt, and two police stations were damaged. Many whites fled the surrounding areas of Waaihoek on Sunday night as they feared that they would be attacked. On Monday morning, shop owners responded in a similar manner and closed for the day.[101]

On 20 April, Bloemfontein's 20 000 black residents supported the stayaway.[102] By six that morning, a large crowd had congregated in Harvey Road. They were met with an expanded police blockade that significantly diluted the boundary between the white police and the white civilian population. This blockade included 150 civilian 'special officers' armed with pick-handles; 31 policemen under two officers, armed with revolvers with bayonets fixed; 54 civilian 'special constables' from the District Rifle Association; 130 'special constables' who had volunteered from the Railway and Harbours Regiment Detachment, were also armed with rifles with bayonets fixed.[103] At their rear was a gathering of white civilians, not under any supervision, and some were armed.

Once again Cooper intervened. This time, with the help of Mpinda and Sesing, he tried to 'parley' with the crowd.[104] They managed to gather a group of representatives that met with the town council. Again, Mpinda played a leading role in the meeting and articulated residents' demands – an end to police searches for illicit beer that undermined residents' right to brew beer for their own consumption and justice for Dibi and compensation for his family.[105]

At the meeting with the town council, delegates were informed that unless the crowd had dispersed by three o' clock that afternoon, the police contingent would march through the location to 'restore order'.[106] However, when Mpinda and the other representative returned, the mood of the crowd had shifted, and they proved 'unable to influence the element who had taken charge'.[107] Mpinda, who had played a key role in mobilising residents and organising the stayaway, was not able to convince the crowd to call off the protest action. At ten minutes past three, the police and 'special constables' advanced into the location, attacking protesters with guns and picks.[108] This resulted in the death of a further three residents and 24 people were injured.[109] In addition, 85 men and 12 women were arrested.

ICU leaders showed remarkable political agility in transforming an altercation between beer brewers and police into a stayaway.[110] However, leaders lacked experience in dealing with protest outside the bounds of organised politics and were unable to steer the volatile politics of 'the crowd'[111], with its own political vernacular that tended towards violence. ICU leaders also did not see beer brewers, who worked on their own account, as workers and failed to establish durable linkages with them.

Aftermath

After the riots, there was a bit of an upset when 'Mote turned King's witness against Mpinda in the Commission of Inquiry. (He was briefly expelled as a result). However, the Bloemfontein branch continued to campaign for minimum wages, which was given a major boost with the establishment of Bloemfontein's Native Wages Commission. Representatives were drawn from the town council, Master Builders, Chamber of Commerce, shopkeepers and professional officers as well as four representatives from the Advisory Board and four from the ICU. The ICU stood firm and held out for a minimum wage of 3s 6d. with an immediate rise of 6d, for all those earning 3s 6d and over. However, Advisory Board members undercut the ICU during the negotiations and agreed to a minimum wage of 3s. This determination was not compulsory – and, once again, it probably did not apply to domestic workers. Nevertheless, some employers did increase wages on 1 May 1926. According to both Wickins and Hirson, the ICU's participation in the Commission was counted as one of the ICU's major successes.[112]

However, the victory was short-lived as the national ICU was increasingly drawn into organising rural South Africa. There are indications that the Bloemfontein branch transferred branch fees to the national ICU in 1927, but not in 1928 or 1929.[113] The ICU held its 1928 conference in Bloemfontein, but it appears that by this time the branch and its campaign for a minimum wage had drawn to an end.

Conclusion

The idea that the time had come 'for him and her to unite and stand side-by-side' as equals in the struggle for an Africa that was free of racial oppression and economic exploitation was powerful for its time and held much promise.[114] The Bloemfontein branch flirted with the idea but was unable to organise or relate to proletarian women in any meaningful or sustained manner and did not realise this promise. As the ICU moved into the rural reaches of South Africa, more traditional gender hierarchies and forms of gender domination would be confronted. Bradford reminds us that many rural women did not think that the ICU's red membership card was for them.[115] Yet others, such as those in Natal, refashioned traditional gender ideas to suit their interests and claim sections of the ICU as their own. They drew on their own vernacular forms of protest, which included violence, to confront power directly.

7 The ICU in the Western Transvaal, 1926–1934: Re-Imagining Ideological, Spatial and Political Realities

Laurence Stewart

Introduction

This chapter explores the expanse of the ICU's character and politics in the Western Transvaal and northern parts of the Cape Province (the present-day North West Province) between 1926 and 1934.[1] The unique geographical focus of the ICU's activism disrupts the conventional periodising of its longevity, which lasted in the Western Transvaal until 1934. The extant literature assumes its presence to have ended in 1928–29. The extent of the ICU's activism links to a key question posed by Bonner: 'what was the enduring attraction of the ICU?' He suggests that the answer to this question lies in the 'power of the spoken word', particularly in that the ICU offered workers 'a taste of freedom'. Although presenting this conclusion, he argues that 'how this was served up in different locales and different contexts is obviously a much more complex question'.[2]

This chapter investigates the extent of the ICU's character, politics and longevity in a particular locale, the Western Transvaal, through three innovative forms of their activism: in the oratory of ICU organisers, in the public discussions that the ICU hosted and in the way the ICU challenged spatial segregation. These facets of the ICU's activism highlight its ideology, praxis and participation in local protests. In investigating 'the power of the spoken word', this chapter seeks not only to examine the ICU's speeches and use of language, but the concomitant spatial, ideological and political outcomes of their public meetings and oratory. This embeds Bonner's framing of the ICU's appeal in the political economy of the Western Transvaal and within the context in which the 'spoken word' was articulated.

The political economy of the Western Transvaal in the 1920s and the ICU's expansion

From the mid-1800s, land dispossession had forced black workers in the Western Transvaal into sharecropping, squatting and labour tenancy. By the 1920s, the trend across the countryside was that white farmers were trying to rid their farms of these forms of labour in favour of more productive and profitable relationships; sharecroppers' shares were reduced, as were the land and livestock allowances of squatters and labour tenants. Many of these workers, who were being relegated to wage labour, settled in tightly controlled locations and took up jobs on low-paying diamond diggings. Despite proletarianisation existing on Western Transvaal farms, it was 'stunted' owing to the region's complex political economy. Drought, bad soils and poor world markets meant that conditions were not productive enough for farmers to capitalise their farms. This meant that the usage of sharecropping and tenant labour continued during the first half of the twentieth century and was mediated through paternalism and violence.[3]

These dynamics and incoming changes in rural areas generated responses from black rural workers. This has been framed by both Helen Bradford and Sylvia Neame as a 'rural revolt' which was unfolding in Southern Africa in 1927–1928.[4] The ICU played a pivotal role in the revolt that dominated the countryside, where they managed fairly successfully to both 'piggy-back' on already present fractures in rural areas and also organise campaigns, attach to local struggles, provide support to workers and stoke, as well as provide space for the articulation of, rural anger. From 1926, the ICU had increased their attention on countryside matters, which was facilitated by the relocation of the headquarters from Cape Town to Johannesburg. This prompted their move to the Western Transvaal where they opened branches in Potchefstroom and Mafeking [Mafikeng] in 1926. The ICU's presence in Mafikeng led ICU organisers to Lichtenburg, the site of a major strike in June 1928.

During the Lichtenburg strike, which saw over 5 000 black workers down tools over low wages and poor living conditions, the ICU played a role in organising workers, picketing and negotiating on their behalf. Following the strike, news of the '*Keaubona*' (Sesotho for 'I See You') spread throughout the Western Transvaal.[5] Between late 1928 and early 1929, a host of branches were opened in the towns of Bloemhof, Klerksdorp, Makwassie, Rustenburg, Schweizer-Reneke, Taung, Wolmaransstad and Vryburg. As the ICU hopped from town to town, they gathered large audiences at their meetings.

It was within meetings that the ICU managed to inspire and rouse workers over their difficult plights; at countless meetings held between 1928 and 1934, they excited workers with sharp and politically astute oratory which dreamed of a free future, although with varying degrees of success. In Klerksdorp and Potchefstroom, for example, competition with the African National Congress (ANC) and the Communist Party of South Africa (CPSA) minimised the ICU's constituency and drew them to infighting rather than representing workers' grievances. Towns like Rustenburg, Taung and Vryburg were adjacent to Reserves and this meant that African people were partially shielded from wage labour through limited access to land. By far the most explosive expansion of the ICU was in the farming districts of the South-Western Transvaal, where seasonal workers on the diamond diggings and farmer-diggers carried the messages of the Lichtenburg strike back to farms.[6]

Dynamic and exciting organisers helped facilitate the spread of the ICU in the Bloemhof-Schweizer-Reneke-Wolmaransstad triangle. Robert Makhatini was 'very educated', clever and an independent thinker who operated in this region where he gave exciting speeches and fought on behalf of farmworkers, location residents and those on diamond diggings. Keable 'Mote began his activism in the Orange Free State (OFS) and moved to the Western Transvaal in 1927–1928; he was an energetic and bombastic public speaker who prolifically used meetings to represent workers' grievances and expose the failures of government. Jason Jingoes, who was a Basotho chief, organised the ICU's most powerful and vibrant branch at Makwassie and travelled to surrounding towns representing workers and giving ICU members legal counsel for over six years (from 1928–1934). Clements Kadalie attended numerous meetings in the Western Transvaal where he gave sensational speeches – his name was synonymous with the ICU in the region.[7]

From 1928 ICU organisers like Kadalie and Makhatini delivered speeches in Wolmaransstad, 'Mote held meetings in Bloemhof in 1929, and Jason Jingoes also took control of the branch in Makwassie in 1929. Their speeches and activism rallied sharecroppers and labour tenants; fought for wage increases and better working conditions on farms; challenged paternalism and violence; argued for the abolition of passes and campaigned against the degrading practices of town administrations. The ICU provided legal counsel to dispossessed squatters, sharecroppers, farmworkers and labour tenants, and often fought their own battles against local administrations trying to evict them from locations. In Schweizer-Reneke, the ICU developed a remarkable following where it supported residents who fought against forced removals and for better services and, in turn, residents protected ICU leaders. The longevity of the Schweizer-Reneke branch relied on these interconnections and lasted long enough to include a change of leadership from Robert Makhatini to Henry Maleke from 1929 to 1930.

Despite these branches being buoyed by the genius and oratory of these leaders, they quickly diminished in the face of government repression and farmer violence against ICU members. Fearing the impact of the ICU, racist and Nationalist-aligned local administrations throughout the Western Transvaal policed the movement of workers between farm and town and used the law, and often outdated legislation, to prevent the ICU from holding meetings and organisers from entering and living in towns. This kind of repression forced Jingoes out of the Makwassie location whereafter he moved to Ottosdal and began organising workers there until 1934.

While a more detailed account of the ICU's presence (especially into the 1930s) is covered elsewhere,[8] this chronology shows how the ICU hopped from town to town (it was only in Schweizer-Reneke that the branch outlived an individual organiser) based on the meetings and campaigns of charismatic organisers. The meeting – held in different locales and with different degrees of success – was the central, albeit transitory, means through which they could communicate, give speeches and interact with their supporters. Interest in the ICU revolved around 'the spoken word' of organisers, who criticised and reflected on the political economy of the region. The speeches they gave, the ideology they communicated, the form that the meetings took and the spatial implications of holding such meetings help explain the character, politics and longevity of the ICU in the Western Transvaal.

The ICU's language of freedom

Many farmworkers, sharecroppers, workers on the diamond diggings, labour tenants, unemployed location residents and other labourers heard ICU organisers speak of 'freedom' as they travelled throughout farming districts and small towns in the Western Transvaal. They would stand atop wagon platforms and prophesy a better world. The ICU's language of freedom in the Western Transvaal were grounded in the political economy of the region. ICU officials juxtaposed conditions of future freedom as opposed to slavery, and called for better wages and the inclusion of black South Africans as equal members of an industrialising society.

Their vision of freedom also went beyond a reflection of the political economy or an appeal to the state or farmers for better treatment. At meetings, the ICU and their constituency sang 'Nkosi Sikelel' iAfrika', which resembled a collective call for liberation; they promoted self-determination and they encouraged their members to become educated (or conscientised). This kind of thinking relates to Michael Neocosmos' conception of freedom, defined as thinking 'beyond social location'.[9] David Johnson argues that the ICU 'expressed their own distinctive dream of freedom' and relates their language of freedom to both adventitious and indigenous models. He identifies multiple forms of this language,[10] which are referred to below. The rich oral history material presented shows how pervasive the theme of freedom was in people's memories of the ICU.

Mmereki Molohlanyi, a farmworker in Wolmaransstad, recalled Kadalie speaking in Wolmaransstad sometime in 1927 or 1928. In his speech, Kadalie 'said it was essential that we should be free' and that 'it was high time that we should rid ourselves of the chains of slavery.'[11] ICU organiser, Cecil Sehlabo, visited Rustenburg in October 1929 and encouraged the town's black people, whom he regarded as living in 'slavery', to remember the struggle of Israel in their struggle as workers.[12] Wealthy sharecropper Andries Seiphetlo heard Jason Jingoes talking in Makwassie sometime in 1929, who said to the crowd that 'he was going to liberate [them] from bondage'.[13] Kas Maine's nephew, Baefesi Maine, also heard Jingoes speaking in Makwassie during the early 1930s, saying that 'he was a black representative who would liberate us from slavery'.[14] Selwane Legobathe, who was Kas Maine's sister and stayed on a farm near Bloemhof, listened to Jingoes draw a sharp analogy between the South African situation and slavery:

> He talked about the South African Laws on Blacks, about Blacks enslavement by the whites even about [how] Blacks slavery works. He went on to ask why whites are handling blacks like slaves yet they are the ones working for them. They don't eat well, stay well, yet they work for them.[15]

David Johnson identifies the ICU's language of 'slavery as opposed to freedom' as being a distinct language of freedom the ICU embodied across South Africa. Slavery had both historical and contemporary significance among farmworkers in the

Western Transvaal; white farmers had conducted slave raids in the nineteenth century and paternalism on farms resembled a form of slavery.[16] Further, Bradford argues that Africans regarded labour tenancy, which was the predominant relationship in the countryside, as 'approximated slavery, forced labour or serfdom'.[17]

The discourse of slavery was often counterposed in ICU organisers' visions of the freedom to come. Klerksdorp resident, George Lephadi, heard Kadalie and Keable 'Mote address a crowd in the Klerksdorp location, and he specifically remembered them speaking of freedom. In Lephadi's words: 'they were talking about freedom. They were fighting for our liberation. They said how long had we been slaves, and when would we get a better life. We have been under the Boers, oppressing us.'[18] 'Mote, who was a Christian, drew a link between religion and the abolition of slavery which had Christian millenarian undertones: 'women and men you have a big message to carry, don't play with it; the message is to be free from slavery I shall speak until Jesus Christ sees upon me, we want to kick the slavery away.'[19] There were also ideas about how to become free from oppression and slavery. The proposed 'way to liberty' suggested by Kadalie at a meeting in East London in 1930 'passes through gaol, thorns, aeroplanes, big flying machines and Great Government Authorities'.[20] In a less flamboyant way, Samuel Rampoumanie, an ICU organiser in Potchefstroom, suggested: 'comrades, we cannot expect to get freedom without persecution.'[21]

Solutions to slavery and oppression related to basic political and economic freedoms and ranged from constitutionalism to collective action. In practice, the ICU used the law most effectively in fighting for the freedom of black people. Ottosdal resident Thetheletse Thys summed up Jingoes' role: 'the law would come, it would find that he had fixed everything up'.[22] For some, such as George Lephadi, the solution to 'slavery' espoused by ICU organisers was 'revolution' which, however, would be non-violent: 'their liberation, they said it would be obtained through verbal negotiation. They did not encourage war'.[23] Robert Makhatini echoed the constitutional approach to fighting for freedom when at a meeting in Makwassie 'he said that whites were treating us badly, the law would free us'.[24] In contrast, when ICU local organiser David Leeo spoke in Klerksdorp in 1928, he suggested collective action was key to achieving freedom: 'everybody has his freedom in his own hands. We must organise and speak in one voice. Hertzog will give you damn little. He will give you a damn sjambok.'[25]

One of the distinctive languages of freedom that Johnson identifies within the ICU is freedom in the economic dimension, often related to socialist liberation. In the future society where slavery would be abolished, fair wages were crucial. Motlagomang Maine, who was a member of the CPSA and was married to Kas Maine's brother, Mphaka Maine, heard Jingoes talk 'about freedom, the whites must free blacks and pay them'.[26] The same was the case for Baefesi Maine who recalled Jingoes saying that 'the whites are oppressing the blacks and that they were underpaying the blacks.'[27] For Thabiso Bogopane, who was a migrant labourer between Rustenburg and Johannesburg, 'Kadalie spoke for every black man ... he wanted [that] every black man should be paid. He must also be free'.[28] In other words, economic freedom was central to the ICU's vision of freedom and this relates to Neame's framing of the ICU as radical-democratic (calling for the democratisation of economic and political freedoms).[29]

In July 1928, Makhatini gave a speech at Makwassie where the audience began the meeting singing *Nkosi Sikelel' iAfrika*. When Makhatini opened for questions, he got into an argument with a white farmer, a certain Wentzel. The question of economic freedom lay at the heart of their exchange, which is quoted in full below:

> Mr Wentzel: What is the ICU's highest ideal?
>
> Robert Makhatini: We want to be free.
>
> Wentzel: Be free ... But how exactly do you want to be free, because there are many ways?
>
> Makhatini: White people had flourished – they have nice clothes and machines and money and so on. And black people have no nice clothes, nor do they have money and black people also want their women to wear smart dresses
>
> Wentzel: But how can you say this, black people had worn animal skins before…
>
> Makhatini: […] It is true that we wore animal skins, but everyone wore animal skins. We ate tripe and lived good lives.
>
> Wentzel: Did black people have money and nice clothes which they are all now talking about?
>
> Makhatini: We didn't know what money was, but we had many cows; had much milk to drink and ate meat, we moved around to where we wanted. Now we must work very hard for a pound and for our work.
>
> Wentzel: Why don't you work for cattle anymore?
>
> Makhatini: Back in the days we had a place for our cattle, and nowadays we don't have a place for our cattle. Here at Maquassi, black people have land which is only good enough for two animals.[30]

Here Makhatini articulates two different conceptions of freedom; the first is about the freedom African people had in precolonial society through economic stability, and the second is the freedom to enjoy the benefits of an industrialising society through fair wages. Makhatini thought that a return to precolonial life was impossible considering the extent of colonial conquest and land dispossession, and rather viewed full participation in the 'new' society as the way to freedom. While Makhatini's comments could be seen as limited to freedoms within white society rather than thinking 'beyond their social location', to quote Neocosmos,[31] they present a pragmatic view of the socioeconomic changes resulting from colonisation. Makhatini's wish for black women to wear 'smart dresses' also highlights the influence of Garveyism on ICU leaders. Vinson argues that African Americans were seen as 'alternate models of modernity' where black South Africans 'admired their remarkable journey from slavery to freedom, their educational and socioeconomic advancement, their extraordinary cultural production, their urbane modernity.[32]

Another way in which discourses of freedom were advanced was through the link between the African Methodist Episcopal Church (AMEC) and the ICU. In 1929, Selwane Legobathe stumbled upon Jingoes addressing an ICU meeting in Bloemhof after she attended an AMEC Sunday service.[33] She remarked that the language espoused by Jingoes was not particularly different from that of the AMEC. Legobathe felt that some AMEC preachers (several of whom came from the United States) were also ICU members, and for Legobathe, this was evidenced in the kinds of topics which they both spoke about. Discourses of freedom overlapped between the church and the ICU and, in addition, Legobathe saw the singing of 'Nkosi Sikelel' iAfrika' as part of a joint call for liberation: 'They talked about freedom. They said that if we pray whole heartedly, God will free us. During concerts we sang 'Nkosi Sikelela'. That is why I am saying that those priests were working together with the ICU'.[34] The singing of 'Nkosi Sikelel' iAfrika', while first conceptualised and used in a religious setting, was sung at the first meeting of the South African Native National Congress (SANNC) in 1912. From then on, according to Coplan and Jules-Rosette, the song began to occupy a position at the intersection of 'public religion and popular culture'.[35] The song was used in 1919 'in political street protests' and was commonplace at meetings held by the ANC and 'countless other political organisations', including the ICU. 'Nkosi Sikelel' iAfrika' has come to 'symbolise more than any other piece of expressive culture the struggle for African unity and liberation in South Africa'.[36]

For some workers, the ICU invoked a race consciousness which aimed to secure self-determination and political freedom. According to Andries Seiphetlo, for example, this 'freedom' meant, that 'we [...] rule ourselves'.[37] Rustenburg sharecropper and migrant labourer Israel Matholoe claimed the ICU was fighting for 'freedom from whites'.[38] Neame has argued that different ICU leaders exhibited a race consciousness, which was partially informed by Garveyite influence, and that the Congress movement had self-determination as a central aim.[39]

According to Antonio Gramsci, the importation of ideology from other countries or contexts can impinge on their local effectiveness.[40] Like in the case of the ICU, much of their discourse is borrowed; be it from American ideas of race, slavery and freedom or Christian ideas of liberation. Throughout this chapter, the weapons of language used by the ICU were employed precisely because they were effective among rural workers in the Western Transvaal. As suggested earlier, Neocosmos argues that ideas of freedom emerge within local contexts and crucially present a 'politics of universal humanity', which refer to organic and universal ideas of freedom, justice and equality.[41]

Motlagomang Maine's idea of freedom was inspired by a speech Jingoes gave in 1930 linking freedom to education and conscientisation. In Motlagomang's words, Jingoes exclaimed:

> Look at me, I am educated, I know everything about the world and
> I am free. I learn you are called bobbejaans [baboons]'. [...] when he
> spoke the last words he turned his back... and pulled up the sledge of
> his jacket and said, "look they said we have tails, where do you see one
> on me?".... He went on to say that blacks must feel free and become
> wise, and they must get out of the dark.[42]

The ICU managed to bring about a political consciousness, which was crucial for
most black people as they were 'still blind'.[43] For Motlagomang Maine the key to this
was education: 'blacks must become wise ... and must get out of the dark and take
away the *hoogklap*' (a 'hoogklap' is something that functions as a cover for a person's
eyes, almost like a sleep mask, or a horse's eyes, commonly called blinkers).[44] She
saw the impact of the ICU as educative, helping black farmers like herself to 'have a
clear understanding about life' as the ICU 'brought light to us'.[45] Another prominent
theme in Motlagomang's interview is how Jingoes called out the dehumanising
language of white people, while his description of himself aims to show how black
people can overturn racist stereotypes.

The ICU had a vision of future freedom and ICU organisers would prophesy a better
and freer world. At a meeting in Schweizer-Reneke sometime in the late 1920s,
for example, Kas Maine recollected Kadalie, who gave the promise of freedom to
come: 'the time will come gradually, it cannot be today but a year or fifty or ten,
twenty years, but we will be freed'.[46] The ICU's message of freedom was also found
in booklets and pamphlets that were sold for between 2s and 5s each. Molohlanyi
highlighted how the publications outlined the ways in which 'the boers were ill-
treating blacks' and how the ICU promised to strive for a 'better world for blacks'.[47]
More simply, in the memory of Selwane Legobathe, the books were 'saying that we
shall get freedom'.[48]

Languages of subversion and ridicule

The themes that framed the ICU's subversive language ranged from the exploitation
of black workers to calls for equality and dignity. Selwane Legobathe remembered
Jingoes giving a speech in Bloemhof where he said, 'You whites eat butter forgetting
that it's the black man who is milking for you, herds your cattle. He has not time for
rest, he stays out in the storm, in the rain, you care less when he gets wet out in the
rain.'[49] Jingoes' comment challenged the myth that a generation of white farmers had
been successful without the labour and expertise of black people, and he recognised
the rightful historical position of black sharecroppers who, as Timothy Keegan
suggests, kept white farmers afloat from the early 1900s.[50]

Modise Tsubane was an ICU member who stayed on a farm in the Wolmaransstad
district. He used to attend meetings in Wolmaransstad town and return to his
farm to tell his family about the ICU. On one occasion, his brother Petrus Tsubane
remembered him speak about how 'there is no Apartheid [segregation], and that

the boers and blacks must be one thing. We must share the same meal on the same table. But we never became one thing. The boers did not like the blacks on top of them'.[51] There are two ways in which Modise's words can be read as subversive: the first relates to the fact that white people had an aversion to having black people 'superior' or even equal to them. The second is the antipathy of white farmers to be physically close to black people, as they rejected the idea that black and white people could ever 'be one thing'.

When Kadalie gave a speech in Wolmaransstad in 1928, he turned towards some white women who had attended the meeting and, 'while pointing to them with his fingers', said, 'We have wives who are working for you instead of working for us, their husbands. How will you feel when they will no longer work for you and you are forced to carry a bucket full of water yourself. I can make it happen that you should carry a bucket full of water for yourself.'[52]

Kadalie's suggestion that white women should be doing the work of their black domestic workers was indeed subversive. The comment aimed to shock and ridicule and the net effect on the crowd, as recalled by Mmereki Molohlanyi, was that workers 'cheer[ed] aloud and clap[ped] [their] hands at such bold speeches'.[53] At the same time, it also reflected the prevailing patriarchal norms of society among both white and black people, according to which women were viewed as their husbands' property. Van Onselen suggests that Kadalie's message appealed to 'beleaguered black patriarchs who were in danger of losing their control over family labour'.[54] Sharecroppers and labour tenants needed family labour to effectively fulfil the conditions of their relationships on white-owned farms.

After leaving Lichtenburg during the June 1928 strike, Kadalie gave another speech in Mafikeng in which he ridiculed the opulent lifestyle of white people:

> Look, your wives and children are starving. If a person came to me and told me to go to church when I was hungry, I would tell him to go to hell. The white people have got on their tables; pork, beef, mutton, turkey and some of the damn fools are too lazy to get up and eat it.[55]

As well as mocking, there were more aggressive and antagonistic remarks. Ramakgelo Dinkebogile, a farmer in a reserve area in K***kraal, near Rusten–burg, remembered Kadalie visiting his farm and comparing white people to pigs: 'he would say "if you want to see how a Boer is like, you must get a pig. After scrubbing it you must fetch a boer; you will see that these people are pigs."'[56]

At times Kadalie had a particularly foul mouth. Ishmael Moeng, who was a local CPSA member in Makwassie and worked as a mechanic in Lichtenburg, remembered Kadalie 'shouting' and 'swear[ing] at policemen' during a visit to Makwassie.[57] Lephadi simply remembered ICU organisers 'swearing at whites wherever they go'.[58] When Makhatini was interrupted during a meeting in Bloemhof by a court interpreter named Brewis, Makhatini retorted 'we are no more kaffirs.

Mr. Brewis is a snake.'[59] As Bonner notes, black audiences enjoyed the 'verbal excesses' of ICU organisers and, as ICU Research and Complaints Secretary Doyle Modiakgotla remarked 'audiences rejoiced when the speaker cursed the white man'.[60]

The ICU saved their most aggressive insults for the government. Bonner argues that the 'words used by ICU leaders stung and offended the political establishment [...] from the Prime Minister down'.[61] After a meeting given by 'Mote in Potchefstroom in June 1928, the policemen present noted that 'every member of the force present is ridiculed' and that most of ['Mote's] speech was full of abuse for ministers and officials in general "Mote abuses the Ministers, Police Officers, Magistrates, Municipal Officials and Europeans".[62]

At a meeting in September 1928, 'Mote opened the meeting by ridiculing the Minister of Agriculture, General Kemp, and his role in the 1914 Afrikaner rebellion with the words: 'when they [Kemp and the rebels] were running all over the country like monkeys'.[63] In September and October 1928, 'Mote twice threatened to give both the government and Prime Minister Hertzog a 'sjambok'.[64] In a speech delivered in Lichtenburg in October 1928, Kadalie claimed that he would electorally 'contest' J.B.M. Hertzog's seat as Prime Minister, arguing that, as a Malawian immigrant, he 'could appeal to the Dutch sentiments probably better than Tielman Roos [the Justice Minister, 1924-1929] or General Hertzog'.[65] Kadalie was suggesting that Roos and Hertzog were incompetent even in fulfilling the parochial needs of their constituency.

If politics can be viewed as 'what is seen and what can be said about it, around who has the ability to see and the talent to speak, around the properties of spaces and the possibilities of time', as Ranciére argues, then the inextricable link between politics and speech highlights the potency of the ICU's words.[66] While the ICU's colourful language in the Western Transvaal conformed to patterns identified by Bonner in the Witwatersrand, ICU organisers in the Western Transvaal spoke to the particular political economy of the region. The ICU used subversive language to show the contradictions of spatial segregation, the unequal division of resources relating to the sharecropper-farmer relationship and the use of black family labour by paternalist white patriarchs. Furthermore, they ridiculed the gluttony and selfishness of white farmers and mocked Nationalist Party politicians who stoked the racist sentiments of poor white workers in the Western Transvaal.

Democratising public discussion: The ICU and the public sphere

Habermas' notion of the public sphere has been debated among scholars of the ICU. Keith Breckenridge has suggested that the ICU formed a key part of the public sphere which characterised black politics in the 1920s, to which Phil Bonner responded that the ICU 'harangued' their audiences and public participation was 'for the most part limited to listening and then approving or withholding support'.[67] While both authors highlight the internal politics of the ICU in relation to public discussion, neither engage literature on the stratification of the public sphere and on the plurality of 'public spheres'. Nancy Fraser has argued for the notion of a 'subaltern counter-public' where oppressed groups who are excluded from public discussion form 'parallel discursive spaces'.[68] Further, the public sphere has also been characterised by groups of people who engage on matters of particular interest called 'issue publics'.[69] These latter two notions of a 'subaltern counter-public' and 'issue public' apply to the ICU in the Western Transvaal in a few instances.

Baefesi Maine remembered that in Makwassie farmworkers managed to raise certain issues during meetings. They were able to express issues 'concerning their lives, the way they lived and also the way whites treated them and underpaid them'.[70] Maine further described how farmworkers were able to 'ask [ICU organisers] how they should live in the world', which 'the ICU people explained to them'.[71] Rather than simply 'haranguing' their audiences, on occasions such as the one described, ICU meetings took on the form of a 'counter-public sphere', where audiences and the ICU could engage on matters of general interest, outside the gaze of the state or white farmers. The ICU and workers formed a counter-public because these meetings were severely repressed as they challenged those in power. In contrast to the repression the ICU and their members faced in towns such as Bloemhof, Mphaka Maine noted that 'whites have their own meetings on the farms and we [black people] never question them about those meetings'.[72]

At the meeting in Makwassie in July 1928 discussed earlier, Makhatini invited questions from the audience after his address. White members of the public flung a barrage of questions which Makhatini either denied or refused to comment on. For example, Wentzel asked: 'Is it true that black people are teaching to drive white people into the sea?'; 'Is it true that Kadalie said he would hit [Minister of Justice Tielman] Roos with a sjambok?' Black audience members, one of whom was a municipal official from Bloemhof named Saayman, asked whether ICU members still needed to carry passes, 'What must we make of the red tickets [the ICU's membership cards]? Can we now walk without passes?' Saayman aired his views on the desires and aspirations of black people, 'We don't have the power to fight with the white man. We must try to be one [people], then we can do a lot, we must wear beautiful clothes and then we can be like the white people. White people don't disregard us, it is black people that do.'[73] Although the conversation did not go much further, Saayman's comment was echoed in Makhatini's vision of freedom when he spoke about how black women should 'wear smart dresses' and live like white people in his exchange with Wentzel. In this instance, there appears to have been an interplay between the views of the audience (Saayman) and those of the speaker (Makhatini) and can be viewed as evidence of the egalitarian character of the meeting.

As the meeting continued, there was further questioning from different sections of the audience, with white farmers complaining about black people not adhering to the pass laws, the economic recession and other matters: 'do you know the country has plenty debt', and 'are you against the pass law?'. After Makhatini deflected a number of questions, white farmers turned to making statements such as 'you want to make war, right?', 'you talk too much, why not rather pay your dues'. Makhatini then interjected, 'I will be pleased if the [white] bosses stop asking questions.' At this point, Saayman complained about the treatment of black people by white farmers:

> Saayman: We get nothing from white people, we walk with clothes in tatters, they say that they plough for us, just two acres – not even enough to pay for the tasks that we do.

> Robert Makhatini: I will come here [in] two or three weeks, because I see you have it difficult here. I will come see how you work, I will come and hear your complaints and difficulties... I will go to Johannesburg and say that Maquassi is a bad place.[74]

The discussion was skilfully managed by Makhatini to include the views of black audience members. It included black workers, white farmers and Makhatini/the ICU deliberating across their differences – in terms of opinion, class, race and political affiliation. They discussed issues pertaining to the context of the Western Transvaal like sharecropping, payment of wages, the relationships between workers and farmers and the presence of the ICU. They also spoke about issues relating to national politics and the state – a conversation which was usually the preserve of white people.

Rethinking the ICU's impact on space and spatial relationships in the Western Transvaal

This section analyses the ICU's impact on the production of space in the Western Transvaal in the context of enforced spatial segregation.[75] Henri Lefebvre's theory of the interconnectedness of space is useful to explore the spatial context of the Western Transvaal, which was characterised by both legal and ideological divisions between urban and rural space. The ICU played a role in breaking down ideological and political divisions between town and countryside. In viewing the ICU as a 'mediator' in forging spatial relationships, Lefebvre's theory helps unpack the ICU's role in the producing an interconnectedness between rural and urban.[76]

The spatial politics of farms

In the 1920s, farms in the Western Transvaal were spread in-between towns and their size could range between 1 000 and 7 000 hectares, meaning they were remote and isolated (this is still true today). The isolated nature of these farms both produced and corresponded with rather insular ways of social organisation. In his study of the paternalism and violence on farms in the South-Western Transvaal, Charles van Onselen shows that paternalist relationships predominated and were maintained through youth socialisation, shared language, the granting of material gifts and the integration of servants into the family of the master. On farms, paternalism played a key role in maintaining social order; as Bradford argues, it 'clearly linked individual Africans to their [employer's] families in ways which inhibited the development of tenant protest and independence'.[77] Van Onselen suggests that most studies of paternalism in South Africa emphasised its 'recessive potential', whereas paternalism was in fact characterised by violence from both the master's and servant's side. He further suggests that there were times when 'the black dependent [was] predisposed to question the social reach of the white patriarch'.[78]

A second feature of farms was violence meted out by farmowner onto a farmworker; a feature of farms which goes back to slavery, and in the Western Transvaal links to paternalist violence. Speaking of the general make-up of farms in South Africa, Bradford suggests that it was 'a brutal and bloody world that black farm labourers inhabited in the 1920s'.[79] John Higginson argues that the Western Transvaal countryside was characterised by violence which took on multiple forms: legal or 'formal' violence, which was sanctioned by the state, and extra-legal violence committed by white farmers aiming to protect their often precarious economic position.[80] Proletarianisation, poor world markets and increasing struggles between farmworkers and farm owners meant that both 'legal' and 'extra-legal' violence were used by white farmers to discipline farmworkers. Andries Leeu, a sharecropper in the Western Transvaal, had a direct experience of this violence, and on one occasion was hit by his employer with an axe for being late for work.[81]

The geographical isolation, paternalism and violence on the farms contributed to the perception of the ICU as an urban phenomenon amongst some farm workers, as their oral testimonies show. A farmworker named M. Motete heard about the ICU in Bloemhof and Makwassie, and felt the ICU and other political organisations were not for people on farms: 'Now, most things came with people from towns… They knew about them – we were farm people[;] farm people are farm people. All those things were not there, we knew nothing.'[82] Speaking about the ICU's growth in Bloemhof, Selwane Legobathe noted that 'we the people on farms don't get the news in time. We hear it later.'[83] Kas Maine claimed to not know much about the ICU because he 'was staying on the farms' and 'did not worry much about it.'[84]

The separation between town and farm, and the violent conditions on farms also affected the kinds of politics farmworkers engaged with, inhibiting collective organisation. Kas Maine chose not to join the ICU because 'I was a man of the farm and as such didn't want a quarrel with the whites.'[85] As Bradford notes, 'the norm amongst farm labourers was not overt collective resistance but subterranean individualistic protest'.[86] When Kas Maine was asked about the possibility of striking on farms, he questioned, 'How could they [farmworkers] call for a strike where they had no social standing? How will you be able to strike and you're inside a man's home? Strike inside a man's house, you cannot do that!'[87] Kas Maine's experience informed Charles van Onselen's position that 'strategies of industrial resistance were unsuited to farms, where a paternalistic ethos governed day-to-day relationships'.[88]

Forging new spatial-political connections: The ICU and the disruption of spatial segregation

It is important to recognise that the spatial politics of farms represented a challenge for the ICU in Western Transvaal and other farming districts. Bonner argues that labour tenants, a central constituency of the ICU, were the 'Achille's heel' of the ICU, in that they were 'scattered across thousands of square miles of countryside [and] were virtually impossible to protect'.[89] Moreover, government segregationist legislation sought to enforce spatial divisions between town, diamond digging and countryside through the pass system and this greatly inhibited the ICU's capacity for consistent organisation. While there were significant spatial impediments to the ICU's ability to organise workers, this section explores the extent to which the ICU provided a challenge to the spatial ordering of the Western Transvaal.

Across this region, the ICU held meetings in towns which workers travelled to from farms. Mmereki Molohlanyi travelled with other farmworkers on horse-drawn carts to meetings held in Wolmaransstad on Sundays. At one meeting, Kadalie addressed workers on a wagon-turned-platform in the graveyard of the Wolmaransstad location, which he began by arguing the importance of freedom.[90] Andries Seiphetlo remembered going to meetings in 1929 where he heard Jingoes say that 'we should get more pay, in fact be allowed to own property so that they [black people] could do farming on their own.'[91]

Farmworkers who attended meetings returned to farms and spread the news of the ICU. Motlagomang Maine learnt of the ICU's ideas through her husband Mphaka Maine, who used to travel to meetings in Bloemhof on horseback.[92] Selwane Legobathe had learnt songs like *Nkosi Sikelel' iAfrika* and sang it on the farm where she worked, 'When you sing it, the Boers ask you "'Ken jy daardie ding'" [do you know that thing?]. They did not like it. They would ask you why we sing that song.'[93] Modise Tsubane attended meetings in the town of Wolmaransstad and returned to his farm to tell his family about the ICU. After one meeting he mentioned, 'if we are staying on the farm with our span, we must divide the land in such a way that the white man have [sic] his own ploughing fields and the black man his own fields, and our livestock must graze in the same fields.'[94]

The ICU also used existent spatial connections to their advantage. Throughout the Western Transvaal, ICU meetings were often held strategically after AMEC's Sunday morning services. Members of the church used to 'walk directly across the way to a Union meeting', which were set up deliberately after the Sunday services. Selwane Legobathe remembered a meeting held by Jingoes in Bloemhof, 'It was the time we went for Holy Communion Service at Bloemhof. Now on the very same Sunday there was an ICU meeting. Now after our service we went to the meeting just to see'.[95] The ICU both used already existing connections and created new ones between town and farm. Local administrations in the Western Transvaal used the Native Urban Areas Act of 1923 and, in the case discussed below, outdated legislation to enforce urban segregation; they harassed workers for passes and 'special passes' and deliberately barred the ICU from holding meetings. In March 1929, Makhatini held a meeting in Schweizer-Reineke and was arrested and taken to the police station for contravening Proclamation No. 1787, an outdated law banning public meetings. The crowd who had attended the meeting marched 'in line' in support of Makhatini. Noticing their mood, Police Sergeant Wagner demanded they each produce their tax receipts and passes.[96] These actions further incensed the protesting crowd and forty black women began 'shouting, singing' and threw their shawls (headscarves) onto the ground. They pointed at the group of police who had arrested Makhatini, and, in the words of Sergeant Wagner, 'appeared to call on the powers that be to destroy us'.[97]

The locus of the ICU's political activism was in urban space. Lefebvre argues that while the 'the city and urban sphere are [...] the setting of struggle', they are also, 'the stakes of that struggle'.[98] The struggle over the right to be in urban space is predetermined to erupt in urban areas, 'as the appropriation of space, the development of the urban sphere, the metamorphosis of everyday life, and the transcendence of the conflictual split between city and country all clash heads with the state and with politics'.[99] The request by policemen to see farmworkers' passes was a deliberate means to enforce spatial segregation, and reminded those attending that their presence in urban space was conditional. By throwing their headscarves onto the ground, women in Schweizer-Reneke challenged their exclusion from urban space and is a vivid example of the 'conflictual split between city and country'. Evidence from throughout the country shows that the ICU was perceived as a threat by town administrations that sought to thwart its influence through the application of the pass law and other oppressive measures.[100] Despite repression, the ICU's meetings disrupted the spatial controls of local administrations in the Western Transvaal. The new spatial connections, like meetings, facilitated the movement of people and ideas between town and countryside and disrupted local administrations' control over urban space.

Conclusion

This chapter has used the ICU's experience in the Western Transvaal to generate an embedded and textured explanation for the ICU's longevity. 'The 'power of the spoken word' has been analysed in relation to its concomitant features: 1) the words, concepts and ideology of ICU's organisers; 2) the political form of meetings; and 3) the spatial effects of meetings. These features provide an account of the ICU's attraction which is embedded in the political economy of the Western Transvaal.

The ICU's languages of freedom, subversion and ridicule both gestured towards a new future and sharply critiqued oppression. Speaking to the oppression workers faced on farms, in towns and on diamond diggings, the ICU's appeals to freedom highlighted the need to end slavery, embrace self-determination, obtain economic freedom like better wages, have political representation and for black workers to be included in society on an equal basis. The ICU used subversive language which turned racial and class norms on their head, excavating the exploitative conditions workers faced and using clever language to highlight the need for greater equality. While to a certain extent relying on imported models of discourse and forms of language, the ICU managed to attract a constituency precisely because the ideals they were fighting for were both universal and at the same time relatable to the workers of the Western Transvaal.

The ICU in a few instances hosted public discussions which resembled a 'subaltern counter-public' and an 'issue public' which helped include black people in public discussion. The attendance of ICU meetings had an impact on the spatial politics of the Western Transvaal, which was characterised by the isolated farms governed by a paternalist and violent ethos and government repression in the towns. ICU organisers were able to partially disrupt spatial barriers between farm, town and location both through holding meetings and spreading its ideas.

In general, the ICU struggled to obtain a constituency that they could return to and their tenure in rural towns rarely lasted longer than two years. As ICU organisers moved between towns, their sharp use of language, democratic ideology and a disruption of spatial norms helped attract a transitory constituency. The 'enduring attraction' of the ICU lasted long beyond the ICU's physical presence in the Western Transvaal; all of the interviews included in this chapter were conducted in the 1980s, at least 40 years after the ICU ceased to exist in organisational form. The colourful memories of the ICU's activism point towards the lasting ideological imprint and the relevance of the ICU not least for the 1980s, but today too.

8 The ICU in Port Elizabeth: The Making of a Union-Cum-Protest Movement, 1920–1931

Noor Nieftagodien

Introduction

Port Elizabeth in 1919–1920 was an important locale of black working-class struggles as African and coloured workers campaigned for wage increases and established the Port Elizabeth Amalgamated Industrial and Commercial Coloured and Native Workmen's Union (PEAICCNWU), the first of its kind in the town. The union became the local branch of the ICU and grew exponentially by recruiting members and supporters from various sectors of the local black population. It was then the largest branch in the country. At its origins, therefore, the local ICU was not a conventional trade union but combined characteristics of unions and protest movements. This chapter examines the salient and distinctive characteristics of the ICU in Port Elizabeth and explains its evolution as a union-cum-protest movement in three phases: its effervescent founding as a union (1919–1920), the years of decline and stagnation (1921–1926) and its revival as a protest movement (1927–1931). The ICU's longevity in Port Elizabeth, with considerable support, albeit unevenly across this period, was quite remarkable and challenges the standard view that the movement had disintegrated by the late 1920s.[1] The chapter thus argues against the conventional 'rise and fall' narrative of the ICU and emphasises its role as *the* movement of popular black protests at the time, operating in increasingly difficult political and economic conditions. It was a resistance movement in the making, without any local historical precedents, that pioneered popular protest politics in the region.

Following two years of rapid growth after its establishment, the local branch experienced a period of crisis, seemingly reflecting the trajectory of growth and decline of the national organisation. Various explanations have been posited to account for the problems of the ICU, directed mainly at the perceived weaknesses of its leadership: their financial profligacy, elitism and petty bourgeois background, dictatorial tendencies and inability to formulate effective strategy and tactics.[2] Among the most insightful critiques has been that the ICU failed as a trade union. Communist Party of South Africa (CPSA) member and leading historian of the period, Edward Roux, argued that the ICU's unwillingness to organise mass 'direct action', particularly strikes, against unjust laws prevented the organisation from registering any discernible gains for workers.[3] A generation later, prominent labour historian and unionist, Phil Bonner, criticised the ICU's 'neglect of industrial organisation' and ascribed its ultimate failure to the leadership who prematurely pursued a political strategy before developing an effective trade union strategy.[4]

Baines and Cherry, the leading scholars on Port Elizabeth's working class and movements in this period, have advanced a similar line of argument.[5]

These critical assessments of the ICU are mostly valid but their common framing around an analysis of its rise and decline as a union tends to obscure its evolving character. Launched as a trade union to campaign for a minimum wage, jobs and an eight-hour day, by the mid-1920s, the ICU had been transformed into a popular protest movement that articulated multiple grievances of the oppressed: such as for higher wages, against land dispossession, passes and liquor raids.[6] In her seminal study, Bradford argued that the ICU became the political home of tens of thousands of African rural dwellers, working class and petty bourgeoisie, brought together around the struggle against the national oppression of African people.[7] The ICU's politics and forms of protests were shaped by local circumstances, that is, the socioeconomic character of particular places. Port Elizabeth's distinctive processes of industrialisation and urbanisation, and the consequent nature of its working class, determined both the ICU's core membership and the grievances that animated its protests. African male labourers, who were low paid and precarious, were the primary constituency of the organisation, but coloured workers also joined its ranks. With black workers at its core, the local branch campaigned for improved minimum wages throughout the 1920s. The ICU also mobilised against various unjust laws, which caused other residents from the main locations (Korsten and New Brighton) to rally behind it. Crucially, public assemblies were the main site of its popular protests, attracting thousands of black residents, who participated in its production of nascent emancipatory politics, over a period of more than a decade.

Working-class town

Founded in 1820 as a redoubt of British colonialism in the Eastern Cape, Port Elizabeth from the mid-nineteenth century developed into the Cape Province's leading commercial and financial hub. In the period from 1850 to 1880, the town eclipsed the more established and populous Cape Town in terms of export trade, and was acknowledged as the 'Liverpool of the Cape'.[8] Thereafter, it experienced several years of decline due, in part, to the vagaries of the pastoral economy and inadequate development of the harbour.[9] But this trend was reversed during the First World War when new investment in manufacturing inaugurated a phase of substantial economic expansion.[10] Between 1916/17 and 1919/20 the number of industrial establishments increased by 16% causing industrial employment to grow by 20% compared to the national average of 11%.[11] Footwear and textiles were the main sectors in the 1920s and 1930s, accounting for 34% and 43% of industrial employment respectively in 1920/21 and 1935/36.[12] However, the most significant new development in the town was the establishment in the mid-1920s of car manufacturing plants by the multinational companies, Ford and General Motors. A decade later this sector accounted for more than a third of the town's net output[13] and employed about 6 000 workers.[14] Port Elizabeth, according to Adler, in this period transformed from the 'Liverpool of the Cape' to the 'Detroit of South Africa'.[15]

These processes contributed to the town's distinctive working-class character. From its inception, Port Elizabeth attracted a high number of white workers from various parts of the British Empire. White male workers remained the main source of labour in the secondary economy well into the first half of the twentieth century.[16] Black labour was initially recruited from the surrounding Khoi and Mfengu communities and from the mid-nineteenth century also from a steady influx of coloureds from Cape Town.[17] The colonial wars of conquest introduced a profound change in labour supply as larger numbers of Xhosa people were forced into wage labour.[18] Post-war industrialisation caused the town's population to nearly double between 1921 (82 000) and 1936 (151 000). Although the African population rose by more than 100% in the same period (from 22 000 to 46 300), whites remained the majority until the 1950s, while the coloured population was also relatively high, numbering 35 200 in 1936.[19] A significant proportion of the town's population was permanently urbanised, an important indicator of which was that the ratio of men to women was close to 1:1, reflecting a considerably higher rate of female urbanisation than other industrial towns.[20] The presence of large numbers of settled black workers and their families created a strong sense of belonging in the urban space, thus engendering claims to the city, manifested in demands for higher wages, jobs and housing.[21]

In the second half of the nineteenth century, black workers – African and coloured – organised several strikes to demand higher wages, often winning concessions from employers.[22] White workers began to establish craft unions (eg. printers, engineers and bricklayers) in the 1880s and 1890s,[23] which excluded black workers. Community-based protests began to emerge in the early twentieth century, principally against the planned removal of Africans to the newly established segregated location of New Brighton.[24] Largely spontaneous, this was one of the earliest struggles by urban blacks against forced removals and segregation. At the same time, the town's nascent black petty bourgeoisie (teachers, priests, interpreters and small-scale business owners) established *Imbumba Yama Afrika* to unite Africans to struggle for national rights. Predisposed to moderate politics and to advance their own interests, the elite focused on making representations to the authorities on voters' registration, limiting the issuing of canteen licences and for the establishment of a 'native' management board.[25] Members of this group became involved in the African National Congress (ANC) and dominated black politics in Port Elizabeth in the early twentieth century.

Worker militancy and the birth of the ICU

A new, more radical politics exploded onto the political landscape at the end of the First World War and transformed black protest. Adverse socioeconomic conditions caused by the war, particularly high inflation, triggered a wave of strikes across the country. The Witwatersrand was the epicentre of strikes for higher wages by black workers, notably municipal, railway and mine employees.[26] Similar conditions pertained in Port Elizabeth where the minimum wage of 4s a day for African workers was lower than their real income at the start of the war.[27] A campaign for higher wages launched in 1918 got off to a tepid start with only 35 African and coloured workers going on strike. The following year, however, the number of black workers involved in industrial action surged to 2 708. Municipal workers led these struggles and in July established the Port Elizabeth Municipal Coloured and Native Employees Association. Their successful strike inspired railway and harbours workers to threaten strike action, which immediately won them a wage increase.[28]

The strikes of 1919 were notable for a few reasons. They involved mostly unskilled and low-paid workers in the public sector, who were especially hard hit by inflation. The establishment of a union gave organisational expression to the existing class unity among black workers and was an early manifestation of non-racialism. Although these struggles started at different workplaces – municipality, harbour and railways – the locus of mobilisation soon shifted to the black locations where workers and other residents could meet in large numbers to protest and organise solidarity. The high cost of living adversely affected the black population in general, which explains the broad appeal of the minimum wage campaign. Importantly, the strikes marked a qualitative shift in the contestation between the black population and white authorities in the town, which reached a climax the following year.

In January 1920, two meetings, each reportedly attended by approximately 4 000 people, resolved to demand a minimum wage of 10s per day for black workers and to back this up with a general strike. This figure represented nearly 20% of the town's total black population, a remarkable and unprecedented demonstration of power of the emerging black working class. In order to give greater effect to the mobilisation, workers formed the PEAICCNWU, which claimed a membership in excess of 4 000 and printed more than 12 000 membership cards.[29] Undoubtedly overambitious, it symbolised the enthusiasm and confidence of the moment. Samuel Masabalala, a former teacher and clerk at an insurance company,[30] emerged as the popular leader of this movement. He, Clements Kadalie and Selby Msimang convened the July 1920 conference where the Industrial and Commercial Coloured and Native Workers' (Amalgamated) Union of Africa (ICWU) was founded. The PEAICCNWU affiliated to the ICWU and was renamed the Port Elizabeth Industrial and Commercial Workers' Union of Africa (Port Elizabeth ICWU).[31] It was the first mass-based popular protest movement of the town's black working class and, in pursuing the plan for a general strike, demonstrated its willingness to mobilise the collective power of its constituency to win concessions from the white authorities.

Encouraged by the July conference's endorsement of the demand for a minimum wage of eight shillings for an eight-hour day, Masabalala returned to Port Elizabeth with new energy to mobilise for the proposed general strike. The authorities were alarmed by both the renewed campaign and the popularity of Masabalala whom they labelled a radical agitator. As the date for the action approached, they struck a pre-emptive blow by arresting Masabalala on 23 October 1920. People were outraged and immediately marched to the centre where nearly 3 000 gathered outside the police station to demand his release. White society found this intolerable and was determined to quash this unprecedented expression of black working-class power in the town. Police and white residents opened fire on the protesters, killing 24 people and injuring 126. The massacre sent shockwaves through the town's black population and many reportedly fled the city out of fear. Approximately 30 000 people attended the funeral.[32] It also marked a turning point in the history of the ICU in the town.

Disarray ensued in the Port Elizabeth ICWU. The popular wage campaign was violently smashed and no further mobilisation took place on this front. Angered by the Smuts government's role in the massacre, Masabalala declared his support for J.B.M. Hertzog's National Party in the 1921 election, a contentious statement that caused some consternation in the ranks of the union. The national union deployed Msimang to Port Elizabeth to mediate between the union and white authorities, which intervention was rejected by Masabalala.[33] At the 1921 national conference, Masabalala therefore sided with Kadalie against Msimang, and later that year the two of them convened a conference to constitute a new ICU. This caused a split in the Port Elizabeth branch with the majority joining the newly established ICU. Masabalala was riding the crest of a wave of popularity and was appointed Organiser-in-Chief of the ICU, requiring him to relocate to Cape Town. By 1924, however, poor organisational abilities and personality clashes with other leaders led to his dismissal. Attempts to revive his role as a leader in Port Elizabeth failed and he quickly receded into obscurity.[34] Masabalala's demise seemed to reflect the fortunes of the ICU in Port Elizabeth. At the 1923 national conference, Kadalie complained about the 'desperate muddle' in the branch.[35] The only notable activity was the annual commemoration of the massacre: in 1921, a reported 10 000 people participated in a procession to the cemetery but the following year only 4 000 people attended the event.[36] While these commemorations reflected deep anger among black people and demonstrated widespread support for the ICU, there is little evidence of sustained public activities thereafter.

In the doldrums, 1921–1926

Besides the debilitating effect of the shootings, the ICU had to contend with structural challenges to the unionisation of African workers. Industrial expansion and the concomitant growth of the working class did not lead to a qualitative change in the strategic position of African workers, who, in 1925, constituted only 19% of the town's workforce and mainly as unskilled labour in the municipality, harbour, railways and stores. By comparison, coloureds and whites constituted 29% and 52% respectively of the workforce.[37] Whites usually occupied skilled and semi-skilled jobs but from the mid-1920s they, especially the growing number of Afrikaners, received preferential access to unskilled posts under the 'civilised labour policy'. Companies in the rapidly expanding motor industry prided 'themselves on being able to market vehicles assembled wholly by white labour'.[38] By 1935 the car industry employed 5 400 whites compared to the miserly number of 600 Africans.[39] The other major sectors of the town's economy, leather and food, only employed 800 Africans compared to 1 600 coloureds.[40] Furthermore, the increase of the African population in the 1920s meant more competition for unskilled jobs, making it easier for employers to use the threat of dismissals to enforce workplace acquiescence. The Industrial Conciliation

Act of 1924 excluded Africans from the definition of employee, making it even harder to unionise them. Objectively, therefore, African workers, who comprised the overwhelming membership of the ICU, were in a relatively weak position in the labour market, especially in the secondary industries.

Operating from Korsten and New Brighton, the ICU was able to recruit workers and other residents, which contributed to its initial growth as a general union-cum-protest movement. But in the 1920s, the state sought to tighten restrictions in black urban locations. The Native (Urban) Areas Act of 1923 was the pivotal piece of legislation that paved the way for the establishment of municipal locations under the administration of white officials. In her study of the state's 'location strategy', Robinson examined the various technologies of control instituted by the Port Elizabeth City Council (PECC) after it brought New Brighton under its jurisdiction.[41] Headmen became peace officers and acted as auxiliaries to the municipal police, thus playing an important role in maintaining law and order in the locations. Among their responsibilities was the monitoring of rent payments and registration cards, which determined access to the fenced-off location.[42] This system of surveillance created challenges for political mobilisation in New Brighton. By contrast, Korsten was not subjected to the same administrative restrictions and, consequently, became the main site of the ICU's activities in the 1920s. According to Baines, the PECC prided itself for its 'exemplary treatment of its African population', especially in relation to its more liberal attitude to influx control.[43] Yet, the 1920 shootings and the application of the 1923 Act demonstrated a commitment to segregate and control the black population, reflecting the national process of the consolidation of the white state.

In addition to these external challenges, the local ICU was beleaguered by internal crises, particularly in respect of membership and finances. Organisers continually exhorted attendees at meetings to join because, as one of them warned, 'The ICU will not come to your assistance even if you are sacked without a good reason if you do not become its financial member.' Branch membership was estimated to be between 300 and 600, but only 40 paid subscriptions regularly.[44] Routine financial appeals at meetings and fundraising activities such as bazaars, dances and tea-meetings rarely produced the desired outcome. As a result, the branch was dependent on the cash-strapped national office to pay for its full-time secretary. Allegations of financial irregularities surfaced regularly and in 1927, James Dippa, a leading member, was accused of borrowing money in the ICU's name to set up the Alexandra Native Land Settlements, a scheme designed for him to own land in that township. At the same time, the branch was unable to repay a debt of £70.[45] A year later and after months of not receiving a salary, Henry Blaauw resigned as the branch secretary.[46] Even during periods of heightened activity, the local branch could not raise sufficient funds to address the challenges.

The ICU leadership itself expressed serious doubt about the vitality of the branch and in September 1926 dispatched James La Guma (General Secretary of the ICU) and Alex P. Maduna (Provincial Secretary of the OFS) 'to investigate the cause of the apathy of this Branch, which is getting from bad to worse, financially and otherwise'.[47] Reflecting on the challenges faced by the local ICU after 1920, Baines and Cherry emphasised the inactivity and decline of the organisation, concluding that it was a 'spent force' by the end of the decade.[48] As suggested earlier, their insightful assessments are based mostly on the ICU being a trade union and focuses on the early years of its existence in Port Elizabeth. Yet, even during the period of stagnation, the ICU continued to hold meetings, albeit only episodically. Considering the problems faced by the branch, it is quite remarkable that it retained broad support and continued to be the focal point of black protest. This became more evident from 1927 when the ICU became the conduit for renewed protests by black workers and other residents of the locations.

Emancipatory assemblies

The ICU's activities in Port Elizabeth centred on public meetings that served two overarching purposes: as spaces of expression of popular dissent and as the foundational unit in the organisational architecture of the movement. Usually convened at the Kopjie, an open area in Korsten, meetings were attended by a variety of groups from a relatively small core of paid-up members to non-paying members, general supporters, curious onlookers and police spies. Working class Africans were the principal constituency in these meetings, while coloureds and the petty bourgeoisie seemed to be intermittently involved, although a few of the local leaders were coloured. There is some evidence of the presence of women but they appear as only peripheral actors in meetings. In May 1927, Maduna's wife announced her intention to start a Women's Committee but nothing seemed to have come from this initiative. For most of the period under discussion, meetings occurred irregularly and with uneven attendance, ranging from a few dozen to several hundred. However, the size and frequency of meetings increased, sometimes sharply, when particular grievances ignited widespread indignation and a desire for collective responses. For example, numerous meetings were convened in 1927 as concerns over the Hertzog Bills and struggles for higher wages triggered protests. Up to 600 people attended these meetings, confirming their role as the main spaces for popular mobilisation and emulating the successes of ICU public gatherings throughout the country.

Meetings were popular assemblies where location residents, excluded from the formal political structures, convened to express opposition to various injustices perpetrated by the white minority government. Grievances vented in the meetings ranged from local regulations (permits, beer raids), to national policies (Hertzog Bills, the 'civilised labour policy'), and bread-and-butter issues (wages, jobs, housing). As such, they were the pre-eminent 'sites of contestation'[49] that engendered a sense of collective purpose and mobilisation. The ICU was, of course, not the first to organise protest meetings of black residents in the town, but its assemblies marked a break from the routines sanctioned by the elites.[50] Meetings convened by the local black elite mainly served to channel the concerns of the small number of eligible voters and petty bourgeois to the authorities via appeals and petitions, rather than through confrontations. ICU meetings, by contrast, drew in broader sectors of black society, particularly the working class, and deliberately produced militant and popular collective action.[51] ICU leaders were regarded as fearless critics of white authority, who were prepared to speak truth to power by using indignant language of protest that resonated with the oppressed.

The militancy of ICU protests was particularly evident in the oratory of its leaders, whose speeches were often flamboyant, theatrical, belligerent and infused with radical rhetoric.[52] Maduna played the role of orator-in-chief at local public meetings and proved adept at tapping into the prevailing mood of the local black population. Audiences enthusiastically applauded his verbal assaults against various opponents. Whites were ostracised as 'uncivilised and immoral' because they benefited from the 'civilised labour policy' at the expense of blacks. The Hertzog Bills were lambasted as a 'diabolical policy... out to exterminate the Natives from the face of the earth'.[53] Moderate black leaders were not spared his sharp tongue and even local church leaders who refrained from actively supporting the ICU were castigated: 'I hate ministers, they are filthy persons who misled the people'.[54] For Bonner, the ability of ICU orators to 'rouse passions, to voice anger, to stir indignation' was a crucial reason for the popularity of the meeting.[55] It certainly provides some explanation for the ICU's support in the locations.

ICU leaders also used meetings to articulate the movement's nascent emancipatory politics: a composite protest ideology, drawing inspiration from a variety of political sources, especially nationalism, Garveyism and communism.[56] Various leaders emphasised different aspects of the movement's eclectic ideology, depending on the salience of particular grievances and their own political predispositions. However, the organisation mainly embodied a 'diffuse African nationalism' that expressed the national political interest of the African majority.[57] Thus the constant clarion call of meetings was for unity of the oppressed against white minority rule. Although the main appeal was for 'Natives to unite', in Port Elizabeth, leaders such as Maduna, urged 'Natives and coloureds' to unite. When struggles around wages pre-occupied the ICU, his speeches reflected a distinct communist influence, such as in the February 1927 warning to the government: 'General Hertzog is out to bring a revolution similar to the one which was brought about in Russia in 1917. We are going to revolt not against the government, but against the system of the government'.[58] Two months later, he introduced his speech thus, 'I am prepared to speak this afternoon on *down with the capitalists and bloodsuckers, we want our freedom and country*', and proceeded to deride the government's exploitation of black people.[59] Karl Fredericks, another local organiser, was also enamoured of socialism and for a period concluded meetings with renditions of the *Red Flag*. Communist politics co-existed with religious and millenarian ideas. When local leader, Louis Frans, told a meeting 'the ICU is the greatest church in the world', the audience greeted him with rapturous applause.[60] Joel Magade promised his audience '[t]he ICU wagon is on the way to the Land of Promise...the ICU is your God'.[61] A few months later, he appealed to blacks to unite behind the ICU 'if you want God to listen to your complaints'.[62] This was a common refrain as the ICU struggled with recruitment and fees. Thus, Louis Frans warned a crowd: 'those of you who have not taken membership tickets shall have to do so now, if, you do not do so, you will answer before God for not having made proper provisions for your children.'[63] Although their speeches articulated varied beliefs, local leaders conveyed an overarching political message of dissent that sought to mobilise the ICU's constituencies behind common grievances and promises of alternative futures.

Local gatherings were also pivotal nodal points in the national network of protest meetings that constituted the lifeblood of the movement. Being public in nature and therefore not limited to paid-up members, these assemblies created political connections among large numbers of black people across the country. They were spaces where the political horizons of participants could transcend local preoccupations by simply learning about struggles elsewhere and expressing solidarity with fellow protesters. There were regular reports on ICU activities (mostly its successes), repression by the government and Kadalie's national and international travels. Reports in the *Workers' Herald* also augmented these national connections and contributed to forging an ICU community with broadly shared ideas and purposes. A signal achievement of the ICU was the creation of a national (and sub-regional) protest movement. However, these assemblies were also spatially circumscribed, at least in so far as the protests were mostly confined to the meetings themselves and were rarely translated into political activity beyond the geographic limits of the black locations. The power and militancy generated in these meetings tended to dissipate immediately afterwards rather than being directly channelled to white authorities through, for example, marches, occupations, strikes and memoranda of demands, which constitute the repertoire of social movements' collective action.[64] As a result, and particularly in the late 1920s, the state could afford to ignore most protests because they rarely posed a direct threat. But the authorities remained sufficiently concerned about the ICU to subject it to various forms of repression.

Meetings also played a role in the internal life of the ICU as the foundational space where members and supporters could engage on organisational matters, such as finances, membership and recruitment. Leaders reported on their work in relation to these and other issues, which introduced a degree of accountability to their audiences. Assemblies, often attended by hundreds of location residents, thus contained elements of democratic praxes that characterised new social movements from the 1990s. However, these participatory impulses remained attenuated, as meetings were quite conventional: male leaders dominated proceedings by delivering lengthy orations and reports. In this format, limited opportunities existed for audience participation, although members sometimes harangued leaders with whom they disagreed. These practices reflected the hierarchical relations in the organisation, characterised by a discernible division between a layer of leaders (mostly paid full-timers) and the rank-and-file, reinforced by the fact that the former were often from the ranks of the educated petty bourgeois.[65]

Maduna apparently owned a sizeable house in the Orange Free State and expected similar accommodation in Port Elizabeth. James Dippa, another local leader who was a former mine clerk and later also served on the Advisory Board, made numerous applications for an eating-house. On the other hand, Louis Frans, earned just over £1 for a six-day working week.[66] From the mid-1920s, the union's organisers had become paid officials at levels at least a third higher than the average African mine worker, which, Bradford argued, distanced them from members and opened opportunities for them to climb the social ladder.[67] Concerned about the poor state of the local branch, the national office deployed organisers to the town with the aim of reviving activities. Alex P. Maduna, Karl Fredericks and Joel Magade acted as the representatives of the national leadership with a mandate to resolve internal organisation problems, mainly recruitment of members and the payment of monthly dues. In this sense, they served mainly as a conduit of leaders from the national headquarters, which, in the late 1920s, was pre-occupied with addressing internal challenges, rather than as local leaders of a protest movement.

Reflecting on the 'core practice in the ICU's method' in rural areas, Bradford argued that the mass meetings held transitory attraction, 'followed by dispersal into isolated units without any lasting organisational legacy'.[68] This is a crucial insight that applies to the ICU's activities nationally and points to its inability to create meaningful and sustained organisations, least of all union structures in workplaces, relying instead on ephemeral expressions of power in meetings. Nonetheless, sustained mobilisation occurred when regular meetings were convened to protest on a variety of issues, which transformed the nature of resistance in locations. As discussed in the following section, this was evident in Port Elizabeth during 1927-1928.

New waves of protest, 1927-1928

New energy was injected into the local ICU from early 1927 as a number of grievances emerged that punctured the relative quiescence of the preceding period and produced unprecedented protests by sections of the black population. Inevitably, perhaps, ICU meetings became the primary site of the surge in black resistance, triggered by widespread opposition to Hertzog's infamous Native Bills of 1926. The first protest in Port Elizabeth against the Bills involved a few hundred coloured residents who met on 18 January 1927 to reject the threat to disenfranchise them.[69] It is unclear from the records under whose auspices the meeting was organised but the fact that it was held in the City Hall would suggest that it was not one of the main black opposition organisations. The day after, however, the ICU effectively assumed the leadership of the local campaign when it announced a protest march. Suddenly rejuvenated, it organised seven meetings in ten days, each attended by between 400 and 500 black residents, reflecting the widespread dissatisfaction with the proposed Bills. The opposition movement culminated on 30 January in a march of approximately 400 people to the Post Office, a rare occasion when an ICU protest transcended the parameters of a public meeting and aimed at directly confronting the authorities with a clear demand. However, the campaign quickly lost momentum because local leaders were seemingly disappointed by a lower than expected turn-out. Their negative assessment of the march probably stemmed from a defeatist approach to the possibility of persuading the government to change course. Karl Fredericks told a meeting in 1928 that the passage of the Native Bills was inevitable,[70] an explicit acknowledgement of the ICU's lack of capacity to sustain a political campaign in the face of a recalcitrant government that had become increasingly dismissive of black opinion. Nonetheless, the short-lived burst of activity contributed to the reactivation of the local ICU and the mobilisation especially of workers.

Throughout 1927 and 1928, ICU public meetings once again became important platforms to campaign for improved wages for unskilled African workers who earned half that of their white counterparts. In 1929, African labourers earned a mere 3/- a day, which even employers conceded was too low.[71] Although ICU leaders were behind the demand for an improved minimum wage, their support seemed conditional on workers becoming members:

> ... we are here this afternoon for the purpose of getting better wages for every non-European worker of Port Elizabeth. If you join our union and become a member, we shall see that you get three good meals a day, a good suit of clothes, a decent house to live in and a good decent education for your children.[72]

The ICU's support for improved minimum wages generated considerable enthusiasm and led to the convening of regular gatherings, the main purpose behind which seemed to be to gain access to the Wages Board hearings. Speaking to an audience of more than 400 in March 1927, Kadalie explained that the promulgation of the Wages Act 'was good because it allowed the ICU to campaign for higher wages.'[73] This approach was not without merit, as the successful appeals to the Wages Board hearings in Bloemfontein and East London attested.[74] More than a year later Magade reiterated the basic stance of the ICU on this matter: 'General Hertzog may be very bad but he did one good thing by passing the Wages Act... If you join the Union today, I can get you more money from your employers, and if they refuse to accede to our demands we can involve the aid of the Wages Board.'[75] When the Wages Board sat in Port Elizabeth in 1928, expectations were high that the ICU's campaign for a minimum wage of 6s/6d a day for African workers, double the existing rate, would bear fruit. Hundreds of workers and supporters packed ICU meetings for several weeks hoping the authorities would notice their presence in large numbers and the fiery oratory of the leaders. Despite appeals to the Wages Board, there is no evidence of the ICU having attended the sittings. In fact, the Wages Board was principally concerned with wages of white workers and effectively ignored the conditions of African labourers. The rebuff by the Wages Board was a serious blow to workers and the local ICU, whose campaign rested almost entirely on being able to make representations to the Board. The absence of an alternative strategy to mobilise workers in a campaign aimed directly at employers highlighted the ICU's limited capacity to act as a trade union. Although the protracted mobilisation was a significant achievement, it also underscored both the ICU's strategic weaknesses and the precarious position of African labour in the local economy.

The ICU's response to the implementation of 'Civilised Labour Policy' in the local public sector revealed similar shortcomings. In February 1927, the PECC started replacing black domestic workers with white women in hospitals and schools,[76] and in May, it was reported that black workers in the municipality and harbour were being replaced by white workers. African workers were understandably incensed and turned to the ICU for assistance. Local leaders, such as branch secretary, Blaauw, lambasted the government's 'diabolical' policy and vowed that '[t]he ICU will see that not a single person who is its member is dismissed from work without a reason'.[77] To the disappointment of workers, he reported a week later that lawyers had advised the case of the dismissed workers could not be won because they were daily or weekly paid. In other words, unskilled African workers were dispensable and the ICU was too weak to defend their jobs. Faced by these challenges, the ICU effectively retreated from an issue that adversely affected the position of African labour in the local economy.

In November 1927, harbour workers went on strike against the management's decision to increase their work day by half an hour to ten and half hours (55 hours a week). On November 6, Alexander Ntantiso, a member of the ICU and apparent leader of the strikers, attended a public meeting to appeal for support.[78] Interestingly, he reportedly cautioned against the strike but workers ignored his advice and were determined to flex their collective muscle against the arbitrary intensification of their exploitation. Not surprisingly, they turned to the ICU for solidarity. On two consecutive days more than 700 people, mainly strikers and their supporters, attended the public meetings in solidarity with the workers. But, as had become customary, the local leaders baulked at the prospect of endorsing the strike and reiterated the standard refrain that they could only support workers who were members of the organisation. Blaauw also advised workers to postpone their action to allow Kadalie to travel to the town to assist them. Evidently, the local leaders lacked the confidence to engage in industrial action and deferred to Kadalie's messianic authority which they hoped would force employers to accede to the workers' demand. The proposed intervention did not materialise and, as a result, the workers called off their strike without achieving any concession from the employers.[79]

These events brought into sharp relief the ICU's reticence about strikes, which contrasted with its enthusiasm for workers' struggles in the early period. Kadalie, in 1923, articulated this core characteristic of the union:

> If we have to succeed, we must form ourselves into 'One-Big-Union'. It is just as natural, therefore, that I should present to the workers a real, live, active organisation, which will work, if you will work, fight, if you will fight and which has never turned its back on the enemy.[80]

While such pugilistic rhetoric remained a staple of the ICU's oratory, in the late 1920s, a more conciliatory tone began to emerge that, in fact, shaped the organisation's praxis. This was evident in Tyamzashe's polemical riposte to Edward Roux's criticism of the ICU's lack of militancy. 'The strike weapon', he wrote in the *Workers' Herald* in 1928, 'is only used as a last resort'. This basic observation about trade unionism was, however, lost in a convoluted justification for opposing strikes. According to Tyamzashe, 'no employer or employee should be proud of a strike because it means that there is something rotten somewhere, either on the side of the employers or employees'. Trade unions, he opined, 'should not "look for" or "manufacture" strikes' and it was therefore commendable that the ICU had only used the strike weapon on three occasions since 1919.[81] The retreat from confrontation with authorities also affected the ICU's approach to the poll tax. Depressed wages and growing unemployment caused an increase in the number of Africans defaulting on poll tax payments.[82] In November 1926, 20 people were reportedly arrested for non-payment in one day,[83] a trend that continued in 1927 and 1928. Harry Schultz, a prominent figure in the local branch, sought to link non-payment to low wages, and appealed for unity to fight for higher wages. Again, however, rhetoric did not translate into action, and the ICU eventually appealed to people to pay the poll tax. Maduna even admitted to having paid his poll tax in January 1927.[84]

After nearly two years of campaigning on the issue of minimum wages, the ICU's strategy of relying on protest meetings failed to yield positive results. In 1928, after the national conference, an ordinary member pointedly asked the ICU to give an account of what it had done for members in Port Elizabeth. Confounded by the implicit critique, the meeting remained silent for about two minutes and the local leaders failed to respond.[85] This was in sharp contrast to the vocal protests that usually characterised ICU meetings. An impasse had been reached, causing workers to retreat from the organisation. When the level of African wages again became a contentious issue in 1929, workers ignored the ICU and met directly with the employers. The Council agreed to introduce a marginal increase in the minimum wage for the approximately 1 000 unskilled African municipal labourers but excluded employees of the railways and harbours.[86] It was not until the 1940s that African workers managed to organise trade unions to challenge their precarious status in the local economy. At its founding, the ICU united African and coloured workers but following the 1920 massacre and the decline of unionisation, many semi-skilled coloured workers joined craft unions.[87] This fracturing along racial lines further weakened the local ICU and it seemed, therefore, to have reached the end of the road.

Independent ICU

On the 10 February 1929, 234 attendees at a local ICU gathering heard that Kadalie had resigned, which news Magade dismissed as a false rumour spread by newspapers.[88] A month later, pandemonium erupted when a meeting of 500 people received a report of Kadalie's expulsion from the ICU. All those who spoke expressed strong support for Kadalie. For example, Johnnie Jacobs received enthusiastic applause when he addressed himself to the national leadership: 'We say to you tonight, we want Mr. Kadalie reinstated as General Secretary. Failing to do so, we shall secede from the old ICU and join the new ICU formed by Mr. Kadalie known as the Independent ICU [IICU].' Similar approval met Magade's report that a number of branches had already joined Kadalie. A member of the audience, Walter Mbokoto, waved his *kierie* at Magade saying he was fortunate to support Kadalie otherwise he would have received a good thrashing.[89] After some discussion, it was resolved: 'That this meeting of the PE branch of the ICU ask that Mr. Kadalie be immediately reinstated as General Secretary of the ICU failing to accede to this request this Branch pledges itself to join the IICU led by Mr. Kadalie'.[90] The resolution was unanimously endorsed, and the atmosphere was punctuated with shouts of: 'Away with Ballinger and his loafers!' The meeting signalled the death knell of the ICU and the birth of the IICU in Port Elizabeth. The old ICU quickly disappeared from the local scene, but there was also little evidence of the IICU maintaining the protest activity of the previous period, which reflected the general malaise of the organisation. Then, after nearly two years of inactivity, a sudden and short burst of mobilisation erupted under the banner of the new organisation. In February 1931, approximately 1 000 people attended a meeting, the biggest in more than a decade, to listen to a report by Magade about the strike in East London the previous year. Korsten residents expressed their anger and solidarity with the striking workers. Although this act of solidarity was remarkable, the large number of number of people in attendance probably had more to do with the mounting anger over the deteriorating conditions in the location and the state's increasingly robust efforts to assert control over its residents.

Korsten was established in the late nineteenth century outside the jurisdiction of the Port Elizabeth municipality, and from 1902, fell under the control of a Village Management Board. The location escaped the surveillance that characterised the administration of New Brighton, but the absence of municipal control also resulted in a neglect of housing provision and social services.[91] By 1930, Korsten was terribly overcrowded[92] and the Native Economic Commission (1930-1932) reported that 'Living conditions in some parts were indescribably filthy and insanitary. Most of the houses or shanties are built of wood and iron, the latter term including rusty paraffin tins. The area is very much overcrowded'.[93] Together with Korsten's 'racial mixing' and propensity to protest, these derogatory observations could have been applied to freehold locations across the country. Perceived as troublesome spaces, they represented a visible challenge to the state's objectives of imposing segregation and control in urban areas. Few issues caused the authorities greater consternation than the proliferation of domestic beer brewing, in which women were the main actors. In Korsten, a combination of population growth and increased unemployment made beer brewing an important source of income for African women, who found it even harder than their male counterparts to establish a foothold in the formal economy. In the mid-1920s, the PECC had approved the introduction of beerhalls to undermine domestic beer brewing but abandoned the plan after widespread protests against beerhalls, especially in Durban. However, from the late 1920s, it began more deliberately to formulate plans to bring Korsten under control and in 1931, announced its intention to incorporate the location into the municipality and to remove its African residents. As part of this process the authorities stepped up raids against illegal beer brewing which it regarded as 'the chief cause of lawlessness in Korsten'. These raids were a constant source of friction between the community and law enforcement, and in early February 1931, triggered a large-scale protest. On the morning of 7 February 1931, according to a report by Sergeant Johnston, 69 police took part in the raid, including some reinforcements from other areas. They destroyed 6 000 gallons of beer and arrested 39 people on various charges, including illegal brewing, non-payment of the poll tax and one for assaulting the police during the raid. Johnston expressed the hope that this raid would discredit the 'agitators' because there was no resistance to the raid.[94]

His sanguine assessment of the raid was certainly premature. There may not have been immediate resistance but the raid angered the Korsten community. Despite its weaknesses, the IICU was able, briefly, to become the community's vehicle of protest. On the 20 February 1931 Harry Schultz, now a local leader of the IICU, organised a meeting of 120 people and appealed to them to bring their complaints to the IICU so that it could ensure that the police responsible for the raid be removed from the police station. For good measure, he reiterated the demand for an improved daily minimum wage (of 4s/6d).[95] Two days later 3 000 people attended a protest meeting. Two more meetings of 300 (at Hills Kraal) and 800 (at the Tsabalala Hall) were held on the same day.[96] Together they constituted the single biggest protest by black residents against Port Elizabeth's white authorities since the campaign for higher wages in 1920 and reflected the mounting indignation over the state's plans for Korsten. But this mass mobilisation proved to be short-lived and unravelled due to internecine political disputes. Although the IICU seemed to be the prime movers behind the convening of these mass meetings, an ANC representative (Mvalo) insisted that he wanted to address the crowds. Although the organisers objected, the audience supported his right to do so, but it turned out to be disastrous as he devoted his speech to attacking the leadership of the IICU as being thieves and liars. The ensuing public squabble caused all the meetings to end in disarray and effectively ended any prospect of an organised response to the liquor raids. What may have signalled the beginning of a third period of ICU-led protests, ended in an ignominious collapse of the IICU and, conversely, strengthened the hand of the authorities. In 1932, it was reported that in a period of only four months the police destroyed about 25 711 gallons of beer. Unlike in the previous year, no resistance materialised. Two years later, Kadalie held a few meetings in Port Elizabeth. No more than 40 people attended with Kadalie reportedly drunk at one meeting, after which the authorities warned him to leave the city.[97] After this, there are no records of the ICU's presence in the town.

Conclusion

In the end, the Port Elizabeth branch of the ICU did fall, but more than a decade after the October 1920 massacre. By then the national structure had fragmented and collapsed, leaving only a handful of episodically active sites of protest. The local ICU also suffered from the organisational malaise and strategic shortcomings that afflicted the national movement. It too emphasised protest over organisation, and oratory over strategy, rather than combining these critical elements of resistance to create a viable protest movement, never mind a conventional trade union. Conditions in Port Elizabeth made it particularly difficult to unionise African workers, yet they remained loyal to the ICU. Their struggles for higher wages remained an important source of mobilisation for most of the period, and a spine on which to attach other grievances. Although wages are quintessential workplace matters, they affected large swathes of black residents who, as permanent urbanites, had few other sources of income. As a result, the ICU's protests had a wide appeal. Its meetings merged struggles in the spheres of production and reproduction, thus anticipating the emergence in the 1980s of social movement unions. Except, unlike its historical successors, the ICU did not establish any meaningful workplace-based organisations. Its public assemblies were the lifeblood of protest politics, sites of resistance where black people could defiantly express their opposition to white rule and articulate emancipatory politics, on their own terms. In so doing, it created a template for black working-class resistance in South Africa.

9 'Home Truths' and the Political Discourse of the ICU

Philip Bonner

Introduction

The historical impact of the Industrial and Commercial Workers' Union (ICU) has been immense. It was unquestionably the most widely supported political organisation among blacks in South Africa prior to the African National Congress (ANC) of the 1950s. Its geographical reach was quite extraordinary: it stretched out to touch virtually every black township and hamlet in South Africa, from the gold mines of Pilgrims' Rest to the maize fields of Schweizer-Reyneke to the wheat mills on the banks of the Caledon River that processed the large quantities of grain still produced by the peasantry of Basutoland, and endlessly on.[1] Its historical resonance has been huge. For members of the political leadership of the 1940s which revived the ANC, it was frequently their first and sometimes even formative political experience. One of Govan Mbeki's first political memories is taking minutes at ICU meetings in the Eastern Cape.[2] Walter Ngqoyi, key ANC leader on the East Rand in the early 1950s experienced his political baptism with the ICU.[3] Countless small town political activists of the 1940s and 1950s received their political awakening at the hands of the ICU.[4] At times such influences and links could ramify extraordinarily broadly. Veteran Rand Communist Party of South Africa (CPSA) and ANC leader, David Bopape, recalls attending school at Botshabelo in Middleburg in the late 1920s. Transvaal Indian Congress and Communist Party leader, Dr Yusuf Dadoo, sometimes travelled from Krugersdorp to Middelburg to visit a relative. There, 'he attended the meetings of Clements Kadalie of the ICU ...[and] was highly inspired. Kadalie of the ICU inspired Dr Dadoo, Dadoo in turn inspired me [David Bopape] in the political movement'.[5]

The ICU has, fittingly, attracted a great deal of scholarly attention. It continues to excite interest. Its leadership, its organisational structure, its methods of mobilisation, and the constituencies that it rallied to its support have all been extensively explored. An underlying question in the minds of many scholars who have studied the ICU is what accounted for its extraordinary success. In broad terms the answer is straight forward: it offered a taste of freedom.[6] How this was served up in different locales and different contexts is obviously a much more complex question. Several writers have drawn attention to the power of the language or discourse employed by the leaders of the ICU. Bradford highlights the appeal of 'flamboyant, theatrical... inflammatory orations' delivered by ICU leaders like Clements Kadalie, Keable 'Mote and Thomas Mbeki.[7] La Hausse speaks of the way the ICU leadership of Natal developed 'a language resonant with Durban's labouring classes... a rich syncretic subversive language of protest which incorporates traditional idioms and symbols... [that] fused nationalist rhetoric with traditionalist folklore'.[8] Beinart and Bundy refer to the 'belligerent', 'bombastic' and fiery speeches of Kadalie, 'Mote and others in East London and specifically to 'a mounting Africanist rhetoric' in late 1929 and 1930.[9] Breckenridge posits the emergence of 'something similar to Habermas public sphere amongst the African population of South Africa in the 1910s and 1920s in which the ICU played a prominent role', and 'the development of a form of popular politics that privileged speech per se'.[10] All writers cite extensive passages of the extraordinarily vivid and emotive language that key ICU leaders deployed. Even so, there is no extended or systematic effort in any of these accounts to explore the logic or form of the discourse of these speeches themselves. The imagery evoked and the themes of the speeches are explored with great sophistication and at length. The pattern and purpose of the discourse is by contrast passed over. This is to some degree surprising but is equally understandable as well. An exceptionally rich seam of information exists that documents ICU meetings and ICU speeches, which take the form of police reports. This presents both opportunities and pitfalls. They offer a detailed, textured and absorbing body of data, but also raise the inescapable problem of the degree of bias or occlusion of the information they contain. I can do little better in this paper than to quote Beinart and Bundy on this subject:

> The reports also contain a record of what was actually said: they are essential verbatim or precise accounts of speeches. In some cases, the policemen merely summarised the drift of an address... but more usually they attempted to record the main points and sequence of what they said.

They go on: 'the question... has... been... raised... How trustworthy are the policemen in their accounts? Might they be trying to frame the ICU leaders?' and then conclude:

> So far as we are able to judge, these are not serious problems in using this archival source. The intention of the police reports was to provide an accurate record of what was taking place, rather than to collect evidence for use in court cases. In some cases, more than one report was filed, by different reporters, for the same meeting: their content reveals a high degree of agreement on what was said. Even more convincing corroboration, we believe, comes from prolonged reading of the reports: their internal consistency is striking. Even through their unadorned prose it is possible to recognise the oratorical style of individual speakers; and in reports filed over many months it is possible to identify the way new topics are introduced, explored and elaborated. It would not have been possible for any policemen then serving in the East London SAP to have invented – and sustained – the changing content of these speeches.[11]

In all this, I concur. Provided one subjects this source to the normal canons of historical enquiry of careful linguistic and close textual scrutiny, this source provides an exceptionally illuminating window into our past.

The ICU on the Witwatersrand, 1925–1930

The activities of the ICU on the Witwatersrand have been relatively shallowly researched.[12] Its real growth in this area dates from September 1924, when Kadalie arrived in Johannesburg from Natal. A fledgling branch already existed which had been founded by former Bloemfontein ICU members Thomas Mbeki and Stanley Silwana, with the aid of Eddie Roux and the Young Communist League.[13] Kadalie's presence transformed it virtually overnight. To begin with meetings were held in various Reef locations, but these soon proved 'too slow for my [Kadalie's] taste' and were replaced by mass assemblies in Johannesburg's Market Square on the site of today's Public Library. Workers and other black residents of Johannesburg flocked to ICU meetings to hear Kadalie's giddy rhetoric, his lavish promises and his piercing lampoons of white politicians and state functionaries as well as the 'good boy' black elite. One particular episode helped cement Kadalie's reputation as a resolute tribune of the people. During the course of a public meeting at Market Square Kadalie was summoned by Major Trigger, head of the Criminal Investigation Division (CID), to police headquarters at Marshall (subsequently John Vorster) Square. Trigger was in the middle of counselling Kadalie to abandon public meetings for fear of a Port Elizabeth-style white backlash and riot when the entire assembly from the Market Square meeting arrived outside the police building, having marched there under the leadership of a cherubic 20-year old Thomas Mbeki to secure Kadalie's release. Kadalie had never been arrested, but this did not matter. He was quietly released from the CID offices and his status as an unbowed defier of the authorities was sealed.[14] By the time Kadalie left Johannesburg in November 1924, the Johannesburg branch numbered 1 000 and a satellite branch had been set up in Benoni.[15] Other branches in Germiston and Roodepoort were soon to set up shop.

Kadalie came back to base himself permanently in Johannesburg in January 1925 and transferred the national headquarters of the ICU from Cape Town to Johannesburg in April 1926.[16] The intervening 15 months were the high point of the ICU on the Rand. Its message and the spell-binding oratory in which it was couched made a huge impact on a broad spectrum of the Witwatersrand's heterogeneous labouring poor, yet it still managed to retain an organisational and strategic focus which it lost in later years. Until the middle of 1926, the ICU remained primarily an urban organisation and claimed a membership of predominantly 'urban and detribalised Africans'.[17] The ICU leadership on the Rand also continued to favour a broadly speaking industrial approach. The greater part of its energy and resources continued to be directed towards gaining increases in wages and securing redress for workers for underpayment, unfair dismissal and other forms of victimisation. In 1925, the newly elected Pact Government passed the Wage Act which provided for the establishment of a Wage Board to which groups of workers could apply for improved minimum wages. In theory, the Act and its instruments were colour blind. In practice, its intention was to create a safety net for white workers who could not gain access to the existing industrial council machinery which guaranteed the right to collective bargaining. The ICU had high hopes of the racial impartiality of the Wage Board and placed considerable faith in its capacity to deliver economic redress to low-paid African workers.[18] The prospective and even apparent success of this strategy in Bloemfontein in late 1925–1926, as well as in East London, where actual improvements of black workers' wages were secured, were held up as models to the ICU membership on the Rand by Kadalie and other ICU leaders, and at least until late 1926, appeared to offer a credible strategy.[19]

The ICU also operated a complaints office in Johannesburg, probably from early 1925. This sought redress for individual workers by making written representations to the local office of Native Affairs (often to the Pass Officer) and by instituting the occasional legal action against employers. The available evidence suggests that this met with modest success, but even meagre results made an impact in the oppressive environment in which the ICU worked. The complaints office never confined itself strictly to workplace grievances. In October 1925, for example, Henry Daniel Tyamzashe, the Provincial Secretary, wrote to the authorities to urge action in the case of the attempted rape of a Boksburg nurse when she was on her way to work. The following month he was petitioning the same office on behalf of ICU members from the Cape who had been required to pay the Transvaal poll tax, while a short while after, he was appealing about the wrongful arrest of an ICU member in Western Native Township apparently on a permit charge.[20] Nevertheless, in most cases, the issues taken up were either loosely or specifically work-related, such as the withholding of domestic servants' wages, dismissal without the payment of notice pay, or assault at work.[21] The same emphasis can be seen in the wider activities of the ICU on the Rand. In the course of 1925, it ventured only once onto unambiguously political terrain, and then in a somewhat half-hearted manner. When the Minister of Justice threatened to impose night passes on the Witwatersrand's black female population, it summoned at least one protest meeting but thereafter seems to have been content to let the Transvaal African Congress take up the running.[22]

Substantial numbers of the Witwatersrand's black urban population joined or passed through the ranks of the ICU in 1925 and early 1926. Tyamzashe records a huge surge of support following a successful strike at Maytham's tin factory which was further consolidated when the organisation secured the lease of a large-scale indoor venue on Fox Street, Doornfontein, immediately adjacent to the Doornfontein slums.[23] ICU activist Simon Elias claimed to have joined the ICU in 1925 and to have recruited 500 members from Prospect Township in the course of the year. These examples suggest the basis of ICU support in this period. A few consolidated blocks of membership existed in the Maytham's tin factory on the railway goods yard at Kazerne, due almost wholly to the independent initiatives of powerful shop floor leaders such as Philemon C. Fetsha (Maytham's), or Communist Party activists who worked within the ranks of the ICU (Kazerne).[24]

The bulk of the membership, however, was individual and to some degree scattered, and was drawn from the ranks of store workers, messengers, and those oscillating between self-employment and wage labour, among whom a higher than average rate of literacy prevailed. To take one example, teachers, ex-teachers and separatist church ministers featured prominently among ICU branch leaders and were probably amply sprinkled among the ordinary membership as well.[25] For them in particular, the weekly mass meeting at Workers' Hall served as a magnet and the beacon. From these various constituencies (which from time to time also included considerable numbers of mine workers living in the slums of the Malay location and elsewhere), the ICU could claim a membership of at least 5,800 in Johannesburg and 1 000 elsewhere on the Rand early in 1926.[26] Kadalie himself claimed the not improbable figure of 10 000, a number hugely in excess of that commanded by any other black political or industrial organisation in that region prior to the Second World War.[27]

Such figures nevertheless mask a number of underlying weaknesses which became steadily more apparent in the course of 1926 and 1927. While scores of members joined, only a minority kept up their subscriptions. Areas outside of Johannesburg and distant from Workers' Hall were particularly hard hit. In August 1926, for example, Walter Ngqoyi, the ICU's Benoni branch secretary complained at a meeting called to revive the union, that when the ICU was first brought to Benoni there had been great enthusiasm, but that this had now shrivelled away. Identical sentiments were expressed in the same months in Germiston and Springs.[28]

This gradual wilting of support was due partly to the failure of the union's Wage Board strategy, which became steadily more apparent in late 1926, early 1927, along with its inability to devise any constructive workplace strategy in its place and partly to a mounting sense of disillusionment with the behaviour and general probity of union officials. In January 1926, James La Guma, General Secretary of the ICU and prominent Communist Party member, embarked on a tour of inspection of ICU branches, as mandated by the ICU's Board of Arbitration in October of the previous year. Everywhere he visited he encountered shortcomings and derelictions, not least in Johannesburg. Here he found the National and Provincial Secretary assisted by the office clerk acting in place of an executive (whom he did not meet) and roundly condemned the leasing of the Workers' Hall as 'a menace to the welfare of the branch'.[29] A sanitised version of La Guma's report was presented to the annual conference of the ICU held in Johannesburg in April 1926, thereby shielding Kadalie and his fellow office bearers from further criticism. However, other signs of restlessness at the lack of delivery by the ICU were visible at this meeting, particularly about the organisation's reliance on the Wage Board, in place of which several delegates advocated a general strike.[30] Such rumblings of discontent continued for the rest of the year. In October, an 'acrimonious discussion' erupted at a Johannesburg branch meeting when Communist Party members queried what had happened to monies collected to finance a legal appeal by Kadalie against a conviction under the pass laws.[31] At another branch meeting held shortly afterwards, Philemon Fetsha, stalwart of the Maytham's tin factory strike, charged that members of the ICU were treated with scant courtesy by union officials when attending union offices. Complaints were not taken up promptly and even if such complaints were taken up, the workers concerned were not looked after.[32] Early in 1927 when Sam Dunn arrived in Johannesburg from Natal to take up the Provincial Secretaryship, he denounced the Johannesburg branch as 'a disgrace and a sore.' Certain leaders were addicted to brandy and loose women.[33] Clearly much was wanting in the national office and the provincial centre. Kadalie reacted to these misgivings and criticisms with typical pugnacity and vigour.

At a meeting of the National Council held in Port Elizabeth in December 1926, he proposed that his most vociferous critics, the Communist Party members of the ICU, be expelled. Despite the opposition of both the Cape Town and Johannesburg branches, his proposal won through. Equally significantly, Kadalie and his chief lieutenants also began to contemplate a shift of strategy which would take it on to more unambiguously political terrain. This was advertised as early as January 1926 at the ANC's National Congress, when Kadalie, partly at the behest of the ANC, threatened a general strike on the railways, mines and domestic service, if the recently unveiled Hertzog Bills were passed.[34] In the middle of 1926, when the ICU's fortunes on the Rand were sliding deeper into a trough, both Kadalie and the Provincial Secretary, Thomas Mbeki, again brandished the threat. In meetings in Johannesburg and Benoni, Mbeki advised his audience that a general strike would bring the country to a standstill. At gatherings across the East Rand, Kadalie picked up the same refrain, 'If the natives merely stopped work all the industries would be at a standstill in one minute'.[35] When Kadalie was banned from visiting Natal later in 1926, a general strike of Johannesburg workers was contemplated anew, only to be abandoned at that point as impractical.[36] Once white socialists and the Communist Party were ditched, Kadalie also reached for a more ancient authority for such a deed. 'The Israelites didn't know they were in bondage until [Moses] came and organised them and organised the first strike'.[37] The same threat was issued at the ICU's Durban Conference of April 1927, which was notable for the extremity of the language spoken, when Kadalie and others repeatedly promised that they 'would paralyse South Africa as not a native would work'.[38] One month later they began to present such an action as lying within the realms of reality, claiming that the ICU was 'at present so strong that it is capable of bringing all the industries in the country to a standstill'.[39]

When the idea of a general strike was linked to the quest for the abolition of passes as began to happen from the beginning of 1927, it presented a tremendously potent and appealing vision. Its very utterance was enough to send shivers of expectation down the collective spines of ICU assemblies. From late 1926, Kadalie began to train much of his rhetorical fire power on this single issue. His mind was focused somewhat involuntarily on this question when he was served with a ban by the government which proscribed him from entering Natal. At the ICU Conference which shortly followed, it was resolved to fight this restriction and Kadalie was instructed to break it forthwith. Kadalie was at his best, and the ICU often at its strongest, when Kadalie could project broader political issues on himself. The banning presented just such an opportunity. After a short delay, Kadalie challenged the ban, was convicted by a magistrate in Natal which was then upheld by a ruling in the Pietermaritzburg Supreme Court. Throughout the whole period well-attended meetings were held, subscriptions flowed in, and a new energy began to pulse at least temporarily through the ranks of the Rand's ICU.[40]

While the case was still proceeding, Kadalie repeatedly denounced the whole edifice of the pass system. Rhetorically at least, the ICU shifted gear: 'No strong organisation could exist while the pass laws continued', Kadalie proclaimed, adding that 'He was sick and tired of protests. It was time for action... He wanted to see the spirit of Russia in 1917'.[41] At the first public meeting he addressed after returning to Johannesburg from Natal in November 1926, he gave notice of a new orientation when he announced his intention of 'going out into the country to agitate against the pass laws' and this remained his key preoccupation over the following months.[42] The new thrust also provided a useful foil against the criticisms of the Communist Party members of the ICU's Johannesburg branch. When Kadalie returned from the Port Elizabeth conference at which the communists were expelled, he neatly threaded the two issues together at a branch meeting held in the Workers' Hall. 'The Communist Party and General Hertzog could not prevent him from proceeding with his work. He advised that the ICU would hold a big demonstration throughout the country to protest against the Native Pass Laws'.[43]

Despite the impassioned rhetoric, the initial path that the ICU chose to follow in pursuit of this goal was a legal test case in the courts. At the ICU's Durban Conference in April 1927, this was allied, as we have seen, to the idea of a general strike. The problem with this course of action as ICU leaders well knew was that they possessed neither the organisation nor the following to pull off such a feat. 'A stoppage of work would bring the country to a standstill', but as Thomas Mbeki acknowledged in the second breath 'until they were united, this was impossible to hope for'.[44] In practice, therefore, the general strike and any effective challenge to the pass laws was postponed to some point in the distant future. It functioned as an aspiration, a vision, almost as a mirage shimmering on an ever-retreating political horizon. In some respects, it paralleled the millenarian and sometimes apocalyptic vision described by Bradford, and Beinart and Bundy, as taking hold of the white farm lands and part of the Eastern Cape African reserves.[45] In the urban context, it can best be described as a millenarian syndicalism which could inspire hope but could not secure any immediate relief.

Millennial dreams are of course generally destined to be shattered, as quickly happened in the countryside of the highveld and Natal. In Johannesburg, the collapse of expectation seems to have been by no means as complete. An attack on the pass laws still presented an alluring and perhaps not wholly unattainable vision. On the other hand, it seems improbable that this could have held up indefinitely against the competing attractions of the church and the shebeen. Some other sense of satisfaction had to be provided – which is the subject of the next section of this paper.

'Comrades, friends and government agents ...'

Despite the low level of delivery of the ICU after the first year of its existence on the Rand, and a continuing undercurrent of unease among its members about the probity of top ICU officials, the union continued to exercise a sway over the imaginations of at least some sections of Johannesburg's urban poor. Meetings at the Workers' Hall routinely attracted audiences of 200–400 strong between 1926 and 1928, and particular issues could suck in enormous crowds, as happened at the meeting convened on 27 March 1927 to discuss the Native Administration Bill which 2 000 people attended.[46] This raises a question which has not been addressed sufficiently directly in the literature on the subject: what was the enduring attraction of the ICU? How, given its numerous derelictions and shortcomings, could it display such resilience and buoyancy for nearly five years? The question posed in this section is thus not the more familiar one of why the ICU failed, but the considerably more challenging one of how it was able to succeed for so long.

The key to unlocking this puzzle lies in the power of the spoken word. A tone of mild condescension sometimes creeps into discussions of the public persona of the ICU, and particularly of the often extravagant language used by its leaders. A hint of censure also occasionally intrudes, especially among commentators pursuing their own political agendas.[47] It is as if such verbal excesses are seen as symptomatic of a debilitating bent towards self-indulgence and self-deception among the ICU leadership, which drove them insistently down the road to oblivion. The closer one looks at the ICU's record on the Rand, however, the more difficult it is to escape the conclusion that language itself, excessive or otherwise, was one of the chief political weapons in the arsenal of the ICU – perhaps its singlemost potent resource. Public oratory was used by ICU speakers to rouse passions, to voice outrage, to stir indignation, to inspire confidence, to register a flat collective refusal, to kindle hope and to predict a better future. Words were weapons for leaders of the ICU and were employed with extreme facility, verve and effect. Towards the end of 1928, Richard Zindela, chair of the ICU's branch at Prospect Township, invited his audience to square up to the sad reality of their physical disempowerment: 'as the natives were incapable of fighting the white man', he observed, 'it would be better to engage in a war of words'.[48] Much of the ICU's political leadership on the Rand would probably have echoed the same sentiment at any time after the heady days of 1925.

Keith Breckenridge, in an article on the emergence of a public sphere on the South African gold mines in the 1910s and 1920s, discerns the power of the spoken word much more keenly than most other writers who have studied this period, and highlights 'the development of a form of popular politics that privileged speech per se'. He asserts further that popular politics in the 1920s was organised and mobilised by a self-consciously rational, critical discourse 'in which African men from all across the vast distances of the continent... addressed themselves as confederates and equals for the first time'. Breckenridge presents a credible case for the emergence of a public sphere at meetings attended by groups of gold miners across the Rand, as well as in some of their rural homes through much of the 1920s, while also demonstrating the links that existed between these and the ICU.[49] However, as a way of comprehending the character and dynamics of the ICU meetings on the Rand with which I am concerned, the notion of a developing public sphere is less compelling.

Habermas' notion of the original public sphere is confined to bourgeois men of the enlightenment who engaged in a rational/critical discourse as equals. Only later did this extend, and thereby degenerate, as it drew in a wider proletarian world. Prior to the rise of this initially somewhat socially circumscribed public sphere, participation in public argument depended on 'status and tradition' and public involvement was limited to the capacity to applaud or withhold support.[50] In neither instance did ordinary folks gain access to this realm. Breckenridge himself raises doubts as to the full applicability of the notion of the public sphere to the broader range of African politics in the 1920s.[51] Certainly the typical form of the ICU meetings on the Rand approximates more to a blend of the characteristics of the pre-public and the first-phase public sphere outlined by Habermas. ICU leaders generally harangued their audiences and so elicited little audience participation. This was a discourse confined largely to the world of the petit bourgeoisie. Public involvement, moreover, was for the most part, limited to listening and then approving or withholding support.

I propose an alternative role for the spoken word in the public meetings and the politics of the ICU. Even though this may apply to some extent to political activities and discourse of the ICU nationwide, it primarily refers to the ICU on the Rand. In some accounts the Witwatersrand figures as a kind of model of urban and industrial growth to which all urban centres were destined to some extent to conform. This it emphatically was not. The Witwatersrand was distinct, if not unique, among South African cities (and towns) by virtue of the scale of the gold mining industry, the huge concentrations of migrant labourers that this employed and its extraordinarily polyglot population. No other centre was as ethnically and linguistically diverse, and in this lies its particular specificity. In this peculiar environment, the ICU on the Rand took on its own distinctive and peculiar form.

ICU leaders on the Rand valued the properties of words. For these to be realised in all their rich potential, they had to be heard. Public meetings were a way of ensuring this would happen though in more complex and mediated ways than first meets the eye. In 1926, Clements Kadalie expressed his frustration that the ICU's words of protest at his banning from Natal were not reaching their intended destination. Speeches condemning the banning were 'of no use' he proclaimed, 'unless Roos and Hertzog were there to listen'. He was, he insisted, 'sick and tired of protests'. He wanted to see 'the spirit that prevailed in Russia in 1917'.[52] In so pronouncing, Kadalie was adopting a slightly ingenuous position. ICU leaders were acutely conscious of the audiences they were addressing, both near and far away, and were well aware these were usually heterodox and multiple and often only reached indirectly. Not only did an assortment of members and spectators attend ICU meetings, as Kadalie and other ICU functionaries well knew, but a motley array of reporters, detectives and informers as well. ICU leaders not only tolerated but welcomed the presence of police. Known or suspected detectives were at liberty to take out membership cards, and were ironically among the most faithful subscribers of dues, and it was only after some ICU speakers were charged with incitement in 1928 under the Native Administration Act which had been passed the previous year, that its leaders began to insist that these cards be returned.[53] ICU leaders were obviously aware that detectives and informers were present for the purpose of surveillance but consciously inverted and subverted this function by turning them into a channel of communication.

Foucault argues that in order for police power to be effectively exercised:

> it has to be given the instrument of permanent, exhaustive, omnipresent surveillance, capable of making all visible, as long as it could itself remain invisible. It had to be like a faceless gaze that transformed the whole social body into a field of perception: thousands of eyes posted everywhere, mobile attentions, ever on the alert, a long hierarchical network of [police officers]... observers... secret agents... informers... and prostitutes.[54]

Much of this apparatus of surveillance and control was replicated in the various police departments of South Africa's local and central government. Much of the general thrust of his argument also applies to the South African situation. However, in Foucault's analysis, surveillance operates as a one-way process and little attention is given to the possibility of the exercise being at least partly turned against itself. This may well be because the metaphor of the panopticon and the gaze is so overpowering, while the equally important surveillance exercise of eavesdropping on the spoken word is ignored. Police surveillance of the ICU in South Africa at this time functioned primarily through listening in to meetings and recording the proceedings in reports which might eventually reach the desks of the Minister of Justice or the Prime Minister. ICU speakers partly reconstituted this mode of surveillance into a channel of communication. The agents of surveillance were consciously used to relay sentiments of dissatisfaction, grievance or outrage to their political masters. These were the ICU's 'home truths'. ICU leaders addressing meetings at the Workers' Hall and elsewhere frequently directed their comments to known or suspected detectives or lamented their supposed absence. In April 1926, for example, Professor James Thaele regretted that no CID member or newspaper reporter was present to report his speech at a Johannesburg meeting.[55] In August 1928, Philip Mlite, branch secretary of Boksburg's Stirtonville location, urged his audience 'to invite their friends and also some native constables'.[56] In October 1928, ICU branch leader Alexander Ngobizembe Ngqabeni from Springs expressed regret at a meeting held in Payneville location that 'no Government men were present as what he had to say he wished them to report to their superior officers'.[57] Similar sentiments were expressed on dozens of other occasions.

To ensure that the message was getting through, ICU leaders on the Rand more often than not addressed their audiences in English. Clements Kadalie is well known to have spoken no South African, African language and was thus obliged to use English as his medium of communication. Less well known is that most other ICU leaders on the Rand adopted the same practice, at least up until the end of 1928. On the few occasions in which police reports note the translation of speeches at ICU meetings on the Rand, it is from African languages into English, suggesting that this was unusual and the opposite was the norm.[58] Rand-based ICU leaders such as Thomas Mbeki transported this practice into the small highveld towns of the ICU. Helen Bradford cited an acute observation by Eddie Roux on both this mode of delivery as well as the unexpectedly great impact that it had:

> ... the speaker often rouses his audience to a high pitch of enthusiasm. He speaks the white man's language and wears good clothes; he reads the white man's books and quotes against him;... he carries the war into the enemy's camp. Speaking English with difficulty or not at all, illiterate, clad in a blanket or the cast-off clothes of Europeans, timid, afraid to answer back when he is cuffed or beaten, the native worker looks on and applauds. He identifies himself with his leader. The leader knows what is best and will deliver him out of Egypt.[59]

The expectation that ICU leaders should have a good command of English is amply borne out by the branch election which was held in Johannesburg in 1927 when the barely literate railway worker, John Pearce Sijadu, won the majority of votes, only to be substituted for runner up, Stoffel Mabe, by the meeting's chair, Thomas Mbeki, for no other reason that Sijadu's command of English was poor.[60] Generally the flavour of the language and the metaphors employed indicate that English was the language being used at the majority of ICU meetings and being recorded in police reports for most of the lifespan of the ICU on the Rand.

This pattern only began to change once the ICU entered into a period of accelerated disintegration in 1928–1929. Thenceforth much of the blame for the collapse was placed by ordinary members on English-speaking leaders. Time and again grassroots leaders denounced the 'educated natives' as 'traitors'. 'Do not trust the educated natives of this country,' Joe Sibiya bellowed out on more than one occasion. 'They look solely into your pocket.' 'Leaders were not faithful to their work,' declared Isaac Montoeli. 'They talk English and do not carry passes.' 'Only those who spoke in their own languages could be trusted,' insisted George Quntani. 'The others,' spat out Jacob Mluzi, 'were nothing less than a poison to the organisation.'[61]

ICU leaders in Durban and East London, by contrast, addressed many, if not most, of their meetings in the local languages of isiZulu and isiXhosa.[62] Why then was the Rand so different in this respect? An explanation that is sometimes ventured for the use of English at black political gatherings is that this was a form of snobbery or affectation on the part of the black elite. This may provide some tiny part of the answer but it is the view of this paper that the black elite leaders of the ICU were much less vainglorious than that. Another possible explanation is the polyglot nature of their audiences, but then again, there should have been no insuperable obstacle to translating speeches from isiZulu/isiXhosa to Sesotho or the reverse, and, indeed, this sometimes occurred. In default of any other explanation, it seems likely that some other agenda was being pursued. It is the contention of this paper that English was used as the medium of communication most appropriate to the project of refracting police surveillance back onto its authors. It remains now to demonstrate that this was so.

Part of the reason why ICU rhetoric was so popular (perhaps even to the black detectives who recorded it) was the way in which it set out to outrage and provoke. ICU leaders not only articulated outrage at the innumerable indignities to which the black populace was subject (and to communicate this through police reports) but also sought to insult and offend those responsible for their plight. Missionaries, the Prime Minister, the Minister of Justice, white police and Native Affairs Department functionaries were all targets for ICU leaders' derision and verbal barbs. 'ICU members did not pray with their eyes closed, but open to observe the trickery of ministers'.[63] Pirow and Hertzog were 'political criminals'. White constables were 'the white baboon class' who were so stupid that 'when given a pass they read it upside down'. Pass office officials were only fit to be 'employed in the kitchens'. On the day that passes were burnt, 'Mrs Pirow would empty her own chamber pot'. (Minister of Justice) Pirow was 'the son of a squatter', and so on and on.[64] The professional black elite were also the butt of ICU jibes. Attacks on the 'good boys' of the Bantu Men's Social Centre and the Joint Councils were staple fare at ICU gatherings. Occasionally, a particularly gifted satirist like Thomas Mbeki could conjure up a truly memorable image such as when he derided the behaviour of ANC officials that had taken part in the 1919 delegation to England. Even those who were only dimly conscious of the part played by some of the more conservative elements of the black elite and their missionary mentors in providing sanitised leisure time to the black working class on the Rand could not have failed to relish Mbeki's savage caricature of Solomon Plaatje 'returning from England with a dictionary under the one arm [in some versions 'a bible'] and a bioscope under the other'.[65]

English was the preferred medium of communication in delivering these tirades. Not only did this ensure that nothing was lost in the translation – at the ANC Conference of January 1926, Kadalie opposed the motion of President J.T. Gumede that delegates speak in their own languages on the grounds that interpreted speeches were often misunderstood – but its very use gave particular offence to distant listeners, which expressing the same sentiments in vernacular somehow did not.[66] Cursing or profaning public dignitaries or some cherished cultural icon was a particularly strong part of the ICU's rhetorical repertoire. Using the language of domination to insult the representatives of the oppressor was almost guaranteed to elicit a deep visceral response either from white observers hanging round the fringes of the meetings or from the host of surveillors through whose hands police reports passed. Many ICU speakers were adept at causing this kind of offence, but Kadalie was the arch exponent of this craft. When he contemptuously dismissed the Mayor of Durban as 'that damned fool' or railed at Prime Minister Hertzog as 'that damned bugger... that bloody thief' and even spoke of the day when 'he would get that damned bugger Hertzog by the throat', he knew he was doing more than ruffling feathers in the offices of the state.[67]

Police reports repeatedly recorded particular speakers' 'vituperative' tones and often registered deep offence. Head of the CID, Major Trigger, who monitored the proceedings of the ICU Conference in Durban in April 1927 was outraged and offended by the tone of the entire meeting, and with Kadalie's language in particular, which he described as insulting and 'disgusting'.[68] Black audiences by contrast savoured these verbal excesses and the sense of the offence that they caused to those listening in. As ICU Griqualand West Provincial Secretary, Doyle Modiakgotla, confirmed, 'audiences rejoiced when the speaker cursed the white man'.[69] And cursing in English produced its own particular surge of elation.

If the exercise of surveillance could in some sense be refracted back on its authors, the act of informing emerges in a slightly better light. Informers were after all aiding and abetting in this exercise of reverse transmission. Over the decades, informers have penetrated all black political and generally oppositional organisations, but their activities have rarely been explored. A study of their various and changing roles is long overdue. What follows is a brief exploratory venture into this field. The ICU was riddled by informers at all levels who reported back to a variety of different masters not always confined to the state. Allison Champion first attended ICU meetings as a paid spy of the Chamber of Mines.[70] Alfred Solwazi, chair of the Johannesburg branch between 1926 and 1927, took on his mantle and was subsequently unmasked as a spy working under the direction of Mr McKenzie, the compound manager of Crown Mines, where he was employed as a clerk.[71] His predecessor in the position of Johannesburg branch chair, Benjamin Mazingi, was also drummed out of the ICU on the same charge, though in this instance, he appears to have been spying for the police.[72]

Plain clothes detectives were a ubiquitous presence at ICU meetings. Generally, there were several of them reporting on the same event. Thus when the presciently named Corporal Gethsemene Mhlongo was exposed as a spy and expelled from an ICU meeting in November 1928, two other undercover detectives reported on his expulsion and the course of the subsequent discussions.[73] On one bizarre occasion after the ICU/Independent ICU (IICU) split, an ICU meeting drew an audience of 20 in which number two detectives were included. A month later an IICU meeting at Eastern Native Township drew an audience of 18 including another two undercover police.[74]

The ICU were surprisingly tolerant and unperturbed about the presence of spies in their midst, at least until the passage of the Native Administration Act (dubbed the Sedition Act by ICU speakers) in 1927. At the time of the expulsion of Alfred Solwazi, Allison Champion observed that 'he knew detectives and spies from Taberer, the Chamber of Mines, et cetera were there [he should have] but this was not as bad as spying from within the executive'.[75] Ordinary informing could thus be to some extent condoned. Insofar as it performed the function of communication, it was not necessarily inimical to the ICU. High-level informing, however, was also widespread in the ICU. Two top-level ICU officials can be identified as police spies through the numbers by which they were listed in the agitator lists of the CID which were opened in 1927. It is difficult to see either as fully fledged, cold-blooded traitors. Both are likely to have been trapped into informing bit by bit by their own self-indulgence and penchant for high living. This perhaps explains the leniency with which such informing seems to have been treated at the top level of the ICU. The lifestyle of many ICU leaders left them potentially susceptible to the same fate. Beyond that even high-level informers played a curiously ambivalent role. The CID runner for one of the upper echelon ICU informers just referred to made a highly revealing observation on one occasion when he reported to head office on his charge, noting that 'the informants themselves may, to a certain extent, not be reliable as they themselves agree with the views of the agitators on whom they report'.[76] Maybe even they could to some extent justify their actions to themselves in terms of getting the message through. And where low level, undercover agents were involved, who knows what smiles were playing across their lips when they relayed to their superiors speeches, 'likening General Hertzog to a chimpanzee that is so clever it cannot get caught'.[77]

The words used by ICU leaders stung and offended the political establishment of the Union of South Africa from the Prime Minister down. As early as March 1926, Prime Minister Hertzog introduced into Parliament the Prevention of Disorders Bill (widely known as the Sedition Bill). Its intention was to outlaw inflammatory speeches and publications, and it was directed unambiguously at Kadalie and the ICU. Hertzog's Labour Party allies baulked at the measure fearing that it might eventually be used to infringe the freedom of expression of their own white trade union constituency and the measure was shelved.[78] In March 1927, it reappeared as part of the Native Administration Bill which was passed into law later that year. Among the various provisions of the Act was a prohibition of acts 'done with the intention to promote hostility between different races in the Union'. For an organisation like the ICU whose very lifeblood was the unconstrained resort to verbal abuse, this presented an extremely serious threat. Even before the Act came into force on 1 September 1927, certain members were afraid to speak openly because of the Sedition Bill.[79] Rank-and-file members, according to Thomas Mbeki, were under the impression that the Act would destroy the ICU.[80] They were not alone in this apprehension. Within days of the Act coming into force, Acting General Secretary, Allison Champion, ruled that 'irresponsible speakers could not be allowed to address ICU meetings [as it] would cost the Union thousands of pounds'.[81] So perturbed was ICU militant, Shadrack Kutu, that he advised, 'if they could not open their mouths they would make signs with their eyes.'[82] Prosecutions under the incitement clause did in fact soon seriously constrain ICU speakers' freedom of expression. Railway worker and ICU stalwart, John Sijadu, was first to be arraigned, followed by William Selebogo and half a dozen others. The impact of these prosecutions was instantly felt by the Johannesburg branch of the ICU. Many members left the Union after Sijadu was gaoled, and attendance at meetings perceptibly dropped off. Sijadu took some solace from the knowledge that this showed that their words 'had gone to the heart of the government', but for most this was scant consolation.[83] A brief reprieve was given to the ICU when the Communist Party of South Africa took the conviction of two of its members for incitement on appeal and won the case. However, an almost identical clause was re-enacted in 1930, by which time the Johannesburg ICU was in a state of terminal decline.

The incitement clause of the Native Administration and successor Acts is usually seen as an incidental appendage of the whole apparatus of repression. This gravely underestimates the power of the spoken word. It would no doubt be an overstatement to claim that the incitement clause delivered the death blow to the ICU, but it undoubtedly did grievous bodily harm. Breckenridge argues that this and other legislation, along with the reinforcement of the apparatus of control spelled the end of the public sphere for black workers in South Africa.[84] With the broad thrust of this argument, I would agree. It would be on a substantially different basis that black political parties would re-organise and revitalise themselves a decade or more later.

SECTION C

Factions and Legacies of the ICU

10 Leadership Contestations and Worker Mobilisation in the Early Years of the Twentieth Century: Selby Msimang and the ICU, 1919–1921

Sibongiseni Mkhize

Introduction

This chapter examines Selby Msimang's trade unionism and critically analyses his skills as a leader and a negotiator in Bloemfontein and Port Elizabeth during the 1920s. His mobilisation of municipal workers in Bloemfontein raised his stature and escalated his activism on worker issues to the national level. However, this vital but relatively brief phase of his 70 years of political activism was not without its complications, as Msimang was presented with challenges which compelled him to make tough choices that were often unpalatable to his comrades.

Born in Edendale, Pietermaritzburg, on 13 December 1886, Henry Selby Msimang is best known as one of the founder members of the South African Native National Congress (SANNC) in 1912 and for his acrimonious political rivalry with A.W.G. Champion during the late 1940s, when both were provincial executive members of the African National Congress (ANC) in Natal.[1]

While this chapter primarily focuses on Mismang's activities as a leader of the ICU, the author is cognisant of the consistent upward trajectory in Msimang's agitation against land dispossession, racial discrimination, pass laws, and his community and worker activism in Bloemfontein from 1917 to 1919, which culminated in his arrest and eventually brought him to the attention of other emerging worker leaders in other parts of the country.[2] His association with Clements Kadalie resulted in the formation of the first major union with a national footprint, the Industrial and Commercial Workers Union of Africa, with Msimang as its first president from 1920 to 1921. This period marked the earliest phase of leadership contestations, which became a salient feature of Msimang's political career throughout the twentieth century.

Msimang and community mobilisation in Bloemfontein

Prior to relocating to Bloemfontein in 1917, Msimang had been living in Johannes-burg, Volksrust, Vrede in the Transvaal and Verulam in Natal where he was involved in a variety of activities such as agitating against land dispossession and raising his young family, which had led him to find a job in Verulam.[3] Throughout this period, he lived an economically precarious life, which compelled his wife to move to her family in Bloemfontein. Despite these challenges, Msimang continued to combine local and national political activism by being involved in the SANNC activities. When Msimang followed his wife and relocated to Bloemfontein he became a community spokesperson for socioeconomic challenges facing the people of Waaihoek township. He was the driving force behind the formation of the Location Special Committee, whose aim was to discredit and eventually remove the Native Advisory Board members (blockmen), also known as the Local Advisory Board.[4] He distinguished himself as a meticulous, methodical, militant and disciplined campaigner for social justice and worker mobilisation. His experience while leading community struggles reaffirmed his belief in the connection between community issues and the plight of the workers.

Msimang's consciousness of exploitation began earlier when he had worked on the mines as an interpreter.[5] The socioeconomic upheavals caused by the 1913 Natives Land Act, the First World War and the influenza epidemic in 1918 convinced Msimang that the time was ripe to organise the people on a number of fronts.[6] During an interview in 1960, Msimang argued, 'During the First World War the cost of living had soared so high that the non-Europeans could scarcely make both ends meet. Wages of white workers increased in proportion, while those of the non-Europeans remained static during the whole period of the war.'[7] The indignities which the migrant labour system meted out to the mine workers deepened his understanding of the system of racial discrimination and its various effects, particularly in the economic sphere.[8] He went on to say, 'I saw how a man recruited from his home would already be in debt to the local trader, who was usually also the local labour broker. He would supply the family with food before he left home. The cost of this and transport to the mines would be deducted from his pay.'[9]

Msimang recognised the connection between poverty in the reserves and the migrant labour system. The dire economic conditions after the promulgation of the Land Act and then the debilitating First World War, which was followed by soaring cost of living, cholera, typhoid, an influenza epidemic, drought and widespread animal diseases, worsened the situation.[10] By then, labour formations such as the International Socialist League and the Industrial Workers of Africa had emerged in Johannesburg, Cape Town and Durban.[11] Msimang realised that the dire economic conditions were at the heart of the community's problems in Bloemfontein. The low wages and the hated pass system angered the black community and created an explosive situation in the city.[12] The socioeconomic conditions in Bloemfontein, and his in-laws' support, enabled Msimang to mobilise successfully. Bloemfontein, situated in a largely rural province with a history of racial discrimination, dating back to the days of the Boer Republic, experienced an uncontrolled influx of people who had been evicted from the farms as a result of the Land Act. During this period, the authorities had no formal pass system to control the influx of women from Basutoland, which precipitated their poverty and unemployment in the city as there was insufficient accommodation or jobs for them. The introduction of the passes for women in 1913 led to increased militancy which resulted in the first anti-pass campaigns in that year.[13] Msimang unwaveringly challenged the Native Advisory

Board and the municipal authorities throughout his stay in Bloemfontein. He raised his profile and escalated the momentum of his activism further when in 1918 he founded a newspaper, *Morumioa* (The Messenger), which he used an outlet for local and national political expression.[14] His local community activism blurred the lines between the local community struggles and the national struggles that he engaged in as a member of the SANNC more especially on issues such as wage increases, land dispossession, racial discrimination and African economic emancipation.

From community activism to championing workers' rights

Following his relatively successful community struggles, Msimang turned his attention to organising the workers, the majority of whom were employed by the municipality while most of the others were domestic workers in white households. He realised that their wages were very low, which made it difficult for them to keep up with the rising cost of living. On one occasion, he bravely pointed out to the Bloemfontein City Council that their policy of forcing black people to work for low wages only succeeded in giving rise to resistance and hostility among black domestic servants and labourers. He argued:

> Job satisfaction lay in making us love to work and feel good so that we can improve our status. If workers did not experience positive prospects in their daily labour, had nothing to strive for, one created a working class that did not care what direction their lives took and so endless problems for society in general and the government specifically would be created.[15]

Perhaps somewhat hyperbolically, Msimang added, 'I may say with doubled emphasis that about four-fifths of this location represents a population which has no longer any object in life. What ambitions they originally had had been frustrated by the municipal laws – and when any person has lost hope, he has really nothing to live for.'[16] In later years, when he gave evidence in defence of ANC and SACP leader, Harry Gwala and his nine co-accused in July 1976, Msimang compared the conditions of the time to 'economic slavery'.[17]

The years after the First World War witnessed intense hostility by white labour towards their African counterparts and saw the emergence of African labour protest on a mass scale. Eddie Webster argued:

> Faced with rapid inflation and an average wage for unskilled workers of 2/- to 2/6 per day, African workers began to act spontaneously in defence of their interests. In 1918, 152 'bucket boy' sanitation workers struck for a small rise in pay. In 1920, 40,000 mineworkers went on strike. An abortive attempt at organising African workers into the Industrial Workers of Africa was made by a group of white socialists in Johannesburg. In Bloemfontein, Selby Msimang, an African politician, turned his energies to African labour.[18]

Later in his life, Msimang recalled that he was approached by communists who offered to assist him with organising the workers.[19] He said this despite there being no documented evidence of communist activity in Bloemfontein during this period. He claimed that he turned down the offer because he was opposed to communism. His argument was that his fledgling organisation was not bent on strikes, which the communists favoured.[20] He preferred to generate pressure through mass meetings and benefited immensely from the fact that *The Friend* newspaper, which had covered his activities since his arrival in 1917, always sent a reporter to his meetings.[21] His profound and uncompromising aversion to communism was a recurrent theme throughout his political career. He had a different approach to workers' issues, emphasising the important role to be played by the black educated elite in guiding the workers. His scepticism towards communism was typical of the majority of the SANNC leadership of the time which consisted predominantly of the black Christian educated elite.

During this period, black municipal employees earned two shillings a day.[22] Primarily an administrative town, Bloemfontein did not have a large-scale manufacturing sector to absorb its growing population. There were always more men and women flowing in from the farms and from nearby Basutoland than available jobs. According to Baruch Hirson, 'By 1925 there were approximately 4 000 workers employed in the industry, commercial firms, and government or municipal service'.[23] Many of these men and women worked on the railways or the building trade (the largest employers), the municipality (with over 700 workers), or the commercial and manufacturing firms in the town.[24] Hirson credits Msimang with the improvement in wages – albeit still very low by the time of the Bloemfontein riots of 1925.[25] These were the conditions which made Bloemfontein a fertile ground for Msimang's agitation and the rise of the ICU during the 1920s.

Msimang's agitation on behalf of the community and municipal workers culminated in the riots and his eventual arrest. His arrest in February 1919 exposed the city authorities' attitude towards trade unionism and heightened consciousness regarding the plight of the workers.[26] This also raised his profile and attracted the attention of the leaders of the ICU. Despite the City Council's breach of faith and the hardship that he had endured because of his arrest, Msimang was opposed to strikes, convinced that the workers were not sufficiently organised and ready to face the consequences.[27] While the discontent of African people worried Msimang, he believed that militancy was not always the best policy. When organising the Bloemfontein workers, he consistently urged them not to strike. He was convinced that reasonable dialogue between a delegation of the people's representatives and location officials could best redress the people's grievances. Nevertheless, his activism in Bloemfontein raised his stature as a leader even as his philosophy of trade unionism was tested during his brief but eventful presidency of the Industrial and Commercial Workers Union of Africa in 1920.

A workers' leader: Selby Msimang and the ICU, 1919–1921

As mentioned earlier, Msimang's worker mobilisation and community activism attracted the attention of Clements Kadalie and, for a brief period, it looked as though Msimang would play a prominent role as a workers' leader at national level. This was not a period in his life that Msimang was proud of or comfortable recalling, however. For example, in his unpublished autobiography, Msimang did not discuss in detail about his ICU presidency, choosing instead to focus more on the Port Elizabeth riots and his role 'in averting a second bloodshed.'[28] His deliberate omission might be due to the manner in which he was forced to resign from the labour formation, and the fact that this period in his career was later used by his political adversaries, A.W.G. Champion, as evidence of duplicity and unprincipled leadership.[29]

The period between 1918 and 1920 witnessed the rise of the ICU, a union which later went through rapid decline during the late 1920s.[30] The *South African Labour Bulletin* noted that the Industrial and Commercial Workers Union was the first and biggest of the open trade unions in South Africa. Founded in Cape Town in 1919 by Clements Kadalie, it soon absorbed a number of nascent workers' organisations in other centres and became a national organisation. During and after the first World War, there was a rapid expansion of industry and of the industrial workforce. The ICU satisfied a need amongst these workers for a new kind of organisation, and it grew rapidly.[31]

Within a short space of time, Msimang rose from being a local community leader to a national trade unionist and a skilled negotiator. From 1917 to 1920, Msimang earned a reputation as a courageous and uncompromising fighter. Despite the growth of some sectors, South Africa was not yet a highly industrialised country. The main employers were mines, agriculture and the government, which brought Msimang into close contact with town superintendents, mayors, police, magistrates and chiefs.

The founding of the ICU followed a period of uncoordinated black worker mobilisation that began in the mid-nineteenth century in South Africa. As Webster remarked:

> The trade unions emerged in the early stages of European industrialisation out of the 'spontaneous' attempts by workers to bargain collectively with their employers. The primary purpose of these unions was to maintain and raise wages by limiting competition between workers, preventing undercutting, and applying organisational pressure of employers.[32]

Decades before the formation of the SANNC, Mfengu beach labourers in Port Elizabeth had carried out strike actions from the 1850s to the 1890s, although their mobilisation was not necessarily based on broader class interests but limited to ethnic associations.[33] Worker mobilisation in other parts of the country had manifested itself in ethnic identity rather than overall worker consciousness. Home-group associations were the driving force behind worker mobilisation. Some of the disturbances which occurred were isolated and many were mobilised through tribal structures.[34] African workers in the Witwatersrand mines had engaged in a labour disturbance of one form or another since 1913. The extent of the complex worker mobilisation in Witwatersrand is succinctly articulated in Bonner's paper on the 1920 mine workers' strike.[35] In Durban, too, there were signs of worker mobilisation by the informally organised rickshaw pullers who engaged in work stoppages during the interwar years. The rickshaw pullers' mobilisation was, to a large extent, controlled by prominent Natal ANC leaders, A.W.G. Champion and J.L. Dube, both of whom wielded enormous influence even though as members of the middle-class Christian elite they had an ambiguous relationship with the working class.[36] Webster noted:

> The usual pattern of growth of trade unions in the early stages of capitalist industrialisation is that a small section of the working class – usually craft unions of skilled workers – use the apprenticeship system to create and maintain their scarcity value. This group are sometimes referred to as a 'labour aristocracy' to emphasise the wide gap within the working class.[37]

The scale of mobilisation, nationwide coordination and its class-based ideological position differentiated the ICU's worker mobilisation from earlier worker activism. Peter Limb argues that this could be attributed to the inconsistencies in the SANNC's policies, because of the class composition of its leaders and the effects of ideologies that preached moderation.[38]

When Msimang reflected on the relationship between the SANNC and the workers prior to the formation of the ICU, he argued that only a handful of individuals within the upper echelons of the organisation embraced the workers' struggles, and that the SANNC did not have a cohesive organisational position. Msimang recalled that the SANNC refused to attend the inaugural conference of the ICU and did not even want to have its president address the conference.[39] Although Msimang had urged the SANNC to become involved in these workers' struggles mushrooming in the urban centres in South Africa, its leadership decided to keep aloof and Msimang ascribed its declining popularity during the 1920s its failure to read correctly the balance of forces.[40]

In 1919, Clements Kadalie became a founding member and first secretary of the ICU, which, at that stage, was still a localised union based in Cape Town.[41] However, unlike Msimang's labour organisation, simply called the Workers' Organisation, which was driven largely through his work as chairman of the Location Special Committee, Kadalie's was a fully-fledged trade union.[42] Msimang had heard about the latter's worker organisation through the press. Their good relationship encouraged Kadalie to invite him to the first public meeting of his new union. Msimang would later recall, 'When I was arrested in March 1919 Kadalie started communicating with me. I was invited to address a meeting of the ICU when it was first launched in Cape Town in August 1919.'[43] The meeting took place at the Cape Town City Hall.[44] Msimang's speech was a blazing attack on discriminatory regulations in the Orange Free State, which he said, 'had placed workers in a state of semi-slavery and forced them to organise and stand together.'[45] In the 1970s, Msimang recalled vividly his time with Kadalie:

> I spent ten days with Kadalie, in which I got to know him well. We decided to call a conference of all workers and existing organisations in Bloemfontein the next year. I reported these moves to the ANC conference, but it decided to hold aloof from these activities, and as a result suffered declining popularity.[46]

Subsequently, Msimang and Kadalie agreed to join forces by calling a conference of both of their organisations in Bloemfontein. On his return to the Free State, Msimang formed a parallel ICU in the Free State and became its organiser.[47] However, Msimang's memory of Kadalie was that after spending time with him in Cape Town and working closely with him in founding the ICU, he 'struck him as a man of questionable integrity.'[48]

On 13 July 1920, the two trade union leaders convened a conference at the Wesleyan Church's St John School, in Waaihoek, in Bloemfontein, to form the national ICU.[49] The majority of the conference delegates came from branches in the Free State, Northern Cape and Basutoland that Msimang had founded, or that were under his influence.[50] The rest of the delegates came from Kadalie's Cape Town region, Port Elizabeth, Aliwal North and East London, as well as representatives of the Industrial Workers of Africa. The conspicuous absence of Transvaal and Natal representation was a sign of negligible support for the formation of the ICU in those parts of the country.[51] This cast doubt on the national character of the new trade union because both these provinces had rapidly growing, industrialising economies. Although Msimang wished for Kadalie to be elected as leader, Msimang was elected president of the ICU instead. This was likely caused by the fact that the Bloemfontein delegates were a majority.[52]

Msimang claimed that his main object for mobilising workers was to get the workers' organisation under the SANNC. He was apparently anxious about the potential risk of the growth in power and influence of the workers' movement, potentially eclipsing the SANNC.[53] The SANNC, which was still dominated by the Christian petit bourgeoisie, refused to attend the inaugural meeting of the ICU. Msimang had suggested to Kadalie that the President-General of the SANNC, Sefako Makgatho, should preside at the conference. Kadalie agreed, and Msimang invited Makgatho to open the conference. He did this at a meeting of the SANNC which was held in Queenstown.[54] He also presented a detailed report on the new workers' organisation. His aim was 'to make the ICU an impressive power behind the SANNC'.[55] However, the SANNC's leaders saw things differently and decided not to play an active role in the ICU, which was made clear by Makgatho's refusal to give the keynote address.[56] In the introduction to Kadalie's autobiography, Stanley Trapido argues that 'the SANNC leaders' attitudes to political participation and methods of change had been acquired from missionaries, educationists and paternalistic administrators were committed to a programme of moderate reform, which suited its members who were drawn from the new African middle class'.[57] Limb calls Msimang 'a quintessential "two-caps" leader who was able to bestride SANNC and black union movements'.[58]

At this inaugural ICU congress, a new constitution was adopted. Msimang's decision to chair the meeting infuriated Kadalie who saw this as Msimang's ploy to outmanoeuvre his more powerful and radical Cape branch. Msimang's dominant role, plus the adoption of Msimang's own newspaper, *Morumioa* (The Messenger), as the union's official mouthpiece probably angered Kadalie as well. The chief cause of the dispute, however, was the unexpected rejection of Kadalie's candidacy for the post of secretary of the new organisation.[59] Msimang recalled during an interview in the 1970s:

> At the election of office bearers, I was chosen as President. The position of the Secretary, surprisingly, went to a Kimberley teacher, Mr Mache, in spite of Kadalie having the full backing of the Cape delegation as well as my own support. In protest they left the conference with Kadalie, who took with him all the conference papers, including the draft constitution. I did not wish to confuse the issue for workers and thereby split the movement.[60]

Wickins argues that 'Kadalie could not forgive Msimang for what had happened and stored up in his mind other grievances that would no doubt have been forgotten if their amicable relations had remained undisturbed, though it is rather unlikely that the flamboyant Kadalie and the sober Msimang would have worked in harness for long.'[61] Kadalie later wrote that Msimang 'was driven by self-aggrandisement and had fabricated the Bloemfontein membership and usurped the leadership role from the Cape branch by making Bloemfontein the venue for the launch of the national union'.[62]

Msimang's fame as president and his supporters' joy would, however, be short-lived. Kadalie's failure to be elected either as secretary-general or as a member of the executive management of the organisation left him extremely disgruntled.[63] Consequently, Kadalie retreated to his own regional ICU in Cape Town and, from there, continued to extend the organisation to a mass movement countrywide. What followed was a period of tumultuous rivalry between Msimang and Kadalie, and between the Free State and Cape branches, the consequence of which was the weakening of the national union.[64] During this period, the ICU was still mainly dominated by the Cape branches and had not yet reached the stage of what has been described as a 'mass organisation of diverse occupations and social groups – teachers, domestic servants, dockers, farm labourers and even small traders'.[65] Later, Kadalie complained that the Bloemfontein conference was 'nothing but a plot by

Msimang to allow his local supporters to place him in control of the movement.' He accused Msimang of personal aggrandisement and disparaged his supporters as power-hungry. 'How is it possible,' Kadalie asked bitterly. 'How did a person with Msimang's intelligence not see that he should have politely stood back so that the members of the mother organisation could take precedence by serving on the management of the ICWU?'[66]

Intervention in the Port Elizabeth disturbances of October 1920

Three months after the July conference of the ICU, riots broke out in Port Elizabeth. This mobilised support and raised the popularity of the new trade union.[67] The local leadership of the ICU was at the centre of community and worker mobilisation. Samuel Masabalala, an ICU organiser in Port Elizabeth, had left the conference in Bloemfontein to begin organising in Port Elizabeth among both Africans and Coloured workers. He called on workers to demand 10s a day, which the employers ignored and even refused to recognise the union. Masabalala's call for a strike on 3 October 1920 caused divisions within the Port Elizabeth Industrial and Commercial Workers Union (PEICWU). As a result, moderates within the union rejected his resolution. The City Council attempted to outmanoeuvre the trade union by inviting Walter Rubusana, a noted African leader from East London and a member of the Cape's black Christian elite, to use his influence as a counterbalance against Masabalala. City officials, especially Township Superintendent Evelyn Grattan, considered Rubusana as the ideal counterweight to Masabalala's influence amongst the local African community.[68]

At the invitation of some of the moderate trade union leaders, Rubusana addressed meetings of the PEICWU on 13, 14 and 17 October at which he condemned the strike movement as the work of short-sighted 'agitators' who did not have their best interests at heart.[69] Rubusana was assaulted at the third meeting on 17 October after Masabalala had made an emotive speech. Rubusana alleged that Masabalala had encouraged the crowd to assault him, in spite of the fact that it had been Masabalala and his committee who had ushered him to safety.[70] In a bid to pre-empt the strike action, which the union had called for on 3 November, the authorities arrested Masabalala on 23 October on an assault charge. Upon hearing about this, a large group of workers marched on the courthouse to demand his release. After a long standoff outside the court, the tension finally led to a shooting in which the crowd 'was met by a fusillade of firearms, and 23 people were shot dead'.[71] The official record states that twenty demonstrators and three white bystanders were killed, and 126 people were wounded.[72] *The Argus* stated that the matter was more serious than originally reported and put the number of people killed at 27.[73]

The disturbances polarised Port Elizabeth. The city's white population was alarmed by the shootings and took steps to defend themselves with armed vigilantes, mainly ex-servicemen who augmented police patrols.[74] Similarly, black people were gripped by fear and uncertainty and there was a marked exodus from Port Elizabeth.

As research by Robin Bloch and Gary Baines shows, Port Elizabeth's massive urbanisation, the rise of worker organisations, the rising costs of living, inadequate housing, the history of harassment of Africans who lived in perpetual uncertainty, drought in the African reserves and the authorities' preference for migrant labourers led to a culture of mistrust between Africans and Europeans and a rise in militancy.[75]

Msimang's intervention in the Port Elizabeth disturbances was at the invitation of the Secretary of the PEICWU, Alfred Sidzumo. Recalling the incident 57 years later, Msimang said, 'I was urgently called to Port Elizabeth by the Secretary of the ICU branch. Upon my arrival I heard the workers were planning a strike. I realised here was a very delicate situation, feeling was running high, and the least mistake might end up in bloodbath.'[76] Baines paints a dramatic picture of Msimang's arrival: 'The local press noted the arrival, by train, on the evening of 27 October, of a "new factor in the situation" in the person of the editor of a native paper in the Free State'.[77] Msimang claimed to have been unaware of the gravity of the situation in Port Elizabeth. When he received a call from Sidzumo to come to Port Elizabeth, he did not make further enquiries. Sidzumo had not elaborated in his urgent correspondence, and he claimed that he only realised what was going on in Port Elizabeth when he read the newspaper in the train to Port Elizabeth.[78] Before Msimang left Bloemfontein, he was summoned to the office of the local chief of police who told him that he had been in touch with his counterpart in Port Elizabeth. The Bloemfontein chief of police assured his counterpart that Msimang did not pose any threat.[79]

By the time he arrived, Msimang already had an idea of the volatile situation. Sidzumo met Msimang at the train station and informed him that some members of the trade union committee had deserted Masabalala for fear they might also be arrested. Although Sidzumo told him that the chief of police was waiting for him outside the station, he was relieved when they discovered he was not there. They proceeded to New Brighton for a meeting with Grattan, who wanted to know Msimang's plans. Msimang informed him that he had no plans as he was awaiting a briefing by the local leadership and that he was uncomfortable with negotiating while Masabalala was still in jail. Decades later, Msimang remarked:

> If Masabalala had not gone up to raise the voice of the worker, some worse upheaval or outbreak might have taken place. Masabalala was therefore not the cause of the dissatisfaction, but the volcano was on the point of eruption. It only required something to touch it. The workers had made a demand. It was not for me to pass judgement on these demands.[80]

His view was that the prevailing socioeconomic conditions had led to the deterioration of the situation which resulted in the disturbances, and it was unfair to blame Masabalala.

Despite his initial surprise at the situation with which he was confronted, Msimang consulted the relevant people who included the superintendent, the magistrate and the chief of police. He assured them that he wanted to 'deal with the problem fairly and peacefully'. However, he insisted that, as an 'outsider', he would have to act upon the wishes of the local committee of the ICU.[81] The workers had declared a strike which was scheduled to take place on the following Monday. To avert the strike, he and Sidzumo held a public meeting at which he urged workers to converge on Sunday at the cemetery in the morning and then at a meeting at 2pm.[82] Thereafter, Msimang organised a memorial service for the slain, an astute political move that must have highlighted the unrest's cause and outcome.[83] Msimang requested the mayor and the chief of police to withdraw the police and the army. He wanted to ensure that the crowd was not incited at his public gathering.[84] The police were subsequently withdrawn. The service took place at the Presbyterian Church and, according to Msimang's estimation, was attended by 3000 people.

The fact that the service proceeded peacefully inspired his confidence. It turned out to be a wise tactical move which won him the support of Port Elizabeth's black workers. It is plausible that the service released the pent-up emotions of the large crowd, which was prevailed upon to give up thoughts of retribution and, instead, hope for the realisation of justice. The occasion served to reinforce Msimang's appeal to the workers to return to work the following day.[85] Msimang urged the authorities to give him the opportunity to deal with the matter. He assured the crowd he would discuss Masabalala's release with the authorities. No incident occurred except one, when two white youths appeared. The crowd started shouting at them, so Msimang persuaded them to go away.[86] Msimang was so confident, he gave the resolutions of this meeting to a local newspaper reporter.[87]

The following day Msimang met the mayor, who congratulated him for averting another disaster, and asked him to convene the ICU committee for the wage negotiations against the employers. Msimang was convinced that he was in control of the volatile situation. The ICU committee resolved to demand six shillings for inexperienced, unskilled workers, while a sliding scale for more experienced workers in different categories would need to be negotiated. Msimang thought they had 'achieved something of a success'.[88] Msimang and Sidzumo had managed to win the support of the few conservatives within the PEICWU, whom they convinced to join them as part of the delegation to negotiate with the employers. Nevertheless, Msimang supported Masabalala's stance because he believed the latter was not the cause of the dissatisfaction and continued to defend him during negotiations with employers. Nearly 40 years later he still held the view that a long history of poor working conditions and economic hardship were behind the outburst by the city's black community.[89]

Msimang, as the newly recognised chief representative of the workers, led the negotiations but his lack of knowledge of the local conditions made it difficult for him to put a very convincing case to the employers.[90] While Msimang created a favourable impression because of his apparent moderation, he was clearly uncomfortable with the 10s demand made by the local union, and he would have preferred a 'more realistic' 6s per day, which was considerably less than the 8s minimum wage that the ICU was demanding.[91] He also advocated the minimum wage for untrained workers and argued for wage differentiation on the basis of experience. The above suggestions, together with his suggestion for a grading system according to the standard of worker efficiency, attracted unabated criticism from *The Black Man*, the ICU's radical mouthpiece. It unwaveringly criticised him for his handling of the negotiations, especially for obtaining no assurance from employers that workers would not be victimised for their membership of the union.[92] He was clearly out of tune with Masabalala and the radical wing of the ICU because he preferred to cultivate harmonious relations with the police and city administration.

At a wage negotiation meeting held on 15 November, the employers tabled a compromise settlement of 4s/6d minimum wage offer, which represented an effective 6d increase.[93] This was a moderate increase from the 3/- a day, which was paid during the period 1914 to 1919. Baines argued that in 1914 the minimum wage for unskilled black labour was 2/6 a day and by the end of the First World War these rates had increased to only 3/- a day.[94] Having failed to reach an agreement, the negotiations were adjourned to a later date. Meanwhile, Msimang travelled to Grahamstown to attend Masabalala's court case. He used the opportunity to meet and convince the complainant, Walter Rubusana, to withdraw the charges.[95] His negotiations with Rubusana were fruitful as Masabalala and Rubusana settled out of court, even though the former had called the latter 'a thief, dog and seller of the people.'[96] Thereafter, Msimang met with Masabalala and briefed him on what had happened during his incarceration.

To Msimang's dismay, Masabalala vehemently rejected the compromise offer and announced that he was prepared to fight for a minimum wage of 10/- a day. Masabalala was not only unenthusiastic about Msimang's wage proposal; he unequivocally rejected it. However, Masabalala's radicalism did not win the overwhelming support of the workers. Starfield argues that 'apart from avoiding further bloodshed and leaving the workers better off than they had been, Msimang had effectively weakened Masabalala's leadership'.[97] When Msimang withdrew from the wage negotiations, some of the workers urged him to stay as they no longer trusted Masabalala. Msimang claimed people appreciated his efforts.[98] Baines argues, 'Although Msimang tried to play down the rivalry between the two men, it is obvious that Masabalala resented having to play a junior role to an "outsider".'[99] Masabalala disdainfully accused Msimang of weakening the bargaining position of the local branch of the Union.[100] His views were shared by the ICU's newsletter, *The Black Man,* edited by Samuel Michael Bennet Ncwana, which vigorously condemned the suspension of the strike and appealed to the Port Elizabeth workers to appoint their own leaders and to send the 'intruder', Selby Msimang, back home. Msimang was naïve about the complicated political machinations of Masabalala and Kadalie. He had a limited grasp of mass worker formations and the strategies and tactics adopted by leaders of those organisations in times of crisis. His efforts, mainly shaped by his limited experience of worker agitation in Bloemfontein, were being undermined by his adversaries who had extensive experience in mass worker organisation.

Although Masabalala had continued with his demand for 10/- a day, the workers of Port Elizabeth never gained anything near this, and by 1921, the union was apparently bedevilled by schisms and splits.[101] Msimang, by contrast, believed in a gradualist approach in order to achieve the workers' demands. This clearly showed the early signs of Msimang's pragmatic approach. As a pragmatist, he was convinced a gradual approach would avert further bloodshed and improve relations between racial groups in Port Elizabeth. His intervention in the disturbances had demonstrated the wide schism which existed between him and the rest of the ICU leadership under Kadalie's influence. He was clearly not in control of the union, and he failed to accomplish part of his mission, which was to improve the plight of the workers. As a result, he only succeeded in quelling the disturbances while leaving the root causes of the disturbances unaltered.

Msimang, Kadalie and the struggle for the soul of the ICU

Although Msimang had proved to be a relatively competent negotiator, he was disillusioned by his ongoing tussle with Kadalie and Masabalala's hostility. Towards the end of 1920, when Msimang realised the futility of his efforts to achieve reconciliation and unity, he contemplated resignation. Msimang recalled that he took this decision on his return to Bloemfontein when it became clear Kadalie would not countenance working with him. Nevertheless, Msimang attempted on numerous occasions to reconcile with Kadalie. Msimang wrote to Kadalie to enquire if the latter would reconsider his decision to boycott the ICU. Msimang even tried to entice Kadalie back into the ICU fold by telling him that the secretary had informed him that he could not carry out his functions because his job as a teacher restricted his political activities.[102] Msimang argued that he felt they could not run two parallel organisations as it would confuse the people and weaken the workers' struggle. In his autobiography, Kadalie caustically claimed to have rescued the situation from Msimang, and that he and Masabalala drew closer, resulting in Kadalie's invitation to the commemoration of the 1920 disturbances as one of its main speakers.[103]

Msimang and Kadalie had divergent visions as far as the ICU was concerned. Msimang wanted the workers' movement to fall under the control of the SANNC while Kadalie had ambitions of an independent trade union. Kadalie saw the ICU as a vehicle through which he could become one of the prime movers in African politics. He had a dream of becoming the 'Marcus Garvey of Africa.'[104] Kadalie tended to speak with what he felt was an American accent, hence some of his followers' belief that he was the embodiment of Marcus Garvey.[105] It was clear from his speeches and his rhetoric demonstrated that he was influenced by the Africa for Africans Movement which was inspired by Garvey. Because of this perceived association with America, many rural people believed ICU organisers were African Americans coming to liberate them.[106] This was even though the Garvey influence had gradually waned from the mid-1920s. For Msimang, the ICU work represented part of his duties as a member to the SANNC; and he claimed that he had no aspirations to enhance his stature. It was apparent that the antagonism between the two leaders was deep-seated and every action by either was inexorably leading towards a titanic clash which reached a crescendo in 1921.

In July 1921, Msimang delivered his last presidential address at the conference of the ICU, which was held in Cape Town in an attempt to achieve unity between the national ICU and Kadalie's Cape Town-based faction.[107] The address was later published in the *Cape Times*. His statement captured the essence of his belief in moderation and warned against radicalism. He warned delegates about hasty actions such as uninformed strikes instead of pursuing passive resistance and urged them to organise 'patiently and vigorously so that they could end their difficulties'.[108] By then, Msimang was already convinced that the chasm between himself and Kadalie could not be closed. Even when Msimang went to Cape Town for the ICU Congress, he and Kadalie failed to reconcile. Kadalie did not even attend the conference. A meeting was arranged for the two leaders to try and resolve their differences, but they still could not reach an amicable solution. Msimang realised that the future of the workers' movement was at stake and stepped down so that Kadalie could lead. He claimed to have told him:

> Kadalie, rather than running two parallel organisations which are engaged in one particular objective, why not you take over, I withdraw? I will tell my people in the Free State that you have taken over. I would not like two identical organisations to exist in the country.'[109]

Kadalie unashamedly accepted Msimang's proposal, unfazed by the fact that he had essentially manoeuvred a coup against a democratically elected leader. This signalled the triumph of populism over pragmatism. Kadalie became National Secretary, Masabalala became the National Organiser and 'a Cape Town nominee' became President.[110] In 1922, Msimang left for Johannesburg but continued to pursue African trade unionism through presentations to commissions and writing articles in newspapers.

Msimang's acrimonious relationship with the leadership of the ICU did not end with his resignation in 1921. A lesser-known incident of historical erasure happened during the 1940s, which signalled that the fight for the soul of the ICU did not end in the 1920s. Sometime during the 1940s, Henri Danielle Tyamzashe, who had been the Complaints and Research Secretary, as well as editor of ICU newspapers, wrote an unpublished manuscript on the history of the ICU, titled *Summarized History of the Industrial and Commercial Workers Union of Africa (ICU)*. In his version, Tyamzashe completely erased Msimang from the history of the ICU.[111] Tyamzashe was Kadalie's close ally and defended him against accusations of mismanagement although some passages in the *Summarised History* are critical of Kadalie.[112] However, Tyamzashe's narrative prompted William Ballinger to write to *Umteteli* in March 1929 to correct the former, accusing him of portraying Kadalie as the sole founder of the ICU.[113] By the time the manuscript was written, Msimang had relocated to Natal and, while engaged in another struggle with another former ICU leader, had long severed ties with the ICU, while Kadalie had been expelled in 1929 for alleged embezzlement.[114]

While Msimang may not have been a successful and popular leader of the ICU, he claimed to have been concerned about the sustainability of the trade union, going to the extent of handing over funds from his own community development scheme to the union. His constant worries about the economic precariousness of the African people permeated his political activities and dominated his activism during the 1940s, 1950s and 1960s.[115] If his version of history is to be believed, he devised a self-help scheme throughout the Orange Free State, which was later taken over by the ICU.[116] His idea was to get communities to raise and keep funds as a reserve that would enable them to fight their battles against discriminatory laws. To achieve this, he printed membership cards which would be distributed to all the towns in the Free State, and these were handed to those people who contributed to the scheme.[117] He recalled that he raised 'huge sums of money' via this plan.[118] This important gesture, too, was not mentioned in Tyamzashe's version of the ICU's history. Though often overlooked in the writings of the history of the liberation struggle, Msimang's worker and community struggles fundamentally influenced his approach to politics and social justice during his long political career. While Msimang may not have been the subject of a scholarly publication until the completion of my doctoral thesis in 2015, he was extensively interviewed by historians and researchers during the 1960s and 1970s, particularly on the broader aspects of the struggle for liberation.[119] Jane Starfield's MA dissertation, which is a comparative analysis of the autobiographies of R.V. Selope Thema and Msimang, provides a critical analysis of Msimang's political activism. Furthermore, theses, books and journal articles by Peter Wickins and Hellen Bradford on the ICU provide detailed coverage of Msimang's political activities during the 1920s.

Conclusion

While Msimang made history by being the first president of the ICU, he failed to sustain this position due to his stance regarding strikes and boycotts, which brought him into conflict with his fellow trade union leaders. This became evident during his leadership of the community and worker protests in Bloemfontein in 1919 and his intervention during the Port Elizabeth riots of October 1920. While representing the workers, he still believed in the sincerity of the employers, thus placing himself in a position of ambiguity as he often found himself indebted to both parties. He also had the first taste of the complexities of an organisation led by populists who were impatient with his cautious, moderate and thoughtful approach.

At its height, the ICU was seen as a workers' movement that gave South African workers in industrialised parts of the country the capacity to imagine a mass movement that transcended ethnic, rural, urban, class and provincial boundaries. Msimang's brief leadership was characterised by contestations, which dogged the ICU for many years, more especially during the 1920s, the zenith of its popularity through to the 1930s, when its support declined, and it was no longer a giant labour movement.

Msimang's uncompromising pursuit of diplomacy and pragmatism in handling conflicts between workers and employers earned him rebuke from his fellow trade unionists who accused him of being weak. As a person who was responsible for the labour and economic portfolio in the SANNC, Msimang interpreted his trade union leadership as a way of realising the economic emancipation of the workers. His experiences during this period shaped his perspective on African economic emancipation and influenced his activities for many decades during the twentieth century.

11 The Communist Party of South Africa and the ICU, 1923–1931

Tom Lodge

Introduction

Communist engagement with the Industrial and Commercial Workers' Union (ICU) evolved over two phases. First, between 1923 and 1926, this engagement was driven by strategic commands from the Communist International (Comintern) as well as by a growing realisation among communists in South Africa that they should mobilise African workers. While Party leaders began to acknowledge African rights, individuals among the Party's own small black membership joined the ICU. African communists became senior officials in the ICU as well as, more importantly, key organisers, in the smaller rural centres where the Union was recruiting fresh followers.

Consequently, after the expulsion of communist officials from the ICU, the Party continued to pick up support in localities in which Party members themselves had been busy. Communists would emerge at the helm of successful rebellions against taxes and efforts to subject women to pass regulations. Here, communists would appeal to their neighbours as householders, protectors of the family, Christians and members of a subjected race, using very much the same kind of language they had used as ICU organisers.

Influencing and joining the ICU

The Communist Party's effort to influence the ICU began hesitantly. In 1923, the Comintern was instructing its affiliates to form united fronts, that is alliances with potentially sympathetic non-communist organisations. In line with this prescription, South African communists began expressing sympathy for the African National Congress (ANC) and acknowledged the ICU's role in mobilising workers. As Sidney Bunting dutifully conceded, 'national liberation is, in the case of the subject races, the necessary introduction to proletarian revolution'.[1] Party leaders remained divided over whether to organise black workers. Bill Andrews, the most influential Communist within the white labour movement, still maintained that white trade unions would sooner or later acknowledge that their interests would be served through cross racial class solidarity even though 'certain affiliated unions' remained unwilling to countenance such a prospect. He was philosophical about this tension:

> It may be said that these facts reveal inconsistencies and contradictions which is of course true. Life itself is not simple. It is composed of a whole series of compromises, contradictions and apparent inconsistencies. The relationship between man and man, to say nothing of woman, is complex and full of unresolved problems.[2]

Andrews would join the Communist International's executive in Moscow in mid-1923, during a six-month stay. Here he had several meetings with Zinoviev, maintaining 'close contact' with the Comintern's leader throughout his visit, he claimed.[3] The only detail he supplied, though, about any of the Comintern executive meetings he attended was an occasion when the South African Party was reproved for not paying sufficient attention to other left-wing movements elsewhere in Africa.[4] Shortly after his arrival in Moscow, the Comintern would begin preparations for a major 'negro' conference timed to coincide in 1924 with its own fifth Congress. The South African Party was expected to be the main agency through which the Comintern 'would reach the negroes of Southern Africa'.[5] The Comintern informed the South African leadership in November, 'We do not doubt that you are beginning the work among the natives with energy', with the note of asperity that would characterise many its future communications with Johannesburg.[6] Sidney Bunting's response was uncharacteristically defensive. Finding suitable negro delegates among educated Africans, he pointed out, was very difficult.[7]

That may have been the case in 1923. By early 1924, though, members of the Party's Young Communist League (YCL) were helping the ICU to establish its new office in Johannesburg by persuading two key local ICU personalities to join their ranks, Thomas Mbeki and Stanley Silwana. But while Young Communists began enlisting African trade unionists, the Party still remained committed to seeking an accommodation with white labour. The Communist Party did not put up its own candidates in the general election, explaining that they would support the 'Pact' alliance between Labour and Afrikaner nationalists. This was not the time to split opposition to Smuts, the Party's manifesto explained, though communists should not expect radical reforms from the Pact in power.

Whether the Party's main strategic orientation should remain directed at winning over white workers was the key issue at the Party's conference in November 1924. By this stage, the Pact administration had been in power for five months. It had already designated South African Railways a new preserve of protected and privileged employment for unskilled whites. At the conference in November 1924, Party treasurer Frank Glass led the argument in favour of another effort to obtain Labour Party affiliation. At this juncture, Glass and others believed that as the left wing of a labour movement in power, communists would have leverage to extract reforms. But opposition to affiliation won the day. The leadership elections at the conference brought Young Communists into the management committee, including Eddie Roux, appointed as Bunting's deputy in his new role as Party chairman. Their presence reflected a change in the Party's active following. The YCL itself was building new branches outside its original base in Johannesburg.[8] The Party was now younger, better educated, and less likely to attract skilled white workers. As the Young Communists noted, their constituency was unlikely to include many white apprentices: 'the bulk of South Africa's youth, both black and white, stands outside industry'.[9] Andrews retained the CPSA secretaryship, though, and Frank Glass continued to mind the Party finances, but the Party's new programme called for fresh efforts directed at African workers. Communists were now formally committed to building industrial organisation among all workers, 'irrespective of colour'. Yes, they would still seek a united front, but this would be a front of all workers, 'to bring the European and the helot workers together in a united army'.[10] The programme included a list of demands. These for the first time spelled out Communist commitment to the extension of the Cape Franchise to all black South Africans. The programme also called for free compulsory education, votes for white women and the more familiar maxim of equal pay for equal work.

Hardly a radical charter, but in fairness, most communists probably favoured more universal kinds of enfranchisement. As a commentary in *The International* had noted, most Africans were 'exceptionally well qualified' to make sensible voting decisions.[11] Though recruitment of Africans remained selective and limited, tactical and strategic priorities were now different. In February 1925, Bill Andrews resigned from his editorship of *The International* as well as the secretaryship; as he explained 'a difference over tactics has led to his resignation from office'. While he agreed that workers should be unionised 'regardless of colour', he disliked the new emphasis on organising Africans.[12] Frank Glass, who gave up his post as the Party's treasurer, was less diplomatic than Andrews. Africans, he suggested, 'could not possibly appreciate the noble ideals of communism'.[13] He left the Party, one in an exodus that included several influential figures in white labour. Glass charged that the Party had become anti-white.

At the beginning of 1925, the Party started a night school in Ferreirastown.[14] The main organiser of this undertaking was William Thibedi, then also an ICU shop steward.[15] Thibedi was a founding member of the Communist Party. He had also belonged to the International Socialist League, one of the Party's forerunners. Here, Thibedi had been busy in the League-sponsored Industrial Workers of Africa (IWA), a group for black workers. The IWA had been active in Cape Town in 1919, collaborating with the ICU in mobilising black dockworkers. Thibedi was a clergyman's son, an upbringing which he evidently rebelled against judging by the vein of anti-clericalism featuring in his reported speeches.[16] 'Comrades', he would cry, 'we must kick out the missionary and the clergyman. I know because my father is a ------- clergyman.' He continued:

> I know what I am talking about. What is the missionary doing for us? He educates us and then leaves us alone to starve. He points to the sky and tell us, 'By and by, after you're dead, you'll have enough to eat and fine clothes to wear!' That's not good enough for us! We want food to eat and clothes to wear today. Am I right?[17]

Meanwhile the Young Communists League organised their own Euro-African debating society, hoping, presumably, to attract better educated Africans than the workers who would be taught basic literacy in Thibedi's classes. Contributions from African readers began appearing in the columns of *The International*.[18] At this stage, the Party held back from direct organisation of Africans into unions or from any real effort to set up branches in African-inhabited vicinities. Instead, communists worked more actively with African organisations, and especially with the ICU, encouraged by the ICU's proclaimed intention of mounting a 'crusade' for 'One-Big-Union' to embrace all African labour.[19] In fact, its association with the ICU would become its chief preoccupation. In this undertaking, communists continued to take their cues from the Comintern's united front policy and here they could find inspiration in external models. Party strategists drew parallels between their involvement with the Union and the Chinese Party's willingness to defer to and refrain from competing with the nationalist leadership supplied by the Kuomintang.[20] Indeed, Bill Andrews actually appeared as a speaker at a local Kuomintang conference in Johannesburg.[21]

Andrews also spoke at the ICU's formal opening of its new meeting hall in Johannesburg in September 1925, reassuring his hosts that as a 'representative of a very considerable section of the white working class', many white workers welcomed the ICU's efforts to draw 'native workers' into organised labour.[22] Through 1925 and 1926, Sidney Bunting, Eddie Roux and Solly Sachs became familiar speakers at ICU gatherings. Roux in particular developed a friendship with Kadalie, though even the more reserved Bunting would concede to Roux that the ICU leader was 'not yet a bad lot'.[23] Roux had begun attending ICU meetings and fundraiser dances while a student at Wits, making friends with Thomas Mbeki and Stanley Silwana. He also met Kadalie and was enchanted by him. At their first encounter Kadalie took a copy of Swinburne's *Songs before Sunrise* Roux was holding and 'in his gentle high-pitched voice' read some of the verses from 'Messidor':

> Let all that hunger and weep
> Come hither, and who would have bread
> Put in the sickles and reap.[24]

Connections with the ICU went well beyond these relaxed encounters. During 1924 and 1925, cross membership drew the Party closer to the Union. Thomas Mbeki and Stanley Silwana joined the YCL in 1924 and during that year, Mbeki emerged as a pivotal actor in establishing an ICU presence in the smaller centres of the Transvaal, drawing in farmworkers. Meanwhile Silwana worked as a clerk in the Union's office in Cape Town. Eddie Khaile, the ICU's financial secretary, also joined the Communist Party. Here, during 1925, local communists recruited two senior ICU office-holders, James La Guma, the organisation's national secretary as well as its Cape provincial secretary, Johnny Gomas. In 1926, five Party members belonged to the ICU's national council.[25]

Though they occupied conspicuous positions in the Union, communists did not caucus, dividing between a more cautious faction and a more aggressive 'Ginger Group of Young Bloods'.[26] Even so, their influence was considerable. In April 1926, the ICU's removal of its headquarters from Cape Town to Johannesburg made the organisation more accessible for communists. The Party's influence was evident in Clement Kadalie's increasing usage of anti-capitalist rhetoric,[27] and the ICU's movement into the smaller towns and the countryside may have reflected a new conviction among African communists that 'land and peasant questions were of the utmost importance.'[28] The language is from the Party's 1925 conference at which Eddie Khaile told his new comrades that 'The natives especially in the country districts are ripe for organisation.'[29] The Party set up an Agrarian Department in May 1926; three of its six members were ICU officials: Gomas, La Guma and Khaile. A programme of immediate demands included land for peasants, nationalisation of estates and repeal of the Masters and Servants Act. By mid-1926, African communists were sufficiently numerous to constitute a No. 2 Group within the Johannesburg, meeting in Ferreirastown, organising a lecture series, and writing in African languages in the Party newspaper, which had content directed at the Party's new rural following. Much of their educational activity was directed at the ICU; most members of the Group looked forward to changes in their own organisation. As one of their speakers, Joseph Phalane, explained: 'I am a communist not because there are white people in the Communist Party but because that is the Party that will make us free. We want a black Communist Party.'[30]

CPSA promptings were evident at the ICU's annual conference in mid-1925 when it adopted a constitution that included language from the Industrial Workers of the World in its preamble. James La Guma probably helped to draft the document.[31] It was also the case that General Hertzog's introduction in parliament of segregationist legislation shifted ICU's leaders leftwards. After meeting Hertzog, the Union had enthusiastically supported the Pact during its electoral campaigning. ICU leaders would refrain from matching their angry rhetoric with any intentional change in tactics, though, eschewing strikes, and continuing to petition government while still occasionally using the racially irredentist language of Garveyism, language the Party normally condemned. The Party was indulgent though, ready 'to make a fuss of the ICU' as a guest at its Fourth Congress held in Cape Town in December 1925. Here African and Coloured communists were conspicuous. Thibedi would join the Central Executive at this conference. Despite the presence of African communists, the discussions at the meeting included an argument over whether the Party should defend the right of Africans to walk on pavements; certain delegates felt this was an issue on which silence would be more tactful.[32] In a more encouraging vein, in April 1926, Clement Kadalie spoke at a Party public meeting, making warm comments about the Soviet Union and calling on African workers to take part in May Day demonstrations.

Rupture

Cordiality between the two organisations would not last long. The increasing influence communists appeared to enjoy within the ICU alarmed liberal circles. Mabel Palmer, a Fabian and former suffragette, invited Winifred Holtby, the British novelist and Independent Labour Party (ILP) luminary, to tour South Africa, between February and June 1926. Mrs Palmer was well connected, counting George Bernard Shaw and Sidney Webb among her friends. Palmer knew Kadalie slightly and introduced Holtby to the ICU leadership at a meeting in Durban. Holtby, impressed by this encounter, promised to explore British sources of support. In Johannesburg, Holtby stayed with Ethelreda Lewis, herself an author. More politically conservative than Palmer and Holtby, who considered themselves socialists, Lewis was a Smuts supporter, but she was also disliked restrictions on 'native rights in their own native land'. Politically, she was passionately anti-communist, and she was determined to persuade the ICU leader that there could be 'better, safer more stable friends for himself than white communists'.[33] Lewis and her guest agreed that Holtby would on her return to Britain try to secure support for the ICU. True to her word, back in London, Holtby met Arthur Creech-Jones, secretary of the Transport and General Workers Union. Creech-Jones then began corresponding with Kadalie, advising him to join the International Confederation of Free Trade Unions. For Kadalie, this was an attractive prospect. It was becoming clear that despite his own affable relations with Bill Andrews, his application for affiliation with the South African Trade Union Congress would be turned down.[34]

Meanwhile, the Union was struggling to pay the bills for printing its own newspaper on the Party's press; indeed, by November 1926, the press's manager, not a Communist, was refusing to print any further issues of the *Worker's Herald* and had on one occasion thrown the ICU's copy out of the window. A more immediate worry for Kadalie, though, were the criticisms directed at the ICU's leadership by its own Communist officials. In March 1926, James La Guma compiled a report on the Union's mishandling of its finances. Six hundred pounds had been lost the preceding year because of 'inefficiency, dishonesty and unconstitutionalism on the part of the branch and other officials,' La Guma charged. He was especially censorious about some of the provincial secretaries for their misuse of funds. He also criticised Kadalie himself for autocratic behaviour: 'It seemed that a dictatorship is in embryo'.[35] Provincial secretaries should be transferred each year between different provinces, he recommended, and Kadalie should cease his editorship of *The Workers' Herald*.

At the same time, the Communist Party's newspaper, now named *South African Worker*, carried reports by Laurie Greene in Pietermaritzburg, now an ICU member as well as the main personality in a small Communist group active locally. In his despatch, Greene repeated rank-and-file complaints about the national leadership's inactivity and its preference for legalistic methods. The local ICU branch had been at odds with the provincial office over its refusal to forward subscriptions to Durban. As Greene pointed out, most members were too poor to pay their subscriptions and were in any case disinclined to pay for lawsuits when they should be using 'industrial power'.[36]

In Johannesburg, African communists active in the ICU were calling for it to set up sections for specific industries.[37] Such urgings as well as calls from Johnny Gomas for the establishment of a shop-stewards' movement were implicitly threatening to the kind of leadership exercised by most top ICU officials. More explicitly, the *South African Worker* began publishing critical comments about top-echelon venality within the ICU. Police reports indicate an increasingly fractious relationship between the communist-led ICU branch in Johannesburg and the ICU headquarters; at the end of October, Kadalie himself instructed the Johannesburg branch to end its preparations to commemorate the Russian revolution.[38] In September, communists believed they had succeeded in persuading Kadalie to accept an invitation to attend a Comintern-sponsored Conference of Oppressed Nationalities to be held in Brussels. For the Comintern, anti-colonial politics had acquired a fresh strategic importance. The communists would supply the necessary funding, presumably with help from the Comintern. As we have seen, Creech-Jones counselled Kadalie to turn down the invitation, advice which he accepted in the end, though initially he prevaricated. He may also have received vague hints about rewards for any turn against the communists. Meanwhile both La Guma and Eddie Khaile were urging that the ICU call for a general strike to protest the recent enactment of colour bar legislation, a proposal Kadalie felt would be reckless.[39]

On 16 December 1926, at an ICU National Council meeting, Kadalie announced he would not be travelling to Brussels. He accused the Party of interfering in his organisation. A final source of irritation was that La Guma had accepted the Party's nomination to attend the Brussels meeting without seeking permission from Kadalie.[40] La Guma's report had ensured he would have few allies at this meeting, but in any case, he was more widely unpopular within the organisation and perceived as an officious bureaucrat.[41] After an angry exchange with La Guma, the Orange Free State's organisational secretary, Alex Maduna, proposed that no office-holder within the ICU could be a member of the Communist Party. La Guma had highlighted Maduna's venality in his report. The council approved the motion and, on the next day, four communists who were senior ICU office-holders were expelled: James La Guma, Thomas Mbeki, Johnny Gomas and Eddie Khaile. In a press interview, Kadalie explained that the communists were guilty of meddling.[42] Mbeki rescinded his Party membership and continued to work as an ICU organiser as did Stanley Silwana.

Kadalie remained on friendly terms with Bill Andrews though. Andrews spoke at an ICU rally on 5 April 1927 [43] At this stage the ICU was still committed to seeking affiliation with the Trade Union Congress and in this venture, ICU leaders perceived Andrews as an ally within the white South African Trades Union Council (SATUC) leadership. Kadalie also asked Frank Glass who had left the Party in early 1925 to help with the task of auditing the ICU accounts, a necessary preliminary for any kind of local of international affiliation. Glass would work as the ICU's temporary financial secretary for the next 18 months, through 1927 and the first half of 1928. Glass was no longer a Party member, but he still probably thought of himself as a communist and it is likely that he helped to ensure that ICU would still occasionally use anti-capitalist phraseology in its statements.[44] It may have been these rhetorical flickerings that prompted Creech-Jones to write to Kadalie in September 1927 warning against 'being sidetracked by the communists'.[45] Ethelreda Lewis was especially exasperated by Glass's recruitment. She'd been away from Johannesburg when it had happened, and as she informed Holtby, on her return to Johannesburg she discovered, '... that a certain dangerous person called Glass (an ex-tailor who is a communist) has been making hay while the cats [were] away and worming himself into positions of indispensability.[46] Glass had in fact known Kadalie for much longer than Lewis, supporting the ICU's early efforts to organise its following in Cape Town in 1920.[47]

Kadalie remained on good terms with communist individuals. Sylvia Neame suggests the real reason for the break with the Party was not any profound antipathy to the communists in general but rather Kadalie's deteriorating personal relationship with La Guma.[48] Andrews would keep his friendship with Kadalie even after the SATUC turned down the ICU's application for affiliation. Andrews himself really had attempted to persuade his fellow unionists to consent to an ICU affiliation, suggesting in January 1928 that the ICU should reduce its claims about its 100 000 paid-up membership so that white trade unionists would not fear they would be overwhelmed. In any case, he argued, such an adjustment would make affiliation more affordable for the ICU. 'More propaganda was needed', though, 'before affiliation could take place,' he conceded.[49]

That same year (1928), Andrews led an ICU deputation of aggrieved African postal workers, negotiating on their behalf a meeting with the Minister for Posts and Telegraphs, a concession that prompted the subsequent expulsion of the minister, the Labour Party's Walter Madeley, from the cabinet. At the ICU's 1927 April conference, the Communist Party's Sophus Pettersen appeared as a fraternal delegate, as an organiser of the Seaman's Union. Pettersen had in fact helped the ICU establish a presence in Durban's docks. Kadalie favoured Pettersen's attendance at the conference – after all his presence there was a mark of recognition from white labour – but he was excluded by a narrow vote from the conference all the same because he was a communist,[50] for at this meeting, the ICU decided that there should be no cross membership between the two organisations. That it took a whole morning to debate this decision is noteworthy, for the number of communists who belonged to the ICU was small, around a 100 or so, 50 on the Witwatersrand.[51] Two months before, in February in Vereeniging, the entire ICU branch was disowned after it had objected to the expulsions. This tension could well have been a consequence of personal loyalties: the branch had originally been established by Thibedi, who had been trying to organise coal miners in the vicinity.[52] A portion of its membership reconstituted themselves as a communist formation. Almost by accident, for the Party's leadership had not anticipated this rupture, the communists were being drawn and prompted into a new kind of politics. They could no longer extend their influence through an alliance with the ICU. Instead, they would have to build their own following. Intuitively, they looked to the workplaces employing black people as labourers, but they would find most of their African support in townships, in the places in which black South Africans lived.

In her history of the Communist Party, Mia Roth has suggested that towards the end of 1926 and through 1927, the Party's financial fortunes improved and she notes that it made no requests to the Comintern for funding through 1927. Other signals, she thinks, that the Party suddenly became comparatively wealthy, were a series of journeys that Party officials made to Europe as well as its ability to move out of the Trades Hall and rent its own office space. She believes the explanation for this comparative prosperity was that through the agency of Frank Glass, the Party was siphoning funds out of ICU accounts. She notes that in writing to Eddie Roux in December 1926, Bunting referred to a 'regular scramble for free trips'. Glass, she suggests, did not really resign from the Party in 1925 and that this was only a subterfuge that enabled him to remain close to the ICU.[53]

Kadalie, it is quite true, did indeed complain that the communists stole ICU money. His contentions, though, probably had their origins in a dispute with La Guma over the control of funds in a bank account maintained by the Cape Town head-quarters of the ICU which he accused La Guma and other officials of transferring into another account used by Cape Town's ICU branch.[54] In an argument with Roux, Kadalie did not repeat this accusation. Writing on 10 October 1928, he angrily refuted Roux's suggestion that the ICU's financial administration had a history of malpractice:

> You say also the finances of the ICU were bad long before and that you did not like to expose us then. If that is correct, any sensible person will agree with me that your Party is rotten to the core since it connived to a crime. … You are deceitful, because your Party got a lot of moneys from the ICU through your printing press.[55]

Ethelreda Lewis, as we have seen, disliked Frank Glass intensely and she was convinced that he had remained a communist. She suggested to Winifred Holtby in a letter written in April 1928 that Glass had stolen hundreds of pounds from the ICU while pretending to manage the Union's accounts.[56]

It is true that the Party funded at least one journey to Europe in 1927, the fare for the ANC President Joshua Gumede's travel to Brussels.[57] But the other expeditions were either, as in Bill Andrews' case, financed through the trade union organisations or paid for by host organisations. Bunting's comment about 'free trips' rather implies trips for which the Party did not have to raise funds. We know that Comintern financing of its non-Russian affiliates peaked in 1927; for Russians, the strategic significance of the British Imperial parties had increased.[58] We also have a comprehensive picture of the ICU's accounts through the balance sheets prepared by Frank Glass. From May to October 1927, head office income from ICU branches totalled £6203; expenditure, mainly on salaries and printing was slightly higher. Altogether the ICU had in its accounts credit balances totalling nearly £1500.[59] Indeed, after a year of Glass's management, the ICU's National Council noted 'with pleasure the improvement made in the financial position'.[60] At about the same time the Party was compelled to halt publication of its newspaper temporarily because it could not afford it. If the Party, through Glass, was stealing from the ICU, it seems unlikely that it would have been unable to pay its printing bills. The ICU's own in-house chronicler, incidentally, insisted that when communist officials ran the

ICU's finances before 1926, they did so honestly, and that the major abuses occurred after the expulsion of communist office-holders.[61]

From the perspective of the Party's leadership, its effort to constitute a progressive united front through alliance with the ICU had been unrewarding. To be sure, from 1924, Communist Party members held key positions in the ICU. But communists who helped manage the ICU would fail in their efforts to reform the organisation or in their advocacy of strike action. Individual communists such as Thomas Mbeki made a significant contribution in extending the ICU's reach to smaller towns and farms in the Transvaal and the Free State, but this was not a consequence of the Party's directives; before 1928, the Party paid very little attention to the people it called 'rural toilers'.

Building support through the ICU's networks

The Party's activities were focused mainly on urban workers but its connections with the ICU would have given its African members access to networks that extended into agrarian communities, now a target of repressive legislation enacted by the Pact regime. Indeed, it was African Party members, particularly Thomas Mbeki, who through 1926, began building ICU branches among African labour tenants in the Eastern Transvaal, their efforts prompted by tenant protests against the application of the 1926 Masters and Servants Act which lengthened the time they had to work on the landowners' fields.[62]

Sydney Bunting was evidently unaware of the labour tenants' rebellion on South African farms, in which several African communists had been involved as ICU organisers. This was despite the fact that he personally worked quite closely with African members, teaching regularly at the Ferreirastown night school, where despite his formality and general 'awkwardness and angularity', his charges 'worshipped him', apparently.[63] But when it came to decision-making, African members were still on the margins. Thomas Mbeki, the main African communist in the ICU, in any case, had resigned from the CPSA so he could retain his ICU position; but, he may also by this time have been working as a police informer.[64] Eddie Roux, who might well have been better informed than Bunting about the scope of ICU rural activity was studying in Britain in 1927 and 1928.

On 25 March 1927, the Party began its own foray into the field of African labour organisation, now competing with the ICU. A coordinating committee for a new Federation of Native Trade Unions was set up, chaired by Ben Weinbren, with Thibedi as full-time paid organiser and La Guma as secretary. In Moscow in July, Eddie Roux wrote a memo for Comintern providing details of the Federation's membership. He claimed the five affiliates between them had a membership of 1 163. At the same time, the Party began to assertively recruit an African membership setting up branches in Sophiatown, Evaton, Potchefstroom and Vereeniging that would be wholly constituted by Africans. In Vereeniging, the Party incorporated a disaffected ICU branch led by communists whom the Union had expelled;[65] a popular night school helped to swell its local organised following. The ICU branch had originally been established after a visit from Thibedi. In 1929 and 1930, Vereeniging communists were active in local protests against a new lodger's tax and new regulations that required African women living in the township to carry passes. A local member of the Party, Rapatana Tjelele, also helped to establish an embryonic steelworkers union.

In Potchefstroom, the Party grew after Bunting had succeeded in obtaining an acquittal for Thibedi from an incitement charge. As in the case of Vereeniging, the Party's membership would grow to over 1 000 during 1928 as a consequence of communists' engagement in local opposition to the introduction of township lodgers' fees. The similarities between the kinds of preoccupations that animated the Party's new following in these small centres is very striking. In Potchefstroom, Party headquarters directed Edwin Mofutsanyana and Shadrach Kotu in June 1928 to set up a night school. They did their best to instil a systematic structure, but in the end, 'We had a big loose Party and we called them communists.'[66] Local women viewed the fees as an assault on their families as children over the age of 18 living at home would now be taxed. The Party supplied more legal support for people who refused to buy the permits, and local communists, many of them women, organised meetings and a procession of 300 to the court building when non-permit holders were charged. In this vicinity, it was the Party's prestige and its apparent embodiment of an alternative source of authority and power to a repressive local administration that were the sources of its local appeal. As Josie Mpama, one of the local Party leaders, recollected much later: 'When one man asked ... why he should join, the answer was given that he would be able to carry a briefcase, like the organisers do.'[67]

Elsewhere, many of the Party's new followers were farm workers, attracted to the Party for much the same reasons that such people were at that time flocking to the ICU. Meetings among these groups were often held 'in a religious atmosphere', the Party's Central Committee noted in mid-1927,[68] a mood to which the Party's own African organisers responded: 'we speak of the love that you Christians speak of and we believe we should protect that love', Mofutsanyana reassured his listeners at one Party rally.[69] These efforts brought substantial increases in membership. By mid-1928 the Party claimed an organised following of 1 750, 1 600 of whom were not white and by the end of year the total had risen to 3 000.[70] Such claims need to be interpreted cautiously. A visiting Comintern official found in 1931 that membership claims of a similar order were often based on 'one-time contacts'.[71] This may have been the case earlier; ballooning local memberships such as those registered by Party organisers in Potchefstroom were more likely to reflect transient local excitement rather than durable commitment. As the Party itself noted, retrospectively, in 1932, these local followings were usually based on 'loose and indefinite' relationships; the 1 000 people signed up at Potchefstroom were all recruited at a single meeting, and many of these were farmworkers rather than location residents.[72]

As in Vereeniging, communists also recruited members through already established ICU networks in Durban. For example, a major confrontation between Africans, the police and white civilians on 17 June 1929 in Durban followed an unruly demonstration outside the municipal beer hall during a boycott. Police raids in November sought to intimidate tax defaulters. A Communist Party branch was first established in Durban by Party members working within the ICU trying to build support among dockworkers. The branch was reportedly defunct by 1926.[73] The Party then revived its presence in Durban in 1928, recruiting among ICU *yase* Natal members and concentrating on Ndabeni township where the municipality had raised rents. Elsewhere in Natal, one of the new ex-ICU recruits was one of the Union's organisers of labour tenants around Pietermaritzburg, former school teacher Gilbert Coka, who had attended Bunting's night school classes and who was, according to the Party's organiser in Pietermaritzburg, storekeeper and one-time ICU adherent, L.H. Greene, a 'born orator'.[74]

Conflict between the authorities and African residents in Durban reflected an increasingly repressive political climate nationally. Global depression in 1929 would halt manufacturing growth and employment would fall. In 1929, the National Party won an electoral majority; now it could dictate terms on policies affecting Africans. There were to be new taxes on urban residents, including African women for the first time. The imposition of lodgers' fees in Potchefstroom in 1928 and in Vereeniging in 1930 heralded what was a wider effort to expand African taxation. These localised developments helped the Party acquire substantial if loosely organised followings in these centres.

During 1930, the Communist Party expanded its Durban following, drawing into its fold former ICU supporters. In Natal generally, taxation increases for Africans were especially high and, in November, armed police conducted tax raids in Durban; searching 8 000 people for proof of payment receipts. Rather unexpectedly the Communist Party had won a council seat in February 1929 in a municipal by-election in Durban Point, with the election of Sophus Pettersen, a Norwegian ship owner and former leader of the Sailor's Union as an independent workers' candidate. Within the ward, Pettersen owned several businesses and he had easy access to the docks and was a familiar figure in the compounds where he addressed workers' meetings. Roux suggested that it was in Durban in 1930 that *Umsebenzi* sales peaked reflecting local sentiment after the taxation raids. That year, the Communist Party was able to offer inspirational leadership to an African working class that had become disillusioned with the ICU *yase* Natal. An alliance between the Union and the Zulu king had proved to be unpopular, failing to shield unemployed men from eviction from the city for having no visible means of subsistence, a new provision under the 1930 amendment of the Urban Areas Act. Engagement of ICU leadership in the newly established Advisory Boards helped detach them from concerns of the 'labouring poor'.[75]

A freshly invigorated Communist Party branch was able to enlist into its ranks a significant number of lower-level ICU officials and thousands of the Union's rank-and-file would join the Party's informal following. A decision by the Party to end the year with a militant protest against the pass laws with mass pass-burnings on Dingaan's Day, 16 December, elicited a massive turn-out in Cartwright Flats, the customary venue for ICU gatherings. As police reported 'a huge crowd, many of them ICU adherent' handed in their passes to Party organisers together with tax receipts, collected in bags and then burnt in a bonfire.[76] As Sifiso Ndlovu has pointed out, the messianic speeches of Johannes Nkosi, as recorded by the police, effectively rooted the communist vision of a black republic in local Zulu nationalist iconography as well as all too recent memories of land dispossession:

> I am native. I am standing in the country of my birth. This country of ours has been stolen. These people have stolen our country and are ruling it. Dingaan was a communist, and he will be there on the Day of Dingaan.... This is the day when we will not forget those who will put them [whites] in hell.[77]

The police broke up the meeting before the burnings could begin and during the confrontation, three people were killed. Nkosi, the Party's main organiser in Durban, a former cook and farm hand, died subsequently in hospital with a fractured skull, most probably from wounds inflicted by policemen.[78] In the aftermath of the Durban protest, 200 of 'the most active communists' were deported. For example, in February 1931, the leader of Durban Clairwood branch, Abraham Nduweni, was banished to Standerton. His branch had been formed in November 1930 when Nduweni led the members of his ICU branch into the CPSA.[79]

Bloemfontein supplied a final example of the way in which communists were able to pick up support through re-animating former networks of ICU activism. Here the key figure was Sam Malkinson, 'the most active communist in the Free State'.[80] That there was a branch at all in Bloemfontein was mainly a consequence of Malkinson's work. Malkinson was a Jewish Lithuanian immigrant. He had first arrived in Bloemfontein in 1914, accompanying his mother from Kaunus, invited by a wealthy uncle. His uncle promised his mother 'he'd make a man' of Sam and he put his 17-year-old nephew to work on his potato farm as a supervisor. Miserably paid and mistreated, Sam ran away after witnessing his uncle sjambokking an African worker. After failing to find work in Johannesburg as a bookkeeper, Sam joined the army. He spent nearly three years fighting in Flanders and was wounded. He tried to reach Russia but the authorities insisted he should return to South Africa. While recovering from his wounds, he had followed the news about the Bolshevik revolution with mounting excitement. After arriving in Cape Town, he joined the Party in 1921 and returned to Bloemfontein in 1923 to work as an accountant. There, in his words, he began 'preaching on a soap box in the location' and with Bunting's encouragement, assembled a Party branch, entirely African, helped by former ICU members including his chief collaborator Isaiah 'Ntele.[81] On good days he could draw a crowd of 400.[82] For the first time he found confidence as a speaker and acceptance among people he admired: 'I loved the Basotho – intelligent people, logical, gentle.'[83] He was banned from attending gatherings after being arrested for sedition but he continued to lead the branch, working through 'Ntele.

Malkinson would visit Bunting at his home in Johannesburg every so often because he 'kept the books' for the Party and each year prepared its financial report. Sam admired Bunting, 'made a hero of him' and maintained with him a lively correspondence, typed on a red ribbon. He fell out with the new Party leader installed at the behest of the Comintern, Douglas Wolton. For Sam Malkinson, Wolton seemed 'a typical Englishman', 'one who sulks if he doesn't like something'. He once asked Malkinson why he hadn't organised the Bloemfontein communists into factory groups as Comintern had demanded, and 'he sulked' when Malkinson told him 'there were no workers in Bloemfontein', not in that sense, 'here was only the railway.'[84] Malkinson's exclusion happened in stages. He had annoyed Wolton by challenging his directives on how the Bloemfontein branch should be re-organised. Then he was dropped from the Party leadership, now named the Politburo. Malkinson's ostensible failing was his lack of theoretical clarity, though the real reason may have been his criticisms at Politburo meetings of Wolton's protégé, Albert Nzula's drunken behaviour and anti-semitic language.[85] The Bloemfontein comrades demanded Malkinson's reinstatement. They also complained about Nzula, whom they said had been writing letters about Party matters to an ex-Party member in Bloemfontein whom they thought was now a police informer.[86] This insubordination was sufficient for Malkinson to be expelled for fractionalism, and in Roux's words, 'the Bloemfontein branch was destroyed.'[87]

Conclusion

When communists experienced brief successes in localised centres mobilising followings among black South Africans between 1926 and the early 1930s, they functioned as a militantly popular organisation, not as a class vanguard. The solidarities they appealed to in the language they used at their crowded meetings were to do with race, faith and justice, not class. The men and women making these appeals were usually not factory workers nor even proletarians in the broader sense. Like the ICU's local leadership from whom they were often recruited, communist organisers were often relatively well-educated, sometimes former teachers, storemen, shop assistants and clerks, people who within African urban communities enjoyed a degree of social mobility and independence. As with the ICU's following, the 'loose' communities constituted in African townships by local communists may have collapsed as suddenly as they appeared. However, they set an enduring pattern for future occasions when South African revolutionaries would succeed in finding a public.

12 Illusion and Disillusion: White Women and the ICU][1]

Elizabeth van Heyningen

Introduction

In 1927 Dr C.T. Loram, a 'liberal' expert on African education, said to Ethelreda Lewis, looking at her very closely: 'Will you tell me how it is that Kadalie has always women to help him? You and Mrs Palmer and Miss Holtby in England.'[2] Although Lewis felt that Loram was making an unsavoury insinuation, he raised an interesting question: Why did some of Kadalie's most faithful white support come from these women? And did they make an effective contribution to the ICU? The answers provide fresh insights into attitudes towards the British Empire in the 1920s and 1930s.[3] Further, by re-inserting Lewis, Palmer and Holtby into the history of the ICU, this chapter complements recent scholarship on the role of white women in anti-colonial and anti-racist struggles – for example, Nancy Cunard's remarkable contribution to black internationalism, notably her curating of the anthology *Negro* (1934) and her collaborations with George Padmore.[4]

Intellectual and political background

Winifred Holtby (1898–1935), Ethelreda Lewis (1875–1946) and Mabel Palmer (1876–1958) were all British-born. Palmer and Holtby were both university-educated, Palmer at Glasgow University and Holtby at Somerville College, Oxford. Both carved out successful careers, Palmer as an educationist, Holtby as a journalist and novelist; both were committed to the improvement of women's lives. They were 'old' 'equality' feminists. As Holtby explained, 'The New Feminism emphasises the importance of the "women's point of view", the Old Feminism believes in the primary importance of the human being.'[5]

Before she emigrated to South Africa in 1921, Mabel Palmer, then Mabel Atkinson, had been an active member of the Fabian Society which emphasised social research and gradual political change. After her short-lived marriage ended, Palmer moved to Durban, where she devoted herself to the education of black South Africans. Her research into Natal Indians led to such books as *Natal's Indian Problem* (1945) and *The History of Indians in Natal* (1957).[6] Palmer has been described as 'generous', devoted to black education, especially that of black women. For Shula Marks, she was 'exceptional'. At the same time, Edgar Brookes commented: 'Not unduly swayed by sentimentality, she saw the weaknesses of her charges and applied a devastating common-sense to their complaints'. Marks sees this 'common-sense' as insensitive at times.[7]

Winifred Holtby is best known for her friendship with Vera Brittain, the feminist and pacifist, and for her last novel, *South Riding* (1936).[8] A farmer's daughter, emotionally rooted in the Yorkshire countryside, Holtby's novel, *The Land of Green Ginger*, started just before she left South Africa, hints at the South African influence on her writing for it has echoes of South African farm novels.[9] It offered a visionary perspective on South Africa, a land of dreamy, untold opportunity: 'The Land of Green Ginger – dark, narrow, mysterious road to Heaven, to Fairy Land, to anywhere, anywhere, even to South Africa, which was the goal of all men's longing.'[10]

While the South African landscape had captured Holtby's imagination, her political commitment was inspired by the First World War. In 1922, she wrote to her friend, Jean McWilliam:

> The day of imperialism is passed. I heard its curfew sound when the guns startled the pigeons in Huchenneville orchard on Armistice day. Imperialism is really nothing more than dynamic and aggressive nationality. … Man may be, as Aristotle says, a political animal, but he is also endowed with sufficient self-love to make his duty to his neighbour the subject of a divine commandment, not a natural instinct. In order to acquire a trained social instinct … he has to be educated in cooperation. … What we want now is the transition to a still wider sphere of international cooperation, where empires don't matter, and patriotism becomes parochial, and the service of mankind at large is the only consideration.[11]

But Holtby still believed that Britain had a responsibility toward her colonial subjects: 'However much we like to keep to ourselves, we find that we are willy-nilly our brothers' keepers,' she wrote.[12]

Holtby's commitment to world peace, and to the League of Nations Union, drew her to South Africa in 1926. She spent six months touring the country, promoting the Union's vision of global cooperation. She was introduced to the small group of progressive white South Africans, including Mabel Palmer, and she met Clements Kadalie, the founder of the ICU, whom she described initially as 'the Bolshevistic Zulu Trades Union Leader'. In Durban, she was introduced to A.W.G. Champion, Kadalie's associate.[13] These encounters and her appalled insight into white South African racism provided her with the direction for her life for which she seems to have been searching.[14] Her commitment to South Africa, and the money and time that she devoted to supporting, first the ICU and later, William Ballinger, she came to consider to be her most important legacy, as 'the willing scribe of one permanent movement for releasing the human spirit'.[15]

Ethelreda Lewis was born of a cultivated but impecunious family. Her fortunes altered when she met a Capetonian, Joe Lewis, who was studying science in Cambridge. In

South Africa, she started writing articles for the local press, mainly to supplement her income. In 1925, her first novel, *The Harp*, was published with the assistance of Vera Brittain and Winifred Holtby, to whom she had been introduced by Jean McWilliam. What made Lewis's name, however, was her meeting with a white tramp named Aloysius Smith. He beguiled her with his tales of a roving life and together they wrote his autobiography. *Trader Horn* became a best-seller, particularly in the United States.[16] Both *Trader Horn* and Ethelreda Lewis had dropped into obscurity until they were rescued by the South African academic, Tim Couzens, in 1992.[17] In doing so, he also rescued many of Lewis's papers which cast light on her relationship with Clements Kadalie.[18]

Socialism, imperialism, modernisation and romanticism

Holtby and Palmer were both socialists. Their deliberate decision to support socialism, rather than the liberalism that was the more conventional home of the left-leaning middle classes, arose from the experience of the First World War, which both probably saw as the product of antiquated political structures, from their dislike of big capitalism, and the sense that the societies of the post-war world must build a more equitable society. Their experience as women led them to equate the position of women and black people. One of her life's aims, Holtby told her mother, was 'to see an end to inequalities of all kind, to persuade people "to recognise the human claims of Negroes and Jews and women and all oppressed and humiliated creatures".[19]

Some describe such moderate socialists as 'liberal', defining liberalism by its opposition to Marxist and fascist totalitarianism. Barbara Bush argues that liberal values inform 'the reformist socialism associated with the British Labour Party and the Trade Union Movement'. The liberal dilemma, she suggests, was the difficulty of tackling racism and oppression while remaining committed to a capitalist system that sustained oppression.[20] Certainly all three women deplored the use of violence as a means of change, and they saw revolution as integral to communism. A. Fenner Brockway of the Independent Labour Party in Britain wrote to Lewis in April 1929, agreeing that 'to urge the negroes to follow Communist policy is criminally stupid inviting violence and bloodshed in which the natives would be butchered and crushed'; but he was alarmed that 'the main concern of Dr Lewis and yourself is rather anti-communist than pro-native unionism'.[21] While Holtby's fears of communism in South Africa were at first influenced by Lewis, she moderated her opinion later[22] It is true that Holtby's visit coincided with the period when communists were most active in the ICU. Fanny Klenerman of the Waitresses Union taught English at the ICU adult education school. Holtby and Klenerman probably had much in common, but Holtby considered that, although South African communists could be generous and right-minded, they were armchair theoreticians, lacking practical experience. She described 'a clever Jewish woman communist' [Klenerman] whom she had met in Johannesburg:

> She was a B.A., knew her Marx; had some trade union experience & lots of pluck. But she seemed to think that you could go right ahead with native workers treating them as though they were skilled Europeans with a long Labour tradition behind them. She did not seem to see that they leave behind them instead … a long, long tradition of tribal organisation … The native worker is too near the kraal & the knobkerry yet to understand the long patience necessary for solidarity.[23]

Yet there remained fundamental differences between the views of socialists like Palmer, Holtby and William Ballinger, and those of the liberals of the Institute of Race Relations and the Joint Councils movement, and of such missionaries as Ray Phillips of the American Board of Missions. There is nothing to suggest that Holtby and Palmer, let alone Ballinger, were committed to capitalism. Kristin Ewins sees Holtby as a radical socialist who embraced 'benign imperialism' while the communist writer, Ralph Bates, thought that Holtby had the 'intellectual equipment of the revolutionary rather than the reformist'.[24]

There is an element of paternalism in Holtby's view of social change as evolutionary. She wrote to Fenner Brockway, congratulating him on his attempt to develop links between 'different grades' of socialists. They both stood on the same ladder, she explained, but some rungs apart. Fenner Brockway was concerned with a mature European world. 'In Africa we have to watch the welfare of a child [i.e. Africans], and the process is different and simpler. You don't argue with a child, you take the knife from his hand before you have had time to discover whether it has a sharp edge or not'.[25]

Mabel Palmer expressed herself in similar terms. In an unpublished article, 'The Economics of Transition in Native Life', she commented on the virtues of rural black social organisation but, she argued, whatever its strengths, it could not survive in the modern world. 'What is not understood [is] that we *cannot* preserve it; it can no more co-exist with our money and machine-using civilisation than a horse and a locomotive engine can make use of the same track,' she explained; a 'primitive subsistence economy and modern money and machine economy *can not* exist side-by-side in the same country'.[26]

Like Leonard Woolf, the major British critic of imperialism in the interwar years, Holtby embraced Article 22 of the League of Nations Covenant, which established the Mandates policy. Intended for the benefit of colonies that were inhabited by 'peoples not yet able to stand by themselves under the strenuous conditions of the modern world', the implicit assumption was that, eventually, colonised people were capable of organising themselves, but they needed tutelage in their less advanced stage. South Africa was not a mandate but, for 'benign imperialists' like Holtby the same caveats applied.[27] While the contradictions integral to this argument remained, over time, both Holtby and Woolf came to recognise more clearly the oppression inherent in imperialism.[28]

In a long letter to William Ballinger, Holtby attempted to explain her views on race and class. She equated the labour problems of South Africa with those of Motherwell in Scotland, where Ballinger had been working. She believed that Ballinger's Motherwell experience would assist him in the Transvaal:

> In each case the aristocracy of Labour is frightened of & contemptuous of the lower layer. The more I see of different races & nationalities & classes, the more certain I am that the man with education, opportunities & sufficient wealth for a civilised stand and of living is much the same whatever his colour, & the man living on the margin of subsistence is much the same whatever his race.[29]

Lewis, by contrast, was a romantic conservative, with an Arnoldian perspective on 'The Machine'.[30] As Holtby noted: 'You seem to despise machinery & modern ways, not only for Africans but for themselves – as though there were no virtue in them. I can't accept that. I am glad of the complexity of life; I do not find it hopeless … I do not think that the heart of man is hurt by machinery – only but its ridiculously unintelligent use'.[31] Couzens identifies Lewis as a 'liberal segregationist' and he considers her to be 'a novelist who was to have a more direct effect on South African history than any other woman writer, including Olive Schreiner and, perhaps, even Emily Hobhouse'.[32] What Lewis valued was untamed Africa before it was killed by the Machine Age, destroyed by the 'mean and constant suspicions of Labour born in crowded states, and the cold cruelty of the capitalist'. Her novel, *Wild Deer*, saw Africans, the wild deer, in the grip of the capitalist python. 'Who can save the doomed creature? Who can compass the death of the python? Not the Garveys of this world, themselves helpless in the grip, smeared with the slime, of Western civilisation'[33]

At the same time, Lewis admitted that, in trying to help 'the native find his feet' she had to swallow her conservatism. In Johannesburg, where white capitalists had instituted a 'university of crime', 'it is impossible to keep them savages or educated mission-natives any longer'.[34] But like others who combined this Arnoldian dislike of technology with a paternalistic attitude to the poor, Lewis had no difficulty in holding contradictory opinions. Although she was more aggressively anti-communist than Holtby or Palmer, she considered Sidney Bunting, chairman of the South African Communist Party, to be 'a saint unrecorded in the annals of churches'; she felt that that Bunting had given his life to succour Native workers for 'in a place like Johannesburg there is deliberate and conscious starvation of the black man by the White who uses the Native strength and the gay, laughing nature which is part of the source of that strength to grow rich by'.[35] It is this humane compassion that seems to have shaped Lewis's actions, regardless either of theoretical consistency or of the hostility of her white neighbours.

First contacts

Mabel Palmer was probably the first of these three women to become a supporter of the ICU. In Durban, she was a member of the Joint Council, and it is likely that, through this link, she encountered Kadalie and A.W.G. Champion. Given her Fabian background, it was natural, too, that she should give this dynamic trade union her support. It is not certain when Lewis met Kadalie. Couzens states that this occurred in 1926 and she certainly seems to have met him at the time of Holtby's arrival in Johannesburg in early March 1926.[36]

While she was staying with the Lewises, Holtby wrote to Vera Brittain explaining that she was 'deeply involved' in native affairs. In Durban, she had already met Champion (probably through Mabel Palmer) and told him of the history of English trade unionism, 'begging for patience'. Like Lewis, she worried about the influence of communism on the ICU:

> He [Champion] is reasonable, courteous, patient beyond description; but he has upon him the burden of millions of men, still uneducated, brought into contact on the very worst lines with western civilisation, taught the crudest elements of communism with a dash of militant Bolshevism, & then abandoned to find their own salvation.[37]

What is clear is that Lewis was impressed by what she had heard of Kadalie's early achievements and the trust which so many people had in him. 'They believed in him,' she wrote. 'He had a great following, he was a South African Marcus Garvey.'[38] She was concerned, however, about the kind of support he was getting from whites. In particular, she felt he was being wooed by the Communist Party and she was suspicious of the role that Frank Glass was playing in the organisation.[39] As an outsider and a woman, never a member of the Johannesburg Joint Council or the SAIRR, Lewis was also dubious about white 'liberals'. The 'mission group', she noted, looked suspiciously at any independent African organisation. 'They would have nothing to do with this bad man whom they called an agitator, as indeed he was. Like a ripe plum, he was about to fall into the Communist camp'.[40]

It seems probable that, while Holtby was staying with Lewis, the two women had long discussions about South Africa. In their support for Kadalie and the ICU they found a common cause. One subject that they seem to have discussed was the ICU rejection of liberal approaches. They knew that neither Kadalie nor Champion wanted truck with the Joint Councils or missionaries like Ray Phillips of the American Board Mission. Lewis had taken Holtby to meet Kadalie at the ICU office in Johannesburg; it was 'a queer mixture of self-respect & squalor,' Holtby told Vera Brittain. Kadalie she thought was 'extremist, suspicious, sensitive, vain, sincere'.[41] She came to understand that men like Kadalie, Champion and R.V. Selope Thema were deeply sceptical of the overtures of the 'big men' of the mining world, who were hostile to black trade union organisation, but Kadalie and his associates were equally unresponsive to the white liberals of the SAIRR and the missionaries. The result, Holtby noted, was that the only white people who gave them help were the communists. Holtby was wary of this influence. 'Now Communism with Bertrand Russell means one thing, but this particular brand of communism, undiluted & superimposed upon a peculiar ignorance of history or economics, is quite another thing, & there is sufficient unrest among the native workers about the Colour Bar

Bill to cause real trouble – which might be really nasty'.[42] Unfortunately, white trade unionists saw black trade unionists as a threat rather than as brothers. Holtby deplored this division and she seized upon Lewis's suggestion that concerned whites should reach out to black people more directly. 'Mrs Lewis had a happy idea,' she wrote to Vera Brittain. 'If the native Trade Unionists won't go to the white people, the whites must go to the Trades Unionists.' Lewis herself would keep in close touch with Kadalie, she explained, and 'my job is to keep the ILP and the New Leader people informed of their point of view.'[43]

Kadalie and Ballinger

Between 1926 and 1929 Kadalie visited Lewis regularly.[44] 'I feel so terribly responsible while K. was coming here so often and so desperately,' Lewis told Holtby. Kadalie clearly responded warmly: 'When perplexing questions confront me, I have looked for refuge to your advice,' he told her, and he was grateful. 'My people appreciate, and acknowledge with gratitude, your endeavours,' he added.[45] Lewis hoped that quiet diplomacy might lift from Kadalie's heart 'that despairing solitude of a man who has aimed high but has overestimated his own moral strength'. The two women offered other assistance where they could. Both wrote articles for the *Workers' Herald* and Holtby solicited books on Africa and trade unionism for a library in the Workers' Hall, the ICU headquarters in Johannesburg. Fanny Klenerman remembered it as a 'treasure house', with 'all the literature one could desire on the labour movement'.[46] But Lewis could see that there was trouble brewing and she was convinced that Kadalie needed trained assistance.[47]

This 'curious little side line' as Holtby initially termed it,[48] now absorbed much of her attention. She, Lewis and Palmer built networks of like-minded people, through whom they worked. The South African network was confined to the small number of progressive whites whom Lewis knew – Sarah Gertrude Millin and her lawyer husband, Philip Millin, and Oliver Schreiner, Olive Schreiner's nephew, also a legal man; the pianist Elsie Hall and her husband, Dr Stohr, along with Professor W.M. Macmillan, historian at the University of the Witwatersrand, and R.F.A. Hoernlé, Professor of Philosophy at Wits. Margaret Hodgson, Macmillan's colleague in the Wits History Department, became involved as well. In England, Holtby drew in members of the Independent Labour Party and the Imperialism; Committee of the Labour Party. Particular associates included Dr Norman Leys, who had worked in Kenya and was a fierce critic of British imperialism, Arthur Creech-Jones, the General Secretary of the Transport and General Workers Union; A. Fenner Brockway of the Independent Labour Party; and Frederick Livie-Noble, later secretary of the London Group on African Affairs.[49] Beyond this inner circle was Leonard Woolf, Secretary of the Labour Party Advisory Committee on Imperial Questions. Palmer's Fabian connections contributed links to H.N. Brailsford, the left-wing journalist, and George Bernard Shaw, who visited South Africa in 1932 and 1935. Holtby felt that trade union connections were particularly valuable given black suspicions of paternalistic middle-class whites.[50]

An immediate object of the British trade unionists was to bring Kadalie to Europe for the 1927 conference of the International Labour Organisation in Geneva, where 'native labour' was to be discussed. It would strengthen Kadalie's hand if he could present his case at an international forum, Creech-Jones explained to Holtby.[51] This visit was finally achieved.[52] Apart from the help that Kadalie received from Lewis, in Durban, Mabel Palmer provided him with introductions and ensured that he would be made to feel at home when he arrived in England. 'I like Kadalie more and more the better I know him, & he certainly has got brains,' Palmer told Creech-Jones.[53]

It is clear that, for Kadalie, this visit was a high point in his career. The kindness that he received from Holtby and Creech-Jones eased his way in an unfamiliar Europe. The visit also gave the British labour movement the opportunity to meet Kadalie and to assess him. At first he made a favourable impression, but it was clear to men like Fenner Brockway that the ICU needed trained assistance. 'The danger is a mass paper membership without effective organisation,' Fenner Brockway explained to Creech-Jones.[54] Lewis also felt that the ICU needed trained help – 'there was trouble brewing for his [Kadalie's] Union,' she noted.[55]

While Kadalie was still in England, Creech-Jones redrafted the ICU constitution. Since the ICU had broken with the communists at the end of 1926, when they were expelled from the Union, he removed reference to them, and he urged on Kadalie the need for 'high moral integrity' in the choice of officials.[56] Mabel Palmer hoped that the new constitution would assuage the fears of Natal whites that the ICU was a communist organisation. The fact that the ICU inspiration came from British trade unionism was a new point of view, she explained. This was valuable for heightened tensions between farmers and the ICU in the Greytown district made cooperation between the Durban Joint Council and the ICU more urgent.[57]

Holtby was acutely aware of the difficulties that existed in South Africa; above all, she wanted to see black and white labour movements unite:

> I do most sincerely believe that the first necessity now in South Africa is that there should be a native trade union movement, that it should be allowed to develop, and that it needs profoundly a few years under experienced leadership before it will be strong enough to face any more violent crisis than it has to face now. I believe that its hope lies in association with the white labour movement there, if that can possibly be obtained. I am sure that Kadalie is going on the right lines when he works for this. The gulf between black and white labour must ultimately be fatal to South Africa.[58]

The British toyed briefly with the idea of sending out a stenographer but this was quickly abandoned in favour of a more experienced adviser.[59] Lewis was convinced that a woman would be inappropriate. 'We can't do this with just Mrs Palmer and myself. We must have men. It is only fair to the natives to do so,' she wrote. She grumbled that white South African men were unhelpful. Only Livie-Noble (who had been in South Africa before returning to England) and Edgar Brookes had ever given her the assistance that she had pleaded for. 'And so it has always been when I have looked for help from men,' she complained.[60] Palmer agreed. 'They need some judicious & tactful white trade unionist v. badly. They have got their funds into dreadful confusion & Champion – blundering, good-hearted egoist – has exceeded his powers in various ways,' she explained. Convinced that Creech-Jones would benefit from African experience, she was keen that he should be the ICU adviser. 'All these questions of native labour are going to loom larger & larger in the future,' she urged.[61] But Creech-Jones rejected her plea.

Eventually a young Scot, William Ballinger, offered himself for the post of adviser. The history of William Ballinger's role in the ICU has been recorded elsewhere.[62] For these three women, however, Ballinger's appointment marked a shift in their allegiance. Although many people found him difficult and abrasive, they did not. They valued his blunt honesty, his enthusiasm and his hard work, and they appreciated the sacrifices he was willing to make. He knew little about South Africa, but he appeared to grasp the importance of the job that he would be doing. He explained to Holtby in his letter of application:

> The position in this country [Britain] is such, that a kind of stalemate will develop for some time… In the interval the attempt to exploit the so-called 'Backward Races' will be intensified, and in the years ahead, the Black and Yellow races will develop a Civic and National conscience. If our Black comrades are refused the assistance of their White brothers, then it means a fearful internecine struggle with a certain still further lowering of the Whites' standard of living. Another, and very real danger, is the outbreak of an East-West conflagration, with the Blacks used to Police the European Countries. It may be that whoever takes the post of Secretary to Kadalie, will go under in the maelstrom of Colour hatred, which could easily be fostered during an industrial dispute, but the post undoubtedly offers a splendid chance for someone to anticipate events, get an understanding with the White Unions, and help to put the Black ICU in something like order.[63]

Ballinger arrived in South Africa to find the ICU almost bankrupt. The organisation had not been able to pay his fare to South Africa, so Holtby and Lewis financed the voyage. Ballinger was daunted by the task he faced but he was excited to feel that he could make a real contribution to black South Africa. 'It is good to be alive, in such a period of a people's transition, and especially to have a control of a pulse in their lives; albeit it at present beats feebly.' In the beginning relations with Kadalie were good – 'Kadalie is working like a Trodjan [sic],' he reported.

Relations soon deteriorated and eventually Kadalie established a breakaway union, leaving Ballinger with a weakened Johannesburg section. Over time, he turned to other work on behalf of black people. Strikingly, the ICU had provided a place for black women in a way that the ANC did not, until much later, and Kadalie himself had warm relations with women.[64] Consequently it is not surprising to find that Kadalie's white female supporters did not abandon him immediately. Couzens noted that Lewis continued to defend him, at least until April 1929.[65] In June 1929, Holtby described Kadalie as 'very able' and she attributed ICU problems to the unpropitious South African political climate and the great poverty of black workers.[66] By the early 1930s, however, Kadalie had lost their support and they turned instead to ensuring an income for Ballinger so that he could remain in South Africa. Nonetheless, while Holtby and Lewis probably never fully grasped the pressures that drove Kadalie and continued to measure him by white middle-class standards, their relationship seems to have been 'transformative' in the way that Gopal suggests, setting them both on paths which they might never have walked without this friendship.[67]

What did Clements Kadalie gain from these relationships? His autobiography gives little indication although he speaks kindly of the assistance of these women. He was obviously flattered to know such 'distinguished' women. He did acknowledge that the advice of Lewis and Holtby 'led me to adopt a middle course'; in other words, they encouraged him to repudiate the communists.[68] He also received some personal financial assistance, at least from Lewis. Early in 1928, when Kadalie was confronted by heavy legal fees, arising from an attempt to overturn a government ban from visiting Natal, Lewis, flush with her royalties from *Trader Horn*, gave him £70. 'It was the first time I had felt rich and had caught a glimpse of the power of money. When I see how easy it is for rich men to act and how rarely they do I am amazed and incredulous at the opportunities they let slip of helping the world along,' she explained.[69] Without Holtby's 1926 visit to South Africa, it seems unlikely that he would have built the connections that he did with European trade unionism. Wickins suggests that these women offered him 'a prize for which he had long striven, the integration of his union into the main stream of the labour movement' although the ICU never managed to affiliate with South Africa's white trade unions.[70] Between them, they brought to the notice of the European left the plight of black South African workers. Sadly, though, these were unpropitious years for the left with the Great Depression, the rise of fascism and a world war to follow.

Wild Deer and Mandoa, Mandoa!

There is a footnote to this account. Holtby and Lewis were also novelists and each drew on their ICU experience in novels. Ethelreda Lewis's last book, *Wild Deer*, and Holtby's African tale, *Mandoa, Mandoa!*, were both published in 1933. *Mandoa, Mandoa!* had the misfortune to be published within three months of Evelyn Waugh's *Black Mischief* for both books were satirical novels about colonialism in Africa. Nevertheless *Mandoa, Mandoa!* sold relatively well, breaking into the American market and receiving good critical reviews. Now, it has been largely forgotten and, apart from a handful of exceptions, it has been ignored in recent academic literature.[71] *Wild Deer* shared a similar fate, until it was partly resurrected by Tim Couzens in an edition for which he provided a fine introduction.[72] More recently,

Wild Deer has been examined in a blog by Dr Dan Wylie of Rhodes University. In his view the novel is 'not half bad'. He continues, 'In my view, Lewis's insight, political complexity and stylistic flair are as good as those of her much more famous near-contemporary, Olive Schreiner, if not better'.[73]

Attempting to free herself from the shadow of *Trader Horn*, Lewis wrote *Wild Deer* under a pseudonym, R. Hernekin Baptist. Couzens considers that the novel looked back to the three years when Lewis played a central role in the destiny of South Africa. 'For three crowded years,' she wrote, 'I was able to speak for the Natives … and be reported'.[74] The protagonist, Robert de la Harpe, was clearly based on Paul Robeson, whom Lewis had met. De la Harpe was an African American singer, cultured, sensitive but adrift in a world in which he felt lost; in South Africa he returned to his African roots, finally marrying an innocent young woman from the countryside. Although there is no association, De la Harpe bears a resemblance to Dr Don Shirley in the award-winning film, *Green Book* (2018). (This similarity probably speaks to the enduring nature of the myth of the 'noble savage' for Lewis's depiction of De la Harpe has this element to it, as does *Green Book*.) Couzens considers that there is the ghost of another Othello that haunts the book, in the person of Clements Kadalie. The book was in part an expression of Lewis's disillusionment with Kadalie and in it, she turned her back on urbanising Africa.

Couzens is right to talk of 'ghosts'. De la Harpe bears little resemblance to Kadalie but Johannesburg ('Goldburg'), the destructiveness of mining capitalism and the plight of black workers haunts the book. One quotation must serve to give a sense of Lewis's awareness of the degradation of the compounds:

> There were no women to be bought in the compound. They watched like jackal bitches outside. But in the deep parts of the night there was none to make a man forget the chill of the cement bed, none to make a man forget the weariness of the mine. … He falls lower than any savage, lower than any beast of the forest. He falls, it may be, to those slimy depths in which man craves man.[75]

Winifred Holtby was delighted with *Wild Deer*. She wrote to Lewis: 'Why ever did you say it was not a good book? Such passion, such pity, such superb beauty of colour and feeling. One doesn't come across a book like that in a month of Sundays. … To write anything with such vitality is a splendid achievement'.[76]

Mandoa, Mandoa! is very different from *Wild Deer*. Holtby explained that: 'I want to do something hard, muscular compact, very little emotional, and then the emotion hammered into the style. Metal-work, not water-colour'.[77] The book must have been a surprise to those who knew Holtby as a vivid, generous, energetic and optimistic woman, for it rings more of work emanating from the Bloomsbury group; there are echoes of E.M. Forster's cautious *Two Cheers for Democracy* in it. *Mandoa, Mandoa!* is a more ambitious book than *Wild Deer* for it is a critique of imperialism and of the impact of a Western capitalist, materialist culture on a corrupt pre-industrial society based on slave labour.

The central Mandoan figure, Safi Talal, is partly based on Kadalie. Holtby's depiction of Talal is both sympathetic and cynical. He is described as a prepossessing person. Bill Durrant, the emissary sent to Mandoa by a tour company to prepare for tourists invited to the wedding of the virgin princess, is impressed by him, realising that Talal was a man of 'subtle and profound intelligence'. At the same time, 'Talal was honourable; and he accepted bribes shamelessly. For all his liberality, he gave gifts with the most lively hope of favours to come. ... He lied on principle, frequently and with deliberation. In Mandoa, truth was too rare a coin to be used in current exchange'.[78] The slavery of Mandoan society is equated with the wage slavery of the West. Bill attempts to explain the concept of free labour to Talal:

> Half to himself, he began to describe the way in which British industrial work was carried on. The people were not slaves – but they were not free. They obeyed orders, 'clocked in' to factories, downed tools when the whistle blew, were bullied by foremen, and dismissed at the will of an employer. They ... worked eight or nine hours a day to benefit shareholders they never saw, and to judge by their votes at the last election accepted the situation with complacency. While Bill talked, Talal raised his fine eyebrows and stroked his silky beard.[79]

In descriptions like this, Ewins suggests, Holtby is revealing the inherent barbarism in both cultures.[80] Nor does Holtby offer an unambiguous conclusion. At the end, Bill reflects on this place where he has chosen to stay: 'He saw it as a place of poverty and squalor, without arts, or learning, or dignity, or discipline, or science, a place ruled by a corrupt and irresponsible aristocracy, a place where human effort was subject to a million accidents of nature, of chance, of man's unmerciful caprice'.[81] Lisa Regan notes that the portrait of Bill Durrant was partly based on William Ballinger; both shared a commitment to developing Africa. Despite their disillusion, both remained in Africa although the contribution of both was ambiguous. By remaining in Mandoa, Bill was keeping the airport runway clear, the hotel prepared for future tourists. If the Europeans left, he did not believe that the trappings of civilisation would survive a day. But, while he stayed, he was not wholly useless – 'it meant that he had kept faith, though he knew not with what power; he had prepared the way, he knew not for what event'.[82]

On the whole *Mandoa, Mandoa!* was well received. Harold Laski considered it 'masterly'; and he continued: 'It isn't merely its wit and gaiety of temper. It is even more the power to convey a philosophy of civilisation with a critical insight that has the thinker's knowledge and the artist's detachment. I do congratulate you warmly. You are an asset to social decency'.[83] By contrast, her friend, Dr Norman Leys, disliked it. The Mandoans bore no resemblance to Africans, he complained. 'I don't care a damn who your authorities are. I don't believe in these blood thirsty Sensual Savages'.[84]

Winifred Holtby wrote *Mandoa, Mandoa!* while in the throes of the illness that was to kill her two years later on 29 September 1935. By then she had completed her final novel, *South Riding*, which was to bring her enduring critical acclaim. Almost to the last, she continued to work for Ballinger and Africa. In Johannesburg, she left a legacy in the Winifred Holtby Memorial Library, which was opened in 1940 in Western Native Township, the first library in Johannesburg for black people. It was moved subsequently to Soweto where, sadly, it was burnt down in 1976.

After the death of her beloved husband in 1931, Ethelreda Lewis moved to Port Alfred in the Eastern Cape. She lived out her days in relative obscurity but, in her last years, she devoted her energies and limited income to electioneering for Margaret Ballinger for the 1948 Senate elections where she stood as a 'native' representative.

In Durban, Mabel Palmer continued to work for black education. In 1929, she was elected to the Senate of the University and she was awarded an honorary doctorate for her work in education in 1947. One of the residences of the University of KwaZulu-Natal is named after her.

13 The Romance and the Tragedy of the ICU

David Johnson

Introduction

Were Marx's comment attributed to Hegel that history is repeated 'once as a great tragedy and once as a wretched farce' to be applied to the history of the ICU, we would have to settle upon a different sequence of literary genres: history is told once as an anti-colonial romance and once as a didactic tragedy.[1] Farce is not entirely absent from the historiography of the ICU, but as we shall see, romance and tragedy are the two genres to have most frequently framed its histories.

In discussing the historiography of the ICU, the meanings of 'anti-colonial romance' and 'didactic tragedy' are nuanced, but preliminary definitions are nonetheless required. The anti-colonial romance contains: heroic protagonist(s) (individual anti-colonial leaders or collective movements/organisations); formidable adversaries and obstacles (the agents of the imperial power, the settler/colonial state, local and international capital, and rival parties and leaders); and an optimistic plot-line recording the heroic protagonist's progress in overcoming these obstacles as s/he/they journey from subjugation to freedom.[2] The didactic tragedy – derived from Aristotelian tragedy – comprises: heroic protagonist(s) with a fatal flaw (*hamartia*); a plot in which the hero initially flourishes, but then suffers a reversal (*peripeteia*) and/or discovery (*anagnorisis*) as a result of the fatal flaw; and a final act culminating in suffering/ calamity/ death (*katastrophe*).[3] Whereas the desired effect of anti-colonial romances upon audiences and readers is to inspire other anti-colonial struggles, didactic tragedies aim to educate/warn/admonish those contemplating anti-colonial resistance.

In the conclusion, alternative generic frames to romance and tragedy are considered for the re-writing of the history of the ICU now. Revisiting the historiographical reflections of C.L.R. James, as well as the different versions of his classic, *The Black Jacobins: Toussaint L'Ouverture and the San Domingo Revolution* (1938, 1963), I argue that by disrupting the dominant inherited genres, the history of the ICU in the 1920s can be e-interpreted to speak to the politics of Southern Africa in the 2020s.

The romance of the African toilers

In 1923, Kadalie opened his essay 'A Call from Macedonia' in the radical US magazine, *The Messenger*, with the observation, 'I shall venture to state that the romance of the African toilers has never been written gallantly so as to create attention in the outside labor world, more particularly to reach kinsman and brother, the American Negro'.[4] Addressing this silence, Kadalie proceeds to recount the 'romance of the African toilers', establishing a narrative template for his subsequent accounts of the history of the ICU. First, he casts himself as the heroic embodiment of the African workers' struggle. Writing of himself in the third person, he notes, 'he pursued the path of duty and served his race and the working class'.[5] Secondly, he enumerates the formidable obstacles confronting the ICU: to overcome the divisions between workers ('our chief obstacles here are our various native languages and also the uncultured state of mind of the many thousands of the race'); and to withstand the police violence unleashed upon workers by the segregationist state ('1920 began with struggles for economic emancipation but ended in sorrow, imprisonment and deaths').[6] Thirdly, he expresses total confidence in the capacity of the ICU to overcome all adversity and to progress towards freedom. Kadalie contemplates defeat following the Port Elizabeth killings of 1920 but refuses to capitulate, asking rhetorically, 'Were widows, orphans of the victims of the Port Elizabeth tragedy, and the maimed ones to be denied maintenance by the workers? No!… And since then we cry out: Onward! Onward!'.[7] Could one individual tragedy unsettle romance as the framework for narrating the ICU's history? Kadalie's answer is an emphatic no, as he reverts briskly to his optimistic *telos*, quoting Booker T. Washington: '"the history of the African natives in the Dark Continent seems like the story of a great adventure, in which for my part I am glad to have had a share"'.[8] Washington projects his own personal history of individual and collective self-improvement in the United States on to the history of Africans in Africa, and Kadalie then adopts Washington's projection as an inspirational model for the interwoven history of his own life and that of the ICU.

In subsequent accounts, Kadalie repeated his anti-capitalist/anti-segregationist historical romance with but minor variations. In 1926, he published two such articles in the *Workers' Herald*. In the first, 'The Romance of African Labour', he identifies his destiny and the ICU's as one:

> It was absolutely necessary that the workers should be given a new revolutionary lead at the threshold of a new year, and the onus fell on me to steam off this new line of agitation… All over the country the African workers breathed a new spirit. They exclaimed with one voice: 'We want to be free men and women in the land of our forefathers.'[9]

Of the obstacles confronting the ICU on its journey to freedom, Kadalie begins with the South African Party government of Jan Christiaan Smuts. Characterising the police shootings instigated under Smuts' aegis – the Port Elizabeth killings of 1920; the Bulhoek Massacre of 1921; the Bondelswarts Rebellion of 1922; and the 1922 Rand Strike – as 'a reign of terror', Kadalie describes how '[w]ith our fellow white workers, we had resolved together to rid South Africa of one common enemy, General Smuts, and his Corner House Government'.[10] Claiming credit for the ICU's contribution to J.B.M Hertzog's defeat of Smuts in the 1924 election, Kadalie celebrates a brief moment of triumph: we 'were confident of the fact that the rule of Big Finance was abolished in South Africa, and that automatically prosperity, good government of the people by the people and for the people, would be the watchwords of our sunny land'.[11] However, no sooner had Smuts been seen off than the ICU was confronted by a new enemy – the treacherous Hertzog at the head of the Pact coalition government of the National Party and South African Labour Party. In his 'infamous Smithfield declarations', Hertzog revealed that far from rescuing black and white workers from Big Finance, he intended to abandon black workers, with bills before parliament that would ensure 'that the black men and women of this land should remain forever as "hewers of wood and drawers of water"'.[12] A key strategy of Hertzog's alliance of 'back-velders and capitalist imperialists' was to contain the ICU, specifically to prevent its expansion throughout the country. To this end, a ban on Kadalie's movement was imposed in March 1926, but Kadalie flouted the ban, undertaking in August 1926 a successful tour of Natal, which he describes in racy detail in the second half of the article. His final assessment of the Natal tour reiterates the identification of romantic hero and the masses, culminating in their common victory:

> I am now in the trenches. The enthusiasm of my fellow workers is now very high and encouraging. Messages of sympathy and solidarity pour in from all parts of the country... What is all this? Is democracy going to triumph? It looks like it.[13]

As in his 'Call from Macedonia' article, so too here Kadalie concludes with a quotation, in this case one stanza from a long poem by Walter Scott, the progenitor of the historical romance. The stanza from 'Lord of the Isles' (1814) describes Robert the Bruce killing the English knight De Boune in one-to-one combat on the eve of the Battle of Bannockburn – '"Right on De Boune the while he past/ Fell that stern blow, the first, the last"'.[14] The four lines of Scott's poem distil the essential elements of the historical romance, as well as correspond to the narrative structure of Kadalie's article: Robert the Bruce and Scotland stand for Kadalie and the ICU, and De Boune and the English oppressors stand for Hertzog and the 'back-velders and capitalists'. The vanquishing of De Boune and the victory of Scotland presages the defeat of Hertzog and triumph of the ICU.

In the second *Workers' Herald* article, 'Past and Future', Kadalie shifts register, adopting a mix of Biblical and military language to convey the historical struggles and relentless progress of the ICU. Of the historical betrayals and defeats inflicted in the past by the coloniser, Kadalie writes, 'Alike King David of old, [the white man] is not satisfied with what he possesses, and he will plot to kill Uriah at the battle front. Joab is there to do the job of manslaughter and poor Uriah is dead'.[15] But after centuries of oppression, the black man is fighting back: 'He will gather his unarmed warriors to meet at Bloemfontein at the beginning of the present year. The unarmed army accepts the challenge; thus, we are brought to the trenches and you hear the noise of bombs and aeroplanes'.[16] The adversities faced by the ICU are being overcome, with Kadalie aided by his loyal lieutenants. In 'The Romance of African Labour', Kadalie recounted the breach of his ban and successful speaking tour of Natal in the idiom of a boys' own adventure; here he describes it as a military campaign against Germany:

> At Durban, Commander A.W.G. Champion opens the defensive attack. The enemy is defeated there, five bad by-laws are declared ultra vires. Encouraged by these victories, it is decided that the 'chief of general staff' proceeds to the war zone. Immediately upon his arrival he is captured by the Huns. He is now a war prisoner and will soon be brought before the War Tribunal at the Hague. He is released by the court and the story of his release is a great inspiration to thousands of soldiers.[17]

Looking to the future, Kadalie believes that '[i]f the battle is conducted scientifically, fearlessly and courageously, one cannot but visualise a bright future before the black "Noble Ones"'.[18] And once again, he reaches for a poem to clinch his argument, quoting a stanza from Thomas Carlyle's translation of J.W. Goethe's poem, 'The Masonic Lodge' (1827): '"The future hides in it/ Gladness and sorrow;/ We press still thorow;/ Nought that abides in it/ Daunting us – Onward"'.[19] Goethe's tribute to the spirit of freemasonry thus travels from Enlightenment Germany via Victorian England to the freedom struggles of the ICU in interwar South Africa.

Two years later, when the ICU was disintegrating, Kadalie published a 'Manifesto' which provided a further modified version of the romance of the ICU. As in earlier versions, his own heroic role is emphasised. After describing the founding and early struggles of the ICU, Kadalie returns to his triumphs of 1925, claiming that '[w]ith extraordinary courage and zeal, I went from one place to another preaching INDUSTRIAL UNIONISM and sinking of TRIBAL DIFFERENCES amongst the African workers'.[20] Notwithstanding his successes in such endeavours, Kadalie found himself and the ICU confronting a new obstacle, namely internecine conflict: 'All my energy I utilise to build a MIGHTY TRADE UNION MOVEMENT amongst the Non-European workers. Instead of applauding and backing me, my colleagues are envying my position… In short, my colleagues are jealous of my achievements'.[21] To overcome this fresh challenge, Kadalie proposes two strategies. The first is for his ICU comrades to read a colonial romance – *Bayete! Hail to the King!* (1923) by George Heaton Nicholls: 'In that book, Mr Nicholls puts it clearly how the natives of South Africa supported by coloured people would gain their political and economic freedom by Mass Industrial Organisation'.[22] *Bayete!* is a novel that faithfully repeats the formula established in Rider Haggard's popular romances of the 1880s in which the white hero confronts and ultimately subdues African resistance, restoring the colonial order in the closing pages. In Kadalie's misreading of the novel, the white 'hero' Grim Collingwood and the colonial-settler state are defeated, and the unified African resistance movement led by Balumbata/ Nelson triumphs.[23] In other words, Kadalie subverts the genre of the colonial romance by first reversing the end of the novel, and then by interpreting it as an *anti*-colonial romance that teaches his message of African unity. His second strategy for addressing internecine conflict is of a different order, proposing the reconfiguring of the relationship between leader and masses. Asking 'What is the good of us leaders fighting amongst ourselves when thousands, if not millions, of our people are groaning under oppressive laws?', he pledges his willingness to relinquish his position as leader: 'I am ready to step out and hand over to those [the masses] trust, but I intend to be in the firing line as an ordinary soldier'.[24]

After the fragmentation of the ICU in 1928, Kadalie's references to the history of the ICU no longer fit the genre of the anti-colonial romance. His autobiography, first drafted in 1946, casts the defeats suffered after 1928 not as obstacles to be overcome, but as 'turning-points' and 'humiliations' signalling both the demise of the ICU and the end of his own public career.[25] Kadalie lists many reasons for the disintegration of the ICU: 'the split in the union'; 'the advent of Ballinger'; the attacks on himself 'owing to my being born outside the Union of South Africa'; the tendency of the rank-and-file to revert to tribal loyalties, 'to follow the chief, whether right or wrong'; the inept young men appointed as ICU officials who 'were not suited for public appointment [and] indulged in intoxicants freely'; 'bad financial management'; and 'rivalries amongst its higher officials… unscrupulously engineered by the European elements, backed of course by the powers that be'.[26] For Kadalie, the cumulative effect of these many mistakes and defeats brought the romance of the African toilers to a bitter end.

Before turning to the tragic versions of the ICU's history, it should be registered that in the 1920s, Kadalie was far from alone in framing the story of the ICU as romance. In 1926, the labour historians Ernest Gitsham and James F. Trembath praised Kadalie for using 'his talents and training to serve the cause of the Native worker. He is a popular figure among the Natives everywhere in the Union and he is destined to play an increasingly important part in the Trade Union Movement'; noted the obstacles confronting African trade unionism in the forms of the segregationist legislation and the racism of white workers; and applauded Kadalie's success in recruiting 30 000 members in such a short period, describing such progress as 'remarkable'.[27] In 1928, G.M. Godden provided an even more effusive portrait of Kadalie: 'that very remarkable young Atonga [who] owes his own education, his trained elocution, his powers of organisation, to the years spent at the white man's college at Livingstonia', and who has 'the necessary qualities of leadership, [a] bedrock of experience of native labour [and] a sagacious judgement'.[28] For Godden, the major threat to the ICU was communism, 'an epidemic of Red infection', but thanks to 'the bold and rapid tactics of Kadalie', the CPSA members of the ICU had been purged, ensuring that the unionised African worker could progress towards becoming 'a useful citizen in his own country and a loyal and industrious asset to the British Empire'.[29] Two years later, Leonard Barnes also lauded Kadalie's achievements, hailing the ICU as 'a remarkable monument to his ability, energy, and resolution', and while recognising the challenges facing the ICU, he proclaimed its destiny in florid terms: 'inchoate in design and fumbling in execution though it may be, [the ICU] is none the less an integral part of ['the Native'] struggle towards the light, a moving, and therefore memorable canto in the Bantu national epic'.[30]

Liberal tragedy

Absent from Kadalie's explanation for the demise of the ICI is any hint of self-recrimination. Many early chroniclers of the ICU, however, were more than ready to place the blame for the ICU's collapse at his door. In the late 1920s, A.W.G. Champion, the ICU leader in Natal, published several pamphlets in English and isiZulu that led the way in fundamentally revising the romance of the ICU. Champion's earliest pamphlet, *The Truth About the ICU*, follows the same narrative structure as Kadalie's accounts. He recognises Kadalie's pre-eminence as the founder of the ICU, acclaiming his heroic stature: 'great credit is due to Mr. Clements Kadalie for his pluck, determination, and courageous lonely fight against all opposition'.[31] Next, he enumerates the many obstacles confronting the ICU, emphasising the racist laws passed by the Pact Government, asking 'who is supposed to act as father to the Natives?'[32] He then insists that the ICU will overcome these obstacles and continue its journey to freedom: 'We have no fear, because right and righteousness are on our side. We shall go on doing what we have been doing. . . fighting for increased wages and the economic freedom of all workers'.[33]

Champion's second pamphlet, however, deviates sharply from the romance template, as it characterises Kadalie as the imperfect protagonist responsible for destroying the ICU. Champion locates Kadalie's fatal flaw in his susceptibility to the blandishments of white advisers, a flaw exacerbated by his 1927 tour of Britain and Europe: 'he came back from overseas with a sudden revolutionised mind. He wanted a European private secretary, white girls as shorthand typists ... he was told [by an ICU delegate] that he went away a black man and came back a white man'.[34] In a third pamphlet, Champion concludes with a six-stanza poem, 'Mr Clements Kadalie on the Horizon', which encapsulates Kadalie's transition from romantic to tragic hero. Described at first as 'Our Clements Kadalie once a mighty power/ ... publicly reported in the four/ Corners of the earth', the next stanzas identify Kadalie's flaws – 'loss of tact' and 'autocratic behaviour' – and then the final lines anticipate a tragic death: 'He deserves/ No support from us; let him hang himself'.[35]

At much the same time that Champion was abandoning his image of Kadalie as the heroic embodiment of the romance of African workers, the novelist Winifred Holtby was having similar misgivings. From February to June 1926, Holtby toured South Africa as a representative of the League of Nations Union, meeting Kadalie and Champion, and taking up the cause of the ICU. Her letters and articles from the 1920s and early 1930s provided the basis for a ventriloquised three-chapter account of the ICU in Vera Brittain's *Testament of Friendship* (1940). Like Champion, Holtby was initially impressed by Kadalie, praising his achievements – 'without money, experience or encouragement, he had organised the black and coloured workers into a presentable trade union' – and describing him as 'a remarkable black African from Nyasaland, flamboyant and dramatic, with the demagogue's qualities of leadership'.[36] Holtby highlights the formidable legal obstacles the Pact Government had flung in the path of the ICU, applauding Kadalie's early successes in rousing the African working class to challenge them: 'various repressive measures... gave [Kadalie] plenty of material for an intelligent survey of grievances, and his virulent tirades against the Government stirred the natives to support him'.[37] The momentum generated by the ICU was checked, however, by 'corruption and mismanagement due to the ignorance, inexperience and credulity of the members [and by] unprincipled lawyers fastening on to the Union', as well as by Kadalie's flaws as a leader. His lavish expenditures in England convinced Holtby that 'he was still too inexperienced to realise that the leader of a revolutionary movement must deny himself luxuries'.[38] Holtby did not restrict herself to complaining about Kadalie's flaws to her English audiences; in a personal letter to Kadalie, she first informed him, 'I have heard some criticism... of the lavishness of your expenditure', before contrasting his extravagance – 'the secretary of the ICU himself seems to spend what he likes upon taxis' – with the frugal ways of the '[t]he English labour pioneers, Keir Hardie and his friends, [who] were content with the humblest equipment until they saw their work firmly established'.[39] For Holtby, Kadalie-the-flawed-hero's downfall coincided precisely with the ICU's, so that by the time he was living in East London in the 1930s, he was 'a spent force, declined into a tragic shadow of the self-appointed Messiah who had landed so confidently in England'.[40]

Holtby's tragic reading of Kadalie and the ICU was elaborated by William Ballinger, the Scottish trade unionist she had helped to recruit as an adviser to the ICU. Although Ballinger's view of Kadalie became increasingly critical, he acknowledged his heroic qualities: 'Courage, no one can deny, Kadalie has had – the courage of the demagogue, and the gift of winning the confidence of men – the gift of leadership'.[41] As regards Kadalie's fatal flaw, Ballinger's diagnosis echoed Holtby's: '[The ICU's] leadership was concerned [with] grandiloquent Marcus Garvey ideas not unmixed with racial domination, instead of concentration on sound administration'.[42] Kadalie's fatal ineptitude as an administrator was, however, more than an individual failing; it was a consequence of the ICU's incomplete journey from the African to the European world: 'the ICU of Kadalie's leadership was but a transitional form, possible only at one stage of the advance of his people towards civilisation. It was trade unionism led by a "chief" – the trade unionism of workers only recently transported from tribal life'.[43] Complementing his characterisation of Kadalie as flawed hero, Ballinger followed the conventions of the tragic plot in identifying a *peripeteia* in the ICU's trajectory: 'The beginning of 1925 saw the opening up of the Rand by ICU emissaries. The headquarters were transferred from Cape Town to Johannesburg. This was the beginning of the end'.[44] By over-reaching itself, employing self-seeking officials, and neglecting the bureaucratic labour essential to trade unionism, the ICU sealed its fate. For Ballinger, however, the ultimate tragedy of the ICU resided not so much in the fate suffered by its flawed leaders and corrupt officials but in its failure to seize the moment and lead black workers to freedom: 'Truly nothing more tragic will ever be recorded in history than the chances for the emancipation of the African lost by the ICU officials in 1925'.[45]

Farce

Tragedy was not the only alternative generic framework to romance adopted to narrate the early histories of the ICU; the *Summarised History of the ICU* (1941) by H.D. Tyamzashe conforms much more closely to the genre of farce. Whereas both romance and tragedy endow their protagonists with heroic stature and aspire to uplift or instruct audiences, farce 'inspires hilarity mixed with panic and cruelty in its audience through an increasingly rapid and improbable series of ludicrous confusions, physical disasters, and sexual innuendos among its stock characters'.[46] In Tyamzashe's *Summarised History*, Kadalie's flaws are so extreme that it becomes impossible to read him as any kind of hero: on the one hand, he 'is entitled to a Monument equal to that edifice erected in honour of the late Cecil John Rhodes', and he is 'one of the most… brilliant platform speakers in this country', but on the other hand, 'his brilliance is dimmed by his uncouth and seditious-like utterings… He is simply a woolly-headed volcano of "damns" and "goes-to-hell"'.[47] As regards Kadalie's role in the history of the ICU, Tyamzashe's account of his ejection from Natal by Champion supporters in 1928 provides an instructive contrast to Kadalie's description of his triumphant 1926 tour of Natal. Arriving in Durban to inspect the accounts of the Natal branch of the ICU, Kadalie met with a hostile reception, and was forced to flee to Pietermaritzburg:

> [W]hen the Zulus heard of it, they followed with a big bus of frenzied supporters of Champion. They found [Kadalie] in bed in a secluded part of the city of Maritzburg. They 'arrested' him in bed with his pyjamas on and took him back holus-bolus to Durban IN HIS PYJAMAS; his street clothes followed later on. They forced him to address their meeting at 3 a.m. with his pyjamas on. The question they asked him was, 'Upi Umhlongo?' (Where is Mhlongo – meaning Champion)… But [Kadalie] was again saved by Champion, Batty and the C.I.D. [Detective Arnold] and he was put on the train direct to Johannesburg.[48]

Characterised as a pyjama-clad coward at the centre of the ICU's chaotic unravelling, Kadalie is reduced from hero to stock character in the denouement of a historical narrative that began as romance but mutated not into tragedy but into farce.

Communist tragedy

As in Tyamzashe's *Summarised History*, so too in the early communist accounts of the ICU, Kadalie's flaws were so deep that he failed to amount to a tragic hero. George Padmore, the Caribbean anti-colonial intellectual, contended in *The Life and Struggles of the Negro Toilers* (1931) that Kadalie belonged in the category of 'black reformist trade union leaders', along with 'Randolph and Croswaith in the United States [and] the nationalist reformist misleader, Marcus Garvey'.[49] In Padmore's account of the 1930 East London strike, 'Kadalie, the black traitor… appealed to the workers to obey the law (Masters and Servants Act) and return to work'; and in the Dingaan's Day protests of 16 December 1930, 'Kadalie ... attempted to sabotage the demonstrations of the workers [and] told the workers to be submissive and obey their oppressors'.[50] Following a similar line, Albert Nzula, member of the Communist Party of South Africa (CPSA) and co-author of *Forced Labour in Colonial Africa* (1933), acknowledged the rise of the ICU from humble origins in 1919 to become the largest organisation in Southern Africa, 'uniting 60 000 workers', but like Padmore, he blamed Kadalie squarely for its demise: 'In 1926, the blatant desertion of Kadalie, the union's leader, to the camp of reformism, and the activities of the British TUC adviser, William Ballinger, led to the disintegration of this union'.[51]

By contrast, for Edward Roux, prominent CPSA member in the 1920s and 1930s and pioneering historian of black resistance, Kadalie met fully the requirements of the tragic hero, and his rise and fall – in synchrony with the ICU's – was one of the greatest tragedies of twentieth-century South African history. In *Time Longer than Rope: The Black Man's Struggle for Freedom in South Africa* (1948), Roux acknowledges Kadalie's strengths: '[f]ull of restless energy, a born orator, a capable organiser'; and '[i]ntelligent, versatile, passionate, he possessed those qualities of personality which drew others to him and made him a natural leader to his fellows'.[52] In his posthumously published autobiography, *Rebel Pity* (1970), Roux embellished this sympathetic image of Kadalie, suggesting that 'Kadalie, the tough politician, the leader, the orator who swayed the multitude, was essentially a poet'; and elaborating further, that he 'was a powerful orator... able to rouse enthusiasm and inspire courage in those who had been hopeless'.[53] Having established Kadalie as a leader whose 'life was lived with epic grandeur', Roux identifies the *hamartia* which precipitated his tragic end, namely his gullibility which self-serving white liberals exploited; his 'facile eloquence [and] noisy bluster' when tactically astute leadership was required; and his pusillanimous approach – described by Roux as the ICU's *hamba kahle* tradition – in moments of crisis.[54] In terms that echo Ballinger's analysis, Roux in a private letter to Norman Leys added a sociological angle in trying to account for Kadalie's failure:

> It is not really remarkable that the native leader almost invariably 'goes west' sooner or later. The temptations are strong enough for trade union leaders in Britain. It is just another instance in Africa of the man who has lost one system of social ethics and had not yet acquired a new one.[55]

In other words, Kadalie's tragedy was to be torn not only between his working-class roots and the temptations of middle-class affluence, but also between European and African value systems. Roux reproduces the tragic plot structure in his history of the ICU: the fortunes of Kadalie-the-tragic-hero rise until they reach the *peripeteia* in 1927–1928 (two years later than Ballinger's 'turning point') when 'the ICU reached its zenith and then the crash came', culminating in *katastrophe* at the end of the decade when Kadalie and the ICU disappeared from public life.[56] Roux (again, like Ballinger) emphasises that Kadalie's personal tragedy is exceeded by the collective tragedy suffered by black South Africans as a consequence of the ICU's failures: 'of this tragic tale of Kadalie, the most tragic feature is that the opportunity he thus squandered was unique in the black man's struggle for freedom in South Africa.'[57]

The combination of generosity and critical judgement that produced Roux's tragic account of Kadalie and the ICU was absent in the next communist history of black resistance, *Class and Colour in South Africa, 1850–1950* (1969) by Jack and Ray Simons. Reverting to the Nzula/Padmore line, the Simonses characterise Kadalie as 'an opportunist politician rather than a militant trade union leader'; as politically immature for putting 'his trust in an alliance [the Pact government] between his people's most bitter enemies'; as culpable of abandoning the revolutionary struggle for workers' rights by expelling CPSA members from the ICU in December 1926; as failing time and again to rise 'to the challenge of the workers' militancy', exemplified by the ICU's conciliatory approach to the Lichtenburg miners' strike of June 1928; and as influenced far too easily by white liberals and British trade unionists.[58] Occasionally the Simonses concede that Kadalie advanced the struggle for African workers' rights, but any praise is always swiftly qualified:

> Kadalie aroused the people to an awareness of their economic bondage, awakened a determination to escape from poverty and the stranglehold of colour bars, and fostered trade unionism. He also let the fires burn out behind him as he took his message farther to the north. He and his lieutenants shrank from turning the power they had generated into a weapon against the oppressor.[59]

In such passages, a faint shadow of Roux's tragic-hero Kadalie lingers, as he is characterised as an inspiring hero/leader of the African workers undone by his flaw of timidity, an unwillingness or inability to harness the revolutionary forces he has inspired. Negating such nuanced assessments, however, are the Simonses' many more frequent condemnations of Kadalie's failings, such as their damning conclusion that '[t]here was no real difference between Kadalie and Ballinger; both were autocratic bureaucrats fighting for supremacy, while the rank-and-file were being bled for their support'.[60]

The resilience of romance and tragedy

After the Simonses' chapter in 1969, the writing of South African 'struggle history' was increasingly professionalised, with historians employed at universities coming to dominate the historiography of the ICU.[61] Compared to the historiography of the ICU from Kadalie in 1923 to the Simonses in 1969, these later histories add more empirical details; describe the minutiae of the ICU's record more comprehensively; provide longer footnotes; and draw upon more extensive archival evidence. Such enhancements notwithstanding, they continue to be framed by the alternating genres of romance and tragedy, as the closing paragraphs of the two major monographs of post-1970 ICU historiography attest. The final page of Peter Wickins' monograph, published two years after the Soweto Uprising, oscillates between tragedy and romance. On the one hand, Wickins contrasts the ICU's few victories with its many (tragic) defeats: 'there was nothing but bloodshed, bickering, and extravagance, all ending in bitterness, recrimination, and disillusionment'.[62] On the other hand, he places the ICU and its achievements at the beginning of a (romantic) journey from servitude to freedom, as it 'initiated the first popular movement among Blacks in South Africa [and] explored what avenues were open to it, [even if] if those turned out to be blind alleys'.[63]

In Helen Bradford's monograph, published at the height of the State of Emergency, Wickins's blind alleys are opened up to serve as routes to 'crucial insights, not the least significant of which was to distrust leaders who could not be controlled from below'.[64] And Southern Africa's black working class, stumbling on the first steps of their journey to freedom in Wickins's hesitant romance, are taking more confident strides in Bradford's version of the ICU's history: '[t]hey challenged the world they inhabited, and sought to transform their place in it. If this was the possibility of the past, then how much greater is the promise of the future for a longer-lasting taste of freedom'.[65] In David Scott's terms, the historical accounts of both Wickins and Bradford conform to the anti-colonial romance in that they frame the ICU as a key agent in the black working-class 'movement from Darkness to Light, Bondage to Freedom'.[66]

Beyond romance and tragedy

Does it matter whether the history of the ICU is framed as romance or tragedy? And what are the alternatives? A return to C.L.R. James sheds light on these related questions.

James's few direct comments on Kadalie and the ICU suggest that he was predisposed towards reading their history through a tragic frame. In *A History of Negro Revolt* (1938), for example, James argues that the ICU in Southern Africa was a movement that compared favourably to the revolutionary slave uprising in San Domingo:

> It will be difficult to over-estimate what Kadalie and his partner, Champion, achieved between 1919 and 1926. Kadalie was an orator, tall, with a splendid voice, and at his meetings he used to arouse the Bantu workers to great heights of enthusiasm... The real parallel to this movement is the mass rising in San Domingo. There is the same instinctive capacity for organisation, the same throwing-up of gifted leaders from among the masses... Seen in that historical perspective, the Kadalie movement can be understood for the profoundly important thing it was. After 1926 the movement began to decline... Kadalie lacked the education and the knowledge to organise it on a stable basis – the hardest of all tasks for a man of his origin.[67]

James's account resembles Ballinger and Roux's tragic histories of the ICU: Kadalie was a heroic leader with a *hamartia* (a lack of education and knowledge), and the fortunes of the ICU had risen until a turning point in 1926, when its catastrophic decline commenced.[68]

For James, however, the question of the generic frameworks of his history-writing was subordinate to his more urgent concern with how anti-colonial histories could be attuned to address their contemporary political context(s). Relating this concern to his own work, James was acutely aware of how decisively the political context had influenced his writing of the 1938 version of *The Black Jacobins*. Not only was his life at the time consumed by the campaign against the Italian invasion of Ethiopia, but – in his own words – he wrote the final pages 'in the stillness of a seaside suburb [where] could be heard most clearly and insistently the booming of Franco's heavy artillery, the rattle of Stalin's firing squads and the fierce shrill turmoil of the revolutionary movement'.[69]

Whereas in the 1930s James wrote his anti-colonial histories in solidarity with African freedom struggles, in the 1960s – when he wrote the second edition of *The Black Jacobins,* the political commitments driving his history-writing had shifted to address to challenges and contradictions of post-colonial rule. During the struggle against colonial rule, James had enjoyed comradely relationships with Eric Williams (1911–1981) of Trinidad and Kwame Nkrumah (1909–1972) of Ghana, but after liberation, he had been bitterly disappointed by the failures of both men to deliver the promised democratic-socialist societies.[70] Freedom for Ghana in 1957 and for Trinidad in 1962 had instead been followed by the emergence of comprador elites, endemic corruption, and limited redress of the inequalities produced by colonialism. The more individualised and critical representation of Toussaint in the 1963 version of *The Black Jacobins* reflects James's conviction that the Haitian revolutionary leader's flaws were in the process of being replicated in the actions of contemporary post-colonial leaders like Nkrumah. James explained in a 1971 lecture that both Toussaint and Nkrumah had initially enjoyed close bonds with the masses before going on to betray them:

> Nkrumah built up the party by personal contact with the mass of the population, and then when he became ruler he lost contact with them, and he begins to pass a lot of laws by which he can detain people without trial and so forth. Toussaint did exactly the same.[71]

For James, it had become increasingly clear that leaders from Toussaint and Dessalines to Williams and Nkrumah could as easily betray the masses and broker compromising post-independence deals with the former colonial powers. Histories celebrating the likes of Williams and Nkrumah and framed as uncritical anti-colonial romances should therefore be jettisoned.

How then should the histories of such leaders and their anti-slavery/anti-colonial struggles be (re)written in order to take into account transformed post-colonial context(s)? James is expansive on the topic of which kinds of history-writing should be eschewed. His first target is empiricist histories. Of Benjamin Quarles' 1948 study of Frederick Douglass, for example, he acknowledges 'the years of study [by] this careful, conscientious Negro scholar', but complains that '[m]erely to go on accumulating facts [and seeking] the secret of Douglass in Douglass' personal character, selfishness and ambition' is inadequate: 'historical facts, as facts, can do so much, and no more. They have to be organised in the light of a philosophy of history'.[72] Even more dangerous than the unreflecting accumulation of 'facts', however, are those histories organised in the light of spurious 'philosophies of history' like Stalinism. Of Herbert Aptheker, author of *American Negro Slave Revolts* (1943), for example, James argues that he 'cannot break through the theoretical vice in which he is enclosed [as] he sees the Negro organisations [of the nineteenth century] as early versions of the Stalinist Negro Congress'.[73] Finally, in an unsparing autocritique of *The Black Jacobins*, James regrets his focus on the leaders of the Haitian Revolution at the expense of attending in detail to the thoughts and actions of the masses. Expressing warm praise for Albert Soboul's efforts to re-write the history of the French Revolution centred on the deeds of the *sans-culottes*, 'not Robespierre, Danton and Marat... but the rank-and-file', James argues that the masses in the French and Russian Revolutions 'were anticipated and excelled by the blacks and mulattoes of the island of San Domingo'.[74] Contemplating both the 1938 and 1963 versions of *The Black Jacobins*, James regrets his failure to foreground those 'little local leaders': 'The records are there. I should have put it all in. I didn't. I mean, if I were writing this book today, I would have page after page of that'.[75]

To evade these pitfalls, namely, anti-colonial romances in the service of post-colonial nationalisms; conscientious empiricism oblivious to its political implications; excessive focus on personal psychology; filtering the past through Stalinist lenses; and neglecting the deeds of the masses by fetishising leaders, James proposes a dialectical encounter between the past and the present: 'the time has come to link [Negro histories of resistance] deliberately and consciously with the most progressive historical currents of the day. A heavy price will inevitably be paid if this is not done'.[76] Quite what 'the progressive historical currents of the day' are at any particular moment is up for debate, but what is clear is that James's emphatic judgements severely delimit the conscious or unconscious recycling of either romance or tragedy as the generic frameworks for the (re-)writing of anti-colonial histories. The trajectories of Williams and Nkrumah stand as warnings against the dangers of anti-colonial romances for post-colonial societies, and James's commitment to foregrounding the 'rank-and-file' works directly against casting anti-colonial leaders as tragic heroes.

Recent James scholarship has kept such debates alive, with the key point of reference David Scott's influential argument that the 1938 version of *The Black Jacobins* frames Toussaint as the hero of an anti-colonial romance, whereas the 1963 revised version frames him as a tragic hero.[77] Of the many responses to Scott's productive provocation, the most relevant to the study of Kadalie and the ICU is Jeremy Matthew

Glick's invention of a new syncretic genre he terms 'the Black Radical Tragic', which derives its theoretical vocabulary from Brecht, Fanon, Lukacs, Du Bois, Benjamin and Malcolm X. Glick argues that 'the Black Radical Tragic' exceeds the inherited categories of romance and tragedy, maintaining 'as both aesthetic strategy and political problematic... the individual and the mass in constant dialectical tension'.[78] Beyond the happy endings of the romance (the defeat of slavery, the triumph of the proletariat, the end of apartheid) and the fatal final acts of tragedy (the death of Toussaint/Trotsky/Lumumba/Sobukwe), a new aesthetics and new politics can thus be staged.

Conclusion

What does a return to James (and James scholarship) suggest for the writing of the history of the ICU a century after its demise and three decades after the formal end of apartheid? As the changes in text and context between the two editions of *The Black Jacobins* and James's historiographical reflections amply demonstrate, '[h]istory and our use of history move'.[79] The history of the ICU – and our uses of its history – have certainly moved substantially between the distinct contexts of segregation, apartheid and post-apartheid. To account for such movement, James instructs historians to link histories of resistance to 'the most progressive currents of the day'. Taking up this challenge in relation to the history of the ICU now requires rethinking the ICU archive in relation to contemporary Southern African 'currents'. A preliminary list of currents might include: the material inequalities generated by Southern Africa's capitalist economy; the neo-colonial kleptocracy embedded within the post-apartheid state; the xenophobic discourses unchecked by rainbow nationalism; and the compromises and contradictions fettering the trade union movement. With any (or all) of these currents foregrounded, new histories of the ICU have the potential both to sharpen our critiques of power and to imagine alternative forms of radical community.

About the contributors

Philip Bonner (1945–2017) joined the History Department at the University of Witwatersrand in 1971; was a founding member of the Wits History Workshop in 1977, serving as its chair from 1987 to 2012; was seconded to the Federation of South African Trade Unions to contribute to worker education programmes in 1982; became Professor of Urban and Labour History in 1991; and Chair in Local Histories, Present Realities in 2007. His major monograph was *Kings, Commoners and Concessionaires: The Evolution and Dissolution of the Nineteenth-Century Swazi State* (1983), and he co-authored and co-edited many works on Southern African history, including *Holding their Ground: Class, Locality and Culture in Nineteenth- and Twentieth-Century South Africa* (1989), *Apartheid's Genesis, 1935–1962* (1993), and *Alexandra: A History* (2008).

Anusa Daimon is a Research Associate with the International Studies Group (ISG) at the University of the Free State, Bloemfontein, South Africa. His research interests include migration, transnational ethnic minorities, labour, citizenship, identity, borders, borderlands, culture, state and politics in Southern Africa. He has published on the afore-mentioned themes in numerous referred journals and is, among other research projects, currently working on a book monograph on Malawian migrant communities in Southern Africa. Anusa has also worked closely with the Harry Guggenheim Foundation, the American Council of Learned Societies – African Humanities Program and the Social Science Research Council - African Peacebuilding Network (APN).

Henry Dee is a historian of empire, labour and migration in the twentieth century, working as a Postdoctoral Research Fellow with the ISG at the University of the Free State. He completed a PhD on the life of Clements Kadalie at the University of Edinburgh in 2020 and has published research on the ICU and the broader Malawian diaspora in the *Journal of Southern African Studies*, the *Journal of South African History* and *African Studies*. He is now working on a comparative study investigating how both the ICU and the All-India Trade Union Congress challenged heightening anti-immigrant restrictions and reconceptualised socialist internationalism in the 1920s and 1930s.

David Johnson is Professor of Literature in the Department of English and Creative Writing at The Open University. He is the author of *Shakespeare and South Africa* (1996), *Imagining the Cape Colony: History, Literature and the South African Nation* (2012) and *Dreaming of Freedom in South Africa: Literature between Critique and Utopia* (2019); the principal author of *Jurisprudence: A South African Perspective* (2001); and the co-editor of *A Historical Companion to Post-colonial Literatures* *in English* (2005), *The Book in Africa: Critical Debates* (2015), and *'I See You!' The Industrial and Commercial Workers of Africa, 1919–1930* (2022). He is the General Editor of the Edinburgh University Press series Key Texts in Anti-Colonial Thought.

Peter Limb is an emeritus professor at Michigan State University and Research Fellow, the Gender and Africa Studies Centre, University of the Free State. He has published widely on South African history, satire and anti-apartheid movements. His books include *Historical Dictionary of South Africa* (with Chris Saunders, 2020), *Taking African Cartoons Seriously* (with Teju Olaniyan, 2018), *The People's Paper: A Centenary History & Anthology of Abantu-Batho* (2012), *Autobiography & Selected Works of A.B. Xuma (2012), The ANC's Early Years* (2010), and *Nelson Mandela* (2008). His articles have appeared in the *Journal of Southern African Studies* and *African Studies*. His current research includes the political history of the Free State, the ICU, the Communist Party of South Africa, and Ilanga lase Natal.

Tom Lodge is an emeritus professor in the Politics Department at the University of Limerick and a member of the Royal Irish Academy. Between 1978 and 2005, he worked at the University of the Witwatersrand, where he was Professor of Political Studies. He is the author of *Black Politics in South Africa since 1945* (1983), *South African Politics since 1994* (1999), *Politics in South Africa: From Mandela to Mbeki* (2002), *Mandela: A Critical Life* (2006) and *Sharpeville: An Apartheid Massacre and its Consequences* (2011). His latest book is *Red Road to Freedom: A History of the South African Communist Party, 1921–2021* (2021).

Sibongiseni Mkhize studied at the University of Natal, Pietermaritzburg, and holds a PhD in history from the University of the Witwatersrand. His area of interest is the twentieth-century history of KwaZulu-Natal, with particular focus on biographical studies and political mobilisation in the Natal midlands during the 1950s and the 1980s. He is the author of *Principle and Pragmatism in the Liberation Struggle: A Political Biography of Selby Msimang* (2019). He has also been involved in research on arts, culture and heritage in South Africa, as well as on the evolution of traditional leadership in Durban. He is former head of the Market Theatre and Robben Island Museum and is currently the Chief Executive Officer of the South African State Theatre.

Tshepo Moloi is a senior lecturer and subject-head of the History Department at the University of the Free State. He obtained his MA and PhD in History from Wits University. Moloi is the co-editor of *Guerrilla Radios in Southern Africa: Broadcasters, Technology, Propaganda Wars and the Armed Struggle* (2020) and the author of *Place of Thorns: Black Political Protest in Kroonstad since 1976* (2015). He contributed chapters to the various volumes of *The Road to Democracy in South Africa*, edited by the South African Democracy Education Trust. Moloi is the editor of *New Contree* and deputy president of the South African History Society. His research interests include histories of liberation struggle in South and Southern Africa.

Noor Nieftagodien is the South African Research Chair in Local Histories, Present Realities and is the Head of the History Workshop at the University of the Witwatersrand. His research covers popular insurgent struggles, public history, youth politics and local history. He is the co-author, with Phil Bonner, of books on the history of Alexandra, Ekurhuleni and Kathorus. Current research projects include histories of popular movements and the local state in the Vaal Triangle, non-racial sport, and the Congress of South African Students. He serves on the boards of the South African History Archives, the Socioeconomic Rights Institute, and the Alternative Information and Development Centre, as well as the journal, *African Studies* and the social justice magazine, *Amandla!*.

Laurence Stewart is currently transforming his MA thesis into several academic journal articles. He completed his MA degree in 2021 on the ICU at the University of the Witwatersrand, analysing its character and politics in the former Western Transvaal. He works as a research assistant, using archival and analytical skills to search archives and libraries across Gauteng. His research interests include workers' histories, histories of environmental change, and more generally, the history of twentieth-century South Africa.

Chitja Twala is an Associate Professor (Department of History) and Vice-Dean (Faculty of the Humanities) at the University of the Free State. He is the author of eight chapters (co-authored two) in *The Road to Democracy in South Africa: Vol. 4 (1970–1990)*. He is the recipient of Andrew Mellon Foundation and the National Institute of Humanities and Social Sciences Grants. His research field is liberation history and the history of the Bantustans. He has been awarded several visiting/research fellowships: Harvard University (USA); Kwame Nkrumah Institute of African Studies at the University of Ghana (Accra); and the University of California, Los Angeles (USA).

Nicole Ulrich is a social/labour historian based in the Department of History, University of Fort Hare, Eastern Cape. She has published widely on the organisation, political ideas and identities of the labouring classes in Southern Africa and their location in global traditions of radicalism and flows of labour. She has held a visiting fellowship (Centre of African Studies) at the University of Cambridge and is currently serving as a Corresponding Editor for the *International Review of Social History*.

Elizabeth van Heyningen is an Honorary Research Associate in the History Department, University of Stellenbosch. Her research interests encompass the history of Cape Town, the history of colonial women, and the social history of medicine. Her many publications include: *The Concentration Camps of the South African War: A Social History* (2013), a monograph that was shortlisted for the Sunday Times Alan Paton Prize; the co-authored (with Vivian Bickford-Smith and Nigel Worden) *Cape Town. The Making of a City* (1998) and *Cape Town in the Twentieth Century* (1999); and the co-edited *Selections from the Letters of President M.T. Steyn, 1904–1910* (2017).

Lucien van der Walt is in the Sociology Department at Rhodes University, Director of the Neil Aggett Labour Studies Unit, and affiliated with the Wits History Workshop. His books include *Anarchism and Syndicalism in the Colonial and Post-colonial World, 1880–1940* (2010) and *Politics at a Distance from the State* (2018). He has published widely, including in *African Studies*, the *Canadian Journal of History, Capital and Class*, the *Global Labour Journal, Labor History, Labour, Capital & Society*, and *Mundos del Trabalho*. He was Southern African editor for the *International Encyclopedia of Protest and Revolution* (2009), and winner of the Labor History and CODESRIA PhD prizes.

Notes

Introduction

1   The ANC's membership never rose above 4, 000 until the 1940s (see P. Landau, '"Johannesburg in Flames": The 1918 Shilling Campaign, *Abantu-Batho*, and Early African Nationalism in South Africa', in P. Limb, ed., *The People's Paper: A Centenary History of 'Abantu-Batho'* (Johannesburg: Wits University Press, 2012), 277), and the CPSA claimed 1 750 members in 1928, rising to a peak of 3 000 in 1929, before plunging to about 100 in April 1931 (see A. Drew, *Discordant Comrades: Identities and Loyalties on the South African Left* (Aldershot: Ashgate, 2000), 132). In global terms, the ICU compared favourably with Marcus Garvey's Universal Negro Improvement Association (UNIA), which had about 300 000 members (see R.T. Vinson, *The Americans are Coming! Dreams of African American Liberation in Segregationist South Africa* (Athens OH: Ohio University Press, 2012), 9.

2   H. Bradford, *A Taste of Freedom: The ICU in Rural South Africa, 1924–1930* (New Haven CT: Yale University Press, 1987), 278.

3   By far the most substantial post-apartheid reassessment of the ICU to date is Sylvia Neame's *The Congress Movement: The Unfolding of the Congress Alliance, 1912–1961. Vols 1–3* (Cape Town: HSRC Press, 2015). As the title of Neame's three-volume work indicates, however, the ICU's significance remains subordinated to that of the Congress Alliance.

4   N. Mandela, 'Address to rally in Cape Town on his release from prison', 11 February 1990, http://db.nelsonmandela.org/speeches/pub_view.asp?pg=itemandItemID=NMS016

5   Quoted in A. Klotz, 'Borders and the roots of xenophobia in South Africa', *South African Historical Journal*, 68, 2 (2016), 192 (2016), 192.

6   T. Mbeki, *Africa: The Time has Come* (Cape Town: Tafelberg, 1998), 299.

7   See the published research of the Southern African Migration Project (SAMP), notably, J. Crush, ed., *Beyond Control: Immigration and Human Rights in a Democratic South Africa* (Cape Town: IDASA, 1998); and D. McDonald et al., *Challenging Xenophobia: Myths and Realities about Cross-Border Migration in South Africa* (Cape Town: IDASA, 1998).

8   For a sample of the abundant scholarship on anti-foreigner violence in post-apartheid South Africa, see: F.B. Nyamnjoh, *Insiders and Outsiders: Citizenship and Xenophobia in Contemporary Southern Africa* (London: Zed, 2006); M. Neocosmos, *From 'Foreign Natives' to 'Native Foreigners': Explaining Xenophobia in Post-apartheid South Africa, Citizenship and Nationalism, Identity and Politics* (Dakar: CODESRIA, 2010), L.L. Landau et al. (eds), *Exorcising the Demons Within: Xenophobia, Violence and Statecraft in Contemporary South Africa* (Johannesburg: Wits University Press, 2011); and H.L. Madigimisha et al., ed., *Crisis, Identity and Migration in Post-colonial Southern Africa* (Cham, Switzerland: Springer, 2018).

9   Quoted in J. Steinberg, 'Xenophobia and collective violence in South Africa: A note of scepticism about the scapegoat', *African Studies Review*, 61, 3 (2018), 131.

10   Quoted in *'They Have Robbed Me of My Life': Xenophobic Violence Against Non-Nationals in South Africa* (Human Rights Watch, September 2020), 44. Human Rights Watch also point out that the main opposition parties have joined the ANC's anti-immigrant chorus.

11   On the mutations in South and Southern African labour history, see P. Bonner, J. Hyslop and L. van der Walt, 'Rethinking Worlds of Labour. Southern African Labour History in International Context', *African Studies*, 66, 2–3 (2007), 137–68.

12   When referring to these former colonies of Southern Africa – Basutoland (Lesotho), Bechuanaland (Botswana), Northern Rhodesia (Zambia), Nyasaland (Malawi), Portuguese East Africa (Mozambique), Southern Rhodesia (Zimbabwe), South West Africa (Namibia), Swaziland (Eswatini) – we observe henceforth the convention of using the nomenclature of the 1920s.

13   The convention adopted has been to reproduce without endorsing Southern African racial identities like 'black', 'African', ''Native', 'Indian', and 'Coloured'/ 'coloured' because they were integral to the social and political world of the 1920s.

14   The most substantial academic commemoration of the ICU's centenary was the hosting of several panels on the ICU at the Southern African History Society Conference at Rhodes University, Makhanda, 24–27 June 2019. This collection has drawn heavily upon those contributions in attempting to take stock of the ICU and its legacies.

15   Historical accounts of the ANC published in the build-up to its centenary included: P. Limb, *The ANC's Early Years: Nation, Class and Place in South Africa Before 1940* (Pretoria: Unisa Press, 2010); S. Booysen, *The African National Congress and the Regeneration of Political Power: People, Party, Policy* (Johannesburg: Wits University Press, 2011); A. Butler, *The Idea of the ANC* (Johannesburg: Jacana, 2012); S. Ellis, *External Mission: The ANC in Exile, 1960–1990* (Johannesburg: Jonathan Ball, 2012); A. Lissoni, J. Soske, N. Erlank, N. Nieftagodien and O. Badsha, eds, *One Hundred Years of the ANC: Debating Liberation Histories Today* (Johannesburg: Wits University Press, 2012); and the Special Issue of the *South African Historical Journal*, 'The ANC at 100', 64, 3 (2012).

16   For a discussion of this transition, see D. Johnson, 'Anti-Apartheid People's Histories and Post-Apartheid Nationalist Biographies', in A. Choudry and S. Vally, eds, *Reflections on Knowledge, Learning and Social Movements: History's Schools* (London and New York: Routledge, 2018), 88–103.

17   L. Callinicos, *Oliver Tambo: Beyond the Ngele Mountains* (Cape Town: David Philip, 2015 [2004]), 596.

18   Biographies of non-ANC leaders have of course also been published, notably Benjamin Pogrund's *How Can Man Die Better: The Life of Robert Sobukwe* (2006) and Xolela Mangcu's *Biko: A Life* (2012). But the reluctance (or refusal) to look beyond Mandela and the ANC continues – witness, for example, the recent C. Bundy and W. Beinart, eds, *Reassessing Mandela* (London and New York: Routledge, 2021), and P. Landau, *Spear: Mandela and the Revolutionaries* (Athens OH: Ohio University Press, 2022).

19   Also of crucial importance are Sylvia Neame's oral interviews, which several chapters in this volume utilise (University of Witwatersrand Sylvia Neame Papers A 2729).

20   Wits Institute of Advanced Social Research (hereafter IASR) Share Cropping and Labour Tenancy Oral History Project 1979–1987 (hereafter SLTP) AG 2738, Interview No. 65, Lucas Nqandela, 25 August 1982.

21   Wits IASR SLTP AG 2738, Interview No. 227, Charles Kumalo, 25 November 1981.

22   Wits IASR SLTP AG 2738, Interview No. 2, Esther Sibanyoni and Rose Mthimunye, 4 September 1979.

23   In addition to his achievements in Kroonstad, the Basutoland-born 'Mote established seven ICU branches in Basutoland in the late 1920s, thus substantially extending the Union's regional influence.

24   Unpublished at the time of Phil Bonner's death on 24 September 2017, the main text was written, but the references incomplete. The editors are very grateful to Henry Dee for searching down all the references and editing the paper into this final publishable form.

25   Bradford, *A Taste*, 143. For discussions of the ICU's eclectic mix of ideologies and discourses – Christianity, Garveyism, Communism, liberalism, and vernacular knowledges – see D. Johnson, *Dreaming of Freedom in South Africa. Literature between Critique and Utopia* (Edinburgh/ Cape Town: Edinburgh University Press/ UCT Press, 2020), 41–70; and extending to the influences of syndicalism and anarchism on the ICU, see L. Van der Walt, '"One Great Union of Skilled and Unskilled Workers, South of the Zambezi": Garveyism, Liberalism and Revolutionary Syndicalism in the Industrial and Commercial Workers Union of Africa, 1919– 1949' (Vienna: European Social Science History Conference, 23–26 April 2014).

26   Quoted in R. Tabane, 'AMCU: a Group of Vigilantes and Liars, Say Alliance Bosses', *Mail & Guardian*, 13 May 2013. https://mg.co.za/article/2013-05-17-00-amcus-no-union-its-just-vigilantes-and-liars-say-alliance-bosses/ [accessed 15 May 2017].

Chapter 1

1   Earlier versions of this paper were presented at the European Social Science History Conference, the Southern African Historical Society biennial conference, and most recently, the Namibian and Southern African Studies Research Colloquium run by the Centre for African Studies, University of Basel, Basler Afrika Bibliographien and the University of Namibia (UNAM). I would like to thank everyone who has provided feedback and acknowledge funding by Rhodes University and the National Research Foundation (NRF).

2   'Bloemfontein Congress: Delegates Report', *The Black Man*, August 1920.

3   For example, Clements Kadalie apparently hoped that fellow Nyasa, Isa Macdonald Lawrence, then in Mozambique, would establish a branch at the Beira docks. See R. A. Hill ed., *The Marcus Garvey and Universal Negro Improvement Association Papers. Vol. 10, Africa for the Africans, 1923–1945* (Berkeley, CA: University of California Press, 2006), lxvi-lxvii.

4   See W. B. Lyon, 'From Labour Elites to Garveyites: West African Migrant Labour in Namibia, 1892–1925', *Journal of Southern African Studies*, 47, 1 (2021), 52.

5   J. Kimble, *Migrant Labour and Colonial Rule in Basutoland, 1890–1930* (Grahamstown: Institute of Social and Economic Research/ISER, Rhodes University, 1999), 185–86; S. Neame, *The Congress Movement: The Unfolding of the Congress Alliance 1912–1961*, Vol. 1 (Cape Town: HSRC Press, 2015), 168; S. Neame, *The Congress Movement: The Unfolding of the Congress Alliance 1912–1961*, Vol. 2 (Cape Town, HSRC Press, 2015), 244, notes 454, 357, 384–365, 486.

6   Lüderitzbucht until 1920.

7   This dated back to a Dutch claim in 1793.

8   Among which must be counted many of the *mestiços* of Angola and Mozambique.

9   Robert Sambo, quoted in A. Ewing, *The Age of Garvey: How a Jamaican Activist Created a Mass Movement and Changed Global Black Politics* (Princeton: Princeton University Press, 2014), 204.

10   M. van der Linden, 'Transnationalising American Labour History', *Journal of American History*, 86, 3 (1999), 1080–81.

11   L. van der Walt, 'The First Globalisation and Transnational Labour Activism in Southern Africa: White Labourism, the IWW and the ICU, 1904–1934', *African Studies*, 66, 2/3 (2007), 223–51.

12   See, for example, Van der Walt, 2007, 'The First Globalisation and Transnational Labour'; L. van der Walt, '"One Great Union of Skilled and Unskilled Workers, South of the Zambezi": Garveyism, Liberalism and Revolutionary Syndicalism in the Industrial and Commercial Workers Union of Africa, 1919–1949', European Social Science History Conference, Vienna, Austria, 23–26 April 2014.

13   National Archives of Namibia, Windhoek (hereafter NAN) A.0309, 'Trade Union Lüderitzbucht'.

14   There was also a small but significant number of Italian workers: B.C. Moore, S. Quinn, W.B. Lyon and K.F. Hertzog, 'Balancing the Scales: Re-Centring Labour and Labourers in Namibian History', *Journal of Southern African Studies*, 47, 1 (2021), 3, note 40.

15   A. Cooper, 'The Institutionalisation of Contract Labour in Namibia', *Journal of Southern African Studies*, 25, 1 (1999), 124.

16   'The Labour Movement in South West Africa', *The Bolshevik* [Cape Town], January 1921.

17   'The Labour Movement', *The Bolshevik*, January 1921; E. Mantzaris, 'Radical Community: The Yiddish-Speaking Branch of the International Socialist League, 1918–20', in B. Bozzoli, ed., *Class, Community and Conflict: South African Perspectives* (Johannesburg: Ravan Press, 1988), 167.

18   G. van Goethem, *The Amsterdam International: The World of the International Federation of Trade Unions (IFTU), 1913–1945* (Aldershot: Ashgate, 2006), 43.

19   Trade Union Council of South Africa (TUCSA), Part 1, 1915–1954 Papers AH 646 Cc4.8, 'South West Africa, 1928–1930', Historical Papers, University of the Witwatersrand.

20   Personal communications, Giorgio Miescher, 1 October 2020, 18 October 2020 and 9 November 2020. Also noted in D. Henrichsen, 'Liberals and Non-Racism in Namibia's Settler Society? Advocate Israel Goldblatt's Engagement with Namibian Nationalists in the 1960s', in J. Silvester, ed., *Re-viewing Resistance in Namibian History* (Windhoek: University of Namibia Press, 2015), 129 note 5.

21   For example, O. Angula, *SWAPO Captive: A Comrade's Experience of Betrayal and Torture* (Cape Town: Zebra Press, 2018), 24–25, 33, 57, 78; S. Whittaker and H. Boesak, 'Tribute to Kenneth Abrahams', *The Namibian*, 28 April 2017.

22   Moore, Quinn, Lyon and Hertzog, 'Balancing the Scales', 3.

23 R. First, *South West Africa* (Baltimore: Penguin, 1963), 196–97.

24 G. Bauer, *Labor and Democracy in Namibia, 1971–1996* (Athens OH: Ohio University Press/ London: James Currey, 1998), 69.

25 G.A. Pirio, *The Role of Garveyism in the Making of the Southern African Working Classes and Namibian Nationalism* (University of California, mimeo, 1982); reprinted in B. Wood ed., *Namibia, 1884–1984: Readings on Namibia's History and Society* (London: Namibia Support Committee and the SWAPO Department of Information and Publicity, 1984).

26 Ibid., 1, 14, 16–18.

27 Ibid., 259–267.

28 R.A. Hill, ed., *The Marcus Garvey and Universal Negro Improvement Association Papers: Vol 9, Africa for the Africans, 1921–1922* (Berkeley, Cal.: University of California Press, 1995), lxxvii, 204, 269 note 3, 269–270 note 4, 278–279, 311 note 1, 391 note 1, 546, 588; Hill, ed., *The Marcus Garvey and Universal Negro Improvement Association Papers*: Vol. 10, 81–82, 122–23.

29 For example, see Hill, ed., *The Marcus Garvey and Universal Negro Improvement Association Papers:* Vol 10. lvi–lviii, 34–36 notes 9–15; 360 note 3, 619 note 3.

30 Emmett, *Popular Resistance*, 4, 125–134.

31 Ibid., 21,22, 29, 32.

32 'Griqua' in South Africa.

33 B.C. Moore, 'Smuggled Sheep, Smuggled Shepherds: Farm Labour Transformations in Namibia and the Question of Southern Angola, 1933–1975', *Journal of Southern African Studies*, 47, 1 (2021), 100. Also see J. Silvester, 'Black Pastoralists, White Farmers: The Dynamics of Land Dispossession and Labour Recruitment in Southern Namibia, 1915–1955' (PhD thesis, University of London, 1993), 110–111, 224–225, 240–241, 258, 307–310.

34 Silvester, 'Black Pastoralists, White Farmers', 315–316.

35 On the last point, see E. L. P. Stals, *The Afrikaners in Namibia: Who are They? A Collection of Historical Essays about the Afrikaner in Former South West Africa* (Windhoek: Macmillan, 2008), 46.

36 T. Dedering, 'Namibia, Struggle for Independence', in I. Ness et al., eds., *The International Encyclopedia of Revolution and Protest* (Oxford: Wiley-Blackwell, 2001), 2391–94.

37 Stals, *The Afrikaners in Namibia,* 71; G.G. Weigend, 'German Settlement Patterns in Namibia', *Geographical Review*, 75, 2 (1985), 163–64.

38 W. Beinart, 'Cape Workers in German South-West Africa, 1904–1912: Patterns of Migrancy and the Closing of Options on the Southern African Labour Market', *The Societies of Southern Africa in the Nineteenth and Twentieth Centuries*, 11 (London: University of London: Institute of Commonwealth Studies, 1981).

39 W. Hillebrecht, *Lüderitz: A Journey through Time* (Lüderitz: NovaNam, 2017), 21.

40 For example, South African National Archives, Pretoria (hereafter SANA) Native Affairs (hereafter NTS) 2054, 89/280, Recruitment of Labour for Diamond Mines in South West Africa; South West Africa, Native Labour Bureau, 1910–1924, Letter from Director of Native Labour to Secretary for Native Affairs, 23 October 1923.

41 S. Quinn, 'Scalar Claims, Worker Strategies, and "South Africa's Labour Empire" in Namibia, 1943–1979', *Journal of Southern African Studies*, 47, 1 (2021), 63–64.

42 Lyon, 'From Labour Elites to Garveyites', 45 note 36.

43 For example, Cooper, 'Institutionalisation of Contract Labour', 121–38.

44 Johannesburg had a population of 250 000 by 1913: R. Krut, 'The Making of a South African Jewish Community', in B. Bozzoli, ed., *Class, Community and Conflict: South African Perspectives* (Johannesburg: Ravan Press, 1988), 135–36.

45 Lyon, 'From Labour Elites to Garveyites', 37–38, 40–43.

46 Ibid., 45.

47 Weigend, 'German Settlement Patterns', 164.

48 Lüderitzbucht Museum, *Kolmanskuppe: A Journey into the Past* (Lüderitz: n.d.), 2.

49 U. Lindner, 'Transnational Movements between Colonial Empires: Migrant Workers from the British Cape Colony in the German Diamond Town of Lüderitzbucht', *European Review of History—Revue européenne d'histoire*, 16, 5 (2009), 683.

50 O. Levinson, *Diamonds in the Desert: The Story of August Stauch and his Times* (Windhoek: Kuiseb Verlag, 2009), 107.

51 Emmett, *Popular Resistance,* 125.

52 T. Emmett, 'Popular Resistance in Namibia, 1920–1925', in T. Lodge, ed., *Resistance and Ideology in Settler Societies* (Ravan Press, Johannesburg, 1986), 8–16.

53 For an overview, see Van der Walt, 'The First Globalisation', 229–31.

54   NAN IMW 24 6249/1, Strike Lüderitz Diamond Fields, Lüderitz Magistrate, 'Unrest among Natives', Letter to the Secretary for the Protectorate, Windhoek, May 1920.

55 Lyon, 'From Labour Elites to Garveyites', 47–50.

56 A.A. Watts, 'Capitalism and Native Races', *The Call*, 28 December 1918.

57 La Guma, *Jimmy La Guma*, 20–21.

58 NAN IMW 24, 6249/1, Strike Lüderitz Diamond Fields, Lüderitzbucht Chamber of Mines, 'Report on the Strike of the European Workmen of July 1919', 12 August 1919.

59 NAN IMW 24 6249/1, Strike Lüderitz Diamond Fields, Lüderitz Magistrate, 'Unrest among Natives', Letter to the Secretary for the Protectorate, Windhoek, May 1920.

60 An error that several writers, myself included, have reproduced.

61 La Guma, *Jimmy La Guma*, 21.

62 Ibid., 21, 23.

63 NAN ADM 152 C248, Industrial Coloured Workers Union, Lüderitz Magistrate, 'Activities of the Industrial and Commercial Workers Union', Letter to Secretary of the Protectorate, 5 January 1921.

64 La Guma, *Jimmy La Guma*, 20–21.

65 Ibid.

66 Emmett, 'Popular Resistance', 24, 31–32.

67   'Our Agents', *The Black Man*, December 1920.

68   'Bloemfontein Congress: Delegates Report', *The Black Man*, August 1920.

69   Emmett, *Popular Resistance*, 31.

70   Ibid., 126, 136; La Guma, *Jimmy La Guma*, 22.

71   Emmett, *Popular Resistance*, 127.

72   Pirio, *The Role of Garveyism*, 24–25.

73   Industrial and Commercial Workers Union of Africa (ICU), *Third Annual Conference: Official Report of Proceedings* (Cape Town: A. Holder, 1923), 1, 14; Neame, *The Congress Movement, The Unfolding of the Congress Alliance 1912–1961,* Vol. 1 (Cape Town, HSRC Press, 2015), 266, 272–74. The ICU did not hold a conference in 1922. There is an unconfirmed claim that Lüderitz paid £48 into ICU funds in 1926: S.M.B. Ncwana (n.d.), *The ICU Activities: An Exhaustive Inquiry into the Affairs and Policy of the Industrial and Commercial Workers' Union of Africa, both to Trades, Squatters, Farm Labourers and the Manipulation of the Peoples Funds,* 8 (pamphlet held at Wits Sylvia Neame Papers A 2729).

74   Silvester, 'Black Pastoralists, White Farmers', 98.

75   Ibid., 125, 236.

76   For example, NAN SWAA, 1851 A396–10 (vol 1), Native Unrest: Lüderitz and Keetmanshoop (1922–1954), Keetmanshoop Acting Magistrate, 'Faction Fight', Letter to the Secretary for South West Africa, 28 January 1922.

77   ICU, *Third Annual Conference*, 38.

78   NAN LLU 4-3 1 1 W14, Native Societies, Native Unrest (1921–1925), Head Constable and Post Commander Lüderitz, South West African Police, Letter to Lüderitz Magistrate, 21 October 1922.

79   ICU, *Third Annual Conference*, 21.

80   For example, Letter from Gysbert Reitz Hofmeyer, Administrator of South West Africa, to Jan Christiaan Smuts, 18 June 1923, reprinted in Hill, *The Marcus Garvey and Universal Negro Improvement Association Papers,* Vol. 10, 81–82.

81   Lindner, 'Transnational Movements between Colonial Empires', 687.

82   Emmett, *Popular Resistance*, pp. 132–34. Ncwana visited in 1922 but was then in an ICU splinter group, hostile to the Kadalie-linked Lüderitz and Keetmanshoop branches.

83   NAN ADM 152 C248, Industrial Coloured Workers Union, Acting Deputy Commissioner, SWA Police, 'Re: Secret Meetings held by an Educated Cape Boy named Pieterse in Lüderitz', Letter to Secretary of the Protectorate, 29 December 1920.

84   ICU, 1923, *Third Annual Conference*, 38.

85   Emmett 1999, *Popular Resistance*, pp. 132–134.

86   Emmett, *Popular Resistance*, 132–33.

87   Ibid.

88   Kegapilee Moogoris, 'Ezase Jamani (South-West Protectorate)', *Workers' Herald*, 15 November 1926. I would like to thank Henry Dee for drawing this article to my attention.

89   Moogoris, judging by the name, could have been from Bechuanaland or South Africa. A
     small number of 'Bechuanas' and Northern Rhodesians worked on the diamond mines:
     Moore, 'Smuggled Sheep, Smuggled Shepherds', 101 note 31.

90   'Elizabeth Bay Demonstration', *Workers' Herald*, 18 March 1927.

91   T. Emmett, *Popular Resistance and the Roots of Nationalism in Namibia, 1915–1966*, (Basel:
     P. Schlettwein Publishing, 1999), 132.

92   Pirio, *The Role of Garveyism*, 1, 14, 16–18.

93   NAN ADM 152 C248 Industrial Coloured Workers Union, J. La Guma, ICU 'Rules and
     Regulations', n.d., 1, 4.

94   Ibid.

95   NAN 152 C248 Industrial Coloured Workers Union, Press clippings for 25 and 29 October
     1921, *Eastern Province Herald* (Port Elizabeth).

96   Emmett, 'Popular Resistance', 21–22.

97   ICU, *Third Annual Conference*, 35–37.

98   Emmett, 'Popular Resistance', 31.

99   ICU, *Third Annual Conference*, 26.

100 Hill, *The Marcus Garvey and Universal Negro Improvement Association Papers*, Vol 10, 23,
     note 2.

101 The best analysis of these developments remains H. Bradford, *A Taste of Freedom: The ICU
     in Rural South Africa, 1924–1930* (Johannesburg: Ravan Press, 1987).

102 I. Phimister, *An Economic and Social History of Zimbabwe, 1890–1948: Capital Accumulation
     and Class Struggle* (London, New York: Longman, 1988), 200–03; C. van Onselen, *Chibaro:
     African Mine Labour in Southern Rhodesia* (Johannesburg: Ravan Press, 1976), 214–18.

103 See Moore, 'Smuggled Sheep, Smuggled Shepherds', 93–125.

104 Emmett, 'Popular Resistance', 19, 31.

105 Van der Walt, '"One Great Union"'.

106 'The Making of the Working Class, Part Eleven: The ICU Collapses', *FOSATU Worker News*,
     February 1985.

Chapter 2

1   A. Okoth, *A History of Africa: African Nationalism and the Decolonisation Process* (Nairobi:
    Eastern African Educational Publishers, 2006), 126.

2   T. O. Ranger, *Bulawayo Burning: The Social History of a Southern African City 1893–1960*
    (Harare: Weaver Press, 2010), 50.

3   See C. van Onselen, *Chibaro: African Mine Labour in Southern Rhodesia: 1900–1933*
    (Johannesburg: Ravan Press, 1976); I. Phimister, *An Economic and Social History of
    Zimbabwe: 1890–1948: Capital Accumulation and Class Struggle* (London: Longman,
    1988); T.O. Ranger, *The African Voice in Southern Rhodesia* (London: Heinemann,
    1970); T. Scarnecchia, *The Roots of Democracy and Political Violence in Zimbabwe*
    (Rochester: University of Rochester Press, 2008); M.O. West, *The Rise of an African Middle*

Class: Colonial Zimbabwe, 1898–1965 (Indianapolis: Indiana University Press, 2002); B. Raftopoulos, 'The Labour Movement in Zimbabwe: 1945–1965', in B. Raftopoulos and I. Phimister, eds, *Keep on Knocking: A History of Labour Movement in Zimbabwe, 1900–1997* (Harare: Baobab, 1997), 55–90; A. Daimon, 'Ringleaders and Troublemakers': Malawian (Nyasa) Migrants and Transnational Labour Movements in Southern Africa, c. 1910 to 1960', *Labour History*, 58, 5 (2017), 656–75.

4   One of the misplaced files is the National Archives of Zimbabwe (hereafter NAZ) S 1671/2265, Robert Sambo, Organising Secretary of the Industrial and Commercial Workers' Union, Southern Rhodesia. This key file dedicated to Sambo could detail his organisation of the ICU and rabble-rousing activities, his stint in prison and deportation.

5   See P. Nyathi, *Masotsha Ndhlovu* (Harare: Longman, 1998); Scarnecchia, *The Roots of Democracy and Political Violence in Zimbabwe*.

6   A. Daimon, '"TotemlessAliens" The Historical Antecedents of the Anti-Malawian Discourse in Zimbabwe, 1920s–1979', *Journal of Southern African Studies*, 44, 6 (2018), 1095–1114; A. Daimon, 'Settling in Motion as Consciousness: Nyasa (Malawian) Informal Transit across Southern Rhodesia towards South Africa from the 1910s to the 1950s', *African Studies*, 80, 1 (2021), 1–20.

7   O. Kalinga, *Historical Dictionary of Malawi*, 4th Ed. (Plymouth: The Scarecrow Press, 2012), 292.

8   R. Tangri, 'Inter-War Native Associations and the Formation of the Nyasaland African Congress', *Transafrican Journal of History*, 1, 1 (1971), 84–102.

9   Malawi National Archives (hereafter MNA), 'Robert Sambo. An African Pioneer in Self Help', *Livingstonia News*, 14, Jan–March 1927.

10 G. Shepperson, 'Review: *My Life and the ICU: The Autobiography of a Black Trade Unionist in South Africa* by Clements Kadalie and Stanley Trapido', *The Journal of African History*, 14, 1 (1973), 159–61.

11 L. van der Walt, 'The First Globalisation and Transnational Labour Activism in Southern Africa: White Labourism, the IWW, and the ICU, 1904–1934', *African Studies*, 66, 2/3 (2007), 241; B. Pachai, *The Malawi Diaspora and Elements of Clements Kadalie* (Salisbury: The Central African Historical Association, 1969); H. Dee, 'I am a Bad Native': Masculinity and Marriage in the Biographies of Clements Kadalie', *African Studies*, 78, 2 (2019), 185.

12 C. Kadalie, *My Life and the ICU. The Autobiography of a Black Trade Unionist in South Africa* (London: Frank Cass, 1970), 33.

13 Ibid., 35.

14 Van Onselen, *Chibaro*, 121; Daimon, 'Ringleaders and Troublemakers', 656–675.

15 Kadalie, *My Life*, 78.

16 T. Thale, 'Paradigms Lost? Paradigms Regained: Working-Class Autobiography in South Africa', *Journal of Southern African Studies*, 21, 4 (1995), 619; S. Neame, 'Review: *My Life and the ICU: The Autobiography of a Black Trade Unionist in South Africa*', *African Affairs*, 70, 280 (1971), 314.

17 Van der Walt, 'The First Globalisation', 240.

18 NAZ S 3093/1, Kadalie Intelligence Reports - 6/A/1/4, Political Leaders among Southern Rhodesia Natives – Clements Kadalie, CID Bulawayo to the Staff Officer, Salisbury to Chief Staff Office, Defence Force, Salisbury, 9 Mar 1926.

19 Van Onselen, *Chibaro*, 210; Van der Walt, 'The First Globalisation', 242.

20 Van Onselen, *Chibaro*, 210.

21 Scarnecchia, *The Roots of Democracy and Political Violence in Zimbabwe*, 14.

22 Van der Walt, 'The First Globalisation', 241; Ranger, *The African Voice*, 150–53.

23 Van der Walt, 'The First Globalisation', 241.

24 Ibid.

25 A. Ewing, *The Age of Garvey: How a Jamaican Activist Created a Mass Movement and Changed Global Black Politics* (Princeton NJ: Princeton University Press, 2014), 204.

26 Ibid.

27 Ibid.

28 Van Onselen, *Chibaro*, 210; Phimister, *An Economic and Social History of Zimbabwe*, 158.

29 P. Baxter, 'The Amandebele and Modern African Imperial History', http://peterbaxterhistory.com/2011/08/12/the-amandebele-and-modern-african-imperial-history/ [accessed 10 April 2019].

30 Okoth, *A History of Africa*, 126; H. Nelson, *Area Handbook for Southern Rhodesia* (Washington, D.C.: US Government Printing Office, 1975), 30.

31 Phimister, *An Economic and Social History of Zimbabwe*, 158.

32 Okoth, *A History of Africa*, 126.

33 Ibid.

34 South African National Archives, Pretoria (hereafter SANA) Governor-General (hereafter GG) 1566 50/1287, Deportation of R. Sambo from Southern Rhodesia (1928).

35 Ibid.

36 Ranger, *The African Voice*, 150–53.

37 Phimister, *An Economic and Social History of Zimbabwe*, 158; Van der Walt, 'The First Globalisation', 242.

38 NAZ S 482/815/39, ICU of South Africa: Correspondences on ICWU, 1927–1930.

39 Ibid.

40 Ibid.

41 West, *The Rise of an African Middle Class*, 138.

42 Van der Walt, 'The First Globalisation', 241.

43 West, *The Rise of an African Middle Class*, 134.

44 Van der Walt, 'The First Globalisation', 242.

45 Ibid.

46 Ibid.

47 Kadalie, *My Life*, 145.

48 NAZ S 3093/1, Kadalie Intelligence Reports - 6/A/1/4 Political Leaders among Southern Rhodesia Natives - Clements Kadalie, CID Bulawayo to the Staff Officer, Salisbury to Chief Staff Office, Defence Force, Salisbury, 9 Mar 1926.

49 Ibid.

50   West, *The Rise of an African Middle Class*, 134.

51   E. Windrich, 'Rhodesian Censorship: The Role of Media in the Making of a One-Party State', *African Affairs*, 78, 313 (1979), 523–34.

52   West, *The Rise of an African Middle Class*, 138.

53   Ibid.

54   Scarnecchia, *The Roots of Democracy and Political Violence*, 15.

55   NAZ S 482/815/39, ICU of South Africa: Correspondences on ICWU, 1927–1930.

56   Ibid.

57   Ibid.

58   Ibid.

59   West, *The Rise of an African Middle Class*, 135.

60   Ibid.

61   Raftopoulos, 'The Labour Movement in Zimbabwe: 1945–1965', 58.

62   Ranger, *The African Voice*, 150-53.

63   'Trade Unionism in the Crown Colonies', *New Leader*, 15 July 1927.

64   'Round the World', *New Leader,* 30 September 1927.

65   H. Dee, 'Central African Immigrants, Imperial Citizenship and the Politics of Free Movement in Interwar South Africa', *Journal of Southern African Studies*, 46, 2 (2020). 319–37. Wits Historical Papers (hereafter Wits) Trade Union Council of South Africa Part 1, 1915–1954 (hereafter TUCSA) AH 646 Cc4.3, E. J. Khaile to General Secretary, 7 March 1928; University of Cape Town (hereafter UCT) Lionel Forman Papers BC 581 B3.183, C. Kadalie to Prime Minister of Southern Rhodesia, 22 December 1927. See also 'A Blot on British Justice', *Workers' Herald,* 15 July 1927; 'British Labour Party Fight for ICU in S. Rhodesia', *Workers' Herald,* 15 September 1927.

66   Hansard, UK Parliament – Southern Rhodesia (Trade Unions), Vol. 208, 11 January 1927.

67   Ibid.

68   Ibid.

69   UK Parliamentary Debates from Hansard Online - HC Deb 05 December 1927 Vol. 211 cc983-4, http://hansard.millbanksystems.com/commons/1927/dec/05/robert-sambo-deportation#S5CV0211P0_19271205 _HOC_248

70   Ibid.

71   Ranger, *The African Voice*, 151.

72   Kadalie, *My Life*, 125.

73   Ibid.

74   Ibid.

75   'British Labour Party Fight for ICU in Southern Rhodesia', *Workers' Herald,* 15 September 1927.

76   UCT Forman Papers BC 581 B3 1927 3. 183, Circular letter from Kadalie to the Prime Minister, Southern Rhodesia, Re: Deportation of R. Sambo: An ICU agent in Bulawayo, 22 December 1927.

77   'Defiant Letter from Kadalie', *Rhodesia Herald*, 1 February 1928.

78   SANA GG 1566 50/1287, Deportation of R. Sambo from Southern Rhodesia (1928).

79   Ibid.

80   SANA GG 1566 50/1287, Deportation of R Sambo from Southern Rhodesia, R. Sambo to Governor, Zomba, 10 January 1928.

81   SANA NTS 2706 16/301, Prohibited Immigrants: Tropical Natives (1926–1956), Chief Native Commissioner, Natal to Secretary for Native Affairs, 24/11/1927.

82   SANA NTS 2706 16/301, Prohibited Immigrants: Tropical Natives (1926–1956) – Secretary for Native Affairs to Secretary for the Interior, 04 January 1928.

83   Ibid.

84   Ibid; SANA GG 1566 50/1287, Deportation of R. Sambo from Southern Rhodesia, R. Sambo to Governor, Zomba, 10 January 1928.

85   O. Kalinga, 'Jordan Msumba, Ben Ngemela and the Last Church of God and His Christ, 1924–1935', *Journal of Religion in Africa*, 13, 3 (1982), 207-18.

86   J. McCracken, *Politics and Christianity in Malawi, 1875–1940: The Impact of the Livingstonia Mission in the Northern Province* (Blantyre: CLAIM, 2000), 322; J. McCracken, *A History of Malawi: 1859–1966* (Woodbridge: James Currey, 2012), 212; R. Rotberg, *The Rise of Nationalism in Central Africa: The Making of Malawi and Zambia, 1873–1964* (Cambridge, Mass.: Harvard University Press, 1965), 149.

87   Ewing, *The Age of Garvey*, 204.

88   Kalinga, 'Jordan Msumba, Ben Ngemela and the Last Church', 207–18.

89   McCracken, *Politics and Christianity in Malawi*, 322.

90   T.O. Ranger, *The African Churches of Tanzania* (Nairobi: The East Africa Publishing House, 1972), 17.

91   'Defiant Letter from Kadalie', *The Rhodesian Herald*, 1 February 1928.

92   Ranger, *The African Voice*, 152.

93   Nelson, *Area Handbook for Southern Rhodesia*, 30; J. Chikuhwa, *Zimbabwe: The End of the First Republic* (Bloomington: Author House, 2013), 5.

Chapter 3

1   N. Nieftagodien, 'Migrants: Vanguards of the Workers' Struggle?' in P. Delius, L. Philips and F. Rankin-Smith, eds., *A Long Way Home: Migrant Worker Worlds, 1800–2014* (Johannesburg: Wits University Press, 2014), 224–40; M. Hlatshwayo, 'Immigrant Workers and COSATU: Solidarity vs National Chauvinism?', *Alternation*, 7 (2013), 267–93.

2   Numerous historians have questioned the ICU's effectiveness as a trade union. See for example Sylvia Neame's analysis: A. Lissoni, 'Review: *The Congress Movement: The Unfolding of the Congress Alliance, 1912–1961*. Vols 1–3', *African Historical Review*, 47, 2 (2015), 132–52.

3   J. Crush, A. Jeeves and D. Yudelman, *South Africa's Labour Empire: A History of Black Migrancy to the Gold Mines* (Cape Town: David Philip, 1991).

4   H. Dee, 'Central African Immigrants, Imperial Citizenship and the Politics of Free
     Movement in Interwar South Africa', *Journal of Southern African Studies*, 46, 2 (2020),
     319–37.

5   P. Bonner, 'Desirable or Undesirable Basotho Women. Liquor, Prostitution and the
     Migration of Basotho Women to the Rand, 1920–1945', in C. Walker, ed., *Women and
     Gender in Southern Africa to 1945* (Cape Town: David Philip, 1990), 221–50.

6   'Strike of Native Factory Hands', *Rand Daily Mail*, 8 June 1928.

7   South African National Archive (hereafter SANA) Ministry of the Interior (hereafter
     BNS) 1/1/377 194/74, 'Natives from Rhodesia, Bechuanaland, Portuguese East Africa,
     British East Africa, Nyasaland' (1924–1929); BNS 1/1/378 194/74, 'Natives from Rhodesia,
     Bechuanaland, Portuguese East Africa, British East Africa, Nyasaland' (1929–1935); F.
     Malunga, 'Foreign African migrant labour at the Messina Copper Mines, 1905–1960',
     Historia, 47, 1 (2002), 270–90; and Chapter 7 by Laurence Stewart in this volume.

8   Wits Historical Papers (hereafter Wits) Sylvia Neame Papers A 2729, Sylvia Neame interview
     with John Gomas, September 1962; S. Neame, *The Congress Movement: The Unfolding of the
     Congress Alliance, 1912–1961*, Vol. 2 (Cape Town: HSRC Press, 2015), 169. For Malawians
     in Durban, see G.N. Burden, *Nyasaland Natives in the Union of South Africa* (Zomba:
     Government Printer, 1940), 25.

9   SANA Governor-General (hereafter GG) 1566 50/1287, 'Deportation of R. Sambo from
     Southern Rhodesia' (1928), R. Sambo to the Governor, Zomba, 10 January 1928; Z. Groves,
     Malawian Migration to Zimbabwe, 1900–1965: Tracing Machona (London: Palgrave
     Macmillan, 2020).

10   Z. Groves, 'Urban Migrants and Religious Networks: Malawians in Colonial Salisbury, 1920
     to 1970', *Journal of Southern African Studies*, 38, 3 (2012), 497.

11   H. Bradford, 'Getting Away with Murder: Mealie Kings, the State and Foreigners in the
     Eastern Transvaal, c. 1918–1950', in P. Bonner, P. Delius and D. Posel, eds., *Apartheid's Genesis:
     1935–1962*, (Johannesburg: Wits University Press, 1993), 96–125; A. Jeeves, 'Sugar and Gold
     in the Making of the South African Labour System: The Crisis of Supply on the Zululand
     Sugar Estates, 1906–1939', *South African Journal of Economic History*, 7, 2 (1992), 7–33.

12   R.T. Vinson, *The Americans are Coming! Dreams of African American Liberation in
     Segregationist South Africa* (Athens: Ohio University Press, 2012), 78-79; Neame, *Congress
     Movement*, Vol. 1, 450; Wits Neame Papers A 2729, Neame interview with Gomas; SANA
     Commissioner of the South African Police (hereafter SAP) 40 CONF 6/698/19, 'Industrial
     Commercial Union Harbour Branch: Native and Coloured Agitation' (1919–1920).

13   See Lucien van der Walt, Chapter 1 in this volume.

14   P. La Hausse, 'The Message of the Warriors: the ICU, the Labouring Poor and the Making of
     a Popular Culture in Durban', in P. Bonner, I. Hofmeyr, D. James and T. Lodge, eds, *Holding
     their Ground: Class, Locality and Culture in Nineteenth and Twentieth-Century South Africa*
     (Johannesburg: Wits University Press, 1987), 30.

15   T.D.M. Skota, *The African Yearly Register* (Johannesburg: R.L. Esson and Co., 1930), 214;
     S.J. Jingoes, *A Chief is a Chief by the People: The Autobiography of Stimela Jason Jingoes*
     (London: Oxford University Press, 1975), 9.

16 H. Bradford, *A Taste*, 149.

17 C. Kadalie, 'General Secretary's Report for 1924', *Workers' Herald*, 15 May 1925.

18 SANA GG 1566 50/1287, 'Deportation of R. Sambo from Southern Rhodesia' (1928), R. Sambo to Governor, Zomba, Nyasaland Protectorate, 10 January 1928; M. West, *The Rise of an African Middle Class* (Bloomington: Indiana University Press, 2002), 140–144.

19 D. Khosa, 'Coisas Nossas…Clements Kadalie', *Brado Africano*, 27 January 1929; A.D. Lipede, 'Pan-Africanism in Southern Africa, 1900–1960' (PhD thesis, University of York, 1990), 335.

20 Bradford, *A Taste*, 306, 313; P. Wickins, *The Industrial and Commercial Workers' Union of Africa* (Cape Town: Oxford University Press, 1978), 122; L. van der Walt, 'The First Globalisation and Transnational Labour Activism in Southern Africa: White Labourism, the IWW, and the ICU, 1904–1934', *African Studies*, 66, 2–3 (2007), 243.

21 M. Lake and H. Reynolds, *Drawing the Global Colour Line: White Men's Countries and the International Challenge to Racial Equality* (Cambridge: Cambridge University Press, 2008), 72.

22 R. Bright, *Chinese Labour in South Africa, 1902–10: Race, Violence, and Global Spectacle* (London: Palgrave Macmillan, 2013), 39–54; F. Musoni, *Border Jumping and Migration Control in Southern Africa* (Bloomington, Indiana University Press, 2020), 45–75.

23 M. Creswell, *An Epoch of the Political History of South Africa in the Life of Frederic Hugh Page Creswell* (Cape Town: AA Balkema, 1956), 10.

24 S. Katzenellenbogen, *South Africa and Southern Mozambique: Labour, Railways and Trade in the Making of a Relationship* (Manchester: Manchester University Press, 1982), 136–37.

25 'Where is White Labour?', *Forward*, 19 June 1925.

26 J. Klaaren, *From Prohibited Immigrants to Citizens: The Origins of Citizenship and Nationality in South Africa* (Cape Town: UCT Press, 2017), 155.

27 Dee, 'Central African Immigrants'; Bradford, 'Getting Away with Murder'.

28 'Native Immigration into the Union', *Umteteli wa Bantu*, 17 March 1928.

29 Z.K. Matthews, *Freedom for My People* (Cape Town: David Philip, 1981), 62.

30 H.S. Msimang, 'South African Slave Economy', *Umteteli wa Bantu*, 31 March 1928. See also H.S. Msimang, 'Organisation of Bantu Workers', *Umteteli wa Bantu*, 14 February 1925 and 28 February 1925.

31 S.M.B. Ncwana, 'Recruiting of Native Labour', *Imvo Zabantsundu*, 28 April 1925.

32 H.S. Msimang, 'Congress and Blantyres', *Umteteli wa Bantu*, 18 February 1928.

33 *Report of Native Churches Commission* (Cape Town: Government Printers, 1925); J.S. Marwick in *Debates of the House of Assembly: 13th February to 25th July 1925* (Cape Town: Cape Times Ltd, 1925), cols. 2891-2893.

34 'Native Minister's Letter to the Press', *Natal Witness*, 21 January 1928.

35 Wits Neame Papers A 2729 32/11, *Industrial and Commercial Workers' Union of Africa: Third Annual Conference: Official Report of Proceedings* (Cape Town: A. Holder, 1923); 'UNIA', *Umteteli wa Bantu*, 7 November 1925.

36 Neame, *Congress Movement*, Vol.1, 396.

37 West, *Rise of an African Middle Class*, 135.

38   West, *Rise of an African Middle Class*, 142–43; Bradford, *A Taste*, 149, 306.

39   C. Kadalie, *My Life*, 161.

40   SANA Ministry of Justice (hereafter JUS) 916 1/18/26, 'The African World: Police Reports: Part 5', report on ICU meeting at Port Elizabeth, 2 January 1927.

41   'Shedding Crocodile Tears', *Workers' Herald*, 27 March 1926.

42   'South African Labour Congress', *Workers' Herald*, 2 April 1925; SANA GG 1566 50/1287, 'Deportation of R. Sambo from Southern Rhodesia', R. Sambo to Governor, Zomba, 10 January 1928.

43   Wits Neame Papers A 2729, Graham Neame interview with Theo Lujiza, c. February 1969.

44   'Miss Makanya', *Workers' Herald*, 28 April 1926. Translated from isiZulu by Fundile Majola.

45   N. Erlank, 'Christianity and African Nationalism in South Africa in the First Half of the Twentieth Century', in A. Lissoni, J. Soske, N. Erlank, N. Nieftagodien and O. Badsha, eds., *One Hundred Years of the ANC: Debating Liberation Histories Today* (Johannesburg: Wits University Press, 2012), 77–96; H. Langworthy, *'Africa for the Africans': The Life of Joseph Booth* (Blantyre: CLAIM, 1996), 413.

46   'Dr Rubusana's Downfall', *Black Man*, 1, 5 (November 1920); L. Callinicos, *Working Life, 1886–1940* (Johannesburg: Ravan Press, 1987), 115.

47   J. Gomas, 'The Workers and the Capitalists at Loggerheads', *Workers' Herald*, 15 October 1925.

48   C. Kadalie, 'The Old and the New Africa', *Labour Monthly*, 9, 10 (October 1927), 624–31.

49   'ICU Manifesto', *Ilanga lase Natal*, 12 October 1923.

50   A.B.S. Ngaleka, 'Some Aspects of the Colour Problem', *Workers' Herald*, 2 April 1925.

51   Ibid.

52   'Recruiting System', *Black Man*, 1, 5, November 1920; 'Recruitment System', *Workers' Herald*, 21 July 1923.

53   'The Slavery of Recruited Labour', *International*, 11 August 1923.

54   Ibid.

55   Neame, *Congress Movement*, Vol. 1, 294.

56   Skota, *Yearly Register*, 146. Many thanks to Jeanne Penvenne for advice on Dulela.

57   'The New Trade Unionism', *Workers' Herald*, 28 April 1926.

58   Kadalie, *My Life*, 72.

59   Neame, *Congress Movement*, Vol. 2, 158; Wits A 2744 A.W.G. Champion, *Autobiography*, 68.

60   K. Breckenridge, '"We Must Speak for Ourselves": The Rise and Fall of a Public Sphere on the South African Gold Mines, 1920 to 1931', *Comparative Studies in Society and History*, 40, 1 (1998), 71–108.

61   'ICU Programme for 1928', *Workers' Herald*, 12 May 1928.

62   'ICU Transvaal Organiser Exposes Recruiting System', *South African Worker*, 26 November 1926.

63   C. Kadalie, 'National Secretary's Report for 1925', *Workers' Herald*, 28 April 1926.

64   'The News and the Doings of the ICU', *Workers' Herald*, 20 February 1925; C. Kadalie, 'General Secretary's Report for 1924', *Workers' Herald*, 15 May 1925.

65   'Dual Passive Resistance', *African World*, 30 May 1925.

66   'Fourth African Labour Congress', *Workers' Herald*, 15 May 1926.

67   'Undoing Themselves', *Ilanga lase Natal*, 10 February 1928.

68   Bradford, *A Taste*, 313.

69   Neame, *Congress Movement,* Vol. 2, 364–365; 'Chief Motsoene of Basutoland', *Workers' Herald*, 29 September 1928.

70   Neame, *Congress Movement*, Vol. 2, 70–73; 'Fourth African Labour Congress', *Workers' Herald*, 15 May 1926; 'Eighth Annual Congress of the ICU', *Workers' Herald*, 12 May 1928.

71   SANA JUS 915 1/18/26, 'The African World: Police Reports: Part 1', CID to Deputy Commissioner, 1 May 1926.

72   'A Wrong Righted', *Workers' Herald*, 15 December 1926.

73   SANA JUS 916 1/18/26, 'The African World: Police Reports: Part 6', Report on ICU meeting at Witbank, 23 January 1927.

74   SANA JUS 918 1/18/26, 'Native Agitation: Reports On: Part 11', Report on ICU meeting in Johannesburg, 21 August 1927 ICU.

75   Breckenridge, '"We Must Speak for Ourselves"'.

76   SANA JUS 921 1/18/26, 'Native Agitation: Reports On: Part 19', Report on ICU meeting in Johannesburg on 8 July 1928.

77   T.W. Thibedi, 'Workers' Life', *South African Worker*, 23 July 1926.

78   'Replacement on the Railways', *Workers' Herald*, 15 October 1925.

79   'Conditions of Native Workers at Railways', *South African Worker,* 8 October 1926.

80   H.D. Tyamzashe, 'A Huge Labour Struggle', *Workers' Herald*, 15 December 1926.

81   Wits Neame Papers A 2729, Graham Neame interview with Theo Lujiza, c. February 1969.

82   See, for example, 'New Government Bill', *Workers' Herald*, 15 October 1925; 'Faction Fights on the Rand Mines', *Workers' Herald*, 20 February 1926; 'A Trade Union Organ', *Workers' Herald,* 15 June 1926; WITS AD 1438 Native Economic Commission B7.6, T. Mbeki and H.D. Tyamzashe, 8087.

83   'No Black Angels', *Rand Daily Mail*, 13 January 1926.

84   'Fourth African Labour Congress', *Workers' Herald*, 15 May 1926.

85   Breckenridge, '"We Must Speak for Ourselves"'.

86   Ibid.

87   Ibid.

88   Bradford, A *Taste*, 148-161.

89   Kadalie, *My Life*, 89.

90   Breckenridge, '"We Must Speak for Ourselves"'.

91   Ibid.

92   Jeeves, 'Sugar and Gold', 18; N. Cope, *To Bind the Nation: Solomon KaDinuzulu and Zulu Nationalism, 1913–1933* (Pietermaritzburg: University of KwaZulu Natal Press, 1993), 210–11.

93   Cope, *To Bind the Nation*, 207–08.

94 M. Mamdani, *Citizen and Subject: Contemporary Africa and the Legacy of Late Colonialism* (Princeton: Princeton University Press, 1996), 71–72, 94–95.

95 UKZN Killie Campbell Manuscripts (hereafter KCM) John Sydney Marwick Papers, 73 J.L. Dube to J.S. Marwick, 24 February 1928.

96 'Flag Delegation', *Ilanga lase Natal,* 26 November 1926.

97 Neame, *Congress Movement*, Vol. 2, 62–63.

98 Champion, *Autobiography*, 112–113.

99 S.M.B. Ncwana, 'The "Umteteli" Recrudesence', *Umteteli wa Bantu*, 24 September 1927.

100 University of Cape Town Special Collections (hereafter UCT) BC 581 Lionel Forman Papers 3.111, A.W.G. Champion to S.M.B. Ncwana, 5 October 1927.

101 'Is it War to the Knife?', *Workers' Herald*, 15 October 1927.

102 SANA JUS 919 1/18/26, 'Native Agitation: Reports On: Parts 12–13', report of ICU meeting in Johannesburg, 1 April 1928.

103 SANA BNS 1/1/377 194/74, 'Natives from Rhodesia, Bechuanaland, Portuguese East Africa, British East Africa, Nyasaland', SAP Elandsputte to Deputy Commissioner of Police, 2 September 1927.

104 SANA JUS 918 1/18/26, 'Native Agitation: Reports On: Part 11', TAC meeting in Western Native Township, 18 September 1927.

105 SANA JUS 918 1/18/26, 'Native Agitation: Reports On: Part 11', ICU meeting in Johannesburg, 18 September 1927. For more on the ANC's African Labour Congress, see Neame, *Congress Movement*, Vol. 2, 333–35.

106 'Tights at the Western Native Township', *Times of Natal,* 29 December 1927; 'Trouble at Western Native Township', *Umteteli wa Bantu,* 31 December 1927; 'Africans versus Africans', *Abantu Batho*, 9 February 1928; H. D. Tyamzashe, 'Past and Present', *Workers' Herald,* 18 February 1928.

107 R.V.S. Thema, 'The Responsibility of Bantu Leadership', *Umteteli wa Bantu*, 21 January 1928; R.W. Msimang, 'Congress Supports Deportation', *Umteteli wa Bantu*, 11 February 1928; S. Plaatje, 'Should the Nyanjas be Deported?', *Umteteli wa Bantu*, 3 March 1928.

108 'Russia Today', *South African Worker*, 30 March 1928; H.D. Tyamzashe, 'Past and Present', *Workers' Herald*, 18 February 1928.

109 'African Congress and ICU Co-operation', *Workers' Herald*, 17 March 1928.

110 'Russia Today', *South African Worker*, 30 March 1928.

111 H.S. Msimang, 'Congress and Blantyres', *Umteteli wa Bantu*, 18 February 1928.

112 SANA Government Native Labour Bureau (hereafter GNLB) 400 55/1, 'Communism in the Union', Report of TAC meeting in Marabastad, 20 January 1929.

113 SANA JUS 921 1/18/26, 'Native Agitation: Reports On: Part 19', Report on ICU meeting in Johannesburg, 8 July 1928.

114 'Kadalie Resignation', *Workers' Herald*, 5 May 1929.

115 WITS Neame Papers A 2729, Graham Neame interview with Theo Lujiza, c. February 1969.

116 Dee, 'Central African Immigrants'.

117 UCT William Ballinger Papers BC 347 A5 II.1, C. Kadalie, 'Manifesto', 9 July 1928; Champion, *Autobiography*, 100–101.

118 Kadalie, 'Manifesto'.

119 Kadalie, *My Life*, 222.

120 Wits William Ballinger Papers A 410 C2.3.7, A.W.G. Champion to W.G. Ballinger, 21 July 1928.

121 J.G. Coka, 'The Story of Gilbert Coka', in M. Perham, ed., *Ten Africans* (London: Faber and Faber, 1936), 303; Neame *Congress Movement*, Vol. 2, 518.

122 'Clements Kadalie Resigns Secretaryship of ICU', *Star*, 25 January 1929.

123 SANA JUS 923 1/18/26, 'Native Agitation: Reports on: Part 27', Report of IICU meeting in East London, 24 August 1930.

124 South African National Archives, Cape Town (hereafter WCA) East London Magistrate (1/ELN) 86 C3, 'Native Unrest', Report of ICU of Africa meeting in East London on 8 December 1929; Report of ICU of Africa meeting in East London, 23 December 1929.

125 SANA GNLB 400 55/1, 'Communism in the Union', Report of ICU of Africa meeting at Parys location, 18 August 1929. I am grateful to Peter Limb for forwarding this document.

126 H.A. Lamprecht and J.G. Strydom, *Debates of the House of Assembly: 17th January to 31st May 1930* (Cape Town: Cape Times Ltd, 1930), col 2339–2386.

127 K. Motsoakai, 'Portuguese Native Labour on the Rand', *Umsebenzi*, 21 January 1933.

128 Wits, Frank Lucas Papers, Native Economic Commission AD 1769 175, 211–12.

129 Klaaren, *From Prohibited Immigrants*, 152–184.

130 WCA Chief Native Commissioner (hereafter CCK) 21 N1/9/3, 'Independent Industrial and Commercial Workers Union', Sgt Mandy to District Commandant, 14 June 1932.

131 Kadalie, *My Life*, 127.

132 Ibid., 222.

Chapter 4

1   In Afrikaans (as in Dutch) a 'dorp' is a village or small, especially country, town; 'dorpie', the diminutive, signifies an even smaller settlement. In South African English, dorp can connote a place marked by backward or less progressive thinking. The terms well evoke Free State settlements where the ICU sought to gain a precarious base.

2   P. Wickins, *The Industrial and Commercial Workers' Union of Africa* (Cape Town: Oxford University Press, 1978); H. Bradford, *A Taste of Freedom* (Johannesburg: Ravan Press, 1987); T. Moloi, 'Black Politics in Kroonstad' (PhD thesis, University of the Witwatersrand, 2012); S. Mkhize, *A Political Biography of Selby Msimang* (Cape Town: BestRed, 2019); S. Neame, *The Congress Movement*, 3 Vols. (Cape Town: HSRC Press, 2015).

3   P. Wickins, 'The Industrial and Commercial Workers Union of Africa' (PhD thesis, University of Cape Town, 1973), 368; P. Bonner, '"Home Truths" and the Political Discourse

of the ICU' (Cape Town: University of the Western Cape, South African Historical Society Conference, 11–14 July 1999), 11, 14; M. Hawkins, 'Memel: An Exploratory Study of the Workings and Economic Dynamics of a Very Small South African Town' (MSc thesis, University of the Witwatersrand, 2012), 11; J. Butler, *Cradock* (Charlottesville: University of Virginia Press, 2017); T. Moloi, *Place of Thorns* (Johannesburg: Wits University Press, 2015).

4   W. Beinart and C. Bundy, *Hidden Struggles in Rural South Africa* (Johannesburg: Ravan Press, 1987); C. Murray, *Black Mountain* (Edinburgh: Edinburgh University Press, 1992); T. Keegan, *Rural Transformations in Industrialising South Africa* (Johannesburg: Ravan, 1987); B. Hirson, *A History of the Left in South Africa* (London: Tauris, 2005); H. Haasbroek, 'Die Swart Loongeskil van 1926 in Bloemfontein', *New Contree* 76 (2016), 171–92; P. Rich, 'Managing Black Leadership' in I. Hofmeyr, D. James, T. Lodge, eds., *Holding Their Ground* (Johannesburg: Ravan Press, 1989), 177–200.

5   G. Rudé, *Paris and London in the Eighteenth Century* (London: Collins, 1970), C. Tilly, *Contentious Performances* (Cambridge: Cambridge University Press, 2008), xi, 21; Bradford, *A Taste*, 77ff; R. Hilton, *English and French Towns in Feudal Society* (Cambridge: Cambridge University Press, 1992), xi.

6   Neame, *Congress*, Vol. 2, 309–31; C. van Onselen, *The Seed is Mine* (Cape Town: David Philip, 1996).

7   Wits Institute for Advanced Social Research (hereafter IASR), Sharecropping and Labour Tenancy Project (hereafter SLTP), AG 2738, N. Makume, 10 June 1982 6; T. Manoto, 24 February 1980 7ff; J. Mosina, 8 April 1980 14; P. Masike, 24 February 1980, 31; J. Molete, 26 February 1980, 6ff; L. Rakabaele, 26 April 1989, 3ff; T. Keegan, *Facing the Storm* (London: Zed Press, 1988), 22; L. Boswell, *Rural Communism in France, 1920-39* (Ithaca: Cornell University Press, 1998), 243.

8   Bradford, *A Taste*, 115; Keegan, *Rural Transformations,* 79–86; C. le Roux, *Die Verhouding tussen Blank en Nie-Blank in die Oranjerivierkolonie, 1900–10* (Pretoria: Government Printer, 1986), 105; South African National Archives, Bloemfontein (hereafter VAB) Native Affairs (hereafter NAB) 1 66/A/05, Magistrate Philippolis to Native Adviser: 'Treatment of Natives by Some Farmers', 22 July 1905.

9   VAB Orange River Colony (hereafter ORC), *Census 1904* 3–16; *SA Year-Book 1904*, 331; *Municipal Year Book 1922*, 223ff, *1926–7*, 271, *1928-9*, 3–8; *Census 1921*, 16, 58–61; A. van Rensburg, *Die Geskiedenis van Bethlehem 1864–1964* (Bethlehem: Stadsraad, 1964), 169.

10   VAB ORC, *Annual Report Mines Dept. 1903–8*; *Report of Coal Commission* (1921) 3, 8; C. Richards, *The Iron and Steel Industry in South Africa* (Johannesburg: Wits University Press, 1940), 8, 132; South African National Archives, Pretoria (hereafter SANA), Governor-General (hereafter GG) 50/1014, 'Native Labour Statistics returns for 1922'; *Braby's OFS Directory*, 1922, 610; *Select Committee on Railways and Harbours* (SC 3–22) 187; *Official Labour Gazette*, 3, 15 (1927), 239; P. Bonner, 'Desirable or Undesirable Basotho Women?' in C. Walker, ed., *Women and Gender in Southern Africa to 1945* (Cape Town: David Philip, 1990), 229.

11   'Report', *Labour Gazette* 1, 2 (1925), 267; *Social and Industrial Review*, 3, 18 (1927), 601; 'Jagersfontein's Treatment', *Imvo Zabantsundu*, 20 June 1895; VAB NAB 2 N 54/06, 'Complaints of Certain Natives on the Cornelia Mine' and CO 170 3440/03, 'Cornelia Mine: Strike'; VAB ATG 2 543/08, 'Alleged Illegal Arrest and Trial of Natives'; 'Natives on

the Warpath: Voorspoed Mine Rising'; 500 Marching on Kroonstad', *Rand Daily Mail*, 10 December 1907; Trouble at Vo[o]rspoed Mine', *Diamond Fields Advertiser*, 11 February 1910; SANA Department of Justice (hereafter JUS) 5/83/20, 'Native Unrest Jagersfontein'.

12   'Render unto Ceasar[sic]', *Umteteli wa Bantu*, 17 September 1927.

13   'Non-European Workers' Conference: Formation of One Big Union', *Friend*, 14 July 1920; SANA, South African Police (hereafter SAP) 40 CON F6/698/19, 'ICU Harbour…'; 'ICWU', *Umteteli wa Bantu*, 4 June 1921.

14   T.D.M. Skota, *African Yearly Register* (Johannesburg: Esson, 1930), 180; J. Mancoe, *The Bloemfontein Bantu and Coloured People's Directory* (Bloemfontein: White, 1934), 33, 70; *Native Economic Commission 1930–2* (hereafter *NEC*), Evidence 18 July 1930; P. Limb, *The ANC's Early Years* (Pretoria: Unisa Press, 2010), 268ff; Wickins, 'The Industrial', 72; J. Mogaecho, 'Mangaung le Litiro tsa ICU', *Workers' Herald*, 27 March 1926, 'National Secretary's Report', *Workers' Herald*, 28 April 1926; 'Non-European Workers' Conference', *Friend*, 14 July 1920; Bradford, *A Taste*, 83; VAB 4/8/1/81, Wages Committee Minutes, 22 February 1926, Minutes of Town Council Bloemfontein (hereafter MBL); 'Away with Pass Laws', *Star*, 8 April 1927; 'Not Clear about Communism', *Rand Daily Mail*, 10 April 1928; *NEC*, February 1931.

15   'Mote, 'The ICU in the Eastern Free State', *South African Worker*, 3 December 1926; 'ICU Leaders in Orange Free State', *South African Worker*, 8 July 1927; UCT Ballinger Papers BC 347 D3 I 1.1, E. Roux to N. Leys, 16 September 1928.

16   'The Right to Organise', *Umteteli wa Bantu*, 10 October 1927; R. Thema, 'Homeless Wanderers', *Umteteli wa Bantu*, 22 October 1927; *Braby's*, 1922, 46, 70.

17   Wickins, 'The Industrial', 190; UCT Forman Papers BC 2.7; J. La Guma, 'General Secretary's Report of Inspection of Branches', 6 March 1926; 'Mokhatlo oa Basebetsi', *Leselinyana*, 30 Pulungona 1923; 'Mote, 'Agriculture for the Bantu', *Umteteli*, 29 July 1922, H.E. M[abille], 'Tsa South Africa', *Leselinyana*, 22 Pherekhong 1926; 'Litaba tsa Free State', WH, 15 February 1927; 'Free State Activities and New Determin-ation amongst Workers', *Workers' Herald*, 6 April 1927; Neame, *Congress*, Vol. 2, 322.

18   R.V.S. Thema, 'Homeless wanderers', *Umteteli wa Bantu*, 22 October 1927; C. Kadalie, *My Life and the ICU: The Autobiography of a Black Trade Unionist in South Africa* (London: Frank Cass, 1970), 69; E. Roux, 'Agrarian Revolt in South Africa', *Labour Monthly*, 10, 1 (1928), 60.

19   Hawkins, 'Memel', 89; SANA Government Native Labour Bureau (hereafter GNLB) 400 55/1, 'ICU Meeting held in Verkykerskop 30 June 1929'.

20   Mancoe, *Directory*, 69–70, 102; R. Dumah, 'Agricultural Course', *Izindaba Zabantu*, 1 May 1922; Bradford, *A Taste*, 113; SANA GNLB 400 55/1, 'ICU Meeting at Kestell, 17 February 1929' and 'Meeting at Kestell, 17 March 1929'.

21   'Tsa South Africa', *Leselinyana*, 10 Hlakola 1928; SANA GNLB 400 55/1, 'Meeting at Memel, 14 April 1929' and 'Meeting in Memel, 7 July 1929'; SANA GNLB 399 55/1, Vrede 'Native Unrest', 16 December 1929.

22   SANA GNLB 400 55/1, Kromhof. 'Native Agitators Meeting 13/1/29 Christina', 12 March 1929.

23   L. Bank, 'The Failure of Ethnic Nationalism: Land, Power and the Politics of Clanship on the South African Highveld 1860–1990', *Africa*, 65 (1995), 565–91; H. Colson, 'Harrismith: Position of Natives', 8 October 1926, SANA Native Affairs (hereafter NTS) 1756, 46/276;

'Litaba tsa Foreisetata', *Umteteli wa Bantu*, 9 August 1924; 'ICU Propaganda Campaign', *South African Worker*, 17 September 1926; 'Mote, 'The ICU in Eastern Free State'; SAP NTS 7606 27/328, Harrismith Reports 15, 19 October, 2 November 1926.

24 Bradford, *A Taste*, 80, 305; WITS Neame Papers A 2729, Kadalie to 'Mote, 27 July 1929; 'Mote to Kadalie, 15 August 1929, 'Papers from 'Mote 1962'; SANA GNLB 400 55/1 'Native Agitators', Harrismith, 16 January 1929; Wickins, 'The Industrial', 374; 'Mote, 'Plight of "Free" State Natives', *Umteteli wa Bantu*, 7 November 1931; 'Tsa Qoaqoa', *Umteteli wa Bantu*, 23 May 1931; Sihloaelli, 'E Witzies Hoek', *Umsebenzi*, 30 November 1933; J. S[elepe] 'Tsa Witsieshoek', *Umsebenzi*, 10 February 1934; ICS Basner Papers, H. Basner to B. Hirson, 7 May 1975; H.M. Basner, *Am I an African?* (Johannesburg: Witwatersrand University Press, 1993), 86.

25 UCT Forman Papers BC 581 3.140, 'Mote to Champion 31 October 1927; Neame, *Congress* Vol. 2, 472; *Workers' Herald*, 6 April 1927, quoted in Neame *Congress*, Vol. 2, 322; SANA GNLB 400 55/1, Ficksburg, 'ICU meeting, 10 February 1929'; WITS Neame Papers A 2729, Kadalie to 'Mote, 27 July 1929.

26 Wickins, 'The Industrial', 390; SANA GNLB 400 55/1, Paul Roux, 'Native Unrest', 3 March 1929; 'Go Tsamaea ke go Bona', *Umteteli wa Bantu*, 31 May 1930; WITS ICU Records A 924 A4.2.4, W. Ballinger 'The Industrial and Commercial Workers Union of Africa', 1933, 3 and 'ICWU (ICU) Records, 1925–47'.

27 VAB CO 559 933/3, 'Petition from Eastern Branch Native Vigilance Association', 1909; Wickins, 'The Industrial', 386; Mancoe, *Directory*, 102; 'Mote, 'ICU in Eastern Free State'; S.J. Jingoes, *A Chief is a Chief by the People* (London: OUP, 1975), 100–7; 'Branch News', *Workers' Herald Weekly News Bulletin*, 21 November 1928; 'Mote, 'Khoebo ea Batala Foreiseiata', *Umteteli wa Bantu*, 26 December 1931.

28 VAB SOO 1/1/41 N8/10 OFS Education Dept, Correspondence 15 and 21 September 1927; SANA GNLB 399 55/1, 400 55/1, Vrede. 'Native Unrest', 18 December 1928, 18 February 1929; SANA GNLB 400 55/1, 'Reports on a meeting at Vrede, 28 April 1929'; 'Native Horsemen Demonstrate', *Umsebenzi*, 27 June 1930; Dumah, 'South African Native Farm Tenants', *Negro Worker*, 1, 4/5 (1931), 10–12.

29 Wits Neame Papers A 2729, 'Mote to IICU 21 August 1929, to Kadalie 15, 20 August 1929.

30 Wickins, 'The Industrial', 384.

31 Mancoe, *Directory*, 102–103. D. D. T. Jabavu, ed., *Minutes of the All African Convention* (Lovedale: Lovedale Press, 1936), 29; Lady Porcupine [Johanna Phahlane], 'Bloemfontein News', *Bantu World*, 19 September 1936.

32 J. Wells, *We Now Demand!* (Johannesburg: Witwatersrand University Press, 1993), 60-62; VAB MBE (Bethulie) 1/4/4 MB1/4/4/4, J. Cloete to Town Clerk (TC) Bethulie 27 July 1926, TC Bethulie to Cloete 18 Aug 1927, A. Finger to TC, 26 August 1926, D. Smith to Cloete 29 Oct 1928, reply of TC 16 November 1928.

33 VAB MBE 1/4/4, MB1/4/4/4TC, Bethulie to Cloete 8 Feb 1929, I. Letali to TC, Cloete to TC 18 February 1929, TC to Cloete 16 January 1932, 'Public Meeting in Location 6 February 1929'; Wickins, 'The Industrial', 391.

34 Mancoe, *Directory*, 102; SANA GNLB 400 55/1, Bethulie. 'Absolom Gaduka [Goduka], Meeting held at Bethulie, 8–9 December 1928'; 'Meeting at Bethulie, 9 December 1928'.

35   SANA GNLB 400 55/1, Bethulie. 'Meeting at Bethulie 21 April 1929'.

36   SANA GNLB 399 55/1, Bethulie, 'Meeting at Bethulie 30 April 1930', 'Native Agitators: Meeting Bethulie, 7 May 1930'.

37   SANA GNLB 400 55/1, Philippolis, 17 April 1929, 'S. Elias Meeting held at Philippolis, 16 April 1929', CID Kroonstad, 27 May 1929, 'Native Unrest OFS'.

38   'Ezase Alvani', *Umteteli wa Bantu*, 11 August 1928; WITS Ballinger Papers A410 C2g, Leeuw to W. Ballinger, 10 March 1937; SANA NTS 7606 27/328 'Mote to SNA, 10 November 1927; SANA NTS 7606 31/328, Zastron meeting reports 13 February 1927 by Tshepe 22 February 1927, S. Kuolane 20 February 1927; Tshphe, 'Seka Senya', *Umteteli wa Bantu*, 26 February 1927.

39   Wells, *We Demand*, 60, Mancoe, *Directory* 102; 'ICU Notes', *Umteteli wa Bantu*, 28 January 1928.

40   UCT Forman Papers, BC 581 3.147, 'Mote to Champion, 3 November 1927,.

41   S. Mutla in Bloemfontein penned pro-ICU songs: D. Coplan, *In Township Tonight*, 2nd Ed. (Chicago: University of Chicago Press 2008), 161; SANA GNLB 400 55/1, Bultfontein. 'Native ICU Meeting', 27 January 1929; Bradford, *A Taste*, 305; ICU Minutes 1927 in Wickins, 'The Industrial', 599; SANA GNLB 400 55/1, Ladybrand, 'Meeting by Native ICU Agitator', 2 February 1929, 17 March 1929; Mancoe, *Directory*, 102–3.

42   'ICU', *Kroonstad Times*, 28 October 1927; WITS Ballinger Papers A 410, 'Statement of Income ICU, 21 June 1929'; 'Dream of the ICU', *Frankforter*, 3 February 1927; 'Naturelle hou vergadering: Mote Preek Sosialisme', *Frankforter*, 23 December 1926; Moloi, 'Black Politics', 76; *Friend*, 12 May 1927, cited in Neame, *Congress Movement*, Vol. 2, 501; Wits Ballinger Papers A 410 C2g, Mancoe, 'Withholding of Wages', March 1931, Letters to magistrates, Parys, 15 September 1930 and Heilbron 15 December 1930; Moroe, 'Resurrection of the ICU?' *Bantu World*, 9 July 1932; 'Moroe Wins Appeal', *Umsebenzi*, 31 March 1934.

43   SANA GNLB 400 55/1, Petrus Steyn. 'Independent ICU meeting 21 April 1929'; SANA GNLB 399 55/1, Villiers. 'Meeting of ICU', 21 July 1930; Mancoe, *Directory*, 101; SANA GNLB 400 55/1, Edenville, Reports on ICU meetings 17 February, 10 March, 24 March 1929; SANA CID GNLB 399 55/1, Kroonstad, 'Communism', 11 December 1929.

44   UCT Ballinger BC 347 A5.7.14/5, 'ICU Thema Report', 12 May, 6 June 1930; 'Bokhoba Free State', *Leselinyana*, 18 Phupu 1930.

45   'Unity Movement', *Umteteli wa Bantu*, 16 May 1931; 'Mote, 'The "Reds" and Natives', *Umteteli wa Bantu*, 3 October 1931; 'ICU Unity?', *Umteteli wa Bantu*, 1 July 1933; 'Bloemfontein Brevities', *Free State Advocate*, 6 November 1937; 'ICU and S.A.R. Workers Union, *Umteteli wa Bantu* 27 May 1939.

46   'Branch News', *Workers' Herald Weekly News Bulletin*, 21 November 1928.

47   Bonner, Chapter 9 of this volume; Bonner, 'The Rise and Fall of the ICU: A Case of Self-Destruction?' in E. Webster, ed., *Essays in Southern African Labour History* (Johannesburg: Ravan Press, 1978), 116.

Chapter 5

1   T.R.H. Davenport and C. Saunders, *South Africa: A Modern History,* 5th Ed. (Basingstoke: Macmillan, 2000), 315.

2   D. Serfontein, *Keurskrif vir Kroonstad: 'n Kroniek van die Onstaan, Groei en Vooruitsgte van 'n Vrystaatse Plattelandse Dorp* (Kroonstad: Stadsraad, 1990), 451.

3   T. Moloi, *Place of Thorns: Black Political Protest in Kroonstad Since 1976* (Johannesburg: Wits University Press, 2015), 20–23.

4   H. Bradford, *A Taste,* 69.

5   H. Dee, '"I am a Bad Native": Masculinity and Marriage in the Biographies of Clements Kadalie', *African Studies,* 78, 2, (2019), 183–204.

6   P.L. Wickins, 'The Industrial and Commercial Workers' Union of Africa' (PhD thesis, University of Cape Town, 1973).

7   S.W. Johns, 'Trade Union, Political Pressure Group, or Mass Movement?: The ICU of Africa', in I.R. Rotberg and A.A. Mazrui, eds, *Protest and Power in Black Africa* (New York: Oxford University Press, 1970), 746–7.

8   P. Ntantala, *A Life's Mosaic: The Autobiography of Phyllis Ntantala* (Berkeley: University of California Press, 1992), 83.

9   T. Keegan, *Facing the Storm: Portraits of Black Lives in Rural South Africa* (Cape Town and Johannesburg: David Philip, 1988).

10   P.N. de Kay, *Notre Dame under the Southern Cross* (Johannesburg: Ravan Press, 1984), 52–53.

11   H. Phillips, '"Black October": The Impact of the Spanish Influenza Epidemic of 1918 on South Africa' (Johannesburg: University of the Witwatersrand Government Publication, 1990), 166; also see Serfontein *Keurskrif,* 357.

12   T.R.H. Davenport, 'The Triumph of Colonel Stallard: The Transformation of the Natives (Urban Areas) Act between 1923 and 1937', *South African Historical Journal,* 2, 1, (2009), 78.

13   J.S.M. Setiloane, *The History of Black Education in Maokeng, Kroonstad* (Pretoria: HSRC, 1997), 3.

14   T. Moloi, Interview with Hilda 'Mantho' Motadinyane, Sunday Times Oral History Project (hereafter STHP), 7 December 2006.

15   Setiloane, *The History of Black Education,* 4.

16   Ibid., 3.

17   T. Moloi, 'The Emergence and Radicalisation of Black Political Formations in Kroonstad, 1915–1957', *New Contree,* 67 (2013), 174.

18   P. Wickins, 'One Big Union Movement among Black Workers in South Africa', *International Journal of African Historical Studies,* 7, 3 (1974), 403.

19   H. Bradford, 'Mass Movements and the Petty Bourgeoisie: The Social Origins of ICU Leadership, 1924–1929', *The Journal of African History,* 25, 3 (1984), 300.

20   M. Botha, 'Exploring Sense of Place as a Restorative Urban Planning Tool: Marabastad, Kroonstad as a Case Study' (MA thesis, North-West University, Potchefstroom, 2018), 124.

21 Setiloane, *The History of Black Education*, 3.

22 Ntantala, *A Life's Mosaic*, 83.

23 Ibid., 84.

24 Moloi, *Place of Thorns*, 14.

25 T. Moloi, Interview with John Setiloane, Maokeng, Kroonstad, 14 February 2014.

26 I. Schapera, ed., *Western Civilisation and the Natives of South Africa: Studies in Culture Contact* (London: Routledge, 1934), 176

27 T. Moloi, Interview with Parkies Seteloane, Maokeng, Kroonstad, 7 December 2006.

28 Ibid., 19.

29 Bradford, 'Mass Movements', 298–299.

30 Moloi, *Place of Thorns*, 16.

31 Ibid., 17.

32 Bradford, 'Mass Movements', 305.

33 F. Meli, *A History of the ANC: South Africa Belongs to Us* (Harare: Zimbabwe Publishing House, 1988), 53.

34 P. Limb, *The ANC's Early Years: Nation, Class, and Place in South Africa before 1940* (Pretoria: UNISA Press, 2010), 220.

35 Moloi, 'The Emergence and Radicalisation of Black Political Formations', 73.

36 N. Nieftagodien, 'The Implementation of Urban Apartheid on the East Rand, 1948–1973: The Role of Local Government and Local Resistance', (PhD thesis, University of the Witwatersrand, Johannesburg, 2001), 197.

37 Moloi, 'The Emergence', 179–180.

38 Johns, 'Trade Union', Political Pressure Group, or Mass Movement? 712.

39 P. Rich, 'Managing Black Leadership: The Joint Councils, Urban Trading and Political Conflict in the OFS, 1925-1942', in P. Bonner, I. Hofmeyr, D. James and T. Lodge, eds, *Holding Their Ground: Class, Locality and Culture in Nineteenth- and Twentieth-Century South Africa* (Johannesburg, Ravan Press, 1989), 184.

40 Wits Joint Council of Europeans and Africans Collection AD 1433 CK 5.3, Kroonstad Joint Council, 'Letter from Father Martin to Rheinallt-Jones'.

41 *The Road to Democracy: South Africans telling their stories, 1, 1950–1970, South African Democracy Education Trust* (Hollywood: Tsehai Publishers, 2008), 33.

42 Wickins, 'The Industrial and Commercial Workers' Union of Africa', 195.

43 Moloi, 'The Emergence and Radicalisation of Black Political Formations', 173.

44 Ibid., 175.

45 Ibid., 174.

46 Wickins, 'The Industrial and Commercial Workers' Union of Africa', 196–197.

47 Ibid., 197.

48 Moloi, 'The Emergence and Radicalisation of Black Political Formations', 173.

49 Ibid., 175.

50 Johns, 'Trade Union, Political Pressure Group, or Mass Movement?' 716.

51 Wickins, 'The Industrial and Commercial Workers' Union of Africa', 342–386.

52 See H. Dee, 'J. C. Scott, Black Artists and the Cultural Politics of 1920s Johannesburg', SAhistory.org.za, accessed, 8 October 2021, 9.

53 Wits T. D. M. Skota Papers A 1618 C4-2-008, 'Who's Who: Yearly Register'; and Setiloane *Black Education*.

54 Bradford, *A Taste*, 9.

55 Johns, 'The Trade Union, Political Pressure Group, or Mass Movement?', 729.

56 South African National Archives, Bloemfontein (hereafter VAB), SOO 1/1/47, No. 8/10 1946; also see 'Native organisation: another meeting of the ICU at the Location', *The Parys Post*, 10 May 1927.

57 Keegan, *Facing the Storm*, 54.

58 On the attacks and killings of black people on the farms in the Free State, see M. J. Murray, 'The natives are always stealing: White vigilantes and the 'Reign of Terror' in the Orange Free State, 1918-1924', *The Journal of African History*, 30, 1 (1989), 107–123.

59 Keegan, *Facing the Storm*, 54.

60 Wickins, 'The Industrial and Commercial Workers' Union of Africa', note 560.

61 T. Moloi, Interview with John Setiloane.

62 Dee, 'I am a Bad Native', 189.

63 Ibid., 189–90.

64 Ibid., 189.

65 Bradford, 'Mass Movements', 301.

66 Ibid., 300–301.

67 Ibid. Italics mine.

68 Dee, 'I am Bad Native', 191.

69 Wickins, 'The Industrial and Commercial Workers' Union of Africa', 443; In 1927, the ICU utilised Cowley's law firm to challenge the evictions of the Union members in Durban and other areas.

70 Johns 'The Trade Union, Political Pressure Group, or Mass Movement?', 732–733.

71 Wickins, 'The Industrial and Commercial Workers' Union of Africa', 468.

72 Ibid.

73 J. and R. Simons, *Class and Colour in South Africa, 1850-1950* (International Defence and Aid Fund for Southern Africa, 1983), 363.

74 Ibid.

75 Wickins, 'The Industrial and Commercial Workers' Union of Africa', 494.

76 Simons, *Class and Colour*, 373; and Wickins, 'The Industrial and Commercial Workers' Union of Africa', 496.

77 Simons, *Class and Colour*, 373.

78 Dee, '"I am Bad Native"', 189.

79 Simons, *Class and Colour,* 365.

80 Johns, 'The Trade Union, Political Pressure Group, or Mass Movement?', 732.

81 Wickins, 'The Industrial and Commercial Workers' Union of Africa', 542.

82 Dee, '"I am a Bad Native"', 192.

83 Davenport and Saunders, *A Modern History,* 315.

84 Wickins, 'The Industrial and Commercial Workers' Union of Africa', Note 560.

85 Keegan, *Facing the Storm,* 54.

86 Simons, *Class and Colour,* 367.

87 'Kroonstad's News', *Umeteli wa Bantu,* 14 September 1929.

88 Johns, 'The Trade Union, Political Pressure Group, or Mass Movement?', 746.

89 'Kroonstad's News', *Umteteli wa Bantu,*14 December 1929.

90 Moloi, 'The Emergence and Radicalisation of Black Political Formations', 176.

91 R. Edgar, *The Making of an Africanist Communist: Edwin Thabo Mofutsanyane and the Communist Party of South Africa, 1927-1929* (Pretoria: UNISA Press, 2005).

92 Moloi, 'The Emergence and Radicalisation of Black Political Formations', 181.

93 Wits Joint Council of Europeans and Africans Collection AD 1433 CK5.3, Kroonstad Joint Council: 'Letter from Father Martin to Rheinallt-Jones', 27 October 1931.

94 Johns, 'The Trade Union', 747.

Chapter 6

1 'Non-European Workers Conference: Formation of the One Big Union', *Friend,* 14 July 1920.

2 South African National Archives (hereafter SANA) Ministry of Justice (hereafter JUS) 412 5/86/35, Inquest Proceedings, Mr Streak: Testimony of Juliet Litholo, 6 May 1925, 10.

3 N. Gasa, 'Let Them Build More Gaols' in N. Gasa, ed. *Women in South African History: Basus'iimbokodo, Bawel'imilambo/They Remove Boulders and Cross Rivers* (Cape Town: HSRC Press, 2007), 132.

4 D. Johnson and H. Dee, *'I See You': The Industrial and Commercial Workers' Union of Africa, 1919–1930* (Cape Town: Historical Publications Southern Africa, 2022), xxvii, 13–16 and 21–27; see also H. Dee, '"I am a Bad Native": Masculinity and Marriage in the Biographies of Clements Kadalie', *African Studies,* 78, 2, (2019), 185, 189.

5 H. Bradford, *A Taste,* 274. See also P. la Hause, 'Drinking in a Cage: The Durban System and the 1929 Beer Hall Riots', *Africa Perspective,* 20 (1982), 63–75.

6 Ibid.

7 J. Wells, *We Now Demand! The History of Women's Resistance to Pass Laws in South Africa* (Johannesburg: Wits University Press, 1993), 23.

8 Self-employed who do not hire others on a consistent basis.

9 J. Hyslop, 'E.P. Thompson in South Africa: The Practice and Politics of Social History in an Era of Revolt and Transition, 1976–2012', *International Review of Social History,* 61 (2016), 95–116; M. van der Linden, *Workers of the World: Essays Towards a Global Labour History*

(Leiden: Brill, 2008).

10   There is research underway dealing with coercion under the research network 'Worlds of Coercion in Work' led by Juliane Schiel and Johan Heinsen.

11   S. Federici, unpublished excerpt from 'Precarious labor: A feminist viewpoint' [2006] https://caringlabor.wordpress.com/2010/07/29/silvia-federici-precarious-labor-and-reproductive-work/ (accessed 1 November 2021).

12   K. Schoeman, *Bloemfontein: Die Onstand van n Stad, 1846–1946* (Pretoria: Human and Rousseau, 1980), 184.

13   Schoeman, *Bloemfontein,* 184; D. Krige, 'Bloemfontein' in A. Lemon, ed., *Homes Apart: South Africa's Segregated Cities* (London: Paul Chapman Publishing/Bloomington: Indiana University Press/Cape Town: David Philip: 1991), 105.

14   P. Bonner, "'Desirable and Undesirable Basotho Women". Liquor, Prostitution and the Migration of Basotho Women to the Rand, 1920–1945', in C. Walker, ed. *Women and Gender in Southern Africa to 1945* (Claremont: David Philip, 1990), 228–229.

15   South African National Archives, Bloemfontein (hereafter VAB) Minutes of Town Council, Bloemfontein (hereafter MBL), 1/2/4/1/4, Superintendent, 20 October 1922.

16   Wells, *We Now Demand,* 25; Schoeman, *Bloemfontein,* 130.

17   Wells, *We Now Demand,* 25–26.

18   VAB MBL 1/2/1/1/4, Superintendent, 3 August 1920.

19   Schoeman, *Bloemfontein,* 35.

20   Ibid., 218–219, 224.

21   Schoeman, *Bloemfontein,* 285.

22   VAB MBL 1/2/4/1/4, Minutes of the Native Affairs Committee (hereafter NAC), 3 May 1920.

23   Ibid., 223.

24   Ibid.

25   Wells, *We Now Demand,* 35.

26   Schoeman, *Bloemfontein,* 85.

27   Wells, *We Now Demand,* 22.

28   Ibid., 36.

29   Ibid.

30   VAB MBL NAC 1/2/4/1/4, 3 May 1920 and Schoeman, *Bloemfontein,* 280 and VAB MBL 1/2/4/1/3, Minutes of a Meeting by Employers of Labour, 5 December 1919.

31   'A Woman's View', *The Friend,* 8 July 1919.

32   VAB MBL NAC 1/2/1/1/4, Letters from Town Clerk and Treasurer to The Secretary for Native Affairs, 25 February 1919 and 1 November 1920.

33   P. L. Wickins, 'The Industrial and Commercial Workers Union of Africa', (PhD Thesis, University of Cape Town, 1973), 150.

34   'Commission of Inquiry: Native Riots in Bloemfontein.' *Government Gazette,* 11 September 1925, 479.

35   VAB MBL 1/2/1/1/4, Advisory Board Constitution (n.d.).

36   VAB MBL 1/2/1/14, Superintendent, 19 April 1920 and 1 September 1920.

37   'Native Trouble: Bloemfontein Case', *The Star*, 3 March 1919.

38   Schoeman, *Bloemfontein,* 280.

39   'Native Labour: Local Demand for Minimum of Four and Sixpence', *The Friend*, 17 February
      1919; and 'Bloemfontein Natives: Action delayed to meet employers, *The Friend*,
      24 February 1919.

40   Schoeman, *Bloemfontein*, 281

41   'Native Labour: Local Demand for Minimum of Four and Sixpence', *The Friend*, 17 February
      1919.

42   Wickins, 'The Industrial and Commercial Workers Union of Africa', 135

43   'Bloemfontein Natives', *The Friend*, 24 February 1919.

44   SANA Native Affairs (hereafter NTS) 215 768/18/173, Letter to the Secretary for Native
      Affairs from the Magistrate, 26 February 1919.

45   'Trouble among Natives: Serious Disturbance at Bloemfontein', *Cape Times*, 3 March 1919.

46   Ibid.

47   Ibid.

48   Ibid.

49   'Native Lawlessness in Bloemfontein', *The Friend*, 3 March 1919.

50   'Bloemfontein Natives', *The Friend*, 7 March 1919.

51   Ibid.

52   'Msimang's Arrest', *The Friend*, 12 March 1919.

53   'The Ice Broken', *The International*, 7 March 1919.

54   P. Wickins, 'The One Big Union Movement among Black Workers in South Africa', *The
      International Journal of African Historical Studies*, 7, 3, (1974), 393.

55   Ibid.

56   Ibid.

57   Wickins, 'The One Big Union', 394.

58   SANA JUS 248/5/242/16, Native Unrest in the Orange Free State, Report, District
      Commandant, Criminal Investigation Department, OFS, 'Native National Congress,
      Bloemfontein, 12, 13, 21 July 1929: Native Unrest in the OFS' 'Non-European Workers
      Conference: Formation of the One Big Union', *The Friend*, 14 July 1920.

59   Bradford, *A Taste*, 4. See also T. April, 'Theorising Women: The Intellectual Contribution of
      Charlotte Maxeke to the Struggles for Liberation in South Africa (PhD thesis, University of
      Cape Town, 2012)

60   Ibid.

61   'The ICU Female Branch', *The Black Man*, September 1920.

62   'Bloemfontein Branch', *Workers' Herald*, 25 September 1923.

63   'Workers of Africa', *Workers' Herald*, 25 September 1923.

64 'Bloemfontein Branch', *Workers' Herald*, 25 September 1923.

65 Wickins, 'The One Big Union', 409.

66 Ibid.

67 Schoeman, *Bloemfontein*, 280.

68 'My Impression of the Free State Capital', *Workers' Herald*, 22 October 1923.

69 'Bloemfontein Workers Make a Move', *Workers' Herald*, 9 January 1925.

70 'Bloemfontein Workers Demand Increased Wages', *Workers' Herald*, 2 April 1925.

71 'Native Demands: Minimum Wages Bill Asked For: Message for 1925: "Be Free Men and Women in South Africa"', *Workers' Herald*, 20 February 1925.

72 'The Bloemfontein Disturbance and the ICU', *Workers' Herald*, 15 May 1925.

73 SANA JUS 412 5/86/25, Riots in Bloemfontein Location (Inquest) Magistrate Mr Streak, 6 May 1925 (witness testimony). (Hereafter Inquest, 6 May 1925), 13.

74 Ibid.

75 Inquest, 6 May 1925, 7.

76 Inquest, 6 May 1925, 4 and 8.

77 Ibid.

78 Inquest, 6 May 1925, 10.

79 Inquest, 6 May 1925, 13.

80 'Commission of Inquiry: Native Riots in Bloemfontein', *Government Gazette*, 11 September 1925, 473.

81 VAB MBL 1/2/4/2/4, Letter from the 'Native Women of Waaihoek' to the Native Affairs Committee, 8 December 1920.

82 VAB MBL 1/2/4/1/4, Superintendent, 1 December 1920.

83 Inquest, 6 May 1925, 9.

84 VAB MBL 1/2/4/1/4, Superintendent Report, 20 September 1921.

85 Inquest, 6 May 1925, 4 and 8.

86 Ibid., 4, 13.

87 Ibid., 19-21.

88 Ibid., 9.

89 B. Hirson, 'The Bloemfontein Riots, 1925: A Study in Community Culture and Class Consciousness', The Societies of Southern Africa in the Nineteenth and Twentieth Centuries, 13 (London: University of London, Institute of Commonwealth Studies, 1982–1983), 83.

90 Ibid.

91 Inquest, 6 May 1925, 22.

92 Ibid., 15.

93 Ibid., 23, 220.

94 Ibid., 33.

95   Ibid.

96   Ibid., 34

97   Ibid.

98   Ibid.

99   Hirson, 'The Bloemfontein Riots, 1925', 84.

100 Ibid.

101 Hirson, 'The Bloemfontein Riots, 1925', 84; 'Commission of Inquiry', 475.

102 Hirson, 'The Bloemfontein Riots, 1925', 85.

103 SANA JUS 412 5/86/25, Report from the Deputy Commissioner, South African Police, OFS Division, 21 April 1925. 4.

104 Inquest, 6 May 1925, 34

105 Ibid.

106 SANA US 412 5/86/35, Finding of the Court, Magistrate Streak, 30 April 1925, 3.

107 SANA JUS 412, 5/86/25, Report from the Deputy Commissioner, South African Police, OFS Division, 21 April 1925. 3.

108 Ibid.

109 SANA JUS 412, 5/86/25, Letter to the Secretary for Justice, 21 April 1925.

110 Hirson, 'The Bloemfontein Riots, 1925', 91–94.

111 Hirson uses this term, which he derives directly from the archival sources and as such reflects that understanding of those who witnessed events.

112 Hirson, 'The Bloemfontein Riots, 1925', 93.

113 Wickins, 'The Industrial and Commercial Workers' Union of Africa', 384, 388

114 'Bloemfontein Branch' and 'Workers of Africa', *Workers' Herald*, 25 September 1923.

115 Bradford, *A Taste*, 261.

Chapter 7

1   The region encompassing parts of the former Western Transvaal and Cape Province will be termed 'Western Transvaal' for brevity.

2   See Chapter 9 by Phil Bonner in this volume.

3   H. Bradford, 'A Taste of Freedom: Capitalist Development and Response to the ICU in the Transvaal Countryside' in B. Bozzoli, ed., *Town and Countryside in the Transvaal: Capitalist Penetration and Popular Response* (Johannesburg: Ravan Press, 1983), 131–36.

4   For reference to the rural revolt, see: S. Neame, *The Congress Movement*, Vol. 2 (Cape Town: HSRC Press, 2015), 275–391; H. Bradford, *A Taste*, 6–9, 33.

5   C. van Onselen, *The Seed is Mine: The Life of Kas Maine, a South African Sharecropper, 1894–1985* (New York: Hill and Wang, 1996), 146.

6   Ibid.

7   Wits Institute of Advance Social Research (hereafter IASR) Share Cropping and Labour Tenancy Oral History Project 19791987 (hereafter SLTP) AG 2738, Interview No. 52, Kas Maine, 2 November 1982; T. Karis, A. Bugg-Levine, M. Benson, G. Gerhart and T. Barnes, eds, *From Protest to Challenge: A Documentary History of African Politics in South Africa, 1882–1990,* Vol. 4 (Johannesburg: Jacana Media, 2017), 344; S.J. Jingoes, *A Chief is a Chief by the People: The Autobiography of Stimela Jason Jingoes* (London: Oxford University Press, 1975).

8   L.F.R. Stewart, '"I See you in the Soil": The ICU in the Western Transvaal, 1926–1938' (MA thesis, University of the Witwatersrand, 2021).

9   M. Neocosmos, *Thinking Freedom in Africa: Toward a Theory of Emancipatory Politics* (Johannesburg, Wits University Press, 2017), 27. Neocosmos argues that 'thinking freedom' is an act where the 'expression of the objective is transcended or punctured'.

10 D. Johnson, 'Clements Kadalie, the ICU, and the Language of Freedom', *English in Africa* 42, 3 (2015): 43–69; D. Johnson, *Dreaming of Freedom in South Africa: Literature Between Critique and Utopia* (Cape Town: UCT Press, 2020), 56–62.

11 Wits IASR SLTP AG 2738, Interview No. 100, Mmereki Molohlanyi, 19 April 1984.

12 'Tsa Rustenburg [In Rustenburg]', *Workers' Herald*, 15 October 1927.

13 Wits IASR SLTP AG 2738, Interview No. 166, A. Seiphetlo, 9 September 1987.

14 Wits IASR SLTP AG 2738, Interview No. 146, B. Maine, 22 April 1986.

15 Wits IASR SLTP AG 2738, Interview No. 152, Selwane Legobathe, 9 July 1986.

16 F. Morton, 'Slave-raiding and Slavery in the Western Transvaal after the Sand River Convention' *African Economic History* 20 (1992), 99–118; C. van Onselen, 'The Social and Economic Underpinning of Paternalism and Violence on the Maize Farms of the South-Western Transvaal, 1900–1950', *Journal of Historical Sociology* 5, 2 (1992), 127–60.

17 Bradford, *A Taste*, 40, 43.

18 Wits IASR SLTP AG 2738, Interview No. 239, G. Lephadi, 27 May 1987.

19 SANA JUS 922 1/18/26 Vols 22–24, Report compiled by SAP Constable Brewis at Bloemhof sent to the District Commandant of the SAP at Potchefstroom, 28 November 1928.

20 Johnson, 'Clements Kadalie', 56.

21 SANA JUS 920 1/18/26 Vols 16–18, Report of the SAP at Potchefstroom to the District Commandant at Potchefstroom, 9 May 1928.

22 Wits IASR SLTP AG 2738, Interview No. 165, Thys Theteletsa, 9 September 1987.

23 Wits IASR SLTP AG 2738, Interview No. 239, G. Lephadi.

24 Wits IASR SLTP AG 2738, Interview No. 30, Kas Maine, 2 July 1980.

25 SANA JUS 920 1/18/26 Vols 16-18, Report from the SAP at Klerksdorp in Charge to the District Commandant of the SAP at Potchefstroom, 3 July 1928.

26 Wits IASR SLTP AG 2738, Interview No. 154, Motlamogang Maine, 23 October 1986.

27 Wits IASR SLTP AG 2738, Interview No. 146, B. Maine.

28 Johnson, *Dreaming of Freedom*, 66; WITS IASR SLTP AG 2738, Interview No. 55, T. Bogopane, 11 September 1981.

29 S. Neame, *The Congress Movement*, Vol. 1, (Cape Town: HSRC Press, 2015), 1–11.

30 SANA JUS 921 1/18/26 Vols 19–21, Report compiled by the Maquassi police Sergeant, 29 July 1928.

31 Neocosmos, *Thinking Freedom*, 27.

32 R. Vinson, *The Americans are Coming!: Dreams of African American Liberation in Segregationist South Africa* (Ohio: Ohio University Press, 2012), 2, 6.

33 Wits IASR SLTP AG 2738, Interview No. 152, Selwane Legobathe.

34 Ibid.

35 D. Coplan and B. Jules-Rosette, 'Nkosi Sikelel' iAfrika and the Liberation of the Spirit of South Africa', *African Studies* 64, 2 (2005), 285.

36 D. Coplan, *In Township Tonight!: South Africa's Black City Music and Theatre* (Chicago: Chicago Press, 2008), 46.

37 Wits IASR SLTP AG 2738, Interview No. 166, A. Seiphetlo.

38 Wits IASR SLTP AG 2738, Interview No. 318, Mathabeng Mathuloe, 29 July 1981.

39 Neame, *The Congress Movement*, Vol. 1, 36, 400–401.

40 A. Gramsci, *Selections from the Prison Notebooks of Antonio Gramsci*, trans. Q. Hoare and G. Nowell Smith (London: Lawrence and Wishart, 1971), 182.

41 Neocosmos. *Thinking Freedom in Africa*, ix, xi, xxii.

42 Motlagomang suggested in a later interview that it was actually 'Mote who gave this speech, but there is no other evidence to decisively say it was one or the other (Wits IASR SLTP AG 2738, Interview No. 154, Motlagomang Maine).

43 Wits IASR SLTP AG 2738, Interview No. 155, Motlagomang Maine, 25 November 1986.

44 Ibid.

45 Ibid.

46 Wits IASR SLTP AG 2738, Interview No. 30, Kas Maine.

47 Wits IASR SLTP AG 2738, Interview No. 100, Mmereki Molohlanyi.

48 Wits IASR SLTP AG 2738, Interview No. 152, Selwane Legobathe.

49 Ibid.

50 T. Keegan, *Facing the Storm: Portraits of Black Lives in Rural South Africa* (Cape Town: David Phillip, 1988), 29–31.

51 Wits IASR SLTP AG 2738, Interview No. 149, Petrus Tsubane, 1 June 1986. Petrus' use of the word 'apartheid' related to the context of the interview – South Africa in 1986.

52 Wits IASR SLTP AG 2738, Interview No. 136, Mmereki Molohlanyi, 28 June 1985.

53 Ibid.

54 Van Onselen, *The Seed is Mine*, 150.

55 SANA JUS 920 1/18/26 Vols 16–18, Report received by the Divisional Officer at Kimberly from the SAP at Mafeking, 21 June 1928.

56 Wits IASR SLTP AG 2738, Interview No. 48, R. Dinkebogile, 28 July 1981.

57 Wits IASR SLTP AG 2738, Interview No. 258, I. Moeng, 31 March 1987.

58 Wits IASR SLTP AG 2738, Interview No. 239, G. Lephadi

59 SANA JUS 517 6044/29 - 6180/29 - 6175/29, Notes taken of Makhatini addressing a meeting at Bloemhof, providing a speech (Notes taken by Brewis, 2 June 1929).

60 Bonner, chapter 9 in this volume.

61 Ibid., 17.

62 SANA JUS 920 1/18/26 Vols 16–18, Report from the Criminal Investigation Department in Potchefstroom to the District Commandant of the South African Police at Potchefstroom, 25 June 1928.

63 SANA JUS 921 1/18/26 Vols 19–21, Report compiled by the SAP at Maquassi to the District Commandant of the SAP at Potchefstroom, 10 September 1928.

64 Ibid.

65 'The Lichtenburg Outburst', *Umteteli wa Bantu*, 3 November 1928, 3.

66 J. Ranciére, *The Politics of Aesthetics* (London: Bloomsbury, 2004), 8.

67 J. Habermas, 'The Public Sphere: An Encyclopedia Article' in M. Durham and D. Kellner, eds., *Media and Cultural Studies: Key Works* (Oxford: Blackwell Publishing, 2006), 73–74.

68 N. Fraser, 'Rethinking the Public Sphere: A Contribution to the Critique of Actually Existing Democracy', *Social Text*, 25/26 (1990), 67.

69 G. Charles and L. Fuentes-Rohwer, 'Habermas, the Public Sphere, and the Creation of a Racial Counterpublic', *Michigan Journal of Race and Law*, 21 (2015), 1–21.

70 Wits IASR SLTP AG 2738, Interview No. 146, B. Maine.

71 Ibid.

72 Ibid.

73 SANA JUS 921, 1/18/26 Vols 19–21, Report compiled by the Maquassi police sergeant, 29 July 1928.

74 Ibid.

75 P. Maylam, 'Explaining the Apartheid City: Twenty Years of South African Urban Historiography', *Journal of Southern African Studies* 21, 1 (1995): 19–38; and N. Nieftagodien, 'The Place of "The Local" in History Workshop's Local History', *African Studies* 69, 1 (2010), 45, 57–58.

76 Lefebvre argues that spaces are a product of the interaction between space, on the one hand, and nature, people, events, social and productive relationships, on the other. He terms it 'interpenetration'; this chapter labels it as interconnectedness. H. Lefebvre and D. Nicholson-Smith, *The Production of Space* (Oxford: Blackwell, 1991), 11–12, 77, 88, 403.

77 Bradford, *A Taste*, 43.

78 Van Onselen, 'The Social and Economic Underpinning', 38.

79   Bradford, *A Taste*, 55.

80   J. Higginson, *Collective Violence and the Agrarian Origins of South African Apartheid, 1900–1948* (Cambridge: Cambridge University Press, 2014), 6.

81   Wits IASR SLTP AG 2738, Interview No. 21, Andries and Lydia Leeu, 24 February 1980.

82   Wits IASR SLTP AG 2738, Interview No. 168, M. Motete, 10 September 1987.

83   Wits IASR SLTP AG 2738, Interview No. 145, Selwane Legobathe, 27 March 1986.

84   Wits IASR SLTP AG 2738, Interview No. 30, Kas Maine.

85   Ibid.

86   Bradford, *A Taste*, 49.

87   Wits IASR SLTP AG 2738, Interview No. 45, 24 February 1982.

88   Van Onselen, 'The Social and Economic Underpinning', 147.

89   P. Bonner, 'The Decline and Fall of the ICU: A Case of Self-Destruction?' in E. Webster, ed., *Essays in Southern African Labour History*, Vol. 1 (Johannesburg: Ravan Press, 1978), 116.

90   WITS IASR SLTP AG 2738, Interview No. 136, Mmereki Molohlanyi.

91   WITS IASR SLTP AG 2738, Interview No. 166, A. Seiphetlo.

92   WITS IASR SLTP AG 2738, Interview No. 155, Motlagomang Maine, 25 November 1986.

93   WITS IASR SLTP AG 2738, Interview No. 152, Selwane Legobathe.

94   WITS IASR SLTP AG 2738, Interview No. 149, Petrus Tsubane

95   Wits IASR SLTP AG 2738, Interview No. 152, Selwane Legobathe.

96   SANA JUS 517 6044/29 - 6180/29 - 6175/29, Letter from the Sergeant of the SAP at Schweizer-Reneke to the District Commander of the SAP at Potchefstroom, 6 May 1929.

97   Ibid.

98   Lefebvre, *The Production of Space*, 386.

99   Ibid., 387.

100 A *Workers' Herald* article in June 1927, noted that branch secretaries and ICU organisers were increasingly being apprehended for contravening pass laws. 'Annual Review of Work', *Workers' Herald*, 17 June 1927, 3.

Chapter 8

1   Similar arguments have been posited by W. Beinart and C. Bundy, 'The Union, the Nation, and the Talking Crow: The Ideology and Tactics of the Independent ICU in East London', University of the Witwatersrand, African Studies Seminar Paper, 1985: and L. Stewart, '"I See You" in the Soil: The Industrial and Commercial Workers' Union (ICU) in the Western Transvaal, 1926–1934'. (MA thesis, University of the Witwatersrand, 2021).

2   For example, P. Bonner, 'The Decline and Fall of the ICU – A Case of Self-destruction?', in E. Webster, ed., *Essays in Southern African Labour History*, (Johannesburg: Ravan Press, 1978), 114–20; E. Roux, *Time Longer than Rope: A History of the Black Man's Struggle For*

Freedom in South Africa (Madison: The University of Wisconsin Press, 1964), 161–167, 197; P. L. Wickins, 'The Industrial and Commercial Workers' Union of Africa' (PhD thesis, University of Cape Town, 1973); J. and R. Simons, *Class and Colour in South Africa, 1859–1950* (International Defence and Aid Fund for Southern Africa, 1983), 353–386.

3   Roux, *Time Longer than Rope,* 160.

4   Bonner, 'The Decline and Fall of the ICU', 115–117. Chapter 9 in this volume by Bonner offers a re-assessment.

5   G. Baines, 'The Port Elizabeth Disturbances of October 1920' (MA thesis, Rhodes University, 1988), and J. Cherry, 'The Making of an African Working Class, Port Elizabeth, 1925–1963' (MA thesis, University of Cape Town, 1993).

6   H. Bradford, *A Taste,* 3.

7   Ibid, 94.

8   See G. Adler, 'From the "Liverpool of the Cape" to "The Detroit of South Africa": The Automobile Industry and Industrial Development in the Port-Elizabeth-Uitenhage Region', *Kronos* (November 1993), 17–43.

9   Baines, 'The Port Elizabeth Disturbances', 12–13; A. Mabin, 'The Rise and Decline of Port Elizabeth, 1850–1900', *The International Journal of African Historical Studies,* 19, 2 (1986), 298.

10   Baines, 'Port Elizabeth Disturbances', 12–13.

11   Baines, 'New Brighton, Port Elizabeth', c.1903-1953: The History of an Urban African Community' (PhD thesis, University of Cape Town, 1994), 16.

12   Baines, 'Port Elizabeth Disturbances', 15.

13   Baines, 'New Brighton, Port Elizabeth', 16.

14   Cherry, 'Making of an African Working Class', 21.

15   Adler, 'From the "Liverpool of the Cape"', 20.

16   Cherry, 'Making of an African Working Class, 23–26.

17   Y. Agherdien, A.C. George and S. Hendricks, *South End As We Knew* It (Port Elizabeth: Western Research Group, 1997), 4.

18   Mabin, 'The Rise and Decline of Port Elizabeth', 281.

19   Cherry, 'Making of an African Working Class', 8.

20   Baines, 'New Brighton, Port Elizabeth', 19.

21   Cherry, 'Making of an African Working Class', 48–49.

22   Baines, 'Port Elizabeth Disturbances', 57.

23   A. Mabin, 'Strikes in the Cape Colony, 1854–1899' University of the Witwatersrand, African Studies Seminar Paper, 1983, 15.

24   J. Kirk, 'A "Native" Free State at Korsten: Challenge to Segregation in Port Elizabeth South Africa 1901–1905', *Journal of Southern African Studies,* 17, 2 (1991), 316–319.

25   A. Odendaal, 'Even White Boys Call Us "Boy"! Early Black Organisational Politics in Port Elizabeth', *Kronos,* 20, (1993), 5–6.

26   P. Bonner, 'The Transvaal Native Congress 1917–1920: The Radicalisation of the Black Petty Bourgeoisie on the Rand', in S. Marks and R. Rathbone, eds, *Industrialisation and Social Change in South Africa* (London: Longman, 1982), 270–313.

27   Baines, 'Port Elizabeth Disturbances', 63–64.

28   Ibid., 70–71.

29   Ibid., 72–84.

30   Wickins, 'The Industrial and Commercial Workers' Union of Africa', 142.

31   Bradford, *A Taste*, 3, 84.

32   Baines, 'Port Elizabeth Disturbances', 101–133.

33   Ibid., 169–172.

34   Ibid., 178–181.

35   ICU, Third Annual Conference, 'Official Report of Proceedings', 17–25 January 1923, 25.

36   'Port Elizabeth Branch: Lest We Forget', *Workers' Herald*, 22 October 1923.

37   Baines, 'New Brighton, Port Elizabeth', 14–15.

38   Ibid., 18–19.

39   Ibid., 21–39.

40   Ibid., 21.

41   J. D. Robinson, 'The Power of Apartheid. State Power and Territoriality in South African Cities. Port Elizabeth. 1923–1971' (PhD thesis, University of Cambridge, 1990).

42   Baines, 'New Brighton, Port Elizabeth', 74–75.

43   Ibid., 33.

44   SANA JUS 1/18/26 Vol. 16, Police report of ICU meeting on 18 March 1928.

45   SANA JUS 1/18/26, Police report of ICU meeting on 5 June 1927.

46   SANA JUS 1/18/26 Vol. 18, Police report of ICU meeting on 1 July 1928.

47   SANA JUS 1/18/26 Vol. 4, Police report of ICU meeting on 5 September 1926.

48   Cherry, 'Making of an African Working Class', 53; and Baines, 'Port Elizabeth Disturbances', 182.

49   D. Porta and M. Dani, *Social Movements: An Introduction*, 2nd Ed. (Malden: Blackwell Publishing, 2006), 168

50   Ibid., 167

51   Sarah Bruchhausen, 'Emancipatory Politics and the Mpondo Revolts' (MA thesis, Rhodes University, 2016), 77–88, drawing on R. Guha, *Elementary Aspects of Peasant Insurgency in Colonial India* (Delhi: Oxford University Press, 1983), 2.

52   Bradford, *A Taste*; P. Bonner, '"Home Truths" and the Political Discourse of the ICU', Chapter 9 in this volume; P. La Hausse, 'The Message of the Warriors. The ICU, the Labouring Poor and the Making of a Popular Political Culture in Durban, 1925–50', in P. Bonner, I. Hofmeyr, D. James and T. Lodge, eds, *Holding Their Ground* (Johannesburg: Witwatersrand University Press, 1989), 19–57.

53   SANA JUS 1/18/26 Vol. 5, police report of ICU meeting on 16 February 1927.

54   SANA JUS 1/18/26 Vol. 18, police report of ICU on 8 August 1928.

55   Bonner, "'Home Truths'".

56   Bradford, *A Taste*; D. Johnson, *Dreaming of Freedom*.

57   Bradford, *A Taste of Freedom*, 93.

58   SANA JUS 1/18/26 Vol. 5, Police report of ICU meeting on 16 February 1927.

59   SANA JUS 1/18/26 Vol. 5, Police report of ICU meeting on 28 April 1927.

60   SANA JUS 1/18/26 Vol. 20, Police report of ICU meeting of 2 December 1928.

61   SANA JUS 1/18/26 Vol. 19, Police report of ICU meeting of 25 November 1928.

62   SANA JUS 1/18/26 Vol. 28, Police report of ICU meeting of 10 January 1929.

63   SANA JUS 1/18/26 Vol. 19, Police report of ICU meeting of 29 November 1928.

64   Porta and Dani, *Social Movements*, 168.

65   Bradford, *A Taste*, 64.

66   SANA JUS 1/18/26 Vol. 17, police report of ICU meeting on 27 May 1928.

67   Bradford, *A Taste*, 85–87.

68   Ibid., 88.

69   SANA JUS 1/18/26 Vol. 17, Police report of meeting held in the City Hall by Coloured community on 18 January 1927.

70   SANA JUS 1/18/26 Vol.17, Police report of ICU meeting on 25 May 1928.

71   South African National Archives, Cape Town (hereafter WCA), 3/PEZ, Minutes of meeting of representatives of organised bodies employing native labour, held on 14 November 1929.

72   SANA JUS 1/18/26 Vol.16, Police report of ICU meeting on 24 April 1928.

73   SANA JUS 1/18/26 Vol. 16, Police report of ICU meeting on 4 March 1927.

74   Beinart and Bundy, 'The Talking Crow', 13; and Bonner, Chapter 9.

75   SANA JUS 1/18/26 Vol. 21, Police report of ICU meeting on 18 November 1928.

76   SANA JUS 1/18/26, Vol. 21, Police report of ICU meeting on 15 February 1927.

77   SANA JUS 1/18/26 Vol. 9, Police report of ICU meeting on 29 May 1927.

78   SANA JUS 1/18/26 Vol. 9, Police report of ICU meeting on 6 November 1927.

79   SANA JUS 1/18/26, Vol. 9, Police report of ICU meeting on 14 November 1927.

80   Clements Kadalie, 'What of the future?', *Workers' Herald*, 21 July 1923.

81   'Communists' futile attempt to capture the ICU', *Workers' Herald*, 30 November 1928.

82   The government imposed a poll tax on African men to generate income and to force them into wage labour.

83   SANA JUS 1/18/26 Vol. 4, Police report of ICU meeting on 2 November 1926.

84   SANA JUS 1/18/26 Vol. 16, Police report of ICU meeting on 7 May 1928.

85   SANA JUS 1/18/26 Vol. 17, Police report of ICU on 15 May 1928

86   Cherry, 'Making of an African Working Class', 54–56

87   Ibid., 57.

88   SANA JUS 1/18/26, Vol. 28, Police report of ICU meeting on 10 February 1929.

89   SANA JUS 1/18/26 Vol. 28, Police report of ICU meeting on 18 March 1929.

90   Ibid.

91   J. Robinson, 'The Politics of Urban Form: Differential Citizenship and Township Formation in Port Elizabeth, 1925–1945', *Kronos* 20 (1993), 46–48.

92   WCA 3/PEZ 1/3/2/15/5, Minutes of NAC meeting of 16 April 1931.

93   SANA CAD, Union of South Africa, Report of the Native Economic Commission, 1930–1932, 83–484.

94   SANA JUS 1/18/26 Vol. 31, Police report of raid in Korsten on 7 February 1931.

95   SANA JUS 1/18/26 Vol. 31, Police report of IICU meeting of 20 February 1931.

96   SANA JUS 1/18/26 Vol. 31, Police reports of IICU and IICU meetings held on 22 February 1931.

97   WCA GNLB 401, Police report of IICU meetings of 26 November and 29 November 1934.

Chapter 9

1   For major recent works on the ICU see: H. Bradford, *A Taste of Freedom: The ICU in Rural South Africa, 1924–1930* (London: Yale University Press, 1987); P.L. Wickins, *The Industrial and Commercial Workers' Union of Africa* (Cape Town: Oxford University Press, 1978); W. Beinart and C. Bundy, 'The Union, the Nation and Talking Crow', in W. Beinart and C. Bundy, eds, *Hidden Struggles in Rural South Africa: Politics and Popular Movements in the Transkei and Eastern Cape, 1890–1930* (Johannesburg: Ravan Press, 1987), 270–318; P. La Hausse, 'The Message of the Warriors: The ICU, the Labouring Poor and the Making of a Popular Political Culture in Durban, 1925–50', in P. Bonner, I. Hofmeyr, D. James and T. Lodge, eds, *Holding Their Ground: Class, Locality and Culture in Nineteenth- and Twentieth-Century South Africa* (Johannesburg: Ravan Press, 1989). For the ICU at Pilgrims Rest, see P. Bonner and K. Shapiro, 'Company Town, Company Estate: Pilgrim's Rest, 1910–1932', *Journal of Southern African Studies*, 19, 21 (1993), 171–202; at Schweitzer-Reyneke, C. van Onselen, *The Seed is Mine: The Life of Kas Maine, A South African Sharecropper, 1894–1985* (Cape Town: David Philip, 1996); at Caledon River, personal communication, James Christie of Fairiedale, Wepener, June 1999.

2   P. Bonner, Interview with Govan Mbeki, Johannesburg, May 1996.

3   South African National Archives, Pretoria (SANA) Ministry of Justice (hereafter JUS) 915 1/18/26 'Police Reports re Native Meetings: Part 3', Divisional Criminal Investigation Officer, Witwatersrand Division to Deputy Commissioner South African Police, Witwatersrand, 24 August 1926 (hereafter referred to as CID reports).

4   H. M. Basner *Am I an African? The Political Memoirs of H.M. Basner* (Johannesburg: Witwatersrand University Press, 1993).

5   P. Bonner, Interview with David Bopape, Tsakane, 31 May 1982.

6   Bradford, *A Taste*, 278.

7   Ibid. 92–93.

8   La Hausse, 'Message of the Warriors', 31, 33, 45.

9   Beinart and Bundy, 'The Union', 287–292.

10   K. Breckenridge, '"We Must Speak for Ourselves": The Rise and Fall of the Public Sphere on the South African Gold Mines, 1920–1930', *Comparative Studies in Society and History*, 40, 1 (1998), 73, 76.

11   Beinart and Bundy, 'The Union', 287–292.

12   Little other than Wickins, *Industrial and Commercial Workers' Union*.

13   E. Roux, *S.P. Bunting: A Political Biography* (Johannesburg: Commercial Printing Company, 1944), 70.

14   C. Kadalie, *My Life*, 67–69.

15   Kadalie, *My Life*, 69; SANA Municipality of Benoni (hereafter MB) 1/2/15 'Mins GPFLC', Benoni, 22 March 1927.

16   Wickins, *Industrial and Commercial Workers' Union*, 86–91.

17   Ibid., 117.

18   Ibid., 82–83, 86.

19   Ibid., 86–89.

20   SANA Government Native Labour Bureau (hereafter GNLB) 363 140/25, 'Complaints of Members of the Industrial and Commercial Workers Union about Payment of Transvaal Tax'; GNLB 363 150/25, 'Strike of Natives at Maytham's Tinware Factory, Mayfair'; GNLB 249 305/16/89, 'Industrial and Commercial Workers Union: Assault on Woman at Boksburg Hospital'; GNLB 245 227/16/80, 'Industrial and Commercial Workers Union: Complaint about the action taken by the complaints office in relation to the claim by Native Jacob against his employer'.

21   SANA GNLB 363 150/25, 'Strike of Natives at Maytham's Tinware Factory, Mayfair'; 'Walls of Jericho Falling!', *Workers' Herald*, 15 December 1926.

22   K. Eales, 'Patriarchs, Passes and Privilege', in Bonner et al., *Holding Their Ground*, 118–124.

23   Wits Saffery Papers AD 1178 B B5, H.D. Tyamzashe, *Summarised History of the Industrial and Commercial Workers' Union of South Africa* (East London, unpublished, c. 1941).

24   Tyamzashe, *Summarised History*; SANA GNLB 363 150/25, 'Strike of Natives at Maytham's Tinware Factory, Mayfair'.

25   Bonner, 'Unity and Division', 19–22.

26   Breckenridge, '"We Must Speak for Ourselves"', 96–7; calculated on the basis of Kadalie's claim that if all members paid their subscriptions' the union would receive £600 a month (SANA JUS 915 1/18/26, 'Police Reports re Meetings of Natives: Part 2', CID report, 1 May 1926).

27   SANA JUS 915 1/18/26 'Police Reports re Meetings of Natives: Part 2', CID report, June 1926.

28   SANA JUS 915 1/18/26 'Police Reports re Meetings of Natives: Part 3', CID report, 12 August 1926.

29   UCT Lionel Forman Papers BC 581 B.2.7, J. La Guma, General Secretary's Report on

Inspection of the Branches, 6 March 1926.

30 Wickins, *Industrial and Commercial Workers' Union*, 97–99.

31 SANA JUS 916 1/18/26, 'Police Reports re Meetings of Natives: Part 4', CID report, 2 November 1926.

32 SANA JUS 916 1/18/26, 'Police Reports re Meetings of Natives: Part 4', CID report, 29 November 1926.

33 SANA JUS 916 1/18/26, 'Police Reports re Meetings of Natives: Part 7', CID report, 29 March 1927.

34 Wickins, *Industrial and Commercial Workers' Union*, 106–108; JUS 915 1/18/26, 'Police Reports RE Meetings of Natives: Part 1', Report of Private Informer, 5 January 1926.

35 SANA JUS 915 1/18/26, 'Police Reports re Meetings of Natives: Part 2', CID report, 1 May 1926; JUS 915 1/18/26, 'Police Reports re Meetings of Natives: Part 3', CID Report, 12 August 1926.

36 SANA JUS 916 1/18/26, 'Police Reports re Meetings of Natives: Part 4', CID report, 11 November 1926.

37 SANA JUS 916 1/18/26, 'Police Reports re Meetings of Natives: Part 5', CID report, 6 January 1927.

38 SANA JUS 917 1/18/26, 'Native Agitation: Reports On: Part 8', CID report, 22 April 1927.

39 SANA JUS 917 1/18/26, 'Native Agitation: Reports On: Part 9', CID report, 6 June 1927.

40 Wickins, *Industrial and Commercial Workers' Union*, 100–102.

41 SANA JUS 916 1/18/26, 'Police Reports re Meetings of Natives: Part 4', CID report, 7 October 1926.

42 SANA JUS 916 1/18/26, 'Police Reports re Meetings of Natives: Part 4', CID report, 29 November 1926.

43 SANA JUS 916 1/18/26, 'Police Reports re Meetings of Natives: Part 5', CID report for 6 January 1927

44 SANA JUS 915 1/18/26, 'Police Reports re Meetings of Natives: Part 3', CID report, 12 August 1926.

45 Bradford, A *Taste*, 213–245; Beinart and Bundy, 'The Union', 308–314.

46 SANA JUS 916 1/18/26, 'Police Reports RE Meetings of Natives: Part 7', CID report, 29 March 1927.

47 Wickins, *Industrial and Commercial Workers' Union*; Bonner, 'Rise and Fall of the ICU'.

48 SANA JUS 922 1/18/26, 'Native Agitation: Reports On: Part 22', CID report, 12 December 1928.

49 Breckenridge, '"We Must Speak for Ourselves"', 73, 76.

50 C. Calhoun, 'Introduction: Habermas and the Public Sphere', in C. Calhoun, ed., *Habermas and the Public Sphere* (Cambridge, Mass.: MIT Press, 1992), 1–48.

51 Breckenridge, '"We Must Speak for Ourselves"', 75.

52 SANA JUS 916 1/18/26, 'Police Reports re Meetings of Natives: Part 4', CID report, 7 October 1926.

53 SANA JUS 922 1/18/26, 'Native Agitation: Reports On: Part 22', CID report, 12 December 1928.

54 M. Foucault, *Discipline and Punish: The Birth of the Prison* (Harmondsworth: Penguin, 1979), 214.

55 SANA JUS 915 1/18/26, 'Police Reports RE Meetings of Natives: Part 2', CID report, 1 May 1926.

56 SANA JUS 921 1/18/26, 'Native Agitation: Reports On: Part 20', CID report, 26 August 1928.

57 SANA JUS 921 1/18/26, 'Native Agitation: Reports On: Part 21', CID report, 19 October 1928.

58 SANA GNLB 400 55/1, 'Communism in the Union: Part 5', CID report, 10 June 1929.

59 Bradford, *A Taste*, 86; quoting E. Roux, 'Agrarian Revolt in South Africa', *Labour Monthly*, 10:1 (1928), 59.

60 SANA JUS 918 1/18/26 'Native Agitation: Reports On: Part 10', CID report, 3 August 1927.

61 SANA JUS 923 1/18/26 'Native Agitation: Reports On: Part 27', CID reports, 25 September 1930 and 13 August 1930, JUS 923 1/18/26 'Native Agitation: Reports On: Part 25', CID report, 16 April 1930.

62 La Hausse, 'Message of the Warriors', 20, 29, 31, 33, 45; Beinart and Bundy, 'The Union', 278.

63 SANA JUS 915 1/18/26, 'Police Reports re Native Meetings: Part 3', CID report, 24 August 1926.

64 We have been unable to track down the sources of these particular quotations.

65 SANA JUS 918 1/18/26, 'Native Agitation: Reports On: Part 12', CID report, 30 November 1927.

66 S. Johns, ed., *From Protest to Challenge. A Documentary History of African Politics, Vol 1. Protest and Hope, 1882–1934* (Stanford: Hoover Institution Press, 1987), 294.

67 SANA JUS 917 1/18/26, 'Native Agitation: Reports On: Part 8', CID report, 22 April 1927.

68 SANA JUS 917 1/18/26, 'Native Agitation: Reports On: Part 8', CID report, 22 April 1927.

69 SANA GNLB 400 55/1, 'Communism in the Union: Part 5', CID report, 10 May 1929.

70 Kadalie, *My Life*, 87–8, note by S. Trapido.

71 SANA JUS 917 1/18/26, 'Native Agitation: Reports On: Part 9', CID report, 6 June 1927.

72 SANA JUS 918 1/18/26, 'Native Agitation: Reports On: Part 10', CID report, 3 August 1927; Kadalie, *My Life*, 67.

73 SANA JUS 922 1/18/26, 'Native Agitation: Reports On: Part 22', CID report, 12 December 1928.

74 SANA GNLB 400 55/1, 'Communism in the Union: Part 5', CID reports, 29 April 1929 and 10 July 1929.

75 SANA JUS 917 1/18/26, 'Native Agitation: Reports On: Part 9', CID report, 6 June 1927.

76 SANA JUS 915 1/18/26, 'Police Reports re Meetings of Natives: Part 1', Sub-Inspector, SAP to Deputy Commissioner, SAP, Bloemfontein, 7 January 1926.

77 SANA JUS 915 1/18/26, 'Police Reports re Meetings of Natives: Part 2', CID report, 1 May 1926.

78 Wickins, *Industrial and Commercial Workers' Union*, 93, 98.

79   Wickins, *Industrial and Commercial Workers' Union*, 123.

80   SANA JUS 918 1/18/26, 'Native Agitation: Reports On: Part 11', CID report,
     16 September 1927.

81   Ibid.

82   Ibid.

83   SANA JUS 922 1/18/26, 'Native Agitation: Reports On: Part 22', CID report, 12 December 1928.

84   Breckenridge, '"We Must Speak for Ourselves"', 101–108.

Chapter 10

1   For a detailed study of Msimang's political career see S.M. Mkhize, 'Class Consciousness,
     Non-racialism and Political Pragmatism: A Political Biography of Henry Selby Msimang,
     1886–1982', (PhD thesis, University of the Witwatersrand, 2015); See also S.M. Mkhize,
     Principle and Pragmatism in the Liberation Struggle: A Political Biography of Selby Msimang
     (Cape Town: HSRC Press, 2019).

2   Mkhize, *Principle and Pragmatism in the Liberation Struggle*, 24–51.

3   Mkhize, 'Class Consciousness, Non-racialism and Political Pragmatism', 61–77.

4   South African National Archives, Bloemfontein (hereafter VAB) Minutes of Town Council
     Bloemfontein (hereafter MBL) 1/2/4/1/3, Minutes of an ordinary meeting of the Native
     Affairs Committee, 17 June 1918. See also H.J. Haasbroek, 'The Native Advisory Board of
     Bloemfontein, 1913-1923', *Navorsinge van die Nasionale Museum*, 19, 1 (2003), 81–88.

5   UKZN Alan Paton Centre (hereafter APC), John Aitchison Collection (hereafter JAC),
     APC/PC14/1/2/2, Manuscript of Unpublished Autobiography of H. Selby Msimang by John
     Aitchison, 1971–1972.

6   S. Hindson, 'Selby Msimang and Trade Union Organisation in the 1920s', *Reality: A Journal
     of Liberal and Radical Opinion*, 9, 1 (1977), 3.

7   H.S. Msimang, 'Mr H. Selby Msimang tells how it all started – 50 Years of the Road to
     Liberty', *Contact*, 2 April 1960.

8   Hindson, 'Selby Msimang and Trade Union Organisation', 4.

9   WITS Institute for Advanced Social Research Records (hereafter IASR) AG 2738–53, Tim
     Couzens interview with Selby Msimang, 18 June 1974.

10   L. Switzer, 'The Ambiguities of Protest in South Africa: Rural Politics and the Press during
     the 1920s', *International Journal of African Historical Studies*, 23, 1 (1990), 87.

11   A. Drew, *Between Empire and Revolution: A Life of Sidney Bunting, 1873–1936* (London:
     Pickering and Chatto, 2007), 93–104, 105–110; A. Drew, *Discordant Comrades: Identities and
     Loyalties on the South African Left* (Pretoria: Unisa Press, 2002), 38–40, 49.

12   H.J. Haasbroek, 'H. Selby Msimang, Kampvegter vir Swart Belange in Bloemfontein,
     1915–1922', *Culna*, 54 (June 1999), 1.

13   For detailed research see J. Wells, *We Now Demand! The History of Women's Struggles against
     Passes in South Africa* (Johannesburg: Wits University Press, 1993) and P. Bonner, 'Desirable

or Undesirable Basotho Women? Liquor, Prostitution and the Migration of Basotho Women to the Rand, 1920–1945', in C. Walker, ed., *Women and Gender in Southern Africa to 1945* (Cape Town: David Philip, 1990), 221–250.

14   Mkhize, 'Class Consciousness, Non-racialism and Political Pragmatism', 85–87.

15   H.J. Haasbroek, 'Die Rol van Henry Selby Msimang in Bloemfontein, 1917–1922', *Navorsinge van die Nasionale Museum*, 16, 3 (2000), 39.

16   Haasbroek, 'Die Rol van Henry Selby Msimang', 39.

17   Natal Archives Bureau (hereafter NAB), Pietermaritzburg Supreme Court Records (hereafter PSCR) 1/1/1004 Vol. 32, Record 12, Case Number: cc 108/76: State v Themba H. Gwala and 9 others, Evidence of Selby Msimang, July 1976.

18   E. Webster, 'Champion, the ICU and the Predicament of African Trade Unions', *South African Labour Bulletin*, 1 (1974), 7.

19   UKZN JAC APC/PC14/1/2/2, Manuscript of Msimang Autobiography, 94. Although Msimang mentioned Eddie Roux, this is not likely to have been the case because Roux would have been 17 at the time. Perhaps he had contact with Roux during the 1930s when he was CPSA full-time organiser.

20   UKZN JAC APC/PC14/1/2/2, Manuscript of Msimang Autobiography, 94.

21   Mkhize, 'Class Consciousness, Non-racialism and Political Pragmatism', 80–95.

22   UKZN JAC APC/PC14/1/2/2, Manuscript of Msimang Autobiography, 95.

23   B. Hirson, 'The Bloemfontein Riots, 1925: A Study in Community Culture and Class Consciousness', *The Societies of Southern Africa in the Nineteenth and Twentieth Centuries*, University of London, Institute of Commonwealth Studies, 1982–1983, 90.

24   Hirson, 'The Bloemfontein Riots, 1925', 90.

25   Ibid.; See also G. Coka, 'The Story of Gilbert Coka of the Zulu Tribe of Natal, South Africa', in M. Perham, ed., *Ten Africans* (London: Faber and Faber, 1936), 300–301, and 'Masterpiece in Bronze: Henry Selby Msimang', *Drum*, June 1954.

26   Mkhize, 'Class Consciousness, Non-racialism and Political Pragmatism', 87–94; See also H.J. Haasbroek, 'Henry Selby Msimang en die loonagitasie van 1919 in Bloemfontein', *Indago*, 32 (2016), 119–131.

27   UKZN JAC APC/PC14/1/2/2, Manuscript of Msimang Autobiography, 95.

28   UKZN JAC APC/PC14/1/2/2, Manuscript of Msimang Autobiography, 102–106.

29   Mkhize, 'Class Consciousness, Non-racialism and Political Pragmatism', 242–277.

30   See, P.L. Wickins, 'The Industrial and Commercial Workers Union of Africa' (PhD thesis, University of Cape Town, 1973); H. Bradford, *A Taste of Freedom: The ICU in Rural South Africa, 1924–1930* (Johannesburg, Ravan Press, 1987); P. Bonner, 'The Decline and Fall of the ICU – A Case of Self Destruction?', *South African Labour Bulletin*, 1, 6 (1974), 38–43; P. Wickins, 'The One Big Union Movement Among Black Workers in South Africa', *International Journal of African Historical Studies*, 7, 3 (1974), 391–416; H. Bradford, 'Mass Movements and the Petty-Bourgeoisie: The Social Origins of the ICU leadership', *Journal of African History*, 25 (1984), 295–310.

31   'The ICU', *South African Labour Bulletin*, 1, 6 (1974), 4.

32   Ibid., 6.

33   G. Baines, 'The Port Elizabeth Disturbances of October 1920', *Reality,* 18, 5 (1986), 12.

34   S. Moroney, 'Mine Workers Protest on the Witwatersrand, 1901-1912', *South African Labour Bulletin* 3, 5 (1977), 15–19.

35   Bonner, P. 'The 1920 Mineworkers Strike' (University of the Witwatersrand, Wits History Workshop, 3–7 February 1978.

36   R. Posel, 'The Durban Ricksha-Pullers' Strikes of 1918 and 1930', University of Natal, Conference on the History of Natal and Zululand, July 1985.

37   'The ICU', *South African Labour Bulletin,* 1, 6 (1974), 6.

38   P. Limb, *The ANC's Early Years: Nation, Class and Place in South Africa before 1940* (Pretoria: Unisa Press, 2010), 484.

39   UKZN JAC APC/PC14/1/2/2, Manuscript of Msimang Autobiography, 138.

40   Hindson, 'Selby Msimang and Trade Union Organisation', 14.

41   Ibid.; H. Bradford, 'Mass movements and the petty bourgeoisie', 295–310; Kadalie, *My Life and the ICU: The Autobiography of a Black Trade Unionist in South Africa* (London: Frank Cass, 1970), 39-49.

42   Kadalie, *My Life,* 40–49.

43   Hindson, 'Selby Msimang and Trade Union Organisation', 5.

44   Killie Campbell Africana Library, Killie Campbell Audio-Visual (hereafter KCAL KCAV) 355/ Selby Msimang, Transcript of an interview with Selby Msimang, 25 July 1980.

45   H.J. Haasbroek, 'Die Rol van Henry Selby Msimang', 60.

46   Hindson, 'Selby Msimang and Trade Union Organisation', 14.

47   J. Simons and R. Simons, *Class and Colour in South Africa, 1850–1950* (London: IDAF, 1983), 225–26.

48   UKZN JAC APC/PC14/1/2/2, Manuscript of Msimang Autobiography, 140.

49   This was the same venue where the African National Congress was founded in January 1912.

50   Kadalie disputed the existence of the branches Msimang claimed to have organized. See Kadalie, *My Life,* 40–49.

51   Wickins, 'The Industrial and Commercial Workers Union of Africa', 61–63; Haasbroek, 'Die Rol van Henry Selby Msimang', 60.

52   Kadalie, *My Life,* 14.

53   UKZN KCAL KCAV 355/ Selby Msimang, Transcript of an interview with Selby Msimang, 25 July 1980.

54   Msimang repeated this when he gave evidence in the trial involving Harry Gwala and 9 others in 1976, NAB PSCR 1/1/1004, Vol. 32, Record 12, Case Number: cc 108/76.

55   UKZN KCAL KCAV 355/Selby Msimang: Transcript of an interview with Selby Msimang, 25 July 1980.

56   UKZN JAC APC/PC14/1/2/2, Manuscript of Msimang Autobiography, p. 138.

57   Kadalie, *My Life,* 13.

58   Limb, *The ANC's Early Years,* 226.

59   Kadalie, *My Life*, 14.

60   Hindson, 'Selby Msimang and Trade Union Organisation', 5.

61   Wickins, 'The Industrial and Commercial Workers Union', 150–51; See also P. La Hausse, 'Ethnicity and History in the Careers of Two Zulu Nationalists: Petros Lamula (c.1881–1948) and Lymon Maling (1889–c.1936)' (PhD thesis, University of the Witwatersrand, 1992), 91.

62   Wickins, 'The Industrial and Commercial Workers Union', 151–152.

63   Simons and Simons, *Class and Colour in South Africa*, 241.

64   Haasbroek, 'Die Rol van Henry Selby Msimang in Bloemfontein, 1917-1922', 61.

65   Webster, 'Champion, the ICU and the Predicament of African Trade Unions', 12.

66   Haasbroek, 'Die Rol van Henry Selby Msimang' 61.

67   See also G. Baines, 'The Port Elizabeth Riots of October 1920' (MA thesis, Rhodes University, 1988); Wickins, 'The Industrial and Commercial Workers Union of Africa'; Kadalie, *My Life*, 15–16 and 50–53; and K. I. Watson, 'A History of the South African Police in Port Elizabeth, 1913–1956' (PhD thesis, Rhodes University, 1999), 250–56.

68   For a detailed study of Rubusana see, S.J. Ngqongqo, 'Mpilo Walter Benson Rubusana (1858–1910): The Making of the New African Elite in the Eastern Cape' (MA thesis, University of Fort Hare, 1997).

69   Baines, 'The Port Elizabeth Disturbances', 92–93.

70   R. Bloch, 'The High Cost of Living: The Port Elizabeth Disturbances of October 1920', *Africa Perspective,* 19 (1981), 49; See also Wickins, 'The One Big Union Movement Among Black Workers in South Africa', 391–416; G. Baines, 'From Populism to Unionism: The Emergence and Nature of Port Elizabeth's Industrial and Commercial Workers Union, 1918–1920', *Journal of Southern African Studies,* 17, 4 (1991), 679–716; G. Baines, 'Port Elizabeth History: A Select Annotated Bibliography', *South African Historical Journal,* 38, 1 (1998), 252–269; and Baines, 'The Port Elizabeth Disturbances', 12–15.

71   Hindson, 'Selby Msimang and Trade Union Organisation', 6.

72   Simons and Simons, *Class and Colour in South Africa*, 241–242.

73   'Riot at Port Elizabeth – Police Fire on Native Mob', *The Argus*, 26 October 1920.

74   Baines, 'The Port Elizabeth Disturbances', 13.

75   Bloch, 'The High Cost of Living', 39-59; G. Baines, 'The Control and Administration of Port Elizabeth's African Population, c.1834-1923', *Contree* 26 (October 1989), 15–21; A. Appel, 'Housing in the Late Nineteenth and Early Twentieth-century Port Elizabeth', *Contree*, 37, 1995, 18–28.

76   Hindson, 'Selby Msimang and Trade Union Organisation', 6.

77   Baines, 'The Port Elizabeth Disturbances', 128.

78   UKZN JAC APC/PC14/1/2/2, Manuscript of Msimang Autobiography, 102.

79   Ibid., 103.

80   UKZN JAC APC/PC14/1/2/2, Manuscript of Msimang Autobiography, 105.

81   Baines, 'The Port Elizabeth Disturbances', 129.

82   UKZN JAC APC/ PC14/1/2/2, Manuscript of Msimang Autobiography, 103.

83 J. Starfield, '"Not Quite History"': The Autobiographies of H. Selby Msimang and R.V. Selope Thema and the Writing of South African History', *Social Dynamics: A Journal of Social Sciences*, 14, 2 (1988), 33.

84 UKZN JAC APC/PC14/1/2/2, Manuscript of Msimang Autobiography, 104.

85 Baines, 'The Port Elizabeth Disturbances', 130.

86 Starfield, "Not Quite History", 33.

87 UKZN JAC APC/PC14/1/2/2, Manuscript of Msimang Autobiography, 104.

88 Hindson, 'Selby Msimang and Trade Union Organisation', 6.

89 UKZN JAC APC/PC14/1/2/2, Manuscript of Msimang Autobiography, 105.

90 Baines, 'The Port Elizabeth Disturbances', 131.

91 UKZN APC/PC14/1/2/2 – JAC: Manuscript of Msimang Autobiography, 104.

92 Baines, 'The Port Elizabeth Disturbances', 131.

93 Ibid., 132

94 Baines, 'The Port Elizabeth Disturbances of October 19120, Reality, 13.

95 UKZN JAC APC/PC14/1/2/2 – JAC: Manuscript of Msimang Autobiography, 104.

96 Starfield, 'Not Quite History", 33.

97 Ibid.

98 UKZN JAC APC/PC14/1/2/2: Manuscript of Msimang Autobiography, 104.

99 Baines, 'The Port Elizabeth Disturbances', 135.

100 See also Kadalie, *My Life,* 15.

101 Bloch, 'The High Cost of Living', 49.

102 UKZN KCAL KCAV 355/Selby Msimang: Transcript of an interview with Selby Msimang, 25 July 1980.

103 Kadalie, *My Life*, 15.

104 He professed this ambition in his letter to Bennett Ncwana, editor of *The Black Man*, on his wish to be 'the great African Marcus Garvey' (UKZN KCAL KCM J.S. Marwick Papers 8315, 74, Clements Kadalie to S.M. Bennett Ncwana, 20 May 1920; WITS IASR AG 2738–81, Tim Couzens interview with Selby Msimang, 5 June 1977; Bradford, *A Taste*, 5; R.A. Hill and G.A. Pirio, '"Africa for the Africans": The Garvey Movement in South Africa, 1920–1940', in S. Marks and S. Trapido, eds., *The Politics of Race, Class and Nationalism in Twentieth Century South Africa* (London: Longman, 1987), 215.

105 Hill and Pirio, 'Africa for the Africans', 215–16.

106 Ibid., 215.

107 Simons and Simons, *Class and Colour in South Africa*, 266.

108 Address by Selby Msimang, President of the ICU, July 23, 1921, in T. Karis and G. Carter, *From Protest to Challenge: A Documentary History of African Politics in South Africa, Vol. 1: Protest and Hope, 1882–1934* (Stanford, Hoover, 1972), 318.

109 UKZN KCAL KCAV 355/ Selby Msimang, Transcript of an interview with Selby Msimang, 25 July 1980.

110 See Kadalie, *My Life*, 15. For a detailed picture of the complex 'horse trading' which took place during the conference, see Wickins, 'The Industrial and Commercial Workers Union of Africa', 151–52.

111 Wits Saffery Papers AD 1179, H.D. Tyamzashe, *Summarized History of the Industrial and Commercial Workers Union of Africa (ICU)* (Unpublished typescript, 1941), 1–8.

112 H.D. Tyamzashe, 'A friendly critic', *Umteteli wa Bantu*, 16 January 1926.

113 W. Ballinger, *Umteteli wa Bantu*, 9 March 1929.

114 Wits Saffery Papers AD 1179, *ICU Weekly News*.

115 Mkhize, 'Class Consciousness, Non-racialism and Political Pragmatism', 179–213.

116 Hindson, 'Selby Msimang and Trade Union Organisation', 4; JAC, APC/PC14/1/2/2, Manuscript of Msimang Autobiography, 97.

117 WITS IASR AG 2738–78, Tim Couzens interview with H. Selby Msimang, 2 June 1974.

118 Hindson, 'Selby Msimang and Trade Union Organisation', 5.

119 Mkhize, 'Class Consciousness, Non-racialism and Political Pragmatism', 1–32.

Chapter 11

1   S. Bunting, 'A Helots' Bill of Rights', *The International*, 1 June 1923.

2   University of the Western Cape (hereafter UWC) Mayibuye Archive W. H. Andrews Papers MCH06 3-3-265, W. H. Andrews, 'The South African Trades Union Congress and the Industrial Organization of the Non-European Workers'.

3   W.H. Andrews, 'How it's Done', *The International*, 27 June 1924.

4   'News from Comrade Andrews', *The International*, 24 August 1923.

5   A. Davidson, I. Filatova, V. Gorodnov and S. Johns, eds., *South Africa and the Communist International, Volume 1: Socialist Pilgrims to Bolshevik Footsoldiers, 1919–1930*, (London: Frank Cass, 2003), 131.

6   Ibid., 133.

7   A. Drew, *Discordant Comrades: Identities and Loyalties on the South African Left* (Aldershot: Ashgate, Aldershot, 2000), 71.

8   'Young Communist Notes', *The International*, 1 February 1924.

9   'Black and White', *The Young Worker*, January 1924.

10 Davidson et al, eds., *South Africa and the Communist International*,137.

11 'Votes for (Native) Women', *The International*, 22 February 1924.

12 A.B. Lerumo, *Fifty Fighting Years* (London: Inkululeko Publications, 1980), 52.

13 E. Roux, *Time Longer than Rope* (London: Victor Gollancz, 1948), 69.

14 Ibid., 197.

15 H. Bradford, *A Taste*, 78.

16 'International May Day in Johannesburg', *The International*, 3 May 1918.

17 R.E. Philips, *The Bantu are Coming: Phases of South Africa's Race Problem* (London: Student Christian Movement Press, 1930), 45–46.

18 See, for example, the letter from J.N. (from Nancefield), 'Slavery in South Africa' and the article 'Labour vs. Labour', *The International*, 22 February 1924.

19 'Native views of Coalition', *The International*, 11 July 1924.

20 J. Grossman, 'Class Relations and the Communist Party of South Africa 1921–1950' (PhD thesis, University of Warwick, 1985), 119.

21 Ibid., 120.

22 *The Star*, 7 September 1925 (cutting in UCT, Forman Papers, BC 581, B1.3). Andrews appeared at the meeting in his capacity as secretary of the South African Association of Employees' Organisations.

23 S. Johns, 'Marxism-Leninism in a Multi-Racial Environment: The origins and early history of the Communist Party of South Africa', 1914–1932 (PhD thesis, Harvard University, 1965), 355.

24 E. Roux and W. Roux, *Rebel Pity: The Life of Eddie Roux* (London: Rex Collings, 1970), 39.

25 Bradford, *A Taste*, 78.

26 Peter Wickins, *The Industrial and Commercial Workers' Union of South Africa* (Cape Town: Oxford University Press, 1978), 97–99.

27 Musa [one of Kadalie's pseudonyms], 'Am I My Brother's Keeper', *Workers' Herald*, 20 February 1926.

28 Bradford, *A Taste*, 1.

29 S. Neame, *The Congress Movement: The Unfolding of the Congress Alliance, 1912–1961*, Vol. 2 (Cape Town: HSRC Press, 2015), 315.

30 Neame, *The Congress Movement,* Vol. 2, 205.

31 Wickins, *The Industrial and Commercial Workers' Union*, 83–84.

32 Drew cites documentation in the Comintern files in *Discordant Comrades*, 77.

33 Wickins, *Industrial and Commercial Workers' Union*, 104.

34 J. Simons and R. Simons, *Class and Colour in South Africa, 1850–1950* (Harmondsworth: Penguin, 1967), 369–271.

35 UCT Forman Papers BC 581 B.2.7, J. La Guma, General Secretary's Report on Inspection of the Branches, 6 March 1926.

36 L. Greene, 'Pietermaritzburg Notes', *South African Worker*, 6 August 1926; L. Greene, 'Pietermaritzburg Notes', *South African Worker*, 13 August 1926.

37 Neame, *The Congress Movement,* Vol. 2, 207–208.

38 Neame, *The Congress Movement,* Vol. 2, 212.

39 Wickins, *The Industrial and Commercial Workers' Union*, 108.

40 Ibid., 106.

41 Ibid., 111.

42 Neame, *The Congress Movement* Vol. 2, 219.

43 Wickins, *The Industrial and Commercial Workers' Union*, 131.

44   Wickins, *The Industrial and Commercial Workers' Union,* 136.

45   UCT Forman Papers BC 581 B3.87, Creech Jones to Kadalie, 15 September 1927.

46   WITS, ICU Records, A 924 A6.1, Ethelreda Lewis to Winifred Holtby, 4 February 1928.

47   *The Star,* 7 September 1925 (cutting in UCT Forman Papers BC 581, B1.3).

48   Neame, *The Congress Movement,* Vol. 2, 214–15.

49   UWC Mayibuye Archive, W.H. Andrews Papers MCH06 3-3-265, W.H. Andrews, 'The South African Traders Union Congress and the Industrial Organization of the Non-European Workers', 5.

50   Wickins, *The Industrial and Commercial Workers' Union,* 131–32; Neame, *The Congress Movement* Vol. 2, 249.

51   Neame, *The Congress Movement* Vol. 2, 226.

52   A. Drew, *Discordant Comrades,* 82; Neame, *The Congress Movement* Vol. 2, 225.

53   M. Roth, *The Communist Party of South Africa: Racism, Eurocentricity and Moscow, 1921–1950* (Partridge, no place of publication, 2016) 72–77.

54   Wits Sylvia Neame Papers A 2729, Johnny Gomas interviewed by Sylvia Neame, 1962.

55   Wits Edward Roux Papers, A 2667, B1. 8.

56   Cited in Drew, *Discordant Comrades,* 79.

57   Wits Sylvia Neame Papers A 2729, Rebecca Bunting interviewed by Sylvia Neame, 32.

58   A. Thorpe, 'Comintern "control" of the Communist Party of Great Britain', *English Historical Review,* 113, 452 (1998), 649–650.

59   UCT Forman Papers BC 581 B2 143, Statement showing ICU Head Office Income and Expenditure, 1 May to 31 October 1927.

60   UCT Forman Papers BC 581 B3.168, ICU National Council meeting Minutes, 18–25 November 1927.

61   Wits Saffrey Papers AD 1178 B5 1941 H. D. Tyamzashe, 'Summarised History of the ICU', 21.

62   Neame, *The Congress Movement,* Vol. 2, 320.

63   B. Sachs. *Multitude of Dreams* (Johannesburg: Kayor Publishing House, 1949), 136.

64   SANA. Document found by Bob Edgar: Letter written by Mbeki as an informer to DHC Boy, 20 January 1930.

65   Neame, *The Congress Movement,* Vol. 2, 225.

66   R. Edgar, *Edwin Thabo Mofutsanyana and the CPSA, 1927–1939* (Pretoria: University of South Africa, 2005), 9.

67   J. Wells, 'The Day the Town Stood Still: Women in Resistance in Potchefstroom, 1912–1930', in B. Bozzoli, ed., *Town and Countryside in the Transvaal* (Johannesburg: Ravan Press, 1983), 269–307.

68   Drew, *Discordant Comrades,* 85.

69   Edgar, *Edwin Thabo Mofutsanyana,* 11–12.

70   Johns, 'Marxism-Leninism', 399.

71   Roth, *The Communist Party of South Africa,* 94–95.

72   Edgar, *Edwin Thabo Mofutsanyana*, 10.

73   Neame, *The Congress Movement*, Vol. 2, 185.

74   Wits Edward Roux Papers AH 2667, B2L, H. Greene to Douglas Wolton, 2 January 1929. See also G. Coka, 'The Story of Gilbert Coka', in M. Perham, ed., *Ten Africans* (London: Faber and Faber, 1963), 313.

75   P. La Hausse, 'The message of the warriors: The ICU, the labouring poor and the making of a popular political culture in Durban, 1925–1930' in P. Bonner et al, eds, *Holding Their Ground* (Johannesburg: Ravan Press 1989), 19–57.

76   S. Ndlovu, 'Johannes Nkosi and the Communist Party of South Africa: Images of Blood River and King Dingaan, 1920s–1930', *History and Theory*, 39, 4 (2000), 111–31, 121.

77   Ndlovu, 'Johannes Nkosi and the CPSA', 121–122.

78   Sachs, *Multitude of Dreams*, 155.

79   Grossman, 'Class Relations', 193.

80   Roux, *Rebel Pity*, 98.

81   Wits Sylvia Neame Papers, AD 2729, Sam Malkinson interviewed by Sylvia Neame, 1964, 6.

82   Wits Edward Roux Papers A 2667 B2, Sam Malkinson to S. P. Bunting, 30 November 1929.

83   Wits Sylvia Neame Papers, AD 2729, Sam Malkinson interviewed by Sylvia Neame, 1964, 7.

84   Ibid., 7–10.

85   A. Drew, *Between Empire and Revolution: A Life of Sidney Bunting, 1873–1936* (London: Pickering and Chatto, 2007), 205.

86   Drew, *Discordant Comrades*, 122.

87   Roux, *Rebel Pity*, 98.

Chapter 12

1   My thanks go to Dr Sylvia Vietzen who has generously made her research on Mabel Palmer available to me. Diana Wall, the widow of Tim Couzens, has, equally generously, allowed me to use Tim Couzens' research material. I could not have written this chapter without their contributions. I should also like to thank Tanya Barben who first suggested Winifred Holtby as a research topic.

2   Hull History Centre (hereafter HHC): Tim Couzens (hereafter TC), HCL D2 11/50, Extract of a letter from E. Lewis, 14 December 1927. See also R.D. Heyman, 'C.T. Loram: A South African Liberal in Race Relations', *International Journal of African Historical Studies*, 5, 1, (1972), 41–50; R. Hunt Davis, 'Charles T. Loram and an American Model for African Education in South Africa', *The African Studies Review*, 19, 2, (1976), 87–99. The Winifred Holtby collection is held by the Hull History Centre, Hull, Yorkshire. Those listed as 'HHC, WH' have been inventoried relatively recently; those labelled 'TC, HCL' come from Tim Couzens' papers, which he accessed before the current inventory existed.

3   The role of women in the history of the ICU is also discussed by Nicole Ulrich in Chapter 7 of this volume. This chapter concentrates on three white women's relationships with the

ICU; for the histories of black women in the ICU and for Kadalie's personal relationships, see D. Johnson and H. Dee, eds, 'I See You': The Industrial and Commercial Workers' Union of Africa, 1919–1930 (Cape Town: Historical Publications Southern Africa, 2022), xxvii–xxviii, 13–16, and 21–27; and H. Dee, "'I am a Bad Native": Masculinity and Marriage in the Biographies of Clements Kadalie', African Studies, 78, 2 (2019), 183–204.

4 See P. Gopal, Insurgent Empire: Anticolonial Resistance and British Dissent (London: Verso, 2019), 296–316; J. Marcus, Hearts of Darkness: White Women Write Race (New Brunswick, NJ: Rutgers University Press, 2004), 119–49; and L.T. Winkiel, 'Nancy Cunard's Negro and the Transnational Politics of Race', Modernism/ Modernity, 13, 3 (2006), 507–530.

5 W. Holtby, 'Feminism Divided', Yorkshire Post, 26 July 1926, in P. Berry and A. Bishop, eds., Testament of a Generation: The Journalism of Vera Brittain and Winifred Holtby (London: Chatto & Windus, 1985), 47–40. See also H.L. Smith, ed., British Feminism in the Twentieth Century (Aldershot: Edward Elgar, 1990), 47–49, 85–87. Deidre Beddoe sees the interwar years as anti-feminist, largely relegating women to the home; see D. Beddoe, Back to Home and Duty: Women Between the Wars, 1918–1939 (London: Pandora, 1989), 1–5, 136–137.

6 Cited in S. Marks, ed., Not Either an Experimental Doll: The Separate Worlds of Three South African Women (Pietermaritzburg: Natal University Press, 1987), 3. See also S. Vietzen, 'Beyond School: Some Developments in Higher Education in Durban in the 1920s and the Influence of Mabel Palmer', Natalia, 14 (1984), 51; S. Vietzen, 'Mabel Palmer and Black Higher Education in Natal 1936–1942, Journal of Natal and Zulu History 6, (1983), 98–114.

7 Marks, Not Either an Experimental Doll, 3, 6–7.

8 The friendship is recorded in V. Brittain, Testament of Youth (London: Gollancz, 1933) and V. Brittain, Testament of Friendship: The Story of Winifred Holtby (London: Macmillan, 1940), as well as in several collections of letters.

9 Holtby was familiar with Olive Schreiner's writing and she knew Pauline Smith's work on rural life in South Africa. See, especially, J.M. Coetzee, 'Farm novel and "plaasroman" in South Africa', English in Africa, 13, 2 (Oct. 1986), 1–19. Lisa Regan compares The Land of Green Ginger with Olive Schreiner's Story of an African Farm in L. Regan, Winifred Holtby's Social Vision: 'Members One of Another' (London: Routledge, 2012), 75–76.

10 W. Holtby, The Land of Green Ginger (London: Virago, 2011 [1927]), 9–10; Regan, Winifred Holtby's Social Vision, 54–55.

11 W. Holtby, Letters to a Friend (London: Collins, 1937), 87–88. Holtby had met Jean McWilliam while serving as a member of the WAAC in France in 1918. McWilliam emigrated to South Africa, becoming headmistress of Pretoria Girls' High School. M. Shaw, The Clear Stream: A Life of Winifred Holtby (London: Virago, 1999), 77–82.

12 W. Holtby, 'Better and Brighter Natives', Nation and Athenaeum, 23 November 1929, in Berry and Bishop, Testament of a Generation, 181–185.

13 HHC, Winifred Holtby (hereafter WH)/6/6.1/07/04c, Winifred Holtby to Vera Brittain, 15 March 1926.

14 Shaw, The Clear Stream, 11, 38, 113, 169. Holtby made this point repeatedly in her letters to Jean McWilliam. See Holtby, Letters to a Friend, 54, 70, 137, 202, 312–3.

15 Shaw, The Clear Stream, 185; Brittain, Testament of Friendship, 198–257.

16 Trader Horn: The Ivory Coast in the Earlie. (London: Jonathan Cape, 1930 [1927]).

17 T. Couzens, *Tramp Royal: The True Story of Trader Horn* (Johannesburg: Witwatersrand University Press, 1992).

18 Ibid., 1–8, 444–57; T. Couzens, 'Introduction', in E. Lewis, *Wild Deer* (Cape Town: David Philip, 1984 [1933]), v–xxxii.

19 UCT Ballinger Papers, BC 347 D2 I 3, A. Fenner Brockway to Ethelreda Lewis; also cited in Shaw, *The Clear Stream*, 11.

20 B. Bush, *Imperialism, Race and Resistance: Africa and Britain, 1919–1945* (London: Routledge, 1999), 12, 182–3. Marion Shaw also describes Ethelreda Lewis as 'liberal'. *The Clear Stream*, 171.

21 Cited in Shaw, *The Clear Stream*, 170; E. Roux, *Time Longer than Rope: A History of the Black Man's Struggle for Freedom in South Africa* (Madison, Wisc.: University of Wisconsin Press, 1964), 160.

22 Shaw, *The Clear Stream*, 170, 177–8. For the role of communism in the ICU, see A. Drew, *Discordant Comrades: Identities and Loyalties on the South African Left* (London, Routledge, 2019), 79–86.

23 UCT Ballinger Papers BC 347 D1 I 1.1.4, Winifred Holtby to William Ballinger, 20 April 1928. The reference was to Fanny Glass, née Klenerman, who 'greatly admired' Holtby. V. Belling, '"More than a shop". Fanny Klenerman and the Vanguard Bookshop in Johannesburg', *Jewish Affairs* (2017), 1–8; Drew, *Discordant Comrades*, 78–9.

24 K. Ewins, 'The Idea of Africa in Winifred Holtby's "Mandoa, Mandoa!"', *The Review of English Studies*, New Series, 63, 258, (2012), 118–38; R. Bates, 'Winifred Holtby', *Left Review*, 2 (1935), 49, cited in Ewins, 'The Idea of Africa', 128; W. Holtby, *Mandoa! Mandoa! A Comedy of Irrelevance* (London: Virago, 1982 [1933]).

25 UCT Ballinger Papers BC 347 D1 I 2.2, Winifred Holtby to Fenner Brockway, 26 April 1929; Shaw, *The Clear Stream*, 173.

26 UKZN Killie Campbell African Library (hereafter KCL) KCM 17591, Unpublished typescript, M. Palmer, 'The Economics of Transition in Native Life'.

27 L. Woolf, *Imperialism and Civilization* (London: Hogarth, 1928); L. Woolf, *Empire and Commerce in Africa: A Study in Economic Imperialism* (London: Allen & Unwin, 1920); The League of Nations Union, Article 22, *The Covenant of the League of Nations*, 28 June 1919; Ewins, 'The Idea of Africa', 123.

28 Ewins, 'The Idea of Africa', 121, 122, 124–6.

29 UCT Ballinger Papers BC 347 D1 I 1.1.4, Winifred Holtby to William Ballinger, 20 April 1928.

30 M. Arnold, *Culture and Anarchy: An Essay in Political and Social Criticism* (London: Smith Elder, 1869).

31 Cited in Shaw, *The Clear Stream*, 173. On Holtby's modernism, see also Ewins, 'The Idea of Africa', 123.

32 T. Couzens, 'Introduction' to *Wild Deer*, vii. Peter Wickins considers that 'to term Mrs Lewis a liberal would be far from accurate', P.L. Wickins, *The Industrial and Commercial Workers' Union of Africa* (Cape Town: Oxford University Press, 1978), 104.

33 Lewis, *Wild Deer*, 103.

34 UCT Ballinger Papers BC 347 D2 I 1, Ethelreda Lewis to Dr E.P. Keppel and J. Bertram.

35 Lewis, 'Stranger Within My Gate', 93. UCT Ballinger Papers BC 347 D1 I 1.1.12. It would seem that Lewis kept the ICU going at some points through personal loans (see also the letter from William Ballinger to Winifred Holtby, 14 August 1928).

36 Couzens, 'Introduction' to *Wild Deer*, vii–viii.

37 HHC WH/6/6.1/07/04a, Winifred Holtby to Vera Brittain, 3 March 1926, 8 March 1926.

38 Lewis, 'Stranger Within My Gate', 88–9.

39 On Frank Glass, see B. Hirson, 'Death of a revolutionary: Frank Glass/Li Fu-Jen/John Liang 1902–1988', *Searchlight South Africa*, 1, 1 (1988), 28–41; Drew, *Discordant Comrades*, 79.

40 Several writers assert that Lewis was a member of the Johannesburg Joint Council but she denied it. Lewis, 'Stranger Within My Gate', 89, 107.

41 HHC WH/6/6.1/07/04c, Winifred Holtby to Vera Brittain, 15 March 1926.

42 HHC WH/6/6.1/07/07a, Winifred Holtby to Vera Brittain, 6 June 1926.

43 Ibid.; Lewis, 'Stranger Within My Gate', 89–90.

44 In his autobiography Kadalie noted that 'The year 1926 was a very important one in the history of the ICU'. C. Kadalie, *My Life and the ICU: The Autobiography of a Black Trade Unionist in South Africa* (London: Frank Cass, 1970), 86.

45 TC, HHC HCL d4 f7, Ethelreda Lewis to Winifred Holtby, 25 July 1928; UCT Ballinger Collection BC 347 D1 I 1.5, Clements Kadalie to Ethelreda Lewis, 21 June 1927.

46 Drew, *Discordant Comrades*, 81.

47 HHC HCL D2 11/50 58, Extract of letter from Ethelreda Lewis, 14 December 1927.

48 HHC HCL WH/6/6.1/07/07a, Winifred Holtby to Vera Brittain, 6 June 1926.

49 In South Africa Livie-Noble had been one of the founders of the SAIRR. The London Group on African Affairs was established in 1930, partly at the instigation of Rheinallt Jones of the SAIRR. https://archives.bodleian.ox.ac.uk/repositories/2/resources/1018, accessed 30 April 2020.

50 HHC WH/4/4.3/02a, Winifred Holtby to Mabel Palmer, 23 September 1926; S. Vietzen, 'Fabian connections: Bernard Shaw in Natal, 1935', *Natalia*, 38 (2008), 8–26. Holtby's letter lists the names of a number of these networks.

51 TC, HHC HCL D2 11/50, Arthur Creech Jones to Winifred Holtby, 19 February 1927.

52 Wickins, *The Industrial and Commercial Workers' Union*, 129–44; Kadalie, *My Life and the ICU*, 102–23.

53 TC, HHC HCL D2 11/50, Mabel Palmer to Arthur Creech Jones, 26 April 1927; TC: HCL D2 11/50, Mabel Palmer to Arthur Creech Jones, 4 May 1927, Arthur Creech Jones to Mabel Palmer, 20 May 1927, Arthur Creech Jones to Mabel Palmer, 28 June 1927.

54 TC, HHC HCL D2 11/50, A. Fenner Brockway to Arthur Creech Jones, 19 August 1927.

55 Lewis, 'Stranger Within My Gate', 90.

56 Wickins, *The Industrial and Commercial Workers' Union*, 106–8; TC, HHC HCL D2 11/50, Arthur Creech Jones to Charles Roden Buxton, 21 October 1927.

57 TC, HHC HCL D2 11/50, Mabel Palmer to Arthur Creech Jones, 7 March 1928; TC, HCL D2 11/50, Arthur Creech Jones to Mabel Palmer, 29 March 1928.

58 HHC WH/4/4.3/03b, Winifred Holtby to Fenner Brockway, 25 August 1927.

59 TC, HHC HCL D2 11/50, A. Fenner Brockway to Arthur Creech Jones, 4 November 1927; TC, HCL D2 11/50, Arthur Creech Jones to A. Fenner Brockway, 8 November 1927; TC, HCL D2 11/50, A. Fenner Brockway to Arthur Creech Jones, 22 November 1927.

60 TC, HHC HCL D2 11/50, Extract of letter from Ethelreda Lewis, 14 December 1927.

61 TC, HHC HCL D2 11/50, Mabel Palmer to Arthur Creech Jones, 14 December 1927. Ethelreda Lewis, who disliked Champion and his influence – a 'dangerous-tempered man' – hoped that Kadalie would get rid of him. TC, HHC HCL D2 11/50, Extract of letter from Ethelreda Lewis, 14 December 1927.

62 Wickins, *The Industrial and Commercial Workers' Union*; Kadalie, *My Life and the ICU*; F.A. Mouton, *Voices in the Desert: Margaret and William Ballinger: A Biography* (Pretoria: Bendic Books, 1997).

63 TC, HHC HCL D2 11/50, William Ballinger to Winifred Holtby, 11 February 1928.

64 See Johnson and Dee, *'I See You!'*, for examples of the personal letters of Holtby to Kadalie (123–25); Lewis to Kadalie (151–52); and Palmer to Lewis (165–66).

65 Couzens, 'Introduction' to *Wild Deer*, x, xii.

66 HHC WH/4/4.3/05b, Winifred Holtby to [unclear], 22 June 1929.

67 Gopal, *Insurgent Empire*, 43.

68 Kadalie, *My Life*, 85.

69 Lewis, 'Stranger Within My Gate', 93. It would seem that Lewis kept the ICU going at some points through personal loans. UCT Ballinger Papers BC 347 D1 I 1.1.12, William Ballinger to Winifred Holtby, 14 August 1928.

70 Wickins, *The Industrial and Commercial Workers' Union*, 105.

71 Ewins, 'The Idea of Africa', 122; D. Johnson, *Dreaming of Freedom in South Africa: Literature between Critique and Utopia* (Cape Town: UCT Press, 2020), pp. 58–60, 60–63; L. Regan, *Winifred Holtby's Social Vision* (London: Taylor and Francis, 2016, 103–34; L. Regan, ed., *Winifred Holtby, "A Woman in Her Time": Critical Essays* (Cambridge: Cambridge Scholars Publishing, 2010), 194–218.

72 Couzens, 'Introduction' to *Wild Deer*.

73 D. Wylie, 'critical diaries', http://danwyliecriticaldiaries.blogspot.com/2019/08/no88-wild-deer-nature-of-neglect.html, accessed 28 April 2020.

74 *Wild Deer*, xxviii; Lewis, 'Stranger Within My Gate', 413.

75 Lewis, *Wild Deer*, 110–1.

76 Lewis, *Wild Deer*, xxiv–xxv.

77 WH to Lady Rhondda, December 1931, in 'Some letters from Winifred Holtby', *Time and Tide*, 25 April 1936, 589, cited in Ewins, 128–9.

78 Holtby, *Mandoa, Mandoa!*, 133, 136–7.

79 Holtby, *Mandoa, Mandoa!*, 139–40.

80 Ewins, 'The Idea of Africa', 132.

81 Holtby, *Mandoa, Mandoa!*, 380.

82 Holtby, *Mandoa, Mandoa!*, 381–2; Regan, *Winifred Holtby's Social Vision,* 119–120.

83 TC, HHC HCL D2 8/47, Harold J. Laski to Winifred Holtby, 5 July 1933.

84 TC, HHC HCL D2 8/47, Norman Leys to Winifred Holtby, 16 February 1933.

Chapter 13

1 K. Marx, Letter to Friedrich Engels, 3 December 1851: K. Marx and F. Engels, *Selected Correspondence* (London: Lawrence and Wishart, 1965), 62. The better-known version of this line opens *The Eighteenth Brumaire of Louis Bonaparte* (1852). Some year earlier, Marx had framed German history as alternately tragedy and comedy in 'A Contribution to the Critique of Hegel's Philosophy of Right' (1843–1844). See K. Marx, *Early Writings*, ed., L. Colletti (Harmondsworth: Penguin, 1975), 247–248.

2 On the genre of anti-colonial romance, see D. Scott, *Conscripts of Modernity. The Tragedy of Colonial Enlightenment* (Durham NC: Duke University Press, 2004), 59, 70–71, 96. I return to Scott's salient arguments in the conclusion.

3 For a snapshot of how tragedy functions as a didactic/coercive literary genre, see A. Boal, *Theatre of the Oppressed*, trans. C.A. and M-O.L. McBride (London: Pluto, 1979), 36–37. For a taste of the extensive scholarship on tragedy in postcolonial contexts, see A. Quayson, *Tragedy and Postcolonial Literature* (Cambridge: Cambridge University Press, 2021), and on tragedy in South Africa, see D. Johnson, 'Beyond Tragedy: *Otelo Burning* and the Limits of Post-apartheid Nationalism', *Journal of African Cultural Studies*, 26, 3 (2014), 348–351.

4 C. Kadalie, 'A Call from Macedonia', *The Messenger*, September 1923, 813. Kadalie repeated his version of the ICU's history in: 'The Aristocracy of White Labour in South Africa', *The Messenger*, August 1924, 242–43, 262; 'Black Trade Unionism in Africa', *The Messenger*, November 1924, 348–49; 'Political Storms in Africa', *The Messenger*, August 1925, 294, 306; 'The Growth of African Trade Unionism', *The Messenger*, September 1927, 271. For his histories of the ICU for British readers, see 'The Old and the New Africa', *Labour Monthly*, October 1927, 624–631; 'African Trade Unionism', *Lansbury's Labour Weekly,* 12 March 1927, 10–11; 'The Raid on Natal', *Lansbury's Labour Weekly,* 30 April 1927, 6; 'Subjection of Natives in South Africa, *Manchester Guardian*, 23 September 1927, 18; 'Open Letter to Blackpool: South Africa a Slave State?', *New Leader*, 30 September 1927, 8; 'The Black Man's Labour Movement', *Foreign Affairs*, September 1927, 84–85; and 'The African Labour Movement', *Foreign Affairs*, March 1928, 307.

5 Kadalie, 'A Call from Macedonia', 814.

6 Ibid., 814, 822.

7 Ibid., 822.

8 Ibid., 822.

9 C. Kadalie, 'Romance of African Labour', *Workers' Herald*, 14 September 1926. For South African readers, Kadalie repeated his version of the history of the ICU in pamphlets like *The Relation between Black and White Workers in South Africa* (Johannesburg: ICU, 1927), as well as in his 'Evidence Submitted on Behalf of the ICU' to the Economic and Wages Commission at the Workers' Hall in Johannesburg on 19 September 1925 (UCT P.L. Wickins Papers).

10   Kadalie, 'Romance' of African Labour.

11   Ibid.

12   Ibid.

13   Ibid.

14   Ibid.

15   Kadalie, 'Past and Future', *Workers' Herald*, 15 December 1926.

16   Ibid.

17   Ibid.

18   Ibid.

19   Ibid.

20   UCT Ballinger Papers B347 A5II.1.2, C. Kadalie, 'Manifesto, 9 July 1928'.

21   Ibid., 4

22   Ibid.

23   On Kadalie's appropriation of *Bayete!*, see D. Johnson, *Dreaming of Freedom in South Africa. Literature between Critique and Utopia* (Edinburgh/Cape Town: Edinburgh University Press/ UCT Press, 2019), 19–20, 55–56.

24   Kadalie, 'Manifesto', 6.

25   C. Kadalie, *My Life*, 165, 180.

26   Ibid., 221–223.

27   E. Gitsham and J.F. Trembath, *The First Account of Labour Organisation in South Africa* (Durban: E. P. and Commercial Printing, 1926), 169, 124.

28   G.M. Godden, 'Black and White Workers in South Africa', *The Contemporary Review*, 1 July 1928, 753–755.

29   Ibid., 757, 759.

30   L. Barnes, *Caliban in Africa* (London: Victor Gollancz, 1930), 102, 103.

31   A.W.G. Champion, *The Truth About the ICU* (Durban: The African Workers Club, 1928), 24.

32   Ibid., 25.

33   Ibid., 25.

34   A.W.G. Champion, *Mehlomadala: My Experiences in the ICU* (Durban: Crown Printing Press, 1928), 22

35   A.W.G. Champion, *Champion, Kadalie, Dube – Amagama Amatatu* (Durban: The African Workers Club, 1928), 14. Champion's tragic reading of the history of the ICU was echoed in the short entry on the ICU in T.D. Mweli Skota's *African Yearly Register* (Johannesburg: R.L. Esson, 1932), which invokes 'pity', a prerequisite of Aristotelian tragedy, in its conclusion: 'It is a hundred pities that these three sections fail to sink their differences and become one strong organisation again' (430). Another early reading of the ICU's history as tragedy was provided by the first student dissertation on the ICU: Vincent Harold Osborn's 1931 BA dissertation at the University of the Witwatersrand attributes the collapse of the ICU to a fatal error, namely the failure of skilled workers to support the unskilled, concluding via a quotation from John Burns that '"this selfish snobbish desertion by the

higher grades of the lower makes success in many disputes impossible"' ('A Critical Survey of Trade Unionism in South Africa', 18).

36   V. Brittain, *Testament of Friendship. The Story of Winifred Holtby* (London: Virago Press, 1989 [1940]), 236.

37   Ibid., 237.

38   Ibid., 238, 241.

39   UCT Ballinger Papers BC 347 A5X.2.12, W. Holtby to Clements Kadalie, 7 September 1927.

40   Brittain, *Testament*, 247.

41   W. Ballinger, 'In Retrospect', *Umteteli wa Bantu*, 9 March 1929.

42   Wits Ballinger Family Papers A410 C237.3, W. Ballinger, 'A History of the ICU to be Written by W. Ballinger and M. Hodgson (Incomplete), 1930–1934'.

43   Ballinger, 'In Retrospect'.

44   Ballinger, 'A History', 4.

45   Ibid., 5.

46   C. Baldick, *The Oxford Dictionary of Literary Terms*, 4th Ed. (Oxford: Oxford University Press, 2015), online edition.

47   Wits Saffrey Collection AD 1178 B5, H.D. Tyamzashe, *Summarised History of the Industrial and Commercial Workers Union of Africa* (unpublished), 48–49.

48   Ibid., 22. Kadalie provides his version of this incident in *My Life*, 164–165. Kadalie does not mention the indignity of being confronted in his pyjamas even once, emphasizingß instead the police detective Arnold's courage in protecting him 'from the mob'.

49   G. Padmore, *The Life and Struggles of Native Toilers* (London: Red International of Labour Unions, 1931), 5.

50   Ibid., 81, 125. Decades later, in *Pan-Africanism or Communism? The Coming Struggle for Africa* (London: Dobson Books, 1956), Padmore revised fundamentally his assessment of Kadalie, the ICU, and the CPSA's role in the demise of the ICU. He described Kadalie as 'a remarkable young Negro. Like Dr Nkrumah of the Gold Coast, he had many natural gifts, including a pleasant personality and remarkable brilliance as a platform speaker, who never lost the common touch. An able organizer, Kadalie... was able, within next to no time, to sweep aside all the moderate Bantu leaders of the African National Congress. He became the uncrowned king of the black masses. No other Negro in recent South African history has enjoyed the popularity which was Kadalie's at the height of his power. The whites feared him as they feared Dingaan, the last of the Zulu warrior kings' (349). And of the CPSA leaders in the ICU, he argued: 'Although these Communist infiltrators failed in this attempt, they did manage to cause deep disruption within the movement before they were finally expelled in 1926' (350).

51   A.T. Nzula, I.I. Potekhin and A.Z. Zusmanovich, *Forced Labour in Colonial Africa*, ed. R. Cohen, trans. H. Jenkins, (London: Zed Press, 1979 [1933]), 126.

52   E. Roux, *Time Longer than Rope: The Black Man's Struggle for Freedom in South Africa* (Madison: University of Wisconsin Press, 1964 [1948]), 153, 196. Roux rehearsed these same arguments in '"I See You, White Man!"', *Trek*, 18 February 1944, 12, 22, attributing the ICU's ultimate collapse to 'internal disruption' (22).

53   E. and W. Roux, *Rebel Pity: The Life of Eddie Roux* (Harmondsworth: Penguin, 1970), 51, 188.

54 Roux, *Time Longer than Rope*, 170–71, 173.

55 UCT Ballinger Papers BC 347 D3.1, E. Roux to Norman Leys, 16 September 1928. Leys forwarded Roux's letter to Kadalie, who wrote to Roux a month later, refusing his condescending judgments; accusing him of libel and deceit; defending his record and that of the ICU; vituperating the CPSA's efforts; and defending the ICU's reliance on white middle-class advisers: 'you should remember that those who were pioneers of Socialism or Communism, held [sic] from well-to-do-families. For example, Karl Marx, Robert Owen, etc. Messrs Howard Pim, Rheinnalt Jones, etc., are helping the ICU in its fight against the Pass Laws, while your Party is silent' (WITS ICU Records A 924 A.1.3C, Kadalie to Edward Roux, 10 October 1928).

56 Roux, *Time Longer than Rope*, 167.

57 Ibid., 197; E. and W. Roux, *Rebel Pity*, 188.

58 J. and R. Simons, *Class and Colour in South Africa, 1850–1950* (London: International Defence and Aid Fund for Southern Africa, 1983 [1969]), 318, 319, 355–356, 363, 365.

59 Ibid., 364.

60 Ibid., 376.

61 The most important contributions on the ICU have been: S. Johns, 'Trade Union, Political Pressure Group or Mass Movement? The Industrial and Commercial Workers' Union of Africa', in R. I. Rothberg and A. Mazrui, eds, *Protest and Power in Black Africa* (1970); E. Webster, 'Champion, the ICU and the Predicament of African Trade Unions', and P. Bonner, 'The Decline and Fall of the ICU – a Case of Self-Destruction?', *South African Labour Bulletin* 1, 6 (1974); Wickins, *The Industrial and Commercial Workers' Union of Africa* (1978); H. Bradford, *A Taste of Freedom: The ICU in Rural South Africa, 1924–1930* (1987); W. Beinart and C. Bundy, *Hidden Struggles in Rural South Africa. Politics and Popular Movements in the Transkei and Eastern Cape, 1890–1930* (1987); and P. La Hausse, 'The Message of the Warriors: The ICU, the Labouring Poor and the Making of a Popular Political Culture in Durban, 1925–1930', in P. Bonner, ed., *Holding their Ground: Class, Locality and Culture in Nineteenth- and Twentieth-Century South Africa* (1989). There have been several striking exceptions, publications that have tried to address nonacademic/popular readerships rather than exclusively academic audiences: *The ICU* (Salt River: Labour History Group, n.d.); the articles on the ICU by Sylvia Neame (under the pen-name Theresa Zania) in the *African Communist* (116 (1989); 120 (1990); and 123 (1990)); D.D. Phiri's *'I See You' The Life of Clements Kadalie, The Man South Africa, Malawi, Zimbabwe and Namibia Should Never Forget* (Blantyre: College Publishing, 2000); and the pamphlet, *When You Ill-Treat the African People, I See You: A Brief History of South Africa's Industrial and Commercial Workers Union* (Tricontinental Institute for Social Research, Dossier # 20, September 2019). Neame has since elaborated her arguments written for the activist/intellectual readership of the *African Communist* for academic audiences in her three-volume *The Congress Movement: The Unfolding of the Congress Alliance, 1912–1961* (2015).

62 P. Wickins, *The Industrial and Commercial Workers' Union of Africa* (Cape Town: Oxford University Press, 1978), 209.

63 Ibid., 209.

64 H. Bradford, *A Taste*, 277.

65 Ibid., 278.

66 Scott, *Conscripts*, 70.

67 C.L.R. James, *History of Negro Revolt* (London: FACT, 1938), 61–62.

68 James commented on Kadalie at greater length decades later in an interview with Sylvia Neame, repeating his impression of Kadalie as 'a great orator' (WITS Sylvia Neame Papers, H7.17.1, C.L.R. James interviewed by Sylvia Neame, 19 June 1968).

69 C.L.R. James, *The Black Jacobins: Toussaint L'Ouverture and the San Domingo Revolution* (New York: Random House, 1989 [1963]), xi.

70 For James's thoughts on Williams, see his pamphlet *Party Politics in the West Indies* (San Juan, Trinidad: Vedic Enterprises, 1962) and for his thoughts on Nkrumah, see his pamphlet *Nkrumah and the Ghana Revolution* (Westport Conn.: Lawrence Hill and Co., 1977). For a critical assessment of James's initial enthusiasm for Nkrumah, see B. Hirson, 'Communalism and Socialism in Africa: The Misdirection of C.L.R James', *Searchlight South Africa*, 4 (1990), 64–73.

71 C.L.R. James, 'Lectures on *The Black Jacobins*. I. How I Wrote *The Black Jacobins*', *Small Axe*, 8 (September 2000), 78–79.

72 C.L.R. James, 'Key Problems in the Study of Negro History', *The Militant*, 13 February 1950. https://www.marxists.org/archive/james-clr/works/1950/02/problemshtml, accessed 10 August 2021.

73 C.L.R. James, 'Stalinism and Negro History', *Fourth International*, 10, 10 (November 1949), 314. Retrieved from: https://www.marxists.org/archive/james-clr/works/1949/11/stalinism-negro.htm, accessed 10 August 2021.

74 C.L.R. James, 'Lectures on *The Black Jacobins*. III. How I Would Re write *The Black Jacobins*', *Small Axe*, 8 (September 2000), 108.

75 James, 'Lectures III', 109–110. James follows these self-lacerating words with a re-assessment of his experiment in casting Toussaint as tragic hero in the 1963 edition.

76 James, 'Key Problems'.

77 See D. Scott's *Conscripts of Modernity* (2004). Important critiques of Scott include C. Høgsbjerg, *C. L. R. Hames and Imperial Britain* (Durham NC: Duke University Press, 2014), 179–182; J.M. Glick, *The Black Radical Tragic: Performance, Aesthetics and the Unfinished Haitian Revolution* (New York: New York University Press, 2016), 143–147; and R. Douglas, *Making the Black Jacobins: C.L.R. James and the Drama of History* (Durham NC: Duke University Press, 2019), 93–99, 112–116.

78 Glick, *The Black Radical Tragic*, 212–213.

79 C.L.R. James, *Marxism and the Intellectuals* (Detroit: Facing Reality Publishing Committee, 1962). Retrieved from: https://www.marxists.org/archive/james-clr/works/1949/11/stalinism-negro.htm; https://www.marxists.org/archive/james-clr/works/1962/destruction-paper/ch01.htm, accessed 10 August 2021.

Bibliography

Archival Sources (and abbreviations)

Hull History Centre (HHC)
 Winifred Holtby Collection
Malawi National Archives (MNA)
National Archives of Namibia (NAN)
National Archives of Zimbabwe (NAZ)
South African National Archives, Bloemfontein (VAB)
 Advisor of Native Affairs Branch in the Office of the Colonial Secretary
 Colonial Office
 Colonial Secretary: Orange River Colony
 Education Department
 Native Affairs
 Minutes of Town Council, Bethulie
 Minutes of Town Council, Bloemfontein
 Regional Chief Director, Department of Education and Training
 Town Clerk, Bloemfontein
South African National Archives, Pretoria (SANA)
 Boksburg Municipal Archives
 Government Native Labour Bureau
 Governor-General
 Municipality of Benoni
 Native Affairs
 Secretary of Home Affairs
 Ministry of the Interior
 Ministry of Justice
 South African Police
South African National Archives, Western Cape (WCA)
 Chief Native Commissioner
 Magistrate, East London
 Municipality, Port Elizabeth
University of KwaZulu-Natal (UKZN)
 John Aitchison Collection
 Killie Campbell Africana Library

Killie Campbell Audio Visual Collection

J.S. Marwick Papers

Alan Paton Centre and Struggle Archives

University of Cape Town. Special Collections (UCT)

Lionel Forman Papers

William Ballinger Papers

University of London. Institute of Commonwealth Studies (UL)

Basner Papers

University of the Western Cape. Mayibuye Archive (UWC)

W.H. Andrews Papers

University of the Witwatersrand. Historical Papers (Wits)

Ballinger Family Papers

Edward Roux Papers

Frank Lucas Papers

Industrial and Commercial Workers' Union (ICU) Records, 1925–47

Institute for Advanced Social Research. Sharecropping and Labour Tenancy Project

Joint Council of Europeans and Africans Records

Sylvia Neame Papers

Saffery Collection

T.D.M. Skota Papers

Trade Union Council of South Africa Papers

Newspapers and magazines

Abantu-Batho

African World

Argus

Bantu World

Black Man

The Bolshevik

Brado Africano

The Call

Cape Times

Contact

Diamond Fields Advertiser

Drum

Forward

Frankforter

Free State Advocate

Friend

Ilanga lase Natal

Imvo Zabantsundu

The International

Izindaba Zabantu

Kroonstad Times

Leselinyana

Livingstonia News

Mail and Guardian

Manchester Guardian

The Namibian

New Leader

Natal Witness

Negro Worker

The Parys Post

Rand Daily Mail

Rhodesia Herald

South African Worker

The Star

Times of Natal

Umsebenzi

Umteteli wa Bantu

Workers' Herald

The Young Worker

Published Sources

Adler, G. 'From the "Liverpool of the Cape" to "The Detroit of South Africa": The Automobile Industry and Industrial Development in the Port Elizabeth-Uitenhage Region', *Kronos* (November 1993), 17–43.

Agherdien, Y., A.C. George and S. Hendricks. *South End as We Knew It* (Port Elizabeth: Western Research Group, 1997).

Appel, A. 'Housing in the Late Nineteenth- and Early Twentieth-Century Port Elizabeth', *Contree*, 37 (1995), 18–28.

Arnold, M. *Culture and Anarchy: An Essay in Political and Social Criticism* (London: Smith Elder, 1869).

Baines, G. 'The Control and Administration of Port Elizabeth's African Population, c.1834–1923', *Contree*, 26 (October 1989), 13–21.

---. 'From Populism to Unionism: The Emergence and Nature of Port Elizabeth's Industrial and Commercial Workers Union, 1918–1920', *Journal of Southern African Studies*, 17, 4 (1991), 679–716.

---. 'The Port Elizabeth Disturbances of 1920', *Reality: A Journal of Liberal and Radical Opinion*, 18, 5 (1986), 12–14.

---. 'Port Elizabeth History: A Select Annotated Bibliography', *South African Historical Journal*, 38, 1 (1998), 252–269.

Baldick, C. *The Oxford Dictionary of Literary Terms,* 4th Ed. (Oxford: Oxford University Press, 2015 [1990]).

Bank, L. 'The Failure of Ethnic Nationalism: Land, Power and the Politics of Clanship on the South African Highveld 1860–1990', *Africa*, 65, 4 (1995), 565–591.

Barnes, L. *Caliban in Africa* (London: Victor Gollancz, 1930).

Basner, H.M. *Am I an African?: The Political Memoirs of H.M. Basner* (Johannesburg: Witwatersrand University Press, 1993).

Bates, R. 'Winifred Holtby', *Left Review*, 2, (1935), 49–51.

Bauer, G. *Labor and Democracy in Namibia, 1971–1996* (Athens: Ohio University Press/ London: James Currey, 1998).

Beddoe, D. *Back to Home and Duty: Women Between the Wars, 1918–1939* (London: Pandora, 1989).

Beinart, W. and C. Bundy. *Hidden Struggles in Rural South Africa: Politics and Popular Movements in the Transkei and Eastern Cape, 1890–1930* (London: James Currey, 1987).

Belling, V. '"More than a Shop": Fanny Klenerman and the Vanguard Bookshop in Johannesburg', *Jewish Affairs* (2017), 1–8.

Berry, P. and A. Bishop, eds, *Testament of a Generation: The Journalism of Vera Brittain and Winifred Holtby* (London: Chatto and Windus, 1985).

Bloch, R. 'The High Cost of Living: The Port Elizabeth Disturbances of October 1920', *Africa Perspective*, 19 (1981), 39–59.

Boal, A. *Theatre of the Oppressed*, trans. C.A. and M-O.L. McBride (London: Pluto, 1979).

Bonner, P. 'The Decline and Fall of the ICU – a Case of Self-Destruction?', *South African Labour Bulletin*, 1, 6 (1974), 38–43; re-published as 'The Decline and Fall of the ICU: A Case of Self-Destruction?' in E. Webster, eds, *Essays in Southern African Labour History*, *Vol 1* (Johannesburg: Ravan Press, 1978), 114–120.

---. '"Desirable or Undesirable Basotho women?": Liquor, Prostitution and the Migration of Basotho Women to the Rand, 1920–1945' in C. Walker, eds, *Women and Gender in Southern Africa to 1945* (Cape Town: David Philip, 1990), 221–250.

---. 'South African Society and Culture, 1910–1948' in R. Ross, A.K. Mager and B. Nasson, eds, *Cambridge History of South Africa: Vol. 2* (Cambridge: Cambridge University Press, 2012 [2010]), 254–318.

---. 'The Transvaal Native Congress 1917–1920: The Radicalisation of the Black Petty Bourgeoisie on the Rand', in S. Marks and R. Rathbone, eds, *Industrialisation and Social Change in South Africa* (London: Longman, 1982), 270–313.

---. J. Hyslop and L. van der Walt, 'Rethinking Worlds of Labour: Southern African Labour History in International Context', *African Studies*, 66, 2–3 (2007), 137–168.

---. and K. Shapiro. 'Company Town, Company Estate, Pilgrim's Rest, 1910–1932', *Journal of Southern African Studies*, 19, 2 (1993), 171–202.

Booysen, S. *The African National Congress and the Regeneration of Political Power: People, Party, Policy* (Johannesburg: Wits University Press, 2011).

Boswell, L. *Rural Communism in France, 1920–39* (Ithaca: Cornell University Press, 1998).

Bradford, H. 'Mass Movements and the Petty Bourgeoisie: The Social Origins of ICU Leadership, 1924–1929', *The Journal of African History*, 25, 3 (1984), 295-310.

---. 'Getting Away with Murder: Mealie Kings, the State and Foreigners in the Eastern Transvaal, c.1918–1950', in P. Bonner, P. Delius and D. Posel, eds, *Apartheid's Genesis: 1935–1962* (Johannesburg: Witwatersrand University Press, 1993), 96–125.

---. *A Taste of Freedom: The ICU in Rural South Africa, 1924–1930* (Johannesburg: Ravan Press/ New Haven: Yale University Press, 1987).

---. 'A Taste of Freedom: Capitalist Development and Response to the ICU in the Transvaal Countryside' in B. Bozzoli, eds., *Town and Countryside in the Transvaal: Capitalist Penetration and Popular Response* (Johannesburg: Ravan Press, 1983), 128–157.

Breckenridge, K. '"We Must Speak for Ourselves": The Rise and Fall of a Public Sphere on the South African Gold Mines, 1920 to 1931', *Comparative Studies in Society and History*, 40, 1 (1998), 71–108.

Bright, R. *Chinese Labour in South Africa, 1902–10: Race, Violence, and Global Spectacle* (London: Palgrave Macmillan, 2013).

Brittain, V. *Testament of Friendship. The Story of Winifred Holtby* (London: Virago Press, 1989 [1940]).

---. *Testament of Youth* (London: Gollancz, 1933).

Burden, G.N. *Nyasaland Natives in the Union of South Africa* (Zomba: Government Printer, 1940).

Bush, B. *Imperialism, Race and Resistance: Africa and Britain, 1919–1945* (London: Routledge, 1999).

Butler, A. *The Idea of the ANC* (Johannesburg: Jacana, 2012).

Butler, J. *Cradock: How Segregation and Apartheid Came to a South African Town* (Charlottesville VA: University of Virginia Press, 2017).

Calhoun, C. 'Introduction: Habermas and the Public Sphere', in C. Calhoun, ed., *Habermas and the Public Sphere* (Cambridge MA: MIT Press, 1992), 1–48.

Callinicos, L. *Oliver Tambo. Beyond the Ngele Mountains* (Cape Town: David Philip, 2015 [2004]).

---. *Working Life, 1886–1940* (Johannesburg: Ravan Press, 1987).

Cardo, M. *Opening Men's Eyes: Peter Brown and the Liberal Struggle for South Africa* (Johannesburg: Jonathan Ball Publishers, 2010).

Champion, A.W.G. *Champion, Kadalie, Dube – Amagama Amatatu* (Durban: The African Workers Club, 1928).

---. *Mehlomadala: My Experiences in the ICU* (Durban: Crown Printing Press, 1928).

---. *The Truth About the ICU* (Durban: The African Workers Club, 1928).

Charles, G. and L. Fuentes-Rohwer. 'Habermas, the Public Sphere, and the Creation of a Racial Counterpublic', *Michigan Journal of Race and Law*, 21 (2015), 1–21.

Chikuhwa, J. *Zimbabwe: The End of the First Republic* (Bloomington: Author House, 2013).

Coetzee, J.M. 'Farm Novel and "Plaasroman" in South Africa', *English in Africa*, 13, 2 (1986), 1–19.

Coka, J.G. 'The Story of Gilbert Coka of the Zulu Tribe of Natal, South Africa' in M. Perham, ed., *Ten Africans* (London: Faber and Faber, 1936), 273–322.

Cooper, A. 'The Institutionalisation of Contract Labour in Namibia', *Journal of Southern African Studies*, 25, 1 (1999), 121–138.

Cope, N. *To Bind the Nation: Solomon KaDinuzulu and Zulu Nationalism, 1913–1933* (Pietermaritzburg: University of KwaZulu-Natal Press, 1993).

Coplan, D. *In Township Tonight! South Africa's Black City Music and Theatre,* 2nd Ed. (Chicago IL: University of Chicago Press, 2008 [1985]).

Coplan, D and B. Jules-Rosette, B. 'Nkosi Sikelel' iAfrika and the Liberation of the Spirit of South Africa', *African Studies*, 64, 2 (2005), 285–308.

Couzens, T. 'Introduction', in E. Lewis, *Wild Deer* (Cape Town: David Philip, 1984 [1933]).

---. *The New African: A Study of the Life and Work of H.I.E. Dhlomo* (Johannesburg: Ravan Press, 1985).

---. *Tramp Royal: The True Story of Trader Horn* (Johannesburg: University of the Witwatersrand Press, 1992).

Crush, J. ed., *Beyond Control. Immigration and Human Rights in a Democratic South Africa* (Cape Town: IDASA, 1998).

---, A. Jeeves and D. Yudelman. *South Africa's Labour Empire: A History of Black Migrancy to the Gold Mines* (Cape Town: David Philip, 1991).

Daimon, A. '"Ringleaders and Troublemakers": Malawian (Nyasa) Migrants and Transnational Labour Movements in Southern Africa, c.1910 to 1960', *Labour History*, 58, 5 (2017), 656–675.

---. 'Settling in Motion as Consciousness: Nyasa (Malawian) Informal Transit across Southern Rhodesia towards South Africa from the 1910s to the 1950s', *African Studies*, 80, 1 (2021), 1–20.

---. '"Totemless Aliens": The Historical Antecedents of the Anti-Malawian Discourse in Zimbabwe, 1920s–1979', *Journal of Southern African Studies*, 44, 6 (2018), 1095–1114.

Davenport, T.R.H. 'The Triumph of Colonel Stallard: The Transformation of the Natives (Urban Areas) Act between 1923 and 1937', *South African Historical Journal* 2, 1 (1987), 77–96.

---. and C. Saunders. *South Africa: A Modern History,* 5th Ed. (Hampshire and London: Macmillan Press, 2000).

Davidson, A., I. Filatova, V. Gorodnov and S. Johns, eds, *South Africa and the Communist International, Volume 1: Socialist Pilgrims to Bolshevik Footsoldiers, 1919–1930* (London: Frank Cass, 2003).

Dedering, T. 'Namibia, Struggle for Independence', in I. Ness et al., eds, *The International Encyclopedia of Revolution and Protest* (Oxford, Wiley-Blackwell, 2001), 2389–2401.

Dee, H. 'Central African Immigrants, Imperial Citizenship and the Politics of Free Movement in Interwar South Africa', *Journal of Southern African Studies*, 46, 2 (2019), 319–337.

---. '"I am a Bad Native": Masculinity and Marriage in the Biographies of Clements Kadalie', *African Studies*, 78, 2 (2019), 183–204.

De Kay, P.N. *Notre Dame Under the Southern Cross* (Johannesburg: Ravan Press, 1984).

Douglas, R. *Making the Black Jacobins: C.L.R. James and the Drama of History* (Durham NC: Duke University Press, 2019).

Drew, A. *Between Empire and Revolution: A Life of Sidney Bunting, 1873–1936* (London: Pickering and Chatto, 2007).

---. *Discordant Comrades: Identities and Loyalties on the South African Left* (Aldershot: Ashgate Publishing, 2000).

Eales, K. 'Patriarchs, Passes and Privilege: Johannesburg's Middle Classes and the Question of Night Passes for African women', in P. Bonner, I. Hofmeyr, D. James and T. Lodge, eds, *Holding their Ground: Class, Locality and Culture in Nineteenth- and Twentieth-Century South Africa* (Johannesburg: Ravan Press, 1989), 105–140.

Edgar, R. *The Making of an African Communist: Edwin Thabo Mofutsanyane and the Communist Party of South Africa, 1927–1939* (Pretoria: Unisa Press, 2005).

Ellis, S. *External Mission: The ANC in Exile, 1960–1990* (Johannesburg: Jonathan Ball, 2012).

Emmett, T. 'Popular Resistance in Namibia, 1920–1925', in T. Lodge, ed., *Resistance and Ideology in Settler Societies* (Johannesburg: Ravan, 1986), 6–48.

---. *Popular Resistance and the Roots of Nationalism in Namibia, 1915–1966* (Basel: P. Schlettwein, 1999 [1987]).

Erlank, N. 'Christianity and African Nationalism in South Africa in the First Half of the Twentieth Century', in A. Lissoni, J. Soske, N. Erlank, N. Nieftagodien and O. Badsha. eds, *One Hundred Years of the ANC: Debating Liberation Histories Today* (Johannesburg: Wits University Press, 2012), 77–96.

Ewing, A. *The Age of Garvey: How a Jamaican Activist Created a Mass Movement and Changed Global Black Politics* (Princeton NJ: Princeton University Press, 2014).

Ewins, K. 'The Idea of Africa in Winifred Holtby's "Mandoa, Mandoa!"', *The Review of English Studies*, 63, 258 (2012), 118–138.

First, R. *South West Africa* (Baltimore: Penguin, 1963).

Foucault, M. *Discipline and Punish: The Birth of the Prison* (Harmondsworth: Penguin, 1979).

Fraser, N. 'Rethinking the Public Sphere: A Contribution to the Critique of Actually Existing Democracy', *Social Text*, 25/26, 67 (1990), 56–80.

Gasa, N. 'Let Them Build More Gaols', in N. Gasa, ed., *Women in South African History: Basus'iimbokodo, Bawel'imilambo / They Remove Boulders and Cross Rivers* (Cape Town: HSRC Press, 2007), 129–152.

Gish, S. *Alfred B. Xuma: African, American, South African* (Basingstoke: Macmillan, 2000).

Gitsham, E. and J.F. Trembath, *The First Account of Labour Organisation in South Africa* (Durban: E.P. and Commercial Printing, 1926).

Glick, J.M. *The Black Radical Tragic. Performance, Aesthetics and the Unfinished Haitian Revolution* (New York: New York University Press, 2016).

Godden, G.M. 'Black and White workers in South Africa', *The Contemporary Review* (1 July 1928), 753–755.

Gopal, P. *Insurgent Empire: Anticolonial Resistance and British Dissent* (London: Verso, 2019).

Gramsci, A. *Selections from the Prison Notebooks of Antonio Gramsci*, trans. Q. Hoare and G. Nowell Smith (London: Lawrence and Wishart, 1971).

Groves, Z. *Malawian Migration to Zimbabwe, 1900–1965: Tracing Machona* (London: Palgrave Macmillan, 2020).

---. 'Urban Migrants and Religious Networks: Malawians in Colonial Salisbury, 1920 to 1970', *Journal of Southern African Studies*, 38, 3 (2012), 491–511.

Guha, R. *Elementary Aspects of Peasant Insurgency in Colonial India* (Delhi: Oxford University Press, 1983).

Haasbroek, H.J. 'Die Swart Loongeskil van 1926 in Bloemfontein', *New Contree*, 76 (2016) 171–192.

---. 'Henry Selby Msimang en die Loonagitasie van 1919 in Bloemfontein', *Indago*, 32 (2016), 119–131.

---. 'H. Selby Msimang, Kampvegter vir swart Belange in Bloemfontein, 1915-1922', *Culna*, 54 (June 1999), 20–21.

---. 'Die Rol van Henry Selby Msimang in Bloemfontein, 1917–1922', *Navorsinge van die Nasionale Museum*, 16, 3 (2000), 171–192.

Habermas, J. 'The Public Sphere: An Encyclopedia Article', in M. Durham and D. Kellner, eds, *Media and Cultural Studies: Key Works* (Oxford: Blackwell Publishing, 2006), 73–78.

Henrichsen, D. 'Liberals and Non-Racism in Namibia's Settler Society? Advocate Israel Goldblatt's Engagement with Namibian Nationalists in the 1960s', in J. Silvester, ed., *Re-viewing Resistance in Namibian History* (Windhoek: University of Namibia Press, 2015), 127–147.

Heyman, R.D. 'C.T. Loram: A South African Liberal in Race Relations', *International Journal of African Historical Studies*, 5, 1 (1972), 41–50.

Higginson, J. *Collective Violence and the Agrarian Origins of South African Apartheid, 1900–1948* (Cambridge: Cambridge University Press, 2014).

Hill, R.A. ed. *The Marcus Garvey and Universal Negro Improvement Association Papers: Volume 9, Africa for the Africans, 1921–1922* (Berkeley, Cal.: University of California Press, 1995).

---. *The Marcus Garvey and Universal Negro Improvement Association Papers: Volume 10, Africa for the Africans, 1923–1945* (Berkeley, Cal.: University of California Press, 2006).

---. and G.A. Pirio. '"Africa for the Africans": The Garvey Movement in South Africa, 1920–1940' in S. Marks and S. Trapido, eds, *The Politics of Race, Class and Nationalism in Twentieth Century South Africa* (London: Longman, 1987), 209–254.

Hillebrecht, W. *Lüderitz: A Journey through Time* (Lüderitz: NovaNam, 2017).

Hilton, R. *English and French Towns in Feudal Society: A Comparative Study* (Cambridge: Cambridge University Press, 1992).

Hindson, S. 'Selby Msimang and Trade Union Organisation in the 1920s', *Reality: A Journal of Liberal and Radical Opinion*, 9, 1 (1977), 4–6.

Hirson, B. *A History of the Left in South Africa* (London: Tauris, 2005).

---. 'Death of a Revolutionary: Frank Glass/Li Fu-Jen/John Liang 1902–1988', *Searchlight South Africa*, 1, 1 (1988), 28–41.

---. 'Communalism and Socialism in Africa: The Misdirection of C.L.R. James', *Searchlight South Africa*, 4 (1990), 64–73.

Hlatshwayo, H. 'Immigrant Workers and COSATU: Solidarity vs National Chauvinism?', *Alternation*, 7 (2013), 267–293.

Hofmeyr, I. 'Obituary: Professor Phil Bonner (1945–2017)', *Journal of Southern African Studies*, 44, 6 (2018), 1165–67.

Høgsbjerg, C. *C.L.R. James and Imperial Britain* (Durham NC: Duke University Press, 2014).

Holtby, W. 'Better and Brighter Natives', in Berry, P. and A. Bishop, eds, *Testament of a Generation: The Journalism of Vera Brittain and Winifred Holtby* (London: Chatto and Windus, 1985), 181–185.

---. 'Feminism Divided', in P. Berry and A. Bishop, eds, *Testament of a Generation: The Journalism of Vera Brittain and Winifred Holtby* (London: Chatto and Windus, 1985), 47–50.

---. *The Land of Green Ginger* (London: Virago, 2011 [1927]).

---. *Letters to a Friend* (London: Collins, 1937).

---. *Mandoa! Mandoa! A Comedy of Irrelevance* (London: Virago, 1982 [1933]).

---. 'Some Letters from Winifred Holtby', *Time and Tide*, 25 April 1936, 589.

Hughes, H. *First President: A Life of John Dube, First President of the ANC* (Johannesburg: Jacana Media, 2011).

Human Rights Watch, *'They Have Robbed Me of My Life'. Xenophobic Violence Against Non-Nationals in South Africa* (New York: Human Rights Watch, September 2020).

Hunt Davis, R. 'Charles T. Loram and an American Model for African Education in South Africa', *The African Studies Review*, 19, 2 (1976), 87–99.

Hyslop, J. 'E.P. Thompson in South Africa. The Practice and Politics of Social History in an Era of Revolt and Transition, 1976–2012', *International Review of Social History*, 61 (2016), 95–116.

Jabavu, D.D.T. ed., *Minutes of the All African Convention* (Lovedale: Lovedale Press, 1936).

James, C.L.R. *The Black Jacobins. Toussaint L'Ouverture and the San Domingo Revolution* (New York: Random House, 1989 [1963]).

---. *History of Negro Revolt* (London: FACT, 1938).

---. 'Key Problems in the Study of Negro History', *The Militant*, 13 February 1950. Reproduced at https://www.marxists.org/archive/james-clr/works/1950/02/problems.html, accessed 16 September 2019.

---. 'Lectures on *The Black Jacobins*. I. How I Wrote *The Black Jacobins*', *Small Axe*, 8 (September 2000), 65–82.

---. 'Lectures on *The Black Jacobins*. III. How I Would Re-write *The Black Jacobins*', *Small Axe*, 8 (September 2000), 99–112.

---. *Marxism and the Intellectuals* (Detroit: Facing Reality Publishing Committee, 1962). Reproduced at https://www.marxists.org/archive/james-clr/works/1962/destruction-paper/ch01.htm, accessed 10 August 2020.

---. *Nkrumah and the Ghana Revolution* (Westport Conn.: Lawrence Hill and Co., 1977).

---. *Party Politics in the West Indies* (San Juan, Trinidad: Vedic Enterprises, 1962).

---. 'Stalinism and Negro History', *Fourth International*, 10, 10 (November 1949), 314. Reproduced at https://www.marxists.org/archive/james-clr/works/1949/11/stalinism-negro.htm, accessed 10 August 2020.

Jeeves, A. 'Sugar and Gold in the Making of the South African Labour System: The Crisis of Supply on the Zululand Sugar Estates, 1906–1939', *South African Journal of Economic History*, 7, 2 (1992), 7–33.

Jingoes, S.J.*A Chief is a Chief by the People*, J. and C. Perry, eds (London: Oxford University Press, 1975).

Johns, S. ed., *From Protest to Challenge: A Documentary History of African Politics, Vol 1: Protest and Hope, 1882–1934* (Stanford: Hoover Institution Press, 1987).

---. 'Trade Union, Political Pressure Group or Mass Movement? The Industrial and Commercial Workers' Union of Africa', in R.I. Rothberg and A. Mazrui, eds, *Protest and Power in Black Africa* (New York: Oxford University Press, 1970), 695–754.

Johnson, D. 'Anti-apartheid People's Histories and Post-apartheid Nationalist Biographies', in A. Choudry and S. Vally, eds., *Reflections on Knowledge, Learning and Social Movements. History's Schools* (London and New York: Routledge, 2018), 88–103.

---. 'Beyond Tragedy: *Otelo Burning* and the Limits of Post-apartheid Nationalism', *Journal of African Cultural Studies*, 26, 3 (2014), 348–351.

---. 'Clements Kadalie, the ICU, and the Language of Freedom', *English in Africa*, 42, 3 (2015), 43–69.

---. *Dreaming of Freedom in South Africa: Literature between Critique and Utopia* (Edinburgh and Cape Town: Edinburgh University Press/ UCT Press, 2019).

---. Johnson, D. and H. Dee, eds, *'I See You': The Industrial and Commercial Workers' Union of Africa, 1919–1930* (Cape Town: Historical Publications Southern Africa, 2022)

Kadalie, C. 'The African Labour Movement', *Foreign Affairs*, March 1928, 307.

---. 'African Trade Unionism', *Lansbury's Labour Weekly*, 12 March 1927, 10–11.

---. 'The Aristocracy of White Labour in South Africa', *The Messenger*, August 1924, 242–243, 262.

---. 'The Black Man's Labour Movement', *Foreign Affairs*, September 1927, 84–85.

---. 'Black Trade Unionism in Africa', *The Messenger*, November 1924, 348–349.

---. 'A Call from Macedonia', *The Messenger*, September 1923, 813–814, 822.

---. 'The Growth of African Trade Unionism', *The Messenger*, September 1927, 271.

---. *My Life and the ICU: The Autobiography of a Black Trade Unionist in South Africa* (London: Frank Cass, 1970).

---. 'The Old and the New Africa', *Labour Monthly*, October 1927, 624–631.

---. 'Political Storms in Africa', *The Messenger*, August 1925, 294, 306.

---. 'The Raid on Natal', *Lansbury's Labour Weekly*, 30 April 1927, 6.

---. *The Relation between Black and White Workers in South Africa* (Johannesburg: ICU, 1927).

---. 'Subjection of Natives in South Africa, *Manchester Guardian*, 23 September 1927, 18.

Kalinga, O. *Historical Dictionary of Malawi*, 4th Ed. (Plymouth: The Scarecrow Press, 2012 [1980]).

---. 'Jordan Msumba, Ben Ngemela and the Last Church of God and His Christ, 1924–1935', *Journal of Religion in Africa*, 13, 3 (1982), 207–218.

Katzenellenbogen, S. *South Africa and Southern Mozambique: Labour, Railways and Trade in the Making of a Relationship* (Manchester: Manchester University Press, 1982).

Karis, T., A. Bugg-Levine, M. Benson, G. Gerhart and T. Barnes, eds, *From Protest to Challenge: A Documentary History of African Politics in South Africa, 1882–1990*, Vol. 4 (Johannesburg: Jacana Media, 2017).

Karis, T. and G. Carter. *From Protest to Challenge: A Documentary History of African Politics in South Africa, Vol. 1, Protest and Hope, 1882–1934* (Stanford: Hoover, 1972).

Keegan, T. *Facing the Storm: Portraits of Black Lives in South Africa* (London/Cape Town: Zed Press/David Philip, 1988).

---. *Rural Transformations in Industrializing South Africa* (Johannesburg: Ravan Press, 1987).

Kimble, J. *Migrant Labour and Colonial Rule in Basutoland, 1890–1930* (Grahamstown: Rhodes University, Institute of Social and Economic Research, 1999).

Kirk, J. 'A "Native" Free State at Korsten: Challenge to Segregation in Port Elizabeth South Africa 1901–1905', *Journal of Southern African Studies*, 17, 2 (1991), 309–336.

Klaaren, J. *From Prohibited Immigrants to Citizens: The Origins of Citizenship and Nationality in South Africa* (Cape Town: UCT Press, 2017).

Klotz, A. 'Borders and the Roots of Xenophobia in South Africa', *South African Historical Journal*, 68, 2 (2016), 180–194.

Krut, R. 'The Making of a South African Jewish Community', in B. Bozzoli, ed., *Class, Community and Conflict: South African Perspectives* (Johannesburg: Ravan, 1988), 135–159.

La Guma, A. *Jimmy La Guma*, M. Adhikari, ed. (Cape Town, Friends of the South African Library, 1997 [1964]).

La Hausse, P. 'Drinking in a Cage: the Durban System and the 1929 Beer Hall Riots', *Africa Perspective*, 20 (1982), 63–75.

---. 'The Message of the Warriors: The ICU, the Labouring Poor and the Making of a Popular Political Culture in Durban, 1925–50', in P. Bonner, I. Hofmeyr, D. James and T. Lodge, eds, *Holding their Ground: Class, Locality and Culture in Nineteenth- and Twentieth-Century South Africa* (Johannesburg: Witwatersrand University Press, 1987), 19–58.

---. *Restless Identities: Signatures of Nationalism, Zulu Ethnicity and History in the Lives of Petros Lamula (c.1881–1948) and Lymon Maling (1889–c.1936)* (Pietermaritzburg: University of Natal Press, 2000).

Lake, M. and H. Reynolds. *Drawing the Global Colour Line: White Men's Countries and the International Challenge to Racial Equality* (Cambridge: Cambridge University Press, 2008).

Landau, L. L. et al, eds, *Exorcising the Demons Within: Xenophobia, Violence and Statecraft in Contemporary South Africa* (Johannesburg: Wits University Press, 2011).

Landau, P. '"Johannesburg in Flames": The 1918 Shilling Campaign, *Abantu-Batho*, and Early African Nationalism in South Africa', in P. Limb, ed., *The People's Paper: A Centenary History of 'Abantu-Batho'* (Johannesburg: Wits University Press, 2012), 255–281.

Langworthy, H. '*Africa for the Africans*': The Life of Joseph Booth* (Blantyre: Christian Literature Association in Malawi, 1996).

Lefebvre, H. and D. Nicholson-Smith. *The Production of Space* (Oxford: Blackwell, 1991).

Le Roux, Charl. *Die Verhouding tussen Blank en Nie-Blank in die Oranjerivierkolonie, 1900–10* (Pretoria: Government Printer, 1986).

Lerumo, A.B. *Fifty Fighting Years* (London: Inkululeko Publications, 1980).

Levinson, O. *Diamonds in the Desert: The Story of August Stauch and his Times* (Windhoek: Kuiseb Verlag, 2009).

Lewis, E. *Trader Horn: The Ivory Coast in the Earlies. Written at the Age of Seventy-Three with such of the Author's Philosophy as is the Gift of Age and Experience Taken Down and Here Edited by Ethelreda Lewis* (London: Jonathan Cape, 1930 [1927]).

---. *Wild Deer* (Cape Town: David Philip, 1984 [1933]).

Limb, P. *The ANC's Early Years: Nation, Class and Place in South Africa before 1940* (Pretoria: Unisa Press, 2010).

Lindner, U. 'Transnational Movements between Colonial Empires: Migrant Workers from the British Cape Colony in the German Diamond Town of Lüderitzbucht', *European Review of History—Revue européenne d'histoire*, 16, 5 (2009), 679–695.

Lissoni, A.J. Soske, N. Erlank, N. Nieftagodien and O. Badsha, eds, *One Hundred Years of the ANC: Debating Liberation Histories Today* (Johannesburg: Wits University Press, 2012).

Luthuli, A. J. *Let My People Go: An Autobiography of a Great South African Leader* (London: Collins, 1962).

Lyon, W.B. 'From Labour Elites to Garveyites: West African Migrant Labour in Namibia, 1892–1925', *Journal of Southern African Studies*, 47, 1 (2021), 37–55.

Mabin, A. 'The Rise and Decline of Port Elizabeth, 1850–1900', *The International Journal of African Historical Studies*, 19, 2 (1986), 275–303.

Madigimisha, H.L., N.E. Khalema, L. Chipungu, T.C. Chirimambowa and T.L. Chimedza, eds., *Crisis, Identity and Migration in Post-colonial Southern Africa* (Cham, Switzerland: Springer, 2018).

Malunga, F. 'Foreign African Migrant Labour at the Messina Copper Mines, 1905–1960', *Historia*, 47, 1 (2002), 270–290.

Mamdani, M. *Citizen and Subject: Contemporary Africa and the Legacy of Late Colonialism* (Princeton NJ: Princeton University Press, 1996).

Mancoe, J. *The Bloemfontein Bantu and Coloured People's Directory* (Bloemfontein: White, 1934).

Mantzaris, E. 'Radical Community: The Yiddish-Speaking Branch of the International Socialist League, 1918–20', in B. Bozzoli, ed., *Class, Community and Conflict: South African Perspectives* (Johannesburg: Ravan, 1988), 160–176.

Marcus, J. *Hearts of Darkness: White Women Write Race* (New Brunswick, NJ: Rutgers University Press, 2004).

Marks, S. ed., *Not Either an Experimental Doll: The Separate Worlds of Three South African Women* (Pietermaritzburg: University of Natal Press, 1987).

Marx, K. 'A Contribution to the Critique of Hegel's Philosophy of Right', *Early Writings*, L. Colletti, (Harmondsworth: Penguin, 1975), 243–257.

---. and F. Engels. *Selected Correspondence* (London: Lawrence and Wishart, 1965).

Matthews, Z.K. *Freedom for My People* (Cape Town: David Philip, 1981).

Maylam, P. 'Explaining the Apartheid City: 20 Years of South African Urban Historiography', *Journal of Southern African Studies*, 21, 1 (1995), 19–38.

Mbeki, T. *Africa: The Time has Come* (Cape Town: Tafelberg, 1998).

McCracken, J. *A History of Malawi: 1859–1966* (Woodbridge: James Currey, 2012).

---. *Politics and Christianity in Malawi, 1875–1940: The Impact of the Livingstonia Mission in the Northern Province,* 2nd ed. (Blantyre: Christian Literary Association in Malawi, 2000 [1977]).

McDonald, D. et al., *Challenging Xenophobia: Myths and Realities about Cross-Border Migration in South Africa* (Cape Town: IDASA, 1998).

Meli, F. *A History of the ANC: South Africa Belongs to Us* (Harare: Zimbabwe Publishing House, 1988).

Mkhize, S.M. *A Political Biography of Selby Msimang: Principles and Pragmatism in the Liberation Struggle* (Cape Town: BestRed, 2019).

Moloi, T. *Place of Thorns: Black Political Protest in Kroonstad since 1976* (Johannesburg: Wits University Press, 2015).

---. 'The Emergence and Radicalisation of Black Political Formations in Kroonstad, 1915–1957', *New Contree*, 67 (2013), 167–186.

Moore, B.C., 'Smuggled Sheep, Smuggled Shepherds: Farm Labour Transformations in Namibia and the Question of Southern Angola, 1933–1975', *Journal of Southern African Studies*, 47, 1 (2021), 93–125.

---, S. Quinn, W.B. Lyon and K.F. Hertzog, 'Balancing the Scales: Re-Centring Labour and Labourers in Namibian History', *Journal of Southern African Studies*, 47, 1 (2021), 1–16.

Moroney, S. 'Mine Workers Protest on the Witwatersrand, 1901–1912', *South African Labour Bulletin*, 3, 5 (1977), 5–24.

Morton, F. 'Slave-raiding and Slavery in the Western Transvaal After the Sand River Convention', *African Economic History*, 20 (1992), 99–118.

Mouton, F.A. *Voices in the Desert: Margaret and William Ballinger: A Biography* (Pretoria: Bendic Books, 1997).

Murray, C. *Black Mountain: Land, Class, and Power in the Eastern Orange Free State, 1880s to 1980s* (Edinburgh: Edinburgh University Press, 1992).

Murray, M.J. 'The Natives are Always Stealing: White Vigilantes and the "Reign of Terror" in the Orange Free State, 1918–1924', *The Journal of African History* 30, 1 (1989), 107–123.

Musoni, F. *Border Jumping and Migration Control in Southern Africa* (Bloomington IN: Indiana University Press, 2020).

Ndlovu, S. 'Johannes Nkosi and the Communist Party of South Africa: Images of Blood River and King Dingaan, 1920s–1930', *History and Theory*, 39, 4 (2000), 111–31.

Neame, S. *The Congress Movement: The Unfolding of the Congress Alliance, 1912–1961,* Vols 1–3 (Cape Town: HSRC Press, 2015).

---. (pseud. Theresa Zania). 'The ICU and White Parliamentary Parties, 1920–1924', *African Communist*, 120 (1990), 70–83.

---. 'The ICU Reaches its Peak – and Begins to Break Up', *African Communist*, 123 (1990), 68–82.

---. '70th Anniversary of the ICU: Part of the Emerging African Nationalist Movement', *African Communist*, 116 (1989), 33–48.

Neocosmos, M. *From 'Foreign Natives' to 'Native Foreigners': Explaining Xenophobia in Post-apartheid South Africa, Citizenship and Nationalism, Identity and Politics* ((Dakar: CODESRIA, 2010).

---. *Thinking Freedom in Africa: Toward a Theory of Emancipatory Politics* (Johannesburg: Witwatersrand University Press, 2017).

Nelson, H. *Area Handbook for Southern Rhodesia* (Washington: US Government Printing Office, 1975).

Nieftagodien, N. 'Migrants: Vanguards of the Workers' Struggle?' in P. Delius, L. Philips and F. Rankin-Smith, eds, *A Long Way Home: Migrant Worker Worlds, 1800–2014* (Johannesburg: Witwatersrand University Press, 2014), 224-240.

---. 'The Place of "the Local" in History Workshop's Local History', *African Studies*, 69, 1 (2010), 41–61.

Ngqongqo, S. J. 'Mpilo Walter Benson Rubusana', in M. Ndletyana, ed., *African Intellectuals in Nineteenth and Twentieth-Century South Africa* (Cape Town: HRSC Press, 2008), 45–54.

Ngqulunga, B. *The Man who Founded the ANC: A Biography of Pixley ka Isaka Seme* (Johannesburg: Random House, 2017).

Ntantala, P. *A Life's Mosaic: The Autobiography of Phyllis Ntantala* (Berkeley: University of California Press, 1992).

Nyathi, P. *Masotsha Ndhlovu* (Harare: Longman, 1998).

Nyamnjoh, F.B. *Insiders and Outsiders: Citizenship and Xenophobia in Contemporary Southern Africa* (London: Zed Press, 2006).

Nzula, A.T., I.I. Potekhin and A.Z. Zusmanovich, ed, R. Cohen, trans. H. Jenkins, *Forced Labour in Colonial Africa* (London: Zed Press, 1979 [1933]).

Odendaal, A. "Even White Boys Call Us "Boy"! Early Black Organisational Politics in Port Elizabeth', *Kronos*, 20 (1993), 3–16.

---. *The Founders: The Origins of the African National Congress and the Struggle for Democracy in South Africa* (Johannesburg: Jacana Media, 2012).

---. *Vukani Bantu! The Beginnings of Black Protest Politics in South Africa to 1912* (Cape Town: David Philip, 1984).

Okoth, A. *A History of Africa: African Nationalism and the Decolonisation Process* (Nairobi: Eastern African Educational Publishers, 2006).

Pachai, B. *The Malawi Diaspora and Elements of Clements Kadalie* (Salisbury: The Central African Historical Association, 1969).

Padmore, G. *The Life and Struggles of Native Toilers* (London: Red International of labour Unions, 1931).

---. *Pan-Africanism or Communism?: The Coming Struggle for Africa* (London: Dobson Books, 1956).

Phillips, H. '"Black October": The Impact of the Spanish Influenza Epidemic of 1918 on South Africa' (Pretoria: Government Printing Works, 1990).

Philips, R.E. *The Bantu are Coming: Phases of South Africa's Race Problem* (London: Student Christian Movement Press, 1930).

Phimister, I. *An Economic and Social History of Zimbabwe: 1890–1948: Capital Accumulation and Class Struggle* (London: Longman, 1988).

Phiri, D.D. *'I See You': The Life of Clements Kadalie, The Man South Africa, Malawi, Zimbabwe and Namibia Should Never Forget* (Blantyre: College Publishing, 2000).

Porta, D. and M. Dani. *Social Movements: An Introduction,* 2nd Ed. (Malden: Blackwell Publishing, 2020 [2006]).

Quayson, A. *Tragedy and Post-colonial Literature* (Cambridge: Cambridge University Press, 2021).

Raftopoulos, B. and I. Phimister, eds, *Keep on Knocking: A History of Labour Movement in Zimbabwe, 1900–1997* (Harare: Baobab, 1997).

Raftopoulos, B. 'The Labour Movement in Zimbabwe: 1945–1965', in B. Raftopoulos and I. Phimister, eds, *Keep on Knocking: A History of Labour Movement in Zimbabwe, 1900–1997* (Harare: Baobab Books, 1997), 55–90.

Pirio, G.A. 'The Role of Garveyism in the Making of the Southern African Working Classes and Namibian Nationalism' (University of California, mimeo, 1982). Reprinted in B. Wood, ed., 1988, *Namibia, 1884–1984: Readings on Namibia's History and Society* (London: Namibia Support Committee and the SWAPO Department of Information and Publicity, 1984).

Quinn, S. 'Scalar Claims, Worker Strategies, and "South Africa's Labour Empire" in Namibia, 1943–1979', *Journal of Southern African Studies*, 47, 1 (2021), 57–78.

Ranciére, J. *The Politics of Aesthetics* (London: Bloomsbury, 2004).

Ranger, T.O. *The African Voice in Southern Rhodesia* (London: Heinemann, 1970).

---. *The African Churches of Tanzania* (Nairobi: The East Africa Publishing House, 1972).

---. *Bulawayo Burning: The Social History of a Southern African City 1893–1960* (Harare: Weaver Press, 2010).

Regan, L. *Winifred Holtby's Social Vision: 'Members One of Another'* (London: Routledge, 2012).

Rich, P. 'Managing Black Leadership: The Joint Councils, Urban Trading and Political Conflict in the OFS, 1925–1942', in P. Bonner, I. Hofmeyr, D. James and T. Lodge, eds, *Holding Their Ground: Class, Locality and Culture in the Nineteenth- and Twentieth-Century South Africa* (Johannesburg: Ravan Press, 1989), 177–200.

Richards, C. *The Iron and Steel Industry in South Africa* (Johannesburg: Witwatersrand University Press, 1940).

Robinson, J.D. 'The Politics of Urban Form: Differential Citizenship and Township Formation in Port Elizabeth, 1925–1945', *Kronos* (1993), 44–65.

Rotberg, R. *The Rise of Nationalism in Central Africa: The Making of Malawi and Zambia, 1873–1964* (Cambridge MA: Harvard University Press, 1971 [1965]).

Roth, M. *The Communist Party of South Africa: Racism, Eurocentricity and Moscow, 1921–1950* (Johannesburg: Partridge Publishing Africa, 2016).

Roux, E. 'Agrarian Revolt in South Africa', *Labour Monthly*, 10, 1 (1928), 55–62.

---. '"I See You, White Man!"', *Trek*, 18 February 1944, 12, 22.

---. *Time Longer than Rope. The Black Man's Struggle for Freedom in South Africa* (Madison: University of Wisconsin Press, 1964 [1948]).

--- and W. Roux, *Rebel Pity: The Life of Eddie Roux* (Harmondsworth: Penguin, 1970).

---. *S.P. Bunting: A Political Biography* (Johannesburg: Commercial Printing Company, 1944).

Rudé, G. *Paris and London in the Eighteenth Century: Studies in Popular Protest* (London: Collins, 1970).

Sachs, B. *Multitude of Dreams* (Johannesburg: Kayor Publishing House, 1949).

Scarnecchia, T. *The Roots of Democracy and Political Violence in Zimbabwe* (Rochester: University of Rochester Press, 2008).

Schapera, I. ed., *Western Civilisation and the Natives of South Africa: Studies in Culture Contact* (London: Routledge, 1934).

Schoeman, K. *Bloemfontein: Die Onstand van n Stad*, 1846–1946 (Pretoria: Human and Rousseau, 1980).

Scott, D. *Conscripts of Modernity. The Tragedy of Colonial Enlightenment* (Durham NC: Duke University Press, 2004).

Serfontein, D. *Keurskrif vir Kroonstad: 'n Kroniek van die Onstaan, Groei en Vooruitsgte van 'n Vrystaatse Plattelandse Dorp* (Kroonstad: Stadsraad, 1990).

Setiloane J.S.M. *The History of Black Education in Maokeng, Kroonstad* (Pretoria: HSRC Press, 1997).

Shaw, M. *The Clear Stream: A Life of Winifred Holtby* (London: Virago, 1999).

Simons, J. and R. *Class and Colour in South Africa, 1850–1950* (London: International Defence and Aid Fund for Southern Africa, 1983 [1969]).

Simpson, T. 'The ANC at 100', *South African Historical Journal*, 64(3), (2012), 381-392.

Skota, T.D.M. *African Yearly Register* (Johannesburg: R.L. Esson, 1930).

Smith, H.L. ed., *British Feminism in the Twentieth Century* (Aldershot: Edward Elgar, 1990).

South African Democracy Education Trust, eds. *The Road to Democracy: South Africans Telling their Stories, 1950–1970* (Hollywood: Tsehai Publishers, 2008).

Stals, E.L.P. *The Afrikaners in Namibia: Who are They? A Collection of Historical Essays about the Afrikaner in Former South West Africa* (Windhoek: Macmillan, 2008)

Starfield, J. '"Not Quite History": The Autobiographies of H. Selby Msimang and R.V. Selope Thema and the Writing of South African History', *Social Dynamics: A Journal of Social Sciences*, 14, 2 (1988), 16–35.

Steinberg, J. 'Xenophobia and Collective Violence in South Africa: A Note of Scepticism about the Scapegoat', *African Studies Review*, 61, 3 (2018), 119–134.

Swanson, M. ed, *The Views of Mahlathi: Writings of A.W.G. Champion, A Black South African* (Pietermaritzburg: University of Natal Press, 1982).

Switzer, L. 'The Ambiguities of Protest in South Africa: Rural Politics and the Press during the 1920s', *International Journal of African Historical Studies*, 23, 1 (1990), 87–109.

Tangri, R. 'Inter-War Native Associations and the Formation of the Nyasaland African Congress', *Transafrican Journal of History*, 1, 1 (1971), 84–102.

Thale, T. 'Paradigms Lost? Paradigms Regained: Working-Class Autobiography in South Africa', *Journal of Southern African Studies*, 21, 4 (1995), 613–622.

Thorpe, A. 'Comintern "Control" of the Communist Party of Great Britain', *English Historical Review*, 113, 452 (1998), 637–662.

Tilly, C. *Contentious Performances* (Cambridge: Cambridge University Press, 2008).

Van der Linden, M. 'Transnationalizing American Labor History', *Journal of American History*, 86, 3 (1999), 1078–1092.

---. *Workers of the World. Essays Towards a Global Labour History* (Leiden: Brill, 2008).

Van der Walt, L. 'The First Globalisation and Transnational Labour Activism in Southern Africa: White Labourism, the IWW, and the ICU, 1904–1934', *African Studies*, 66, 2/3 (2007), 223–251.

Van Goethem, G. *The Amsterdam International: The World of the International Federation of Trade Unions (IFTU), 1913–1945* (Aldershot, Ashgate, 2006)

Van Onselen, C. *Chibaro: African Mine Labour in Southern Rhodesia: 1900–1933* (Johannesburg: Ravan Press, 1976).

---. *The Seed is Mine: The Life of Kas Maine, A South African Sharecropper, 1894–1985* (Cape Town: David Philip, 1996).

---. 'The Social and Economic Underpinning of Paternalism and Violence on the Maize Farms of the South-Western Transvaal, 1900–1950', *Journal of Historical Sociology*, 5, 2 (1992), 127–160.

Van Rensburg, A. *Die Geskiedenis van Bethlehem 1864–1964* (Bethlehem: Stadsraad, 1964).

Vietzen, S. 'Beyond School: Some Developments in Higher Education in Durban in the 1920s and the Influence of Mabel Palmer', *Natalia*, 14 (1984), 48–58.

---. 'Fabian Connections: Bernard Shaw in Natal, 1935', *Natalia*, 38 (2008), 8–26.

---. 'Mabel Palmer and Black Higher Education in Natal 1936-1942', *Journal of Natal and Zulu History*, 6 (1983), 98–114.

Vinson, R. *The Americans are Coming!: Dreams of African American Liberation in Segregationist South Africa* (Ohio: Ohio University Press, 2012).

Webster, E. 'Champion, the ICU and the Predicament of African Trade Unions', *South African Labour Bulletin*, 1, 6 (1974), 6–13.

Weigend, G.G. 'German Settlement Patterns in Namibia', *Geographical Review*, 75, 2 (1985), 156–69.

Wells, J. 'The Day the Town Stood Still: Women in Resistance in Potchefstroom, 1912–1930', in B. Bozzoli, ed., *Town and Countryside in the Transvaal* (Johannesburg: Ravan Press, 1983), 269–307.

---. *We Now Demand! The History of Women's Resistance to Pass Laws in South Africa* (Johannesburg: Witwatersrand University Press, 1993).

West, M.O. *The Rise of an African Middle Class: Colonial Zimbabwe, 1898–1965* (Indianapolis: Indiana University Press, 2002).

When You Ill-Treat the African People, I See You: A Brief History of South Africa's Industrial and Commercial Workers Union (Tricontinental: Institute for Social Research, Dossier # 20, September 2019).

Wickins, P. *The Industrial and Commercial Workers' Union of Africa* (Cape Town: Oxford University Press, 1978).

---. 'One-Big-Union Movement among Black Workers in South Africa', *International Journal of African Historical Studies*, 7, 3 (1974), 391–416.

Willan, W. *Sol Plaatje: A Life of Solomon T. Plaatje, 1876–1932* (Johannesburg: Jacana Media, 2018).

Windrich, E. 'Rhodesian Censorship: The Role of the Media in the Making of a One-party State', *African Affairs*, 78, 3 (1979), 523–34.

Winkiel, L.T. 'Nancy Cunard's *Negro* and the Transnational Politics of Race', *Modernism/ Modernity*, 13, 3 (2006), 507–530.

Woolf, L. *Empire and Commerce in Africa: A Study in Economic Imperialism* (London: Allen and Unwin, 1920).

---. *Imperialism and Civilization* (London: Hogarth, 1928).

Yap, M. and D. Leong Man, *Colour, Confusion and Concessions: The History of the Chinese in South Africa* (Hong Kong: Hong Kong University Press, 1996).

Unpublished theses

April, T. 'Theorising Women: The Intellectual Contribution of Charlotte Maxeke to the Struggles for Liberation in South Africa' (PhD thesis, University of Cape Town, 2012).

Baines, G. 'New Brighton, Port Elizabeth c.1903–1953: The History of an Urban African Community' (PhD thesis, University of Cape Town, 1994).

---. 'The Port Elizabeth Disturbances of October 1920' (MA thesis, Rhodes University, 1988).

Botha, M. 'Exploring Sense of Place as a Restorative Urban Planning Tool: Marabastad, Kroonstad as a Case Study' (MA thesis, North-West University, 2018).

Bruchhausen, S. 'Emancipatory Politics and the Mpondo Revolts' (MA thesis, Rhodes University, 2016).

Cherry, J., 'The Making of an African Working Class, Port Elizabeth, 1925–1963' (MA thesis, University of Cape Town, 1993).

Grossman, J., 'Class Relations and the Communist Party of South Africa 1921–1950' (PhD thesis, University of Warwick, 1985).

Johns, S., 'Marxism-Leninism in a Multi-Racial Environment: The Origins and Early History of the Communist Party of South Africa', 1914–1932 (PhD thesis, Harvard University, 1965).

La Hausse, P, 'Ethnicity and History in the Careers of Two Zulu Nationalists: Petros Lamula (c. 1881–1948) and Lymon Maling (1889–c.1936)' (PhD thesis, University of the Witwatersrand, 1992).

Lipede, A. D. 'Pan-Africanism in Southern Africa, 1900-1960' (PhD thesis, University of York, 1990).

Meintjes, S, 'Edendale, 1850–1906: A Case Study of Rural Transformation and Class Formation in an African Mission in Natal' (PhD thesis, University of London, 1988).

Mkhize, S.M. 'Class Consciousness, Non-Racialism and Political Pragmatism: A Political Biography of Henry Selby Msimang, 1886–1982' (PhD thesis, University of the Witwatersrand, 2015).

Moloi, T. 'Black Politics in Kroonstad' (PhD thesis, University of the Witwatersrand, 2012).

Ngqongqo, S.J. 'Mpilo Walter Benson Rubusana (1858–1910): The Making of the New African Elite in the Eastern Cape' (MA thesis, University of Fort Hare, 1997).

Nieftagodien, N. 'The Implementation of Urban Apartheid on the East Rand, 1948-1973: The Role of Local Government and Local Resistance' (PhD thesis, University of the Witwatersrand, 2001).

Osborn, V.H. 'A Critical Survey of Trade Unionism in South Africa' (BA thesis, University of Witwatersrand, 1931).

Robinson, J.D., 'The Power of Apartheid: State Power and Territoriality in South African Cities, Port Elizabeth, 1923-1971' (PhD thesis, University of Cambridge, 1990).

Skikna, S.Z., 'Son of the Sun and Son of the World: The Life and Works of R.R.R. Dhlomo' (MA thesis, University of the Witwatersrand, Johannesburg, 1984).

Starfield, J.V, '"Not Quite History": The Autobiographical Writings of R.V. Selope Thema and H. Selby Msimang' (MA thesis, Institute of Commonwealth Studies, University of London,1986).

Stewart, L., '"I See You" in the Soil: The Industrial and Commercial Workers' Union (ICU) in the Western Transvaal, 1926-1934' (MA thesis, University of the Witwatersrand, 2021).

Silvester, J. 'Black Pastoralists, White Farmers: The Dynamics of Land Dispossession and Labour Recruitment in Southern Namibia, 1915-1955' (PhD thesis, University of London, 1993).

Van Diemel, R, 'In Search of Freedom, Fair Play and Justice, Josiah Tshangana Gumede, 1867-1946: A Political Biography' (PhD thesis, University of the Western Cape, 1997).

Watson, K.I, 'A History of the South African Police in Port Elizabeth, 1913-1956' (PhD thesis, Rhodes University, Grahamstown, 1999).

Wickins, P.L. 'The Industrial and Commercial Workers Union of Africa' (PhD Thesis, University of Cape Town, 1973).

Unpublished seminar and conference papers

Beinart, W. 'Cape Workers in German South-West Africa, 1904-1912: Patterns of Migrancy and the Closing of Options on the Southern African Labour Market', *The Societies of Southern Africa in the Nineteenth and Twentieth Centuries*, 11 (London: Institute of Commonwealth Studies, University of London: Institute of Commonwealth Studies, 1981).

Beinart, W. and C. Bundy. 'The Union, the Nation, and the Talking Crow: The Ideology and Tactics of the Independent ICU in East London' (Johannesburg: University of the Witwatersrand, African Studies Seminar, 1985).

Bonner, P. 'The 1920 Mineworkers Strike' (Johannesburg: University of the Witwatersrand, Wits History Workshop, 3-7 February 1978).

---. '"Home Truths" and the Political Discourse of the ICU' (Cape Town: University of the Western Cape, South African Historical Society Conference, 11-14 July 1999).

---. 'Unity and Division in the Struggle: African Politics on the Witwatersrand in the 1920s' (Johannesburg: University of Witwatersrand, African Studies Seminar, 9 March 1992).

Hirson, B. 'The Bloemfontein Riots, 1925: A Study in Community, Culture and Class Consciousness', *The Societies of Southern Africa in the Nineteenth and Twentieth Centuries*, 13 (London: University of London, Institute of Commonwealth Studies, 1982-1983).

Mabin, A. 'Strikes in the Cape Colony, 1854-1899' (Johannesburg: University of the Witwatersrand, African Studies Seminar, 1983).

Posel, R, 'The Durban Ricksha-Pullers' Strikes of 1918 and 1930' (Durban: University of Natal, Conference on the History of Natal and Zululand, July 1985).

Van der Walt, L. '"One Great Union of Skilled and Unskilled Workers, South of the Zambezi": Garveyism, Liberalism and Revolutionary Syndicalism in the Industrial and Commercial Workers Union of Africa, 1919–1949' (Vienna: European Social Science History Conference, 23–26 April 2014).

Oral Interviews

Bonner, P. Interview with David Bopape, Tsakane, 31 May 1982

---. Interview with Govan Mbeki, Johannesburg, May 1996.

Dee, H. Interview with Phil Bonner, Johannesburg, 21 February 2017.

Moloi, T. Interview with Hilda 'Mantho' Motadinyane, Sunday Times Oral History Project, Maokeng, Kroonstad, 7 December 2006.

---. Interview with John Setiloane, Maokeng, Kroonstad, 14 February 2014.

---. Interview with Parkies Seteloane, Maokeng, Sunday Times Oral History Project, Kroonstad, 7 December 2006.

Wits Institute of Advanced Social Research (IASR), Sharecropping and Labour Tenancy Project (SLTP), Oral History Project, 1979-1987.

Online sources

Baxter, P. 'The Amandebele and Modern Imperial History', http://peterbaxterhistory.com/the-amandebele-and-modern-african-imperial-history/, accessed 17 April 2018.

Dee, H. 'J.C. Scott, black artists and the cultural politics of 1920s Johannesburg https://www.sahistory.org.za/archive/js-scott-black-artists-and-cultural politics 1920s johannesburg-henry-dee, accessed 19 August 2020.

Federici, S. 'Precarious labor: A feminist viewpoint' (2006), https://caringlabor.wordpress.com/2010/07/29/silvia-federici-precarious-labor-and-reproductive-work/ accessed, 1 November 2021.

Wylie, D. 'Critical diaries', http://danwyliecriticaldiaries.blogspot.com/2019/08/no88-wild-deer-nature-of-neglect.html, accessed 28 April 2020.

Index